WORLD TRADE ORGANIZATION

Dispute Settlement Reports

2012
Volume V

Pages 2447-2742

CAMBRIDGE
UNIVERSITY PRESS

Shaftesbury Road, Cambridge CB2 8EA, United Kingdom

One Liberty Plaza, 20th Floor, New York, NY 10006, USA

477 Williamstown Road, Port Melbourne, VIC 3207, Australia

314–321, 3rd Floor, Plot 3, Splendor Forum, Jasola District Centre, New Delhi – 110025, India

103 Penang Road, #05–06/07, Visioncrest Commercial, Singapore 238467

Cambridge University Press is part of Cambridge University Press & Assessment, a department of the University of Cambridge.

We share the University's mission to contribute to society through the pursuit of education, learning and research at the highest international levels of excellence.

www.cambridge.org
Information on this title: www.cambridge.org/9781107051256

First published 2014

A catalogue record for this publication is available from the British Library

ISBN 978-1-107-05125-6 Hardback

THE WTO DISPUTE SETTLEMENT REPORTS

The *Dispute Settlement Reports* of the World Trade Organization (the "WTO") include panel and Appellate Body reports, as well as arbitration awards, in disputes concerning the rights and obligations of WTO Members under the provisions of the *Marrakesh Agreement Establishing the World Trade Organization*. The *Dispute Settlement Reports* are available in English. Volumes comprising one or more complete cases contain a cumulative list of published disputes. The cumulative list for cases that cover more than one volume is to be found in the first volume for that case.

This volume may be cited as DSR 2012:V

TABLE OF CONTENTS

Page

United States - Certain Country of Origin Labelling (COOL) Requirements (WT/DS384, WT/DS386)

Reports of the Appellate Body 2449

Cumulative List of Published Disputes 2719

UNITED STATES - CERTAIN COUNTRY OF ORIGIN LABELLING (COOL) REQUIREMENTS

Reports of the Appellate Body
WT/DS384/AB/R, WT/DS386/AB/R*

Adopted by the Dispute Settlement Body on 23 July 2012

United States, *Appellant/Appellee*
Canada, *Other Appellant/Appellee*
Mexico, *Other Appellant/Appellee*
Argentina, *Third Participant*
Australia, *Third Participant*
Brazil, *Third Participant*
China, *Third Participant*
Colombia, *Third Participant*
European Union, *Third Participant*
Guatemala, *Third Participant*
India, *Third Participant*
Japan, *Third Participant*
Korea, *Third Participant*
New Zealand, *Third Participant*
Peru, *Third Participant*
Separate Customs Territory of Taiwan, Penghu, Kinmen and Matsu, *Third Participant*

Present:
Bhatia, Presiding Member
Ramírez-Hernández, Member
Van den Bossche, Member

* The Appellate Body is issuing these Reports in the form of a single document constituting two separate Appellate Body Reports: WT/DS384/AB/R; and WT/DS386/AB/R. The cover page, preliminary pages, sections I through VIII, and the annexes are common to both Reports. The page header throughout the document bears two document symbols, WT/DS384/AB/R and WT/DS386/AB/R, with the following exceptions: section IX on pages CDA-219 to CDA-221, which bears the document symbol for and contains the Appellate Body's findings and conclusions in the Appellate Body Report WT/DS384/AB/R; and section IX on pages MEX-219 to MEX-221, which bears the document symbol for and contains the Appellate Body's findings and conclusions in the Appellate Body Report WT/DS386/AB/R.

TABLE OF CONTENTS

Page

I. INTRODUCTION 2473

II. ARGUMENTS OF THE PARTICIPANTS AND THE THIRD PARTICIPANTS 2481

A. Claims of Error by the United States – Appellant 2481

1. Article 2.1 of the *TBT Agreement* 2481

(a) The Interpretation and Application of Article 2.1 of the *TBT Agreement* 2481

(b) Article 11 of the DSU 2485

(c) The Relevance of the Appellate Body Report in *US – Clove Cigarettes* in this Appeal 2487

2. Article 2.2 of the *TBT Agreement* 2488

(a) Trade-Restrictiveness 2489

(b) The Objective Pursued and the Level at which the United States Considers It Appropriate to Fulfil Its Objective 2489

(c) Whether the COOL Measure Is "More Trade-Restrictive than Necessary to Fulfil a Legitimate Objective" 2491

B. Arguments of Canada – Appellee 2496

1. Article 2.1 of the *TBT Agreement* 2496

(a) The Interpretation and Application of Article 2.1 of the *TBT Agreement* 2496

(b) Article 11 of the DSU 2500

(c) The Relevance of the Appellate Body Report in *US – Clove Cigarettes* in this Appeal 2501

2. Article 2.2 of the *TBT Agreement* 2503

(a) Trade-Restrictiveness 2503

(b) The Objective Pursued and the Level at which the United States Considers It Appropriate to Fulfil Its Objective 2504

(c) Whether the COOL Measure Is "More Trade-Restrictive than Necessary to Fulfil a Legitimate Objective" 2505

C. Arguments of Mexico – Appellee 2511

1. Article 2.1 of the *TBT Agreement* 2511

(a) The Interpretation and Application of Article 2.1 of the *TBT Agreement* 2511
(b) Article 11 of the DSU 2515
(c) The Relevance of the Appellate Body Report in *US – Clove Cigarettes* in this Appeal 2516
2. Article 2.2 of the *TBT Agreement* 2518
(a) Trade-Restrictiveness 2518
(b) The Objective Pursued and the Level at which the United States Considers It Appropriate to Fulfil Its Objective 2518
(c) Whether the COOL Measure Is "More Trade-Restrictive than Necessary to Fulfil a Legitimate Objective" 2520
D. Claims of Error by Canada – Other Appellant 2524
1. "Legitimate Objective" under Article 2.2 of the *TBT Agreement* 2524
(a) The Identification of the Objective 2525
(b) The Legitimacy of the COOL Measure's Objective 2528
2. Less Trade-Restrictive Alternative Measures 2530
3. Article III:4 of the GATT 1994 2533
4. Article XXIII:1(b) of the GATT 1994 2534
E. Claims of Error by Mexico – Other Appellant 2534
1. "Legitimate Objective" under Article 2.2 of the *TBT Agreement* 2535
(a) The Identification of the Objective 2535
(b) The Legitimacy of the COOL Measure's Objective 2537
2. Less Trade-Restrictive Alternative Measures 2538
3. Article III:4 of the GATT 1994 2540
4. Article XXIII:1(b) of the GATT 1994 2542
F. Arguments of the United States – Appellee 2543
1. "Legitimate Objective" under Article 2.2 of the *TBT Agreement* 2544
(a) The Identification of the Objective 2544
(b) The Legitimacy of the COOL Measure's Objective 2549
2. Less Trade-Restrictive Alternative Measures 2551
3. Article III:4 of the GATT 1994 2553

4. Article XXIII:1(b) of the GATT 1994 2554

G. Arguments of the Third Participants 2555

1. Australia 2555

2. Brazil 2557

3. Colombia 2560

4. European Union 2563

5. Guatemala 2569

6. Japan 2570

7. Korea 2571

III. ISSUES RAISED IN THIS APPEAL 2572

IV. BACKGROUND AND OVERVIEW OF THE MEASURES AT ISSUE 2574

A. The COOL Measure 2576

1. Introduction 2576

2. Categories of Origin for Meat 2579

3. Labelling 2580

B. The Vilsack Letter 2585

C. Background Information 2586

V. ARTICLE 2.1 OF THE *TBT AGREEMENT* 2589

A. Introduction 2589

B. Summary of the Panel's Findings 2589

C. Overview of the Issues Raised on Appeal 2593

D. Interpretation of Article 2.1 of the *TBT Agreement* 2594

E. Application of Article 2.1 of the *TBT Agreement*: "Treatment No Less Favourable" 2597

1. Detrimental Impact 2598

(a) "Different Treatment" 2598

(b) Did the Panel Err in Finding that the COOL Measure Has a Detrimental Impact on Imported Livestock? 2600

2. Did the Panel Err under Article 11 of the DSU in Making Certain Factual Findings in the Course of Its Analysis under Article 2.1 of the TBT Agreeement? ... 2607

(a) Segregation and Commingling 2607

(b) The Existence of a Price Differential 2615

3. Does the Detrimental Impact on Imported Livestock Violate Article 2.1? 2622

(a) Arguments on Appeal 2622

(b) Relevant Panel Findings 2624

(c) Does the Detrimental Impact Reflect Discrimination? 2629

VI. ARTICLE 2.2 OF THE *TBT AGREEMENT* 2634

A. Introduction 2634

B. The Panel's Analysis 2636

C. Analysis 2641

1. Article 2.2 of the *TBT Agreement* 2641

2. Did the Panel Err in Finding that the COOL Measure Is Trade Restrictive? 2647

3. Did the Panel Err in Its Identification of the Objective Pursued? 2647

(a) Canada's and Mexico's Other Appeals of the Panel's Approach to Identifying the Objective Pursued 2651

(b) Canada's and Mexico's Claims under Article 11 of the DSU with respect to the Panel's Identification of the Objective Pursued 2653

(c) The United States' Appeal of the Panel's Finding concerning the COOL Measure's "Level of Fulfilment" of Its Objective 2664

(d) Canada's Claim that the Panel Failed to Define the Objective of the COOL Measure at a "Sufficiently Detailed Level" 2666

(e) Summary of Conclusions 2667

4. Did the Panel Err in Finding that the Objective of the COOL Measure Is "Legitimate"? 2667

5. Did the Panel Err in Its Analysis of Whether the COOL Measure Is More Trade Restrictive than Necessary to Fulfil a Legitimate Objective, Taking Account of the Risks Non-Fulfilment Would Create? 2678

6. Completion of the Legal Analysis – Is the COOL Measure More Trade Restrictive than Necessary to Fulfil the Legitimate Objective, Bearing in Mind the Risks that Non-Fulfilment Would Create? 2685

VII. ARTICLE III:4 OF THE GATT 1994 2697

VIII. ARTICLE XXIII:1(B) OF THE GATT 1994 2698

IX. FINDINGS AND CONCLUSIONS CDA-2699

IX. FINDINGS AND CONCLUSIONS MEX-2702

ANNEX I NOTIFICATION OF AN APPEAL BY THE UNITED STATES

ANNEX II NOTIFICATION OF AN OTHER APPEAL BY CANADA

ANNEX III NOTIFICATION OF AN OTHER APPEAL BY MEXICO

ANNEX IV PROCEDURAL RULING AND ADDITIONAL PROCEDURES REGARDING PUBLIC OBSERVATION OF THE ORAL HEARING

CASES CITED IN THESE REPORTS

Short Title	Full Case Title and Citation
Australia – Apples	Appellate Body Report, *Australia – Measures Affecting the Importation of Apples from New Zealand*, WT/DS367/AB/R, adopted 17 December 2010
Australia – Salmon	Appellate Body Report, *Australia – Measures Affecting Importation of Salmon*, WT/DS18/AB/R, adopted 6 November 1998, DSR 1998:VIII, 3327
Brazil – Retreaded Tyres	Appellate Body Report, *Brazil – Measures Affecting Imports of Retreaded Tyres*, WT/DS332/AB/R, adopted 17 December 2007, DSR 2007:IV, 1527
Canada – Pharmaceutical Patents	Panel Report, *Canada – Patent Protection of Pharmaceutical Products*, WT/DS114/R, adopted 7 April 2000, DSR 2000:V, 2289
Chile – Alcoholic Beverages	Appellate Body Report, *Chile – Taxes on Alcoholic Beverages*, WT/DS87/AB/R, WT/DS110/AB/R, adopted 12 January 2000, DSR 2000:I, 281
Chile – Price Band System (Article 21.5 – Argentina)	Appellate Body Report, *Chile – Price Band System and Safeguard Measures Relating to Certain Agricultural Products – Recourse to Article 21.5 of the DSU by Argentina*, WT/DS207/AB/RW, adopted 22 May 2007, DSR 2007:II, 513
China – Auto Parts	Appellate Body Reports, *China – Measures Affecting Imports of Automobile Parts*, WT/DS339/AB/R / WT/DS340/AB/R / WT/DS342/AB/R, adopted 12 January 2009

Short Title	Full Case Title and Citation
China – Publications and Audiovisual Products	Appellate Body Report, *China – Measures Affecting Trading Rights and Distribution Services for Certain Publications and Audiovisual Entertainment Products*, WT/DS363/AB/R, adopted 19 January 2010
China – Raw Materials	Appellate Body Reports, *China – Measures Related to the Exportation of Various Raw Materials*, WT/DS394/AB/R / WT/DS395/AB/R / WT/DS398/AB/R, adopted 22 February 2012
Colombia – Ports of Entry	Panel Report, *Colombia – Indicative Prices and Restrictions on Ports of Entry*, WT/DS366/R and Corr.1, adopted 20 May 2009
Dominican Republic – Import and Sale of Cigarettes	Appellate Body Report, *Dominican Republic – Measures Affecting the Importation and Internal Sale of Cigarettes*, WT/DS302/AB/R, adopted 19 May 2005, DSR 2005:XV, 7367
Dominican Republic – Import and Sale of Cigarettes	Panel Report, *Dominican Republic – Measures Affecting the Importation and Internal Sale of Cigarettes*, WT/DS302/R, adopted 19 May 2005, as modified by Appellate Body Report WT/DS302/AB/R, DSR 2005:XV, 7425
EC – Asbestos	Appellate Body Report, *European Communities – Measures Affecting Asbestos and Asbestos-Containing Products*, WT/DS135/AB/R, adopted 5 April 2001, DSR 2001:VII, 3243
EC – Bed Linen (Article 21.5 – India)	Appellate Body Report, *European Communities – Anti-Dumping Duties on Imports of Cotton-Type Bed Linen from India – Recourse to Article 21.5 of the DSU by India*, WT/DS141/AB/RW, adopted 24 April 2003, DSR 2003:III, 965
EC – Fasteners (China)	Appellate Body Report, *European Communities – Definitive Anti-Dumping Measures on Certain Iron or Steel Fasteners from China*, WT/DS397/AB/R, adopted 28 July 2011
EC – Hormones	Appellate Body Report, *EC Measures Concerning Meat and Meat Products (Hormones)*, WT/DS26/AB/R, WT/DS48/AB/R, adopted 13 February 1998, DSR 1998:I, 135

Short Title	Full Case Title and Citation
EC – Poultry	Appellate Body Report, *European Communities – Measures Affecting the Importation of Certain Poultry Products*, WT/DS69/AB/R, adopted 23 July 1998, DSR 1998:V, 2031
EC – Sardines	Appellate Body Report, *European Communities – Trade Description of Sardines*, WT/DS231/AB/R, adopted 23 October 2002, DSR 2002:VIII, 3359
EC – Sardines	Panel Report, *European Communities – Trade Description of Sardines*, WT/DS231/R and Corr.1, adopted 23 October 2002, as modified by Appellate Body Report WT/DS231/AB/R, DSR 2002:VIII, 3451
EC – Selected Customs Matters	Appellate Body Report, *European Communities – Selected Customs Matters*, WT/DS315/AB/R, adopted 11 December 2006, DSR 2006:IX, 3791
EC – Tariff Preferences	Panel Report, *European Communities – Conditions for the Granting of Tariff Preferences to Developing Countries*, WT/DS246/R, adopted 20 April 2004, as modified by Appellate Body Report WT/DS/246/AB/R, DSR 2004:III, 1009
EC – Trademarks and Geographical Indications (Australia)	Panel Report, *European Communities – Protection of Trademarks and Geographical Indications for Agricultural Products and Foodstuffs, Complaint by Australia*, WT/DS290/R, adopted 20 April 2005, DSR 2005:X, 4603
EC – Tube or Pipe Fittings	Appellate Body Report, *European Communities – Anti-Dumping Duties on Malleable Cast Iron Tube or Pipe Fittings from Brazil*, WT/DS219/AB/R, adopted 18 August 2003, DSR 2003:VI, 2613
EC and certain member States – Large Civil Aircraft	Appellate Body Report, *European Communities and Certain Member States – Measures Affecting Trade in Large Civil Aircraft*, WT/DS316/AB/R, adopted 1 June 2011
Japan – Agricultural Products II	Appellate Body Report, *Japan – Measures Affecting Agricultural Products*, WT/DS76/AB/R, adopted 19 March 1999, DSR 1999:I, 277

Short Title	Full Case Title and Citation
Japan – Alcoholic Beverages II	Appellate Body Report, *Japan – Taxes on Alcoholic Beverages*, WT/DS8/AB/R, WT/DS10/AB/R, WT/DS11/AB/R, adopted 1 November 1996, DSR 1996:I, 97
Japan – Apples	Appellate Body Report, *Japan – Measures Affecting the Importation of Apples*, WT/DS245/AB/R, adopted 10 December 2003, DSR 2003:IX, 4391
Japan – Film	Panel Report, *Japan – Measures Affecting Consumer Photographic Film and Paper*, WT/DS44/R, adopted 22 April 1998, DSR 1998:IV, 1179
Korea – Alcoholic Beverages	Appellate Body Report, *Korea – Taxes on Alcoholic Beverages*, WT/DS75/AB/R, WT/DS84/AB/R, adopted 17 February 1999, DSR 1999:I, 3
Korea – Dairy	Appellate Body Report, *Korea – Definitive Safeguard Measure on Imports of Certain Dairy Products*, WT/DS98/AB/R, adopted 12 January 2000, DSR 2000:I, 3
Korea – Various Measures on Beef	Appellate Body Report, *Korea – Measures Affecting Imports of Fresh, Chilled and Frozen Beef*, WT/DS161/AB/R, WT/DS169/AB/R, adopted 10 January 2001, DSR 2001:I, 5
Mexico – Taxes on Soft Drinks	Panel Report, *Mexico – Tax Measures on Soft Drinks and Other Beverages*, WT/DS308/R, adopted 24 March 2006, as modified by Appellate Body Report WT/DS308/AB/R, DSR 2006:I, 43
Thailand – Cigarettes (Philippines)	Appellate Body Report, *Thailand – Customs and Fiscal Measures on Cigarettes from the Philippines*, WT/DS371/AB/R, adopted 15 July 2011
Thailand – Cigarettes (Philippines)	Panel Report, *Thailand – Customs and Fiscal Measures on Cigarettes from the Philippines*, WT/DS371/R, adopted 15 July 2011, as modified by Appellate Body Report WT/DS371/AB/R
US – Carbon Steel	Appellate Body Report, *United States – Countervailing Duties on Certain Corrosion-Resistant Carbon Steel Flat Products from Germany*, WT/DS213/AB/R and Corr.1, adopted 19 December 2002, DSR 2002:IX, 3779

Short Title	Full Case Title and Citation
US – Clove Cigarettes	Appellate Body Report, *United States – Measures Affecting the Production and Sale of Clove Cigarettes*, WT/DS406/AB/R, adopted 24 April 2012
US – Clove Cigarettes	Panel Report, *United States – Measures Affecting the Production and Sale of Clove Cigarettes*, WT/DS406/R, adopted 24 April 2012, as modified by Appellate Body Report WT/DS406/AB/R
US – Continued Zeroing	Appellate Body Report, *United States – Continued Existence and Application of Zeroing Methodology*, WT/DS350/AB/R, adopted 19 February 2009, DSR 2009:III, 1291
US – COOL	Panel Reports, *United States – Certain Country of Origin Labelling (COOL) Requirements*, WT/DS384/R / WT/DS386/R, circulated to WTO Members 18 November 2011
US – FSC (Article 21.5 – EC)	Appellate Body Report, *United States – Tax Treatment for "Foreign Sales Corporations" – Recourse to Article 21.5 of the DSU by the European Communities*, WT/DS108/AB/RW, adopted 29 January 2002, DSR 2002:I, 55
US – Gambling	Appellate Body Report, *United States – Measures Affecting the Cross-Border Supply of Gambling and Betting Services*, WT/DS285/AB/R, adopted 20 April 2005, DSR 2005:XII, 5663 (Corr.1, DSR 2006:XII, 5475)
US – Gambling	Panel Report, *United States – Measures Affecting the Cross-Border Supply of Gambling and Betting Services*, WT/DS285/R, adopted 20 April 2005, as modified by Appellate Body Report WT/DS285/AB/R, DSR 2005:XII, 5797
US – Large Civil Aircraft (2nd complaint)	Appellate Body Report, *United States – Measures Affecting Trade in Large Civil Aircraft (Second Complaint)*, WT/DS353/AB/R, adopted 23 March 2012
US – Oil Country Tubular Goods Sunset Reviews	Appellate Body Report, *United States – Sunset Reviews of Anti-Dumping Measures on Oil Country Tubular Goods from Argentina*, WT/DS268/AB/R, adopted 17 December 2004, DSR 2004:VII, 3257

Short Title	Full Case Title and Citation
US – Shrimp (Thailand)	Panel Report, *United States – Measures Relating to Shrimp from Thailand*, WT/DS343/R, adopted 1 August 2008, as modified by Appellate Body Report WT/DS343/AB/R / WT/DS345/AB/R, DSR 2008:VII, 2539
US – Steel Safeguards	Appellate Body Report, *United States – Definitive Safeguard Measures on Imports of Certain Steel Products*, WT/DS248/AB/R, WT/DS249/AB/R, WT/DS251/AB/R, WT/DS252/AB/R, WT/DS253/AB/R, WT/DS254/AB/R, WT/DS258/AB/R, WT/DS259/AB/R, adopted 10 December 2003, DSR 2003:VII, 3117
US – Tuna II (Mexico)	Appellate Body Report, *United States – Measures Concerning the Importation, Marketing and Sale of Tuna and Tuna Products*, WT/DS381/AB/R, adopted 13 June 2012
US – Tuna II (Mexico)	Panel Report, *United States – Measures Concerning the Importation, Marketing and Sale of Tuna and Tuna Products*, WT/DS381/R, adopted 13 June 2012, as modified by Appellate Body Report WT/DS381/AB/R
US – Upland Cotton (Article 21.5 – Brazil)	Appellate Body Report, *United States – Subsidies on Upland Cotton – Recourse to Article 21.5 of the DSU by Brazil*, WT/DS267/AB/RW, adopted 20 June 2008, DSR 2008:III, 809
US – Wheat Gluten	Appellate Body Report, *United States – Definitive Safeguard Measures on Imports of Wheat Gluten from the European Communities*, WT/DS166/AB/R, adopted 19 January 2001, DSR 2001:II, 717

PANEL EXHIBITS REFERRED TO IN THESE REPORTS

Panel Exhibit	Title
CDA-1	Farm Security and Rural Investment Act of 2002, Public Law No. 107-171, 116 Stat. 134, section 10816–Country of origin labeling, 533-535
CDA-2	Food, Conservation, and Energy Act of 2008, Public Law No. 110-234, 122 Stat. 923, section 11002–Country of origin labeling, 1351-1354
CDA-3	Interim Final Rule on Mandatory Country of Origin Labeling of Beef, Pork, Lamb, Chicken, Goat Meat, Perishable Agricultural Commodities, Peanuts, Pecans, Ginseng, and Macadamia Nuts, published in *United States Federal Register*, Vol. 73, No. 149 (1 August 2008) 45106, codified as *United States Code of Federal Regulations*, Title 7, Part 65
CDA-4	Interim Final Rule on Mandatory Country of Origin Labeling of Muscle Cuts of Beef (Including Veal), Lamb, Chicken, Goat, and Pork; Ground Beef, Ground Lamb, Ground Chicken, Ground Goat, and Ground Pork, published in *United States Federal Register*, Vol. 73, No. 168 (28 August 2008) 50701, codified as *United States Code of Federal Regulations*, Title 9, Parts 317 and 381
CDA-5	Final Rule on Mandatory Country of Origin Labeling of Beef, Pork, Lamb, Chicken, Goat Meat, Wild and Farm-Raised Fish and Shellfish, Perishable Agricultural Commodities, Peanuts, Pecans, Ginseng, and Macadamia Nuts, published in *United States Federal Register*, Vol. 74, No. 10 (15 January 2009) 2658, codified as *United States Code of Federal Regulations*, Title 7, Parts 60 and 65
CDA-6	Letter sent from the US Secretary of Agriculture, Thomas J. Vilsack, to "Industry Representative[s]", dated 20 February 2009
CDA-10	Country-of-Origin Meat Labeling Act, Hearing on HR 1144 before the Subcommittee on Livestock and Horticulture of the Committee on Agriculture, House of Representatives, 106th Congress, 2nd Session, 26 September 2000

Panel Exhibit	Title
CDA-36	Letter from James Lochner, Senior Group Vice President, Tyson Fresh Meats, Inc. to "Tyson Fresh Meats Cattle Supplier[s]", dated 14 October 2008
CDA-38	Letter from James Lochner, Senior Group Vice President, Tyson Fresh Meats, Inc. to "Valued Customer[s]", dated 14 October 2008
CDA-41	CANFAX, "U.S. Packer procurements policies for Canadian Cattle", updated 24 April 2009
CDA-46	Data on "Total Canadian Cattle Exports as a Percentage of Weekly U.S. Cattle Slaughter", based on USDA APHIS and Market News reports
CDA-57 (BCI)	Witness Statement of Harvey Dann, dated 22 February 2010
CDA-65	USDA, "Country of Origin Labeling Compliance Guide", revised 12 May 2009
CDA-69 (BCI)	Witness Statement of Harold Rempel, dated 11 June 2010
CDA-75 (BCI)	Witness Statement of Duncan Mackey, dated 3 March 2010
CDA-76 (BCI)	E-mail from Gary Machan, Tyson Fresh Meats to Martin Rice, Executive Director, Canadian Pork Council, dated 18 December 2009
CDA-79	Daniel A. Sumner, "Econometric Analysis of the Differential Effects of Mandatory Country of Origin Labeling in the United States on Canadian Cattle Prices and Imports of Canadian Cattle and Hogs into the United States" (16 June 2010)
CDA-81 (BCI)	Witness Statement of John Lawton, dated 22 February 2010
CDA-90 (BCI)	E-mail from Bradley Brandenburg, Director of Cattle Procurement, Tyson Fresh Meats to John Masswohl, dated 6 October 2008
CDA-117	Remy Jurenas, "Country-of-Origin Labeling for Foods", CRS Report for Congress, 7-5700, 18 May 2009
CDA-161	Photographs of COOL labels

Panel Exhibit	Title
CDA-174	Letter from Dennis McGivern, Vice President, Informa Economics, Inc. to Susan Sarich, Deputy Director, Agriculture and Agri-Food Canada, dated 1 September 2010
CDA-192	*FMI Backgrounder*, "Country of Origin Labeling for Food", Food Marketing Institute
CDA-196	Data on "Comparison of U.S. APHIS/AMS and U.S. Census Export Data for Canadian Livestock" (Canadian revision of Panel Exhibit US-107)
CDA-199	Remy Jurenas, "Country-of-Origin Labeling for Foods", CRS Report for Congress, 7-5700, 15 July 2010
CDA-206	Document entitled "Detailed results from regressions quantifying the effects of the COOL measure on Canadian cattle and hogs", comprising tables of estimates using updated data and additional specifications
CDA-211	"2010 National Meat Case Study Methodology", excerpt from 2010 NMCS Research PowerPoint presentation
EU-4	Regulation (EC) No. 1760/2000 of the European Parliament and of the Council of 17 July 2000 establishing a system for the identification and registration of bovine animals and regarding the labelling of beef and beef products and repealing Council Regulation (EC) No 820/97, *Official Journal of the European Communities*, L Series, No. 204 (11 August 2000), 1
MEX-1	Agricultural Marketing Act of 1946, 60 Stat. 1087, *United States Code*, Title 7, section 1621 *et seq.*
MEX-2	Farm Security and Rural Investment Act of 2002, Public Law No. 107-171, 116 Stat. 134, section 10816–Country of origin labeling, 533-535
MEX-3	Food, Conservation, and Energy Act of 2008, Public Law No. 110-234, 122 Stat. 923, section 11002–Country of origin labeling, 1351-1354

Panel Exhibit	Title
MEX-4	Interim Final Rule on Mandatory Country of Origin Labeling of Beef, Pork, Lamb, Chicken, Goat Meat, Perishable Agricultural Commodities, Peanuts, Pecans, Ginseng, and Macadamia Nuts, published in *United States Federal Register*, Vol. 73, No. 149 (1 August 2008) 45106, codified as *United States Code of Federal Regulations*, Title 7, Part 65
MEX-5	Interim Final Rule on Mandatory Country of Origin Labeling of Muscle Cuts of Beef (Including Veal), Lamb, Chicken, Goat, and Pork; Ground Beef, Ground Lamb, Ground Chicken, Ground Goat, and Ground Pork, published in *United States Federal Register*, Vol. 73, No. 168 (28 August 2008) 50701, codified as *United States Code of Federal Regulations*, Title 9, Parts 317 and 381
MEX-6	Final Rule on Mandatory Country of Origin Labeling of Muscle Cuts of Beef (Including Veal), Lamb, Chicken, Goat and Pork, Ground Beef Ground Lamb, Ground Chicken, Ground Goat, and Ground Pork, published in *United States Federal Register*, Vol. 74, No. 53 (20 March 2009) 11837, codified as *United States Code of Federal Regulations*, Title 9, Parts 317 and 381
MEX-7	Final Rule on Mandatory Country of Origin Labeling of Beef, Pork, Lamb, Chicken, Goat Meat, Wild and Farm-Raised Fish and Shellfish, Perishable Agricultural Commodities, Peanuts, Pecans, Ginseng, and Macadamia Nuts, published in *United States Federal Register*, Vol. 74, No. 10 (15 January 2009) 2658, codified as *United States Code of Federal Regulations*, Title 7, Parts 60 and 65
MEX-8	Letter from the US Secretary of Agriculture, Thomas J. Vilsack, to "Industry Representative[s]", dated 20 February 2009
MEX-9	Section 1638 of the Agricultural Marketing Act of 1946, 60 Stat. 1087, *United States Code*, Title 7, section 1621 et seq.

Panel Exhibit	Title
MEX-32	FSIS, Product Labeling: Defining United States Cattle and United States Fresh Beef Products, published on 7 August 2001 in *United States Federal Register*, Vol. 66, No. 152, at p. 41160, codified as *United States Code of Federal Regulations*, Title 9, Parts 317 and 327
MEX-33	Tyson report, "Country of Origin Labeling" (April 2009)
MEX-35	W.F. Hahn, M. Haley, D. Leuck, J.J. Miller, J. Perry, F. Taha, and S. Zahniser, "Market Integration of the North American Animal Products Complex", USDA *Electronic Outlook Report from The Economic Research Service*, LDP-M-131-01 (May 2005)
MEX-37 (BCI)	Affidavit of the Chairman of the Confederación Nacional de Organizaciones Ganaderas (CNOG), dated 17 May 2010
MEX-41	USDA Chart – "Cattle, Beef, Muscle Cuts of Beef, Ground Beef", contained in USDA, "Country of Origin Labeling Compliance Guide", revised 12 May 2009, at p. 17
MEX-42 (BCI)	Letter from a Tyson Fresh Meats, Inc. executive to Tyson cattle suppliers, dated 24 December 2008
MEX-46 (BCI)	Data on cattle procurement showing the terms of trade for Cargill's purchases of Mexican-born cattle (March 2009)
MEX-47	USDA Market News, AL_LS626, weekly news reports from January 2005 to June 2010
MEX-48	Price comparison tables, sourced from USDA website: <http://marketnews.usda.gov/portal/lg>
MEX-49	Country-of-Origin Meat Labeling Act, Hearing on HR 1144 before the Subcommittee on Livestock and Horticulture of the Committee on Agriculture, House of Representatives, 106th Congress, 2nd session, 26 September 2000

Panel Exhibit	Title
MEX-50	Letter from R-CALF USA to US Secretary of Agriculture, Hon. Tom Vilsack and US Trade Representative, Hon. Ron Kirk, "Re: Canada's WTO Complaint Against U.S. COOL Law", dated 16 October 2009
MEX-51	Mandatory Country of Origin Labeling, Hearing before the Committee on Agriculture, House of Representatives, 108th Congress, 26 June 2003
MEX-53	G. Becker, "Country-Of-Origin Labeling For Foods", CRS Report for Congress, 7-5700, 24 February 2009
MEX-55	T. Johnston, "Tyson Cool With Federal Labeling Law", 16 October 2008, available at: < http://www.meatingplace.com>
MEX-64 (BCI)	Letter from a Tyson Fresh Meats, Inc. executive to the President of the Confederación Nacional de Organizaciones Ganaderas (CNOG), dated 9 April 2009
MEX-71	Photographs of labels for US muscle cuts of beef
MEX-87	US Customs and Border Protection, Notice of Proposed Rulemaking on Uniform Rules of Origin for Imported Merchandise, published in *United States Federal Register*, Vol. 73, No. 144 (25 July 2008) 43385, codified as *United States Code of Federal Regulations*, Title 19, Parts 4, 7, 10, 102, 134, and 177
MEX-88	Dermot J. Hayes and Steve R. Meyer, "Impact of Mandatory Country of Origin Labeling on U.S. pork Exports"
MEX-89	107th Congressional Record–House, Statement by Hon. Mr. Lucas (daily ed. 2 May 2002) H2033
MEX-91	107th Congressional Record–Senate, Statement by Hon. Tim Johnson, (daily ed. 8 May 2002) S3998
MEX-92	107th Congressional Record–Senate, Statement by Hon. Mr. Inouye (daily ed. 8 May 2002) S4022
MEX-93	107th Congressional Record–Senate, Statement by Hon. Mr. Wyden (daily ed. 8 May 2002) S4043

Panel Exhibit	Title
MEX-94	Livestock Issues for the New Federal Farm Bill, Hearing before the Committee on Agriculture, Nutrition, and Forestry, US Senate, 107th Congress, 24 July 2001, Statement by Mr. Dennis McDonald, R-CALF USA, at p. 9
MEX-95	R-CALF USA letter from 27 Cattle Associations to members of the US Congress, dated 2 December 2001
MEX-96	Review of the Market Structure of the Livestock Industry, Hearing before the Subcommittee on Livestock, Dairy, and Poultry of the Committee on Agriculture, House of Representatives, 110th Congress, 17 April 2007, Statement of Tom Buis, President, National Farmers Union, at p. 17
MEX-97 (BCI)	Affidavit of the Chairman of the Confederación Nacional de Organizaciones Ganaderas (CNOG), dated 25 October 2010
MEX-101	"Beef Chat: The Wal-Mart Way" (1 June 2003) *Beef*, available at: <beefmagazine.com/mag/beef_walmart/>
MEX-105 (BCI)	Affidavit of the Chairman of the Confederación Nacional de Organizaciones Ganaderas (CNOG), dated 22 December 2010
US-4	Comments of Consumers Union on the USDA AMS Proposed Rule on Mandatory Country of Origin Labeling of Beef, Lamb, Port, Perishable Agricultural Commodities, and Peanuts (20 August 2007)
US-5	Letter from Consumer Federation of America to the USDA AMS Country of Labeling Program, dated 20 August 2007
US-11	"Agriculture, Conservation, and Rural Enhancement Act of 2001", Report of the Committee on Agriculture, Nutrition, and Forestry to Accompany S.1731, Senate Report No. 107-117 (2001), excerpts
US-12	"Food and Energy Security Act of 2007", Report of the Committee on Agriculture, Nutrition, and Forestry on S.2302 with Additional Views, Senate Report No. 110-220 (2007), excerpts
US-13	107th Congressional Record–House, Statement by Rep. John Thune (daily ed. 24 April 2002) H1538

Panel Exhibit	Title
US-14	110th Congressional Record–Senate, Statement by Senator Charles Grassley (daily ed. 5 November 2007) S13761
US-17	Letter from a Public Citizen executive to the FSIS, dated 9 October 2001
US-28	Economic Data on "Cattle, Hog, Beef, and Pork Sectors of Canada, U.S. and Mexico"
US-42	USDA Office of the Chief Economist, "Modeling the Impact of Country of Origin Labeling Requirements on U.S. Imports of Livestock from Canada and Mexico"
US-48	107th Congressional Record–Senate, Statement by Senator Tim Johnson (8 May 2002) S4024
US-53	Letter from Peter D. Sutherland, Director-General of the GATT to Ambassador John Schmidt, Chief US Negotiator, dated 15 December 1993
US-61	107th Congressional Record–Senate, Statement by Senator Tim Johnson (daily ed. 14 December 2001) S13270
US-67	Photographs of labels for muscle cuts of meat
US-84	Letter from the Consumers Federation of America to the FSIS, dated 17 September 2001
US-86	Canadian and Mexican Livestock Market Share, Data from US Department of Commerce and USDA National Agricultural Statistic Service
US-89	"Consumers Union Lauds Mandatory Country of Origin Labeling Finally Implemented on All Fresh Produce, Meat & Poultry in the United States", Consumers Union Press Release, 12 September 2008
US-90	"Statement of CFA's Chris Waldrop on the Implementation of Country of Origin Labeling", Consumer Federation of America Press Release, 30 September 2008
US-95	Photographs of B Label and commingled meat taken at Pick 'n Save in Kenosha, Wisconsin, 18 October 2010
US-96	Photographs of B Label and commingled meat taken at Safeway in Washington, DC, 22 August 2010

Panel Exhibit	Title
US-98	Photographs of B Label and commingled meat taken at Walmart in Austin, Texas, 27 October 2010
US-100	Letter from Food & Water Watch to the USDA, dated 30 September 2008
US 101 (BCI)	Producer Affidavits: Continuous Country of Origin Affidavit/Declarations Provided to USDA in 2009/2010
US-102 (BCI)	Witness Statement of Larry R. Meadows, dated 28 October 2010
US-108	Data on North American cattle and hog prices (sourced from LMIC database for US and Canadian cattle, AMS data for Mexico feeder prices, ERS Exchange Rate database, and Statistics Canada
US-111	TACD, Resolution on Country of Origin Labeling, Doc. No. Food 29-08 (March 2008)
US-113	Letter from Gregory Cook to the USDA, dated 18 July 2007
US-115	Letter from Ross Vincent to the FSIS, dated 2 October 2001
US-116	Letter from Consumers Union to Congress, dated 26 February 2007
US-119	Comments on Mandatory Country of Origin Labeling for Beef, Lamb, Pork, Perishable Agricultural Commodities, and Peanuts, submitted by Charles Rich to the USDA (19 July 2007)
US-120	Comments on Mandatory Country of Origin Labeling for Beef, Lamb, Pork, Perishable Agricultural Commodities, and Peanuts, submitted by Elizabeth Brennan to the USDA (20 August 2007)
US-121	Comments submitted by Sherri Vinton to the USDA (18 November 2003)
US-122	Comments on Mandatory Country of Origin Labeling for Beef, Lamb, Pork, Perishable Agricultural Commodities, and Peanuts, submitted by Richard Leithiser to the USDA (20 August 2007)

Panel Exhibit	Title
US-123	Comments on Mandatory Country of Origin Labeling for Beef, Lamb, Pork, Perishable Agricultural Commodities, and Peanuts, submitted by John and Rita Lesch to the USDA (20 August 2007)
US-124	Comments on Mandatory Country of Origin Labeling for Beef, Lamb, Pork, Perishable Agricultural Commodities, and Peanuts, submitted by Ron Krishner to the USDA (20 August 2007)
US-125	Comments on Mandatory Country of Origin Labeling for Beef, Lamb, Pork, Perishable Agricultural Commodities, and Peanuts, submitted by Jennifer Walla to the USDA (20 August 2007)
US-126	Comments submitted by Dan Downs to the USDA (2 August 2002)
US-144	Data on "Mixed Origin Category D Meat as Percentage of U.S. Imports and Domestic Consumption"
US-145	USDA Country of Origin Labeling Survey (July 2009)
US-148	Christopher G. Davis and Biing-Hwan Lin, "Factors Affecting U.S. Pork Consumption", Electronic Outlook Report from the Economic Research Service, U.S. Department of Agriculture (May 2005)

ABBREVIATIONS USED IN THESE REPORTS

Abbreviation	Description
2002 Farm Bill	Farm Security and Rural Investment Act of 2002, Public Law No. 107-171, section 10816, 116 Stat. 134, 533-535 (Panel Exhibits CDA-1 and MEX-2)
2008 Farm Bill	Food, Conservation, and Energy Act of 2008, Public Law No. 110-234, section 11002, 122 Stat. 923, 1351-1354 (Panel Exhibits CDA-2 and MEX-3)
2009 Final Rule (AMS)	Final Rule on Mandatory Country of Origin Labeling of Beef, Pork, Lamb, Chicken, Goat Meat, Wild and Farm-Raised Fish and Shellfish, Perishable Agricultural Commodities, Peanuts, Pecans, Ginseng, and Macadamia Nuts, published in *United States Federal Register*, Vol. 74, No. 10 (15 January 2009) 2704-2707, codified as *United States Code of Federal Regulations*, Title 7, Part 65—Country of Origin Labeling of Beef, Pork, Lamb, Chicken, Goat Meat, Perishable Agricultural Commodities, Macadamia Nuts, Pecans, Peanuts, and Ginseng (Panel Exhibits CDA-5 and MEX-7)
2009 Final Rule (FSIS)	Final Rule on Mandatory Country of Origin Labeling of Muscle Cuts of Beef (Including Veal), Lamb, Chicken, Goat, and Pork; Ground Beef, Ground Lamb, Ground Chicken, Ground Goat, and Ground Pork, published in *United States Federal Register*, Vol. 74, No. 53 (20 March 2009) 11837, codified as *United States Code of Federal Regulations*, Title 9, Parts 317 and 381 (Panel Exhibit MEX-6)
AMS	Agriculture Marketing Service (of the US Department of Agriculture)
BCI	Business confidential information
Canada Panel Report	Panel Report, *United States – Certain Country of Origin Labelling (COOL) Requirements* (Complaint by Canada) (WT/DS384/R)
Compliance Guide	USDA, "Country of Origin Labeling Compliance Guide", revised 12 May 2009 (Panel Exhibits CDA-65, at p. 17 and MEX-41)

Abbreviation	Description
COOL	Country of origin labelling
COOL measure	COOL statute together with the 2009 Final Rule (AMS)
COOL statute	The Agricultural Marketing Act of 1946, as amended by the 2002 Farm Bill and the 2008 Farm Bill
DSB	Dispute Settlement Body
DSU	*Understanding on Rules and Procedures Governing the Settlement of Disputes*
FSIS	Food Safety and Inspection Service (of the US Department of Agriculture)
GATS	*General Agreement on Trade in Services*
GATT 1994	*General Agreement on Tariffs and Trade 1994*
Interim Final Rule (AMS)	Interim Final Rule on Mandatory Country of Origin Labeling of Beef, Pork, Lamb, Chicken, Goat Meat, Perishable Agricultural Commodities, Peanuts, Pecans, Ginseng, and Macadamia Nuts, published in *United States Federal Register*, Vol. 73, No. 149 (1 August 2008) 45106 (Panel Exhibits CDA-3 and MEX-4)
Interim Final Rule (FSIS)	Interim Final Rule on Mandatory Country of Origin Labeling of Muscle Cuts of Beef (Including Veal), Lamb, Chicken, Goat, and Pork; Ground Beef, Ground Lamb, Ground Chicken, Ground Goat, and Ground Pork, published in *United States Federal Register*, Vol. 73, No. 168 (28 August 2008) 50701 (Panel Exhibits CDA-4 and MEX-5)
Mexico Panel Report	Panel Report, *United States – Certain Country of Origin Labelling (COOL) Requirements* (Complaint by Mexico) (WT/DS386/R)
NAFTA	North American Free Trade Agreement
Panel Reports	Panel Reports, *United States – Certain Country of Origin Labelling (COOL) Requirements*, WT/DS384/R, WT/DS386/R
SPS	Sanitary and Phytosanitary
SPS Agreement	*Agreement on the Application of Sanitary and Phytosanitary Measures*

Abbreviation	Description
Sumner Econometric Study	Daniel A. Sumner, "Econometric Analysis of the Differential Effects of Mandatory Country of Origin Labeling in the United States on Canadian Cattle Prices and Imports of Canadian Cattle and Hogs into the United States" (16 June 2010) (Panel Exhibit CDA-79)
TBT	Technical Barriers to Trade
TBT Agreement	*Agreement on Technical Barriers to Trade*
TRIPS Agreement	*Agreement on Trade-Related Aspects of Intellectual Property Rights*
USDA	US Department of Agriculture
USDA Econometric Study	USDA Office of the Chief Economist, "Modeling the Impact of Country of Origin Labeling Requirements on U.S. Imports of Livestock from Canada and Mexico" (Panel Exhibit US-42)
Vienna Convention	*Vienna Convention on the Law of Treaties*, Done at Vienna, 23 May 1969, 1155 UNTS 331; 8 International Legal Materials 679
Vilsack letter	Letter dated 20 February 2009 from the US Secretary of Agriculture, Thomas J. Vilsack, to "Industry Representative[s]" (Panel Exhibits CDA-6 AND MEX-8)
Working Procedures	*Working Procedures for Appellate Review*, WT/AB/WP/6, 16 August 2010
WTO	World Trade Organization

I. INTRODUCTION

1. Canada, Mexico, and the United States each appeals certain issues of law and legal interpretations developed in the Panel Reports[1], *United States – Certain Country of Origin Labelling (COOL) Requirements* (the "Panel Reports"). The Panel was established on 19 November 2009 to consider complaints by Canada[2] and Mexico[3] regarding certain US country of origin labelling ("COOL") requirements for beef and pork. Both Canada and Mexico challenged the following measures:

(a) the Agricultural Marketing Act of 1946[4], as amended by the "2002 Farm Bill" and the "2008 Farm Bill" (the "COOL statute")[5];

(b) the Final Rule on Mandatory Country of Origin Labeling of Beef, Pork, Lamb, Chicken, Goat Meat, Perishable Agricultural Commodities, Peanuts, Pecans, Ginseng, and Macadamia Nuts[6] (the "2009 Final Rule (AMS)")[7];

---

[1] WT/DS384/R (the "Canada Panel Report"); WT/DS386/R (the "Mexico Panel Report"), 18 November 2011. At the United States' request, the Panel issued its findings in the form of a single document containing two separate reports. This document comprises common sections containing the cover page, table of contents, and sections I to VII (which includes the Panel's findings), and separate conclusions and recommendations in respect of the dispute initiated by Canada and the one initiated by Mexico. (See Panel Reports, para. 2.11)

[2] Request for the Establishment of a Panel by Canada, WT/DS384/8.

[3] Request for the Establishment of a Panel by Mexico, WT/DS386/7 and Corr.1.

[4] 60 Stat. 1087, *United States Code*, Title 7, section 1621 *et seq.*, as amended. See Panel Exhibits MEX-1 and MEX-9.

[5] See Panel Reports, paras. 2.2(a), 2.3(a), 7.13, and 7.77. The statutory provisions of the COOL measure were introduced in the US Congress through the Farm Security and Rural Investment Act of 2002, Public Law No. 107-171, section 10816, 116 Stat. 134, 533-535 (Panel Exhibits CDA-1 and MEX-2) (the "2002 Farm Bill"), which was subsequently amended by the Food, Conservation, and Energy Act of 2008, Public Law No. 110-234, section 11002, 122 Stat. 923, 1351-1354 (Panel Exhibits CDA-2 and MEX-3) (the "2008 Farm Bill"). (Panel Reports, para. 7.77) Both Farm Bills subsequently became part of the Agricultural Marketing Act of 1946, codified as *United States Code*, Title 7, section 1621 *et seq.* (*Ibid.*, para. 7.13) The COOL requirements are contained in section 1638 of Title 7.

[6] Final Rule on Mandatory Country of Origin Labeling of Beef, Pork, Lamb, Chicken, Goat Meat, Wild and Farm-Raised Fish and Shellfish, Perishable Agricultural Commodities, Peanuts, Pecans, Ginseng, and Macadamia Nuts, published in *United States Federal Register*, Vol. 74, No. 10 (15 January 2009) 2704-2707, codified as *United States Code of Federal Regulations*, Title 7, Part 65—Country of Origin Labeling of Beef, Pork, Lamb, Chicken, Goat Meat, Perishable Agricultural Commodities, Macadamia Nuts, Pecans, Peanuts, and Ginseng (Panel Exhibits CDA-5 and MEX-7).

[7] Panel Reports, paras. 2.2(b), 2.2(c), 2.3(c), and 7.14. The term "2009 Final Rule (AMS)" was used by the Panel to distinguish this Rule, promulgated by the Agricultural Marketing Service of the US Department of Agriculture (the "AMS"), from a separate Rule promulgated by the Food Safety

(c) a letter dated 20 February 2009 from the US Secretary of Agriculture, Thomas J. Vilsack, to "Industry Representative[s]"[8] (the "Vilsack letter")[9]; and

(d) the Interim Final Rule on Mandatory Country of Origin Labeling of Beef, Pork, Lamb, Chicken, Goat Meat, Perishable Agricultural Commodities, Peanuts, Pecans, Ginseng, and Macadamia Nuts[10] (the "Interim Final Rule (AMS)").[11]

2. In addition to the above measures, Mexico also challenged the Interim Final Rule on Mandatory Country of Origin Labeling of Muscle Cuts of Beef (Including Veal), Lamb, Chicken, Goat, and Pork; Ground Beef, Ground Lamb, Ground Chicken, Ground Goat, and Ground Pork[12] (the "Interim Final Rule (FSIS)").[13]

3. Generally speaking, the measures challenged by the complainants impose on retailers an obligation to provide origin information on the covered commodities that they sell, including a range of meat products, as well as other agricultural products. The measures also set out the criteria that need to be met for the covered commodities to be labelled as US origin.[14] Canada and Mexico challenged the measures only insofar as they regulate the labelling of beef and pork.[15] For these meat products, origin is defined according to the country or countries in which certain steps in the production of the meat occurr.[16] US origin can only be granted to meat derived from an animal that was exclusively born, raised, and slaughtered in the United States.[17] The measures further set out rules for determining the country or countries of origin of meat when some or all of

---

and Inspection Service of the US Department of Agriculture (the "FSIS"). For the sake of consistency, the Appellate Body will use this same term. Under the 2002 Farm Bill, the AMS was vested with authority over the COOL rulemaking process, complementing the work that the FSIS had been performing in the past. (*Ibid.*, footnote 34 to para. 7.9)

8 Panel Exhibits CDA-6 and MEX-8.

9 Panel Reports, paras. 2.2(d) and 2.3(e).

10 Published in *United States Federal Register*, Vol. 73, No. 149 (1 August 2008) 45106 (Panel Exhibits CDA-3 and MEX-4).

11 Panel Reports, paras. 2.2(b) and 2.3(b).

12 Published in *United States Federal Register*, Vol. 73, No. 168 (28 August 2008) 50701 (Panel Exhibits CDA-4 and MEX-5).

13 Panel Reports, paras. 2.3(d) and 7.18. Although Canada also identified this measure in its request for the establishment of a panel, it decided not to pursue it further in the Panel proceedings. (*Ibid.*, footnote 42 to para. 7.18)

14 Panel Reports, paras. 7.78, 7.81, and 7.89.

15 Panel Reports, paras. 7.64-7.67.

16 Panel Reports, para. 7.255.

17 Panel Reports, para. 7.78.

the relevant production steps (birth, raising, slaughter) involved in the meat production process have taken place outside the United States, and create four different labelling categories for muscle cut meat and one for ground meat.[18] The measures also impose recordkeeping, auditing, and verification requirements on producers along the meat production chain.[19] Different stages of North American livestock and meat production are often performed in more than one country. Both Canada and Mexico export cattle to the United States that are subsequently processed into beef. Canada additionally exports hogs to the United States that are subsequently processed into pork.[20] The factual aspects of these disputes are set forth in greater detail in paragraphs 7.75 to 7.142 of the Panel Reports, and in section IV of these Reports.

4. Both complainants claimed that the challenged measures are inconsistent with Articles 2.1 and 2.2 of the *Agreement on Technical Barriers to Trade* (the "*TBT Agreement*"), and with Articles III:4 and X:3(a) of the *General Agreement on Tariffs and Trade 1994* (the "GATT 1994"). The complainants also raised a non-violation claim under Article XXIII:1(b) of the GATT 1994.[21] More specifically, they argued that the United States' measures accord imported livestock less favourable treatment than that accorded to like domestic livestock in a manner inconsistent with Article 2.1 of the *TBT Agreement* and Article III:4 of the GATT 1994. In their view, compliance with the COOL requirements results in higher segregation costs for imported livestock, which in turn adversely affects the competitive conditions for imported livestock in the US market.[22] They also claimed that the COOL requirements are inconsistent with Article 2.2 of the *TBT Agreement* because their objective is to protect the domestic industry, which is not a legitimate objective, and because, in any event, they do not fulfil the objective identified by the United States.[23] The complainants further alleged that the United States' administration of the COOL requirements is inconsistent with Article X:3(a) of the GATT 1994[24], and that the application of the COOL requirements nullifies or impairs benefits accruing to them under successive rounds of multilateral trade negotiations within the meaning of Article XXIII:1(b) of the GATT 1994.[25] Mexico additionally

---

18 Panel Reports, paras. 7.81 and 7.89.

19 Panel Reports, paras. 7.116-7.120.

20 Panel Reports, para. 7.140.

21 Panel Reports, paras. 3.1 and 3.3.

22 Panel Reports, para. 7.2.

23 Panel Reports, para. 7.3.

24 Panel Reports, para. 7.4.

25 Panel Reports, paras. 7.1 and 7.889.

claimed that the COOL requirements are inconsistent with Articles 2.4, 12.1, and 12.3 of the *TBT Agreement*.[26]

5. The Panel Reports were circulated to Members of the World Trade Organization (the "WTO") on 18 November 2011. In its Reports, the Panel made procedural rulings regarding: (i) additional procedures for the protection of business confidential information ("BCI"); (ii) procedures for open hearings; and (iii) enhanced third party rights.[27] Furthermore, the Panel found the measures identified in paragraphs 1 and 2 above to be within its terms of reference.[28] The Panel, however, decided not to make findings or recommendations on the Interim Final Rule (AMS) and the Interim Final Rule (FSIS), noting that they had expired before the establishment of the Panel.[29] The Panel nonetheless stated that it would consider them, where relevant, in the context of its examination of the parties' claims regarding the other three measures.[30] In addition, the Panel found that the Final Rule on Mandatory Country of Origin Labeling of Muscle Cuts of Beef (Including Veal), Lamb, Chicken, Goat, and Pork; Ground Beef, Ground Lamb, Ground Chicken, Ground Goat, and Ground Pork[31] (the "2009 Final Rule (FSIS)"), which Mexico sought to challenge, fell outside the Panel's terms of reference because it was not mentioned in Mexico's request for the establishment of a panel.[32]

6. The Panel thus stated that it would examine, and make findings and recommendations, with respect to the COOL statute, the 2009 Final Rule (AMS), and the Vilsack letter.[33] The Panel rejected the contention of Canada and of Mexico that the Vilsack letter should be examined together with the COOL statute and the 2009 Final Rule (AMS) as one single measure. Instead, the Panel decided to examine the relevant elements of both the COOL statute and the 2009 Final Rule (AMS) pertaining to the COOL requirements for meat products "as an integral part" of one single measure (the "COOL measure").[34] As for the

---

[26] Mexico claimed that the COOL requirements are inconsistent with Article 2.4 of the *TBT Agreement* because the United States failed to base its technical regulation on a relevant international standard. Mexico also argued that the United States did not take into account Mexico's special needs as a developing country when preparing and applying the COOL requirements, in contravention of Articles 12.1 and 12.3 of the *TBT Agreement*. (Panel Reports, paras. 3.3 and 7.5)

[27] Panel Reports, paras. 2.4-2.8.

[28] Panel Reports, para. 7.21.

[29] The Panel found that making a finding or recommendation on these measures would not "contribute to resolving the current dispute". (Panel Reports, para. 7.34)

[30] Panel Reports, para. 7.34.

[31] Published in *United States Federal Register*, Vol. 74, No. 53 (20 March 2009) 11837 (Panel Exhibit MEX-6), codified as *United States Code of Federal Regulations*, Title 9, Parts 317 and 381.

[32] Panel Reports, para. 7.19.

[33] Panel Reports, para. 7.34.

[34] Panel Reports, para. 7.61.

Vilsack letter, the Panel treated it as a separate measure distinguishable from the COOL statute and the 2009 Final Rule (AMS) "[i]n light of its distinct legal and substantive nature".[35]

7. With respect to Canada's and Mexico's claims under the *TBT Agreement*, the Panel concluded that:

(a) the COOL measure is a "technical regulation" within the meaning of Annex 1.1 to the *TBT Agreement*, whereas the Vilsack letter is not[36];

(b) the COOL measure, in particular in regard to the muscle cut meat labels, violates Article 2.1 because it affords imported livestock treatment less favourable than that accorded to like domestic livestock[37]; and

(c) the COOL measure violates Article 2.2 because it does not fulfil the objective of providing consumer information on origin with respect to meat products.[38]

8. With respect to Canada's and Mexico's claims under the GATT 1994, the Panel concluded that:

(a) it need not make a finding on the COOL measure under Article III:4 in the light of its finding that the same measure violates the national treatment obligation under Article 2.1 of the *TBT Agreement*[39];

---

35 Panel Reports, para. 7.63. The Panel noted, first, that, whereas the COOL statute and the 2009 Final Rule (AMS) are instruments of statutory and regulatory authorities, the Vilsack letter does not have such legal status. Second, the COOL statute and the 2009 Final Rule (AMS) are closely connected to each other in that the latter lays out specificities necessary to implement the contents of the former. By contrast, the Vilsack letter does not have a formal legal link to either the COOL statute or the 2009 Final Rule (AMS). (*Ibid.*, paras. 7.53-7.55)

36 Canada Panel Report, para. 8.3(a); Mexico Panel Report, para. 8.3(a). See also Panel Reports, paras. 7.146-7.216.

37 Canada Panel Report, para. 8.3(b); Mexico Panel Report, para. 8.3(b). See also Panel Reports, paras. 7.275-7.420. The Panel found that the complainants had not established that "the ground meat label under the COOL measure results in less favourable treatment for imported livestock." (Panel Reports, para. 7.437)

38 Canada Panel Report, para. 8.3(c); Mexico Panel Report, para. 8.3(c). See also Panel Reports, paras. 7.565-7.720.

39 Canada Panel Report, para. 8.4(a); Mexico Panel Report, para. 8.4(a). See also Panel Reports, para. 7.807.

(b) the Vilsack letter violates Article X:3(a) because it does not constitute a reasonable administration of the COOL measure[40]; and

(c) having found that the Vilsack letter falls within the scope of Article X:3(a), it refrained from examining whether it is inconsistent with Article III:4.[41]

9. In the light of the above findings of violation, the Panel "refrained from examining [Canada's and Mexico's] non-violation claim[s] under Article XXIII:1(b) of the GATT 1994".[42] The Panel rejected Mexico's claims under Articles 2.4, 12.1, and 12.3 of the *TBT Agreement*, finding that Mexico had not established either that the COOL measure violates Article 2.4 of the *TBT Agreement* or that the United States acted inconsistently with Articles 12.1 and 12.3 of the *TBT Agreement*.[43] In addition, the Panel also rejected Mexico's claim that the United States administered the COOL measure in a non-uniform and partial manner inconsistently with Article X:3(a) of the GATT 1994.[44]

10. At a special meeting held on 5 January 2012, the Dispute Settlement Body (the "DSB") adopted a decision to extend the time period for the adoption of the Panel Reports to no later than 23 March 2012.[45] The DSB adopted this decision following the joint requests by Canada and the United States[46], and by Mexico and the United States.[47] The joint requests were made in view of the "current workload of the Appellate Body" and in order to "provide greater flexibility in scheduling any possible appeal of the panel report[s] in this dispute".[48]

11. On 23 March 2012, the United States notified the DSB of its intention to appeal certain issues of law covered in the Panel Reports and certain legal interpretations developed by the Panel, pursuant to Articles 16.4 and 17 of the

---

[40] Canada Panel Report, para. 8.4(b); Mexico Panel Report, para. 8.4(b). See also Panel Reports, paras. 7.850-7.864.

[41] Canada Panel Report, para. 8.4(c); Mexico Panel Report, para. 8.4(d).

[42] Canada Panel Report, para. 8.5; Mexico Panel Report, para. 8.5. See also Panel Reports, paras. 7.900-7.907.

[43] Mexico Panel Report, para. 8.3(d), (e), and (f). See also Panel Reports, paras. 7.728-7.736 and 7.752-7.804.

[44] Mexico Panel Report, para. 8.4(c). See also Panel Reports, paras. 7.874-7.885.

[45] The DSB decided that it would, no later than 23 March 2012, adopt the Panel Reports unless (i) the DSB decided by consensus not to do so or (ii) Canada, Mexico, or the United States notified the DSB of its decision to appeal pursuant to Article 16.4 of the *Understanding on Rules and Procedures Governing the Settlement of Disputes* (the "DSU"). (WT/DSB/M/310, paras. 9-12)

[46] WT/DS384/11.

[47] WT/DS386/10.

[48] WT/DS384/11; WT/DS386/10.

Understanding on Rules and Procedures Governing the Settlement of Disputes (the "DSU"), and filed a Notice of Appeal[49] and an appellant's submission pursuant to Rule 20 and Rule 21, respectively, of the *Working Procedures for Appellate Review* (the "*Working Procedures*").[50] On 28 March 2012, Canada and Mexico each notified the DSB of its intention to appeal certain issues of law covered in the respective Panel Reports and certain legal interpretations developed by the Panel, pursuant to Articles 16.4 and 17 of the DSU, and each filed a Notice of Other Appeal[51] pursuant to Rule 23 of the *Working Procedures*. On the same day, Canada and Mexico each filed an other appellant's submission.[52] On 10 April 2012, Canada, Mexico, and the United States each filed an appellee's submission.[53] On 13 April 2012, Australia, Brazil, Colombia, the European Union, and Japan each filed a third participant's submission.[54] On the same day, Argentina, China, Guatemala, India[55], Korea, New Zealand, Peru, and the Separate Customs Territory of Taiwan, Penghu, Kinmen and Matsu each notified its intention to appear at the oral hearing as a third participant.[56]

12. On 5 April 2012, the Appellate Body received a joint communication from the participants. In that communication, Canada and the United States requested that the Appellate Body allow observation by the public of the oral hearing, with the understanding that any information that was designated as confidential in the documents filed in the Panel proceedings would be adequately protected in the course of the hearing. Mexico indicated that it did not object to allowing public observation of the oral hearing, but maintained that its position in these proceedings is without prejudice to its systemic views on this matter. On the same day, the Appellate Body invited the third participants to comment in writing on the request by Canada and the United States by noon on 12 April 2012. Australia, Brazil, China, Colombia, the European Union, Guatemala, India, and New Zealand submitted comments. In their comments, Australia, Brazil, China, Colombia, the European Union, and Guatemala did not object to opening the oral hearing to public observation in these disputes.

---

49 WT/DS384/12; WT/DS386/11 (attached as Annex I to these Reports).

50 WT/AB/WP/6, 16 August 2010.

51 WT/DS384/13 and WT/DS386/12 (attached as Annexes II and III, respectively, to these Reports).

52 Pursuant to Rule 23(3) of the *Working Procedures*.

53 Pursuant to Rules 22 and 23(4) of the *Working Procedures*.

54 Pursuant to Rule 24(1) of the *Working Procedures*.

55 Although India appears to have made its notification pursuant to Rule 24(2) of the *Working Procedures* by stating that it would not file a written submission but would appear at the oral hearing, the notification was not received before the 17:00 deadline specified in Rule 18(1) of the *Working Procedures*. Accordingly, the Division treated it as a notification and request to make an oral statement at the hearing made pursuant to Rule 24(4) of the *Working Procedures*.

56 Pursuant to Rule 24(2) of the *Working Procedures*.

Nonetheless, Brazil, Colombia, and Guatemala each maintained that its position in these disputes is without prejudice to its systemic views on this issue, and China indicated that it wished to maintain the confidentiality of its statements at the oral hearing. India expressed the view that the DSU requires appellate proceedings to be confidential and therefore does not allow opening oral hearings to public observation. India further indicated that it wished to maintain the confidentiality of its statements at the oral hearing. On 16 April 2012, the Division hearing this appeal issued a Procedural Ruling accepting the joint request by Canada and the United States to open the hearing to public observation and adopting additional procedures for the conduct of the hearing. The Procedural Ruling is attached as Annex IV to these Reports.[57]

13. In these appellate proceedings, certain filings were made outside of the deadlines prescribed by the *Working Procedures* or by the Division hearing this appeal.[58] The Appellate Body stresses the importance of all participants and third participants adhering to the time-limits for filing documents, in the interests of fairness and the orderly conduct of appellate proceedings.

14. The oral hearing in this appeal was held on 2 and 3 May 2012. Public observation took place via simultaneous closed-circuit television broadcast to a separate room. Transmission was turned off during statements made by those third participants that had indicated their wish to maintain the confidentiality of their submissions. The participants and eight of the third participants (Australia, Brazil, China, Colombia, the European Union, Guatemala, Japan, and Korea) made opening and/or closing statements.[59] The participants and third participants responded to questions posed by the Members of the Division hearing the appeal.

15. On 14 May 2012, the United States requested the Appellate Body to issue two reports in one single document with common descriptive and analytical sections, and separate sections containing findings and conclusions for each complainant. Canada and Mexico were afforded an opportunity to respond to the United States' request, and neither raised any objection to that request.

---

[57] The Panel adopted additional working procedures for the protection of BCI. (Panel Reports, para. 2.4 and Annex E) None of the participants requested the Appellate Body to adopt additional procedures for the protection of BCI in these appellate proceedings, and the Appellate Body has not done so in this appeal.

[58] The Appellate Body notes, for example, that the hard copy of Canada's other appellant's submission, and the electronic copies of Mexico's Notice of Other Appeal, other appellant's submission, and appellee's submission, were not received before the 17:00 deadline specified in Rule 18(1) of the *Working Procedures*.

[59] Canada attached two exhibits to the written copy of its opening statement, but withdrew the exhibits upon objection by the United States. The hard copies of the exhibits were returned to Canada.

16. By letter of 21 May 2012, the Chair of the Appellate Body notified the Chair of the DSB that the Appellate Body would not be able to circulate its Reports within the 60-day period pursuant to Article 17.5 of the DSU, which would expire on 22 May 2012. In the same letter, the Chair of the Appellate Body also informed the Chair of the DSB that the Appellate Body would be unable to circulate its Reports within the 90-day period provided for under the same provision. The Chair of the Appellate Body explained that this was due in part to the size of this appeal, including the number and complexity of the issues raised by the participants. She added that this was also due to the Appellate Body's heavy caseload, scheduling difficulties resulting from the overlap in the composition of the Divisions hearing different appeals at the same time, as well as constraints resulting from the relocation of the Appellate Body and its Secretariat in the context of ongoing renovation work at the Centre William Rappard. The Chair of the Appellate Body informed the Chair of the DSB that the Reports would be circulated no later than 29 June 2012.

II. ARGUMENTS OF THE PARTICIPANTS AND THE THIRD PARTICIPANTS

A. Claims of Error by the United States – Appellant

1. Article 2.1 of the TBT Agreement

17. The United States requests the Appellate Body to reverse the Panel's finding that the COOL measure is inconsistent with Article 2.1 of the *TBT Agreement* with regard to muscle cuts of meat, in particular the finding that the measure accords less favourable treatment to imported livestock than domestic livestock. The United States argues that the Panel's finding was based on "a faulty and unprecedented legal test"[60] for the assessment of less favourable treatment and on a failure to make an objective assessment of facts related to segregation, commingling, and the price differential in the US livestock market.

(a) The Interpretation and Application of Article 2.1 of the *TBT Agreement*

18. The United States submits that, in order to determine whether a measure accords less favourable treatment to imported products under Article 2.1 of the *TBT Agreement*, the Panel should have followed past Appellate Body and panel reports in *Thailand – Cigarettes (Philippines)*, *Korea – Various Measures on*

[60] United States' appellant's submission, para. 52.

Beef, and *Dominican Republic – Import and Sale of Cigarettes*. According to the United States, these reports generally focused on: (i) "whether the measure *itself* treats imported products differently and less favorably than domestic like products on the basis of their origin"[61]; and (ii) "to the extent that there are adverse effects on imported products, whether these effects are attributable to the measure *itself* or are based on external non-origin related factors, such as pre-existing market conditions and the independent actions of private market actors."[62] Such an approach is consistent with the purpose of Article 2.1 of the *TBT Agreement*, which is to avoid protectionism in the form of technical regulations that apply different treatment on the basis of origin. Moreover, it appropriately focuses the inquiry on whether the measure, including its different treatment based on the origin of products, is the reason for any adverse effects on such products, in the same way as the Appellate Body has found, in the context of Article III:4 of the GATT 1994, that there must be a "genuine relationship" between the measure at issue and the adverse impact on competitive opportunities for imported versus like domestic products.[63]

19. The United States maintains that the Panel erred in finding that the COOL measure on its face accords different treatment to imported livestock when it stated that "imported livestock is ineligible for the label reserved for meat from exclusively US-origin livestock, whereas in certain circumstances meat from domestic livestock is eligible for a label that involves imported livestock."[64] The United States emphasizes that the treatment of the products must be different to be less favourable because, "as a matter of logic, treatment that is identical cannot be less favorable".[65] Because the COOL measure treats imported and domestic products identically, however, no different treatment exists, and therefore no less favourable treatment could have been found. The recordkeeping requirements in the COOL measure, which are the only aspect of the measure that directly affects livestock, apply to all US market participants regardless of where they are located and regardless of the type or origin of livestock they produce. Moreover, pursuant to the labelling requirements, retailers must label meat derived from both domestic and imported livestock in the same conditions (that is, they must affix a label to all categories of meat unless one of the exceptions applies). The United States submits that livestock of

---

61 United States' appellant's submission, para. 68 (referring to Appellate Body Report, *Korea – Various Measures on Beef*, paras. 143-148; and Appellate Body Report, *Thailand – Cigarettes (Philippines)*, paras. 128-140). (original emphasis)

62 United States' appellant's submission, para. 68 (referring to Appellate Body Report, *Dominican Republic – Import and Sale of Cigarettes*, para. 96; Panel Report, *US – Tuna II (Mexico)*, para. 7.334; and Panel Report, *Japan – Film*, paras. 10.381 and 10.382). (original emphasis)

63 United States' appellant's submission, para. 72 (quoting Appellate Body Report, *Thailand – Cigarettes (Philippines)*, para. 134).

64 United States' appellant's submission, paras. 57 (quoting Panel Reports, para. 7.295) and 81.

65 United States' appellant's submission, para. 69.

different origins cannot be said to be treated differently simply because the labels ultimately placed on the meat derived from that livestock say different things. The United States adds that the Panel reached its finding regarding the different treatment of *livestock* based on the "commingling flexibility" affecting *meat*, and observes that *meat* is not a product at issue in these disputes.[66] The United States also points out that the complainants never alleged that, on its face, the COOL measure accords different treatment to imported livestock, and that the commingling flexibilities that the Panel relied on as evidence of different treatment were included in the COOL measure at the request of the complainants.

20. The United States alleges that, having wrongly found different treatment, the Panel never linked that finding to its subsequent finding of less favourable treatment. Instead, the Panel "quickly pivot[ed]" to an assessment of whether there is *de facto* less favourable treatment[67], and based its finding that the COOL measure modifies the conditions of competition to the detriment of imported products on the following erroneous conclusions: (i) the COOL measure involves segregation and, consequently, differential costs for imported livestock; and (ii) the compliance costs involved in the COOL measure create an incentive to process domestic livestock, thereby reducing the competitive opportunities for imported livestock. In reaching these conclusions, the Panel failed to examine whether the measure *itself* affected competitive opportunities to the detriment of imports. Instead, the Panel erroneously assessed whether imported livestock are equally competitive with domestic livestock, notwithstanding that nothing in the *TBT Agreement* or the covered agreements requires Members to ensure that imported products and like domestic products are equally competitive. According to the United States, the question for purposes of Article 2.1 of the *TBT Agreement* is rather whether the technical regulation alters the conditions of competition so as to *deny* imported products the ability to compete under the *same* conditions as like domestic products.

21. According to the United States, the Panel wrongly held that less favourable treatment could be demonstrated where the detrimental impact experienced by imported products is caused solely by the decisions of private market participants. The United States highlights the Panel's own finding that segregation is not legally required under the COOL measure. The United States explains that, in promulgating the COOL requirements, it included the commingling provisions to help mitigate the need to make any choices that could have an adverse effect on imports, and that, therefore, any market participant's choice to segregate livestock instead of taking advantage of the commingling

---

66 United States' appellant's submission, para. 57. For a detailed discussion on the commingling provisions under the COOL measure, see section IV of these Reports.

67 United States' appellant's submission, para. 58.

provisions reflects solely the decision of a private market participant. Furthermore, any segregation that occurs equally affects both imported and domestic livestock, because segregation inherently involves separating one type of animal from the other. Therefore, according to the United States, any choice to pass the costs of segregation on to imported livestock, instead of distributing them equally between imported and domestic livestock, is not a choice required by the measure.

22. The United States further contends that even if there were any incentive for market participants to process exclusively domestic livestock—which it contests—this is not due to the COOL measure. The Panel itself essentially acknowledged this in finding that the incentive to process exclusively domestic livestock was related to the following factors: (i) "[l]ivestock imports have been and remain small compared to overall [US] livestock production and demand, and US livestock demand cannot be fulfilled with exclusively foreign livestock"[68]; and (ii) "US livestock is often geographically closer to most if not all US domestic markets, so processing exclusively imported livestock and meat remains a relatively less competitive option."[69] Therefore, the United States argues that, to the extent that they exist at all, adverse effects on imports result from pre-existing market conditions and not from the COOL measure. Thus, in the United States' view, the Panel's analysis of less favourable treatment was "clearly ... inappropriate"[70] because the Panel's conclusion would have been different if these conditions had been different.

23. The United States takes issue with the Panel's efforts to fit its less favourable treatment finding into "the paradigm established by past [panel] and Appellate Body reports".[71] More specifically, the United States argues that the Panel overlooked the fact that, in *Korea – Various Measures on Beef*, the decisions made by private market participants were made on the basis of a legal requirement, not on the basis of any economic incentive or disincentive. By contrast, in the present dispute, market participants have a free choice regarding how to respond to the COOL measure. In addition, the United States submits that, unlike the measure in *Mexico – Taxes on Soft Drinks*, the complaining parties have not asserted that the COOL measure itself singles out imports and discriminates against them on the basis of some neutral characteristic that serves as a "proxy" for imports, and thus acts as a disguised restriction on trade.[72]

---

68 United States' appellant's submission, para. 92 (quoting Panel Reports, para. 7.349).

69 *Ibid.*

70 United States' appellant's submission, para. 92.

71 United States' appellant's submission, para. 93.

72 United States' appellant's submission, para. 95 (referring to Panel Report, *Mexico – Taxes on Soft Drinks*, paras. 8.54-8.58).

24. The United States considers the facts in the present disputes to be very similar to those in *Dominican Republic – Import and Sale of Cigarettes*, in which the Appellate Body found that the Dominican Republic's measure did not accord less favourable treatment to imports because any adverse effects on imports were not compelled by the measure but resulted from the smaller market share of the imported product. However, even though the Panel found the exact same factor to be responsible for the alleged adverse effects on imports in these disputes—that is, smaller market share of imported products—it reached the opposite conclusion to that of the Appellate Body in *Dominican Republic – Import and Sale of Cigarettes* regarding less favourable treatment. Furthermore, the United States recalls the Panel's finding that the costs of segregation under the COOL measure are higher for imports than for domestic products. This, in the United States' view, is simply another way of saying that the unit cost of each import is higher than the unit cost of each domestic like product. Yet, the Appellate Body rejected a similar claim by Honduras in *Dominican Republican – Import and Sale of Cigarettes* and should, for the same reasons, find in these disputes that the COOL measure does not accord less favourable treatment to imports.

25. Finally, the United States contends that the Panel's "faulty legal test" could "have severe unintended consequences" by potentially rendering "common technical regulations" inconsistent with the *TBT Agreement*.[73] This is because nearly all technical regulations impose compliance costs, and such costs are almost never uniform, are affected by external factors, and also depend on how market participants respond. The United States observes that, under the Panel's "speculative cost comparison-based approach", "any Member's COOL requirement could be found to accord less favorable treatment to imported products because it will always be more costly to process products of more than one origin than a single origin (and it is likely that the domestic product in most countries has the highest market share)."[74] Overall, the United States submits that the Panel erred in adopting a cost comparison-based legal framework to find that an origin-neutral measure that applies equally to imported and domestic products accords less favourable treatment merely because the costs of compliance may be higher for some participants due to external factors such as market share, geographic location, and sourcing patterns.

(b) Article 11 of the DSU

26. The United States alleges that the Panel acted inconsistently with its obligation to conduct an objective assessment pursuant to Article 11 of the DSU in assessing the facts relating to segregation, commingling, and the price

---

73 United States' appellant's submission, para. 98.

74 United States' appellant's submission, para. 100. (original underlining omitted)

differential for livestock in the US market, and relied on its erroneous factual findings to reach its ultimate conclusion under Article 2.1 of the *TBT Agreement*.

27. The United States maintains that the Panel erred in finding that the COOL measure necessitates segregation and that this, in turn, necessarily results in higher costs for imported livestock. The COOL measure does not legally require producers to segregate livestock; rather, segregation is but one means of facilitating compliance with the recordkeeping requirements of the COOL measure. The COOL measure also expressly permits the commingling of livestock and meat as an alternative to segregation. The United States claims that, despite acknowledging this, the Panel either ignored or disregarded evidence showing that producers are in fact taking advantage of the commingling flexibilities contained in the measure in order to avoid segregation on a widespread basis. The United States refers to a survey by the US Department of Agriculture (the "USDA") showing that 22% of beef muscle cuts and 4% of pork muscle cuts sold in the United States are labelled "Product of the United States, Canada and Mexico". Given the negligible number of livestock that are born in either Canada or Mexico, raised in the other country, and then slaughtered in the United States—in which case the above label would also be applicable—this evidence shows that "approximately 22 percent of beef sold and 4 percent of the pork sold in the United States is derived from commingled livestock or meat".[75] In addition, the United States alleges that the Panel erroneously dismissed as inconclusive photographs[76] of commingled meat being sold at various locations around the country and an exhibit submitted by Canada showing that "processors are commingling all types of livestock and meat on a wide scale to reduce compliance costs".[77] Similarly, the United States contends that the Panel misinterpreted an affidavit submitted by the United States, which demonstrates that one of the three major US livestock producers is processing commingled animals. Given that the above evidence, together, "indisputably shows significant use of the commingling provisions"[78], the Panel erred in finding that: (i) the COOL measure "necessitates"[79] segregation; and (ii) the COOL measure involves "the identification by origin of *each and every* livestock and piece of meat" throughout the supply chain.[80]

---

75 United States' appellant's submission, para. 106 (referring to United States' response to Panel Question 90, para. 10; and Panel Exhibits US-28, US-144, US-145, and CDA-211).

76 United States' appellant's submission, para. 106 (referring to Panel Exhibits US-67, US-95, US-96, and US-98).

77 United States' appellant's submission, para. 106 (referring to CANFAX, "U.S. Packer procurements policies for Canadian Cattle", updated 24 April 2009 (Panel Exhibit CDA-41)).

78 United States' appellant's submission, para. 107.

79 United States' appellant's submission, para. 107 (quoting Panel Reports, para. 7.327).

80 United States' appellant's submission, para. 108 (quoting Panel Reports, para. 7.336). (emphasis added by the United States)

28. The United States asserts that the Panel also erred in finding that any costs of segregation cannot be passed on to the consumer. In its view, most consumers do not have viable alternatives to the purchase of labelled meat, and thus there is no reason that the retailer cannot pass on at least some portion of the compliance costs to the consumer. The United States alleges that the Panel ignored evidence on the record related to this issue.[81]

29. The United States further challenges the Panel's determination that the COOL measure creates a price differential in the US livestock market between domestic and imported livestock. According to the United States, the Panel considered only the evidence submitted by the complainants, and did not discuss evidence submitted by the United States showing that the prices paid for Canadian and Mexican livestock had been increasing at levels that met or exceeded the price increase for US livestock, and that the price differential between Canadian and US livestock had narrowed, since the adoption of the COOL measure. In addition, the United States argues that, contrary to the Panel's finding, the "Sumner Econometric Study"[82] submitted by Canada does not support the conclusion that the COOL measure affected the price basis of Canadian livestock. Indeed, since the study did not find any price effects on feeder cattle, feeder hogs, or slaughter hogs, the Panel's findings in this respect lack a factual basis.

(c) The Relevance of the Appellate Body Report in *US – Clove Cigarettes* in this Appeal[83]

30. With respect to *US – Clove Cigarettes*, the United States contends that the Appellate Body in that dispute found that there existed a detrimental impact on imported products as a result of the measure at issue, and then inquired as to whether the measure itself provided different treatment to imported products on the basis of their origin. In the United States' view, this inquiry was not meant to provide an exception or to apply an additional test under Article 2.1 of the *TBT Agreement*. Rather, the inquiry performed in *US – Clove Cigarettes* is a way to illuminate the question of whether or not a measure actually treats imports and

[81] United States' appellant's submission, para. 110 (referring to Panel Reports, paras. 7.352, 7.353, and 7.487; and Panel Exhibit CDA-174).

[82] Daniel A. Sumner, "Econometric Analysis of the Differential Effects of Mandatory Country of Origin Labeling in the United States on Canadian Cattle Prices and Imports of Canadian Cattle and Hogs into the United States" (16 June 2010) (Panel Exhibit CDA-79) (the "Sumner Econometric Study").

[83] The United States' appellant's submission was filed prior to the circulation of the Appellate Body report in *US – Clove Cigarettes* and therefore did not contain arguments relating to the Appellate Body's findings in that case. The Unites States addressed the relevance of the Appellate Body report in *US – Clove Cigarettes* to these disputes in its oral statement and responses to questions during the oral hearing.

like domestic products differently. Therefore, in applying the Article 2.1 analysis set out by the Appellate Body, a panel will analyze whether a measure is even-handed to determine whether the measure has a detrimental impact, as well as to determine whether that impact stems exclusively from a legitimate regulatory distinction rather than reflecting discrimination. Ultimately, in the United States' view, the question is whether the measure is even-handed. If it is even-handed, because it does not provide different treatment *in fact*, then it would not breach Article 2.1.

31. Regarding the "legitimate regulatory distinction", the United States points out that it is very important not to confuse this notion with that of legitimate *objectives*. In its view, a Member could have a legitimate objective underlying its measure, but then make illegitimate distinctions within that regulation. In applying this concept to the COOL measure, the United States argues that its measure does not contain a regulatory distinction because there are no different requirements imposed on products, or requirements that some products be labelled and others not. In this respect, the United States emphasizes that the mere fact that the measure identifies the origins of products in order to label them accordingly at retail does not mean that there is a regulatory distinction made between domestic and imported products. Rather, the labels are simply conveying product information that is relevant to the consumer, and different information is conveyed depending on the underlying product.

2. *Article 2.2 of the TBT Agreement*

32. In its analysis of Canada's and Mexico's claims that the COOL measure is inconsistent with Article 2.2 of the *TBT Agreement*, the Panel adopted and applied a three-step test that entailed consideration of whether the complainants had established each of the following:

(a) that the COOL measure is trade restrictive within the meaning of Article 2.2;

(b) that the objective pursued by the United States through the COOL measure is not legitimate; and

(c) if the objective is legitimate, that the COOL measure is more trade restrictive than necessary to fulfil a legitimate objective.[84]

Having conducted its analysis under each of these steps, the Panel found that the COOL measure is inconsistent with Article 2.2.

[84] Panel Reports, para. 7.558.

33. In its appeal, the United States seeks reversal of the Panel's finding of inconsistency under Article 2.2 on three main grounds. First, the United States contests the Panel's finding, under its first step, that the COOL measure is trade restrictive for purposes of Article 2.2. Second, with respect to the second step of its analysis, the United States contends that the Panel mischaracterized its position regarding the level of fulfilment of its objective by relying on partial quotes that omitted key elements of the United States' description of the level at which the United States considers it appropriate to fulfil its objective. In so doing, argues the United States, the Panel "wilfully distort[ed]" and "misrepresent[ed]" the United States' position as to its level of fulfilment, contrary to Article 11 of the DSU.[85] Third, the United States appeals the legal framework adopted by the Panel under its third step to determine whether a measure is more trade restrictive than necessary to fulfil a legitimate objective, including its failure to require the complaining parties to meet their burden to prove that the measure is more trade restrictive than necessary based on the availability of a significantly less trade-restrictive alternative measure. The United States further asserts that the Panel erred in applying its erroneous legal framework by determining that the COOL measure does not fulfil its objective at the level the United States considers appropriate.

(a) Trade-Restrictiveness

34. The United States seeks reversal of the Panel's finding that the COOL measure is trade restrictive. The United States refers to the arguments that it makes in the context of its appeal of the Panel's finding under Article 2.1 of the *TBT Agreement*, namely, that the Panel erred in finding that "the COOL measure negatively affects imported livestock's conditions of competition in the US market in relation to like domestic livestock by imposing higher segregation costs on imported livestock."[86] Because this finding is erroneous, it follows, according to the United States, that for the same reasons, the Panel also erred in finding that the COOL measure is trade restrictive for purposes of Article 2.2.

(b) The Objective Pursued and the Level at which the United States Considers It Appropriate to Fulfil Its Objective

35. The United States considers the Panel to have committed two errors in its analysis of the objective pursued by the United States through the COOL measure and of the level at which the United States considers it appropriate to fulfil that objective. The United States asserts that the Panel: (i) acted

---

[85] United States' appellant's submission, para. 142.

[86] United States' appellant's submission, footnote 187 to para. 124 (referring to Panel Reports, para. 7.574, in turn cross-referencing section VII.D.2 of the Panel Reports).

inconsistently with Article 11 of the DSU because it wilfully distorted and misrepresented the United States' position as to the level at which the United States considers it appropriate to fulfil its objective; and (ii) failed to consider all relevant information regarding the level at which the United States sought to achieve that objective.

36. The United States explains that, in addition to determining what objective a Member pursues, a panel must determine the level at which that Member pursues that objective through the challenged technical regulation. This is distinct from the objective itself. The United States highlights that the sixth recital of the preamble of the *TBT Agreement* confirms that a Member need not achieve its objective at 100%, but that it is up to Members "to decide which policy objectives they wish to pursue and *the levels at which they wish to pursue them*".[87] While this "level" is sometimes loosely referred to as the "level of protection", it is more accurate to think of it as the "level of fulfilment (of the objective)" since the objective may not be "protection" but some other legitimate objective.[88]

37. Referring to various elements of the Panel's analysis, the United States considers that the Panel concluded, based on its characterization of several statements made by the United States, that "the United States had identified in this proceeding that the objective it pursues through the COOL measure and the level at which the United States considers it appropriate to fulfill that objective [is]: '*to provide as much clear and accurate origin information as possible to consumers*'."[89] The United States argues that this identification of the "level of fulfilment" is erroneous because the Panel relied on partial quotes that omitted key elements of the United States' description of the level at which the United States considers it appropriate to fulfil its objective. In particular, the United States points to the complete versions of excerpts from its submissions to the Panel that, in its view, demonstrate that the United States intended to strike a balance between providing information to consumers and minimizing the costs to market participants of implementing the measure.[90] By "selectively editing" the United States' statements, however, the Panel mischaracterized the United States' argument to indicate that it aims to provide as much clear and accurate

---

[87] United States' appellant's submission, para. 133 (quoting Panel Report, *EC – Sardines*, para. 7.120). (emphasis added by the United States)

[88] United States' appellant's submission, para. 124 (referring to, *inter alia*, Panel Reports, para. 7.715).

[89] United States' appellant's submission, para. 131 (quoting Panel Reports, para. 7.620). (emphasis added by the United States)

[90] United States' appellant's submission, paras. 139 and 140 (quoting United States' first written submission to the Panel, paras. 7, 240, and 241; and United States' responses to Panel Question 24, para. 43, and Panel Question 142(a), para. 98).

origin information as possible "*without regard to the cost of doing so*".[91] In doing so, the Panel "wilfully distort[ed] and misrepresent[ed]" the United States' position as to its desired level of fulfilment, contrary to Article 11 of the DSU.[92]

38. The United States further asserts that the Panel erred in its application of Article 2.2 because it failed to consider all of the relevant information regarding the level at which the United States sought to achieve its objective. According to the United States, the true balance between the costs and consumer information provided under the COOL measure is confirmed by the text, structure, and design of the COOL measure, which provides certain information on origin while also allowing commingling, which reduces costs to the market participants. The result of the balance is that the COOL measure does not provide perfect information to consumers on origin in every conceivable scenario, which the United States never maintained it did, or intended to do. Rather, the extent of the information provided through the various labels under the COOL measure reflects the balance that the United States strikes between the provision of information and the costs of providing it. The fact that other countries' country of origin labelling schemes might provide more information does not invalidate the COOL measure, but rather indicates that such countries intended to strike a different balance, as Members are entitled to do under Article 2.2.

(c) Whether the COOL Measure Is "More Trade-Restrictive than Necessary to Fulfil a Legitimate Objective"

(i) The Panel's Legal Framework

39. The United States submits that the Panel erred in the legal framework that it employed at the third step of its Article 2.2 analysis in order to determine whether the COOL measure is "more trade-restrictive than necessary to fulfil a legitimate objective". The Panel effectively found that the United States breached its international obligations because its measure does not fulfil its objective "*enough*".[93] Moreover, the Panel failed to require the complaining parties to meet their burden to prove that the measure is "more trade-restrictive than necessary" based on the availability of a significantly less trade-restrictive alternative measure that also fulfils the objective at the level the United States considers appropriate.

[91] United States' appellant's submission, para. 142. (original emphasis)

[92] United States' appellant's submission, para. 142.

[93] United States' appellant's submission, para. 117. (original emphasis)

40. The United States agrees with the Panel that "the conformity of a measure with the general principle reflected in the first sentence of Article 2.2 must be established based on the elements of the second sentence. In other words, the second sentence explains what the first sentence means."[94] In the United States' view, if the measure pursues an objective considered "legitimate" for purposes of Article 2.2, then that measure is inconsistent with Article 2.2 only if it is "more trade-restrictive than necessary to fulfil" that legitimate objective. To establish that this is the case, a complaining Member must demonstrate that: (i) there is a reasonably available alternative measure; (ii) that fulfils the Member's legitimate objective at the level that the Member considers appropriate; and (iii) is significantly less trade restrictive. The United States asserts that, as with the "parallel provision" in Article 5.6 of the *Agreement on the Application of Sanitary and Phytosanitary Measures* (the "*SPS Agreement*"), "the *key* legal question for Article 2.2 is whether the importing Member could have adopted a less trade-restrictive measure yet still achieve its objective at the chosen level."[95]

41. The United States considers that the Panel erred by adopting a two-stage approach involving, first, an inquiry into whether the measure fulfils the objective and, only if that measure does in fact fulfil that objective, then moving to an examination of whether the measure is more trade restrictive than necessary because there is a less trade-restrictive alternative measure available. According to the United States, like the "parallel provision" in Article 5.6 of the *SPS Agreement*, Article 2.2 of the *TBT Agreement* requires a "single analysis, containing three elements that are to be judged cumulatively".[96]

42. The United States posits that the Panel arrived at its erroneous approach by mistakenly drawing from the interpretative framework under Article XX(b) of the GATT 1994 and the "necessity" case law developed thereunder. In the United States' view, the jurisprudence developed under Article XX is not a useful interpretative guide to the Article 2.2 inquiry. The United States disagrees with the Panel that Article XX of the GATT 1994 is "textually similar" to Article 2.2 of the *TBT Agreement*[97], pointing out that the only similarity between the two texts is the use of the term "necessary". Further, the United States highlights three "important contextual differences"[98] distinguishing the use of the term "necessary" under these two provisions: first, while the question under Article XX is whether the measure *itself* is necessary, Article 2.2 asks whether the

---

[94] United States' appellant's submission, para. 122 (quoting Panel Reports, para. 7.552 (footnote omitted)).

[95] United States' appellant's submission, para. 123 (referring to Appellate Body Report, *Australia – Apples*, para. 356). (original emphasis)

[96] United States' appellant's submission, para. 156.

[97] United States' appellant's submission, para. 159 (quoting Panel Reports, para. 7.670).

[98] United States' appellant's submission, para. 160.

amount of trade-restrictiveness is necessary; second, while the analysis under Article 2.2 involves a comparison of two presumptively WTO-consistent measures, to the extent that alternatives are compared under Article XX, the WTO-inconsistent measure (for which the exception is invoked) is compared to a hypothetical measure that is WTO-consistent; and third, the burden of establishing that a measure is more trade restrictive than necessary under Article 2.2 is with the complainant, which has important consequences given that the burden of proof may be dispositive.

43. The United States also rejects a finding of the Panel that the second and sixth recitals of the preamble of the *TBT Agreement* support the conclusion that the interpretation of Article XX of the GATT 1994 is relevant to an analysis of Article 2.2. While the United States agrees with the Panel that a "close connection" exists between the *TBT Agreement* and Article XX, it is with the second and sixth recitals of the *TBT Agreement*, not Article 2.2 in particular.[99] The reference to a "close connection" is more appropriate in describing the connection between Article XX of the GATT 1994 and Article 5.6 of the *SPS Agreement*, since the *SPS Agreement* is explicitly a development of Article XX(b). Yet, the Appellate Body has not required that the measure be proven "necessary", consistent with Article XX(b), in order to meet the obligation in Article 5.6.[100]

44. The United States considers therefore that the Panel's two-part test that entailed consideration of whether the COOL measure contributed to or fulfilled the objective "*enough*" is in error.[101] Whether a measure makes a "material contribution" to its objective, in the sense that the Appellate Body used the term in *Brazil – Retreaded Tyres*, is not the correct test for purposes of Article 2.2. A measure is not inconsistent with Article 2.2 solely because it fails to make some minimum threshold of contribution to its objective. Rather, the measure is inconsistent only if the complaining party is able to establish that a *significantly* less trade-restrictive alternative measure exists that also makes at least the same level of contribution to the objective. The United States emphasizes that, while a panel's determinations of the objective and of the level at which a Member seeks to fulfil that objective are important for an Article 2.2 analysis, they are not an end in themselves. Rather, they are relevant *in order to* assess whether the complaining party has met its burden of showing that the same level of fulfilment could be achieved by a significantly less trade-restrictive alternative measure. The United States stresses, in this regard, that the relevant question

---

[99] United States' appellant's submission, paras. 159 and 165 (referring to Panel Reports, para. 7.670).

[100] United States' appellant's submission, para. 166 (referring to Appellate Body Report, *Australia – Salmon*, para. 194; and Appellate Body Report, *Australia – Apples*, para. 337).

[101] United States' appellant's submission, para. 167. (original emphasis)

under Article 2.2 is whether the Member could have adopted a less trade-restrictive measure that fulfils the objective at the chosen level of fulfilment, and not whether the Member could have done a better job of designing its measure. Panels are not equipped to undertake the latter type of inquiry. Nor is it appropriate for panels to insert themselves in the place of Members and make their own policy judgements and assessment as to how best to achieve a particular objective within the circumstances of the Member concerned.

45. Finally, with respect to the burden of proof, the United States asserts that the Panel erred in failing to require the complaining parties to meet their burden to prove that the measure is "more trade-restrictive than necessary" based on the availability of a significantly less trade-restrictive alternative measure that also fulfils the objective at the level the United States considers appropriate. According to the United States, such a requirement would be consistent with the Appellate Body's analysis in *Australia – Salmon* of the parallel provision in Article 5.6 of the *SPS Agreement*.[102] In this regard, the United States refers to footnote 3 to Article 5.6 of the *SPS Agreement*, which clarifies that "a measure is not more trade-restrictive than required unless there is another measure, reasonably available taking into account technical and economic feasibility, that achieves the appropriate level of sanitary or phytosanitary protection and is *significantly* less restrictive to trade".[103] In support, the United States refers to a 1993 letter from the Director-General of the GATT to the Chief US Negotiator concerning the application of Article 2.2, stating that, *inter alia*, the *TBT Agreement* "does not concern itself with insignificant trade effects nor could a measure be considered more trade restrictive than necessary in the absence of a reasonably available alternative".[104] According to the United States, this letter constitutes a supplementary means of interpretation, within the meaning of Article 32 of the *Vienna Convention on the Law of Treaties*[105] (the "*Vienna Convention*").

(ii) The Level of Fulfilment Achieved by the COOL Measure

46. Apart from the erroneous legal framework adopted by the Panel, the United States separately appeals the Panel's determination that the COOL

---

[102] United States' appellant's submission, para. 179 (referring to Appellate Body Report, *Australia – Salmon*, para. 194).

[103] Emphasis added by the United States.

[104] United States' appellant's submission, footnote 269 to para. 179 (referring to Letter from Peter D. Sutherland, Director-General of the GATT to Ambassador John Schmidt, Chief US Negotiator, dated 15 December 1993 (Panel Exhibit US-53)).

[105] Done at Vienna, 23 May 1969, 1155 UNTS 331; 8 International Legal Materials 679.

measure does not fulfil its legitimate objective at the level the United States considers appropriate.

47. The United States argues that the Panel failed to take into account that the COOL measure "*completely*" fulfils its objective for meat that carries Label A.[106] According to the United States, it is an "uncontested fact" that meat carrying Label A constitutes at least 71% of the meat sold in the United States.[107] With respect to that label, the COOL measure therefore provides "clear and accurate" information for at least 71% of the meat.[108] Moreover, notwithstanding its various criticisms of the information that Labels B and C provide, even the Panel acknowledged that those labels "provide additional country of origin information that was not available prior to the COOL measure", and that "the COOL measure may have reduced consumer confusion that existed under the pre-COOL measure and USDA grade labelling system".[109] It is also an "uncontested fact", argues the United States, that meat carrying Labels B and C constitutes the vast majority of meat sold without Label A (that is, between 21% and 29% of labelled beef).[110] According to the United States, these contributions to an objective—under any definition—are "material, not merely marginal or insignificant".[111]

48. Instead of taking account of this evidence and focusing on what the COOL measure *could* contribute to its objective, the Panel focused on what the measure *does not do* vis-à-vis the (erroneously identified) chosen level of fulfilment, that is, that the United States aims to provide "*as much clear and accurate* origin information *as possible*".[112] This mistaken approach in turn "forc[ed] the Panel to disregard entirely" the balance that the United States sought to strike between the information provided and the cost of providing it, including the acknowledged fact that, where the COOL measure provides less information, it does so to lower costs to market participants, including Canadian and Mexican producers, which is "an entirely normal regulatory approach".[113]

---

[106] United States' appellant's submission, para. 172. (original emphasis)

[107] United States' appellant's submission, para. 172 (referring to Panel Reports, footnote 941 to para. 7.715).

[108] United States' appellant's submission, para. 173.

[109] United States' appellant's submission, para. 172 (quoting Panel Reports, para. 7.717).

[110] United States' appellant's submission, para. 172 (referring to Panel Reports, footnote 941 to para. 7.715).

[111] United States' appellant's submission, para. 173 (quoting Appellate Body Report, *Brazil – Retreaded Tyres*, para. 210).

[112] United States' appellant's submission, para. 175 (quoting Panel Reports, para. 7.620). (emphasis added by the United States)

[113] United States' appellant's submission, para. 177.

B. Arguments of Canada – Appellee

1. Article 2.1 of the TBT Agreement

49. Canada requests the Appellate Body to reject the United States' appeal of the Panel's finding that the COOL measure is inconsistent with Article 2.1 of the *TBT Agreement*. Canada asserts that the Panel was correct in arriving at this finding, and that the United States' appeal "distorts the Panel's methodical assessment of the COOL measure's effects on the conditions of competition by neglecting key components of the Panel's analysis and misrepresenting others".[114]

(a) The Interpretation and Application of Article 2.1 of the *TBT Agreement*

50. Canada submits that the Panel followed the correct legal approach in its analysis regarding whether the COOL measure accords to imported livestock treatment no less favourable than that accorded to domestic livestock, within the meaning of Article 2.1 of the *TBT Agreement*, and that the Panel's approach is consistent with that of the Appellate Body in *Korea – Various Measures on Beef*. The Panel's approach is also supported by the recent report of the Appellate Body in *US – Clove Cigarettes*, which notes that Article III:4 of the GATT 1994 informs the analysis under Article 2.1 of the *TBT Agreement*, and that the effects on the conditions of competition are the focus under both provisions. Canada highlights that the United States "agrees" that the focus of the analysis under Article 2.1 of the *TBT Agreement* should be "whether the measure *itself* modifies the *conditions* of competition to the detriment of imported livestock (i.e. whether the measure affects the terms under which products compete in the market)".[115] Canada further alleges that, contrary to the United States' argument, a panel is not required to determine whether detrimental impact on imports is related to the origin of the imported product(s), or is a proxy for such origin, in order to find less favourable treatment, as such an approach was rejected by the Appellate Body in *US – Clove Cigarettes*.

51. In Canada's view, by arguing that the COOL measure treats imported and domestic products identically, the United States "conflates" different treatment with discriminatory or less favourable treatment.[116] Canada maintains that the design and structure of the measure, combined with economic logic, "necessitate

---

[114] Canada's appellee's submission, para. 3.

[115] Canada's appellee's submission, para. 36 (quoting United States' appellant submission, para. 62 (original emphasis)).

[116] Canada's appellee's submission, para. 61.

discriminatory treatment" of imported livestock.[117] Canada also contends that the United States "distorts" the Panel's finding when asserting that the Panel relied on "*the commingling flexibility provided with regard to the labeling of meat*" in reaching its finding that the COOL measure, on its face, provides different treatment to imported and domestic livestock.[118] The Panel in fact found that the definitions of the four muscle cut labels under the measure are mutually exclusive, and went on to describe the limited flexibility provided for between the use of Label A and the rest of the labels when commingling is involved. Moreover, the Panel did not erroneously "pivot[]" from the question of different treatment to an assessment of whether there is *de facto* less favourable treatment.[119] Rather, the Panel recognized that differential treatment on the face of the measure does not necessarily constitute less favourable treatment, as indicated by the Appellate Body's findings in *Korea – Various Measures on Beef*. The Panel was correct, therefore, in going on to analyze whether, on the basis of the facts of this case, the different treatment negatively affects the conditions of competition for imported cattle and hogs.

52. Canada maintains that, even if the COOL measure did not treat imported products differently than domestic products on its face, in reviewing the operation of the COOL measure "in practice", the Panel correctly found that, "for all practical purposes, the COOL measure necessitates segregation of meat and livestock according to origin".[120] This finding was the inevitable result of several factual findings made by the Panel, including that the COOL measure, in principle, "prescribes an unbroken chain of reliable country of origin information with regard to every animal and muscle cut", that segregation is "a practical way to ensure" an unbroken chain of reliable information, and that the USDA's own Compliance Guide mentions a "segregation plan" as an "example[] of records and activities that may be useful" for compliance with the COOL measure.[121] The Panel, however, found that this segregation was not *per se* a violation of Article 2.1, and properly moved on to determine whether the COOL measure creates an incentive to process domestic livestock and thereby reduces the competitive opportunities of imported livestock.

---

117 Canada's appellee's submission, para. 7.

118 Canada's appellee's submission, para. 62 (quoting United States' appellant's submission, para. 57). (emphasis added by Canada)

119 Canada's appellee's submission, para. 61 (quoting United States' appellant's submission, para. 58).

120 Canada's appellee's submission, para. 65 (quoting Panel Reports, para. 7.327).

121 Canada's appellee's submission, para. 64 (quoting Panel Reports, paras. 7.317, 7.320, and 7.321, in turn quoting USDA, "Country of Origin Labeling Compliance Guide", revised 12 May 2009 (Panel Exhibits CDA-65, at p. 17 and MEX-41)).

53. With respect to such incentive, Canada argues that the Panel correctly examined the impact of the COOL measure on the market and compared the position of US livestock in the US market with that of imported livestock. In Canada's view, the United States mischaracterizes the Panel's reasoning when it suggests that the Panel did not assess "whether the technical regulation alters the *conditions* of competition so as to deny imported products the ability to compete under the same conditions as like domestic products".[122] On the contrary, the Panel examined whether the COOL measure modifies the conditions of competition to the detriment of imported livestock. In this context, the Panel examined extensive, uncontested evidence establishing that the COOL measure creates disincentives to use Canadian-born or -raised cattle or hogs. The Panel then examined various arguments advanced by the United States, but ultimately found that the COOL measure creates an incentive in favour of processing domestic livestock, and therefore *de facto* discriminates against imported livestock. The Panel rightly considered that it is the "implications" and operation of the contested measure "in the marketplace" that will reveal whether the conditions of competition have been altered to the detriment of imported livestock, and whether there has been a reduction in competitive opportunities for imports.[123] In this regard, Canada further submits that, in assessing the implications of the COOL measure in the marketplace, it was appropriate for the Panel to examine in detail the particular implications of the COOL measure *in the relevant market*.

54. In Canada's view, the United States errs in asserting that certain factors in the market will negate a potential finding that a measure affects the conditions of competition to the detriment of imported products, including the market share held by imports, and the decisions of private market actors. With respect to the market share held by imported livestock, Canada argues that the market share is an appropriate factor for a panel to take into consideration when assessing whether a measure changes the conditions of competition to the detriment of imported products. The Appellate Body has taken the small market share of relevant products into account as a factor in assessing less favourable treatment in several cases.[124] Canada posits that part of the evidence that the conditions of competition were negatively affected in *Korea – Various Measures on Beef* was that the market share of imported beef was small in that relevant market. In *Mexico – Taxes on Soft Drinks*, the fact that imports of the product that was

---

[122] Canada's appellee's submission, para. 68 (quoting United States' appellant's submission, para. 63 (original emphasis)).

[123] Canada's appellee's submission, para. 39 (quoting Appellate Body Report, *US – FSC (Article 21.5 – EC)*, para. 215).

[124] Canada's appellee's submission, para. 43 (referring to Appellate Body Report, *Korea – Various Measures on Beef*, paras. 137 and 139; Panel Report, *Mexico – Taxes on Soft Drinks*, paras. 8.114-8.122; and Appellate Body Report, *US – Clove Cigarettes*, paras. 222 and 224).

favoured (cane sugar sweeteners) had a negligible market share was a relevant factor in the finding of less favourable treatment on non-cane sugar sweeteners. In *US – Clove Cigarettes*, in finding that a ban on all flavoured cigarettes (other than tobacco or menthol) accorded less favourable treatment to imported clove-flavoured cigarettes, the panel and the Appellate Body took into account the small market share of non-clove-flavoured cigarettes also banned under the same measure.

55. Canada also argues that the United States cannot rely on *Dominican Republic – Import and Sale of Cigarettes* to support the proposition that a product's market share should not be taken into account in an analysis regarding less favourable treatment under Article 2.1 of the *TBT Agreement*. In that case, the measure at issue was an origin-neutral bond that was imposed on *all companies* regardless of where they sourced their product, and the differential unit cost accrued because a particular company had a smaller market share and sourced imported products. Under the COOL measure, by contrast, additional segregation costs will apply to all livestock processors who choose to use the imported products regardless of their market share, whereas those processors who choose not to use imported livestock will incur *no* additional costs.

56. Regarding the decisions of private market participants, Canada argues that the Panel was right to determine, like the Appellate Body in *Korea – Various Measures on Beef*, that any decisions by private actors made in order to comply with the COOL measure are not solely the result of their independent business calculations, but are attributable in large part to the economic incentives and disincentives created by the COOL measure. Canada notes that the measure in *Korea – Various Measures on Beef* required retailers to choose whether to sell domestic or imported beef, but allowed them to choose freely between those two options. As the Appellate Body found in that case, however, "the intervention of some element of private choice" did not preclude a finding of less favourable treatment.[125] Rather, it was the measure "itself" that caused private actors to change their behaviour in a way that negatively impacted imported products. Canada emphasizes that, in this dispute, "[t]here was an abundance of uncontradicted specific evidence before the Panel that the COOL measure 'itself' caused private actors to change their behaviour to the detriment of imported cattle and hogs."[126]

[125] Canada's appellee's submission, para. 47 (quoting Appellate Body Report, *Korea – Various Measures on Beef*, para. 146).

[126] Canada's appellee's submission, para. 48 (referring to Panel Reports, paras. 7.374-7.380 and 7.420).

(b) Article 11 of the DSU

57. Canada submits that the United States has not substantiated its claims under Article 11 of the DSU with respect to the facts underlying the Panel's finding of "treatment no less favourable". According to Canada, the threshold for establishing a violation of Article 11 is high, and it is not enough "to simply note a few pieces of evidence that the panel considered, ignore evidence that the panel also considered, and ask the Appellate Body to come to a contrary conclusion" than the panel.[127] Therefore, the Panel's factual findings "must stand".[128] In any event, Canada argues, the Panel's finding that the COOL measure had a negative impact on the conditions of competition for imported cattle and hogs is not only supported by the design and operation of the COOL measure and economic logic, but also by "an abundance" of "uncontested evidence" showing that the COOL measure caused market participants to stop or reduce their purchases of Canadian-born or -raised cattle and hogs.[129]

58. Regarding the extent of commingling in the US market, Canada acknowledges that commingling is happening "to some extent", and points out that it did not argue otherwise before the Panel.[130] Canada argues that, even when commingling is used, however, this does not entirely remove the discriminatory effect of the COOL measure, as the United States suggests. Furthermore, to the extent the United States seeks to argue that commingling is used on a widespread basis in order to avoid segregation, this does not affect the Panel's finding that the COOL measure is inconsistent with Article 2.1 in the many situations in which commingling is not used. Canada emphasizes in this respect that a breach of the national treatment obligation does not depend on a showing that the measure at issue results in less favourable treatment in every instance.

59. With respect to the United States' arguments that the Panel erred in its findings regarding the price differential, Canada submits that the price comparison presented by the United States wrongly starts in 2009, after the

---

[127] Canada's appellee's submission, para. 33.

[128] *Ibid.*

[129] Canada's appellee's submission, paras. 23 and 24. Canada emphasizes that the evidence shows that, as a result of the COOL measure: (i) a considerable discount was applied by major processors to imported livestock; (ii) important processing plants in the United States processed no or less imported livestock; (iii) certain suppliers had to transport imported livestock for longer distances, and faced logistical problems and additional costs; (iv) contractual terms and price differences between imported and domestic livestock changed to the detriment of imported livestock; (v) financial institutions refused to provide credits and loans to Canadian livestock producers; and (vi) imported cattle were excluded from profitable premium beef programmes. (*Ibid.*, para. 23 (referring to Panel Reports, paras. 7.363, 7.374-7.380, and 7.420))

[130] Canada's appellee's submission, para. 18 (referring to Panel Reports, paras. 7.364).

COOL measure had already severely depressed the market for imports. Canada further contends that a moderating of the negative effects of the COOL measure during periods of unusually tight supply is to be expected, and does not mean that the negative effects attributable to the COOL measure have been eliminated. Moreover, Canada points out that the Sumner Econometric Study was expressly found by the Panel to establish a *prima facie* case that the COOL measure negatively and significantly affected the import shares and the price basis for Canadian fed cattle.[131] In contrast, the Panel found that the "USDA Econometric Study"[132] put forward by the United States lacked robustness and did not rebut that *prima facie* case.[133]

(c) The Relevance of the Appellate Body Report in *US – Clove Cigarettes* in this Appeal

60. Canada maintains that the Appellate Body's recent ruling in *US – Clove Cigarettes*, and its finding that in some circumstances Article 2.1 of the *TBT Agreement* permits detrimental impact on imports when it stems exclusively from a legitimate regulatory distinction, is unavailing to the United States in this appeal. Canada considers that, while the Panel did not have the reasoning of *US – Clove Cigarettes* before it, it nevertheless carried out a detailed analysis of the factors indicated by the Appellate Body, and in making its findings "effectively excluded the possibility" that the detrimental impact on imported livestock was the result of legitimate regulatory distinctions that were even-handedly applied.[134]

61. Canada submits that the scope of the "legitimate regulatory distinction" for purposes of Article 2.1 of the *TBT Agreement* should not exceed those that can be justified under Article XX of the GATT 1994. Otherwise, a measure able to survive a challenge under Article 2.1 because its detrimental impact is found to stem from a legitimate regulatory distinction *not* covered under Article XX would nevertheless violate Article III:4 of the GATT 1994, and would *not* be justified under Article XX. Therefore, an expansive reading of what constitutes a legitimate regulatory distinction "will not serve a useful purpose".[135] Canada also points out that, because, in *US – Clove Cigarettes*, the United States had asserted a defence under Article XX of the GATT 1994 in response to Indonesia's claims under Article III:4, it was "appropriate in that case" to consider whether what would otherwise have been a violation of the national treatment obligation in

131 Canada's appellee's submission, para. 26 (referring to Panel Reports, paras. 7.517 and 7.542).

132 USDA Office of the Chief Economist, "Modeling the Impact of Country of Origin Labeling Requirements on U.S. Imports of Livestock from Canada and Mexico" (Panel Exhibit US-42).

133 Canada's appellee's submission, para. 26 (referring to Panel Reports, paras. 7.543-7.545).

134 Canada's appellee's submission, para. 51.

135 Canada's appellee's submission, para. 53.

Article 2.1 could be justified because it pursued "an objective recognized in the GATT as meriting an exception".[136] The United States, however, has raised no Article XX defence in this dispute.

62. Canada submits that, as a matter of logic, it would be incongruous for the United States to claim on appeal that the COOL measure implements a legitimate regulatory distinction, because it did not attempt to justify the measure on the ground of a legitimate objective under the GATT 1994. Canada reiterates that the design, architecture, revealing structure, operation, and application of the COOL measure show that its objective is protectionism, and argues that a regulatory distinction based on such an objective is not legitimate. Even if the Appellate Body rejects this argument, Canada claims that the concept of legitimacy in Article 2.1 does not extend to providing information to consumers. Canada points out that, in *US – Clove Cigarettes*, the Appellate Body relied for its interpretation of Article 2.1 on two "closed lists" of objectives, namely, the sixth recital of the preamble of the *TBT Agreement* and Article XX of the GATT 1994, neither of which includes the objective of providing information to consumers.[137]

63. Canada argues that the design, architecture, revealing structure, operation, and application of the COOL measure establish that the discrimination it causes is not consistent with an even-handed application of a legitimate regulatory distinction. The structure and design of the COOL measure is such that imported livestock can only be used to produce Label B or C meat, whereas meat derived from US-born and -raised animals have exclusive access to Label A, as well as limited access to Label B or C. As a result, the segregation costs and reporting requirements create uneven costs that affect only imported livestock. In addition, the detrimental impact incurred by imported livestock cannot be said to stem exclusively from legitimate regulatory distinctions because the objective that the United States claims to be pursuing—that is, providing consumers with information on where the animal from which the meat is derived was born, raised, and slaughtered—is not reflected in the COOL measure.

64. Canada points to five examples in support of this argument: (i) even though the United States contends that the COOL measure addresses confusion with USDA grade labels, the COOL measure applies to pork, which is not grade-labelled, and not to turkey, which is grade-labelled; (ii) the COOL regime excludes many products from the scope of its coverage; (iii) except for meat produced from certain livestock, almost all products undergoing a significant change in the United States are excluded from the scope of the COOL measure;

---

[136] Canada's appellee's submission, para. 54.

[137] Canada's appellee's submission, para. 56 (referring to Appellate Body Report, *US – Clove Cigarettes*, paras. 96, 100, 101, and 173).

(iv) restaurants, specialty stores (including butchers), and smaller stores are not subject to the COOL requirements; and (v) the information conveyed varies depending on whether the animal was slaughtered in the United States or in another country. Specifically, absent commingling, an animal born and raised in Canada and slaughtered in the United States must be labelled "Product of Canada and the USA", but an animal born and raised in the United States and slaughtered in Canada must be labelled "Product of Canada", and cannot be labelled "Product of Canada and the USA".

2. *Article 2.2 of the TBT Agreement*

65. Canada requests the Appellate Body to reject the United States' appeal in respect of the Panel's analysis and conclusions under Article 2.2 of the *TBT Agreement*. In Canada's view, the Panel correctly articulated the requisite steps of analysis and properly applied them to determine that the COOL measure violates Article 2.2.

(a) Trade-Restrictiveness

66. According to Canada, the United States' appeal against the Panel's finding that the COOL measure is trade restrictive is "extremely cursory, consisting of one sentence and discussion in a footnote ... and does not address the legal reasoning of the Panel in its formulation of this test".[138] Moreover, Canada notes that the success of the United States' appeal depends on the Appellate Body reversing the Panel's finding under Article 2.1 of the *TBT Agreement* that the COOL measure negatively affects the conditions of competition for imported livestock. Should the Appellate Body uphold this finding of the Panel—as requested by Canada—it would not be necessary to undertake any further analysis of the Panel's findings of trade-restrictiveness under Article 2.2.

67. Canada asserts, however, that the converse does not apply. Any reversal by the Appellate Body of the Panel's finding under Article 2.1 would not automatically mean that the COOL measure is not trade restrictive within the meaning of Article 2.2. A measure is trade restrictive if it imposes any restriction on international trade, or restricts trade flows. Canada submits that there is no dispute that the COOL measure imposes limitations on trade: it imposes recordkeeping requirements and additional costs on market participants depending on various factors, and has required participants either to segregate or commingle livestock based on origin. Therefore, even if, contrary to Canada's submissions, the Appellate Body finds that the COOL measure does not

[138] Canada's appellee's submission, para. 75 (referring to United States' appellant's submission, para. 120 and footnote 187 to para. 124).

negatively affect the conditions of competition of imported products, it still restricts international trade.

(b) The Objective Pursued and the Level at which the United States Considers It Appropriate to Fulfil Its Objective

68. Canada urges the Appellate Body to reject the United States' attempts to characterize the objective of the COOL measure as relating to costs. Canada notes that, while the United States appears to appeal essentially the Panel's conclusion that "the objective pursued by the United States through the COOL measure is to provide as much clear and accurate origin information as possible to consumers"[139], it frames its appeal as a mischaracterization of the "U.S. description of its level of fulfillment".[140] Canada observes that the United States does not specify precisely what the Panel should have found the objective (or the "level of fulfilment") of the COOL measure to be, but "appears to argue" that the objective includes an element of cost assessment, and that therefore this element of cost should be a factor in determining whether the COOL measure fulfils its objective.[141]

69. To the extent that the United States is arguing that there is a necessary additional step to determine "level of fulfilment" under the third step of the Panel's analysis, Canada agrees with the United States that the phrase "level of protection" used in other contexts—such as in Article XX of the GATT 1994 and the *SPS Agreement*—is not appropriate under Article 2.2 of the *TBT Agreement*, which instead requires an assessment of the level of fulfilment. Nonetheless, Canada explains that there is no need to determine a theoretical level of fulfilment that the challenged measure is trying to achieve. Rather, as the United States seems to acknowledge[142], the level of fulfilment of a measure must be determined objectively by a panel based on the relevant facts, including the structure and design of the measure, as well as other relevant evidence. Canada further asserts that the reference in the sixth recital of the preamble of the *TBT Agreement* to WTO Members "taking measures ... at the levels [they] consider[] appropriate" indicates that the drafters understood that measures would have "gradations of levels" in attaining their objective.[143] Canada points out, however, that such context should not be used in the way suggested by the United States,

---

[139] Canada's appellee's submission, para. 77 (quoting Panel Reports, para. 7.620).

[140] Canada's appellee's submission, para. 77 (referring to United States' appellant's submission, subheading IV.C.2.a).

[141] Canada's appellee's submission, para. 77.

[142] Canada's appellee's submission, para. 109 (referring to United States' appellant's submission, paras. 126, 134, and 143).

[143] Canada's appellee's submission, para. 102.

namely, to provide a right to WTO Members to assert the level of fulfilment that a technical regulation "seeks" to achieve, rather than to establish their desired level through the level of fulfilment that the technical regulation actually achieves.

70. To the extent that the United States is seeking to change the objective that it identified at the Panel stage, Canada submits that the Appellate Body should reject such attempt, just as the Panel rightly did when the United States sought to do the same at the interim review stage.[144] Canada emphasizes that the United States never raised in its submissions the issue of costs prior to the interim review.[145] In any event, even the excerpts that the United States claims the Panel selectively quoted did not include the issue of costs as part of the objective of the COOL measure.[146] Canada further submits that even if, contrary to arguments in its other appeal[147], the Appellate Body were to uphold the Panel's approach and determine that the objective of the COOL measure is that stated by the United States, it should reject the United States' attempt to revise the identified objective of the COOL measure as relating to costs.

71. Finally, Canada rejects the United States' argument that the Panel failed to make an objective assessment, as required under Article 11 of the DSU. The United States has not established that the Panel failed to address particular evidence relating to the fulfilment of its objective, much less evidence that has a bearing on the objectivity of the Panel's factual assessment, as it is required to do under Article 11 of the DSU. As a result, there is no basis for the Appellate Body to interfere with the Panel's discretion in its determination that the COOL measure "fails to convey meaningful origin information to consumers".[148]

(c) Whether the COOL Measure Is "More Trade-Restrictive than Necessary to Fulfil a Legitimate Objective"

72. Canada observes that much of the United States' appeal under Article 2.2 of the *TBT Agreement* focuses on the question of whether a measure fulfils its objective. While agreeing with the United States that this is a key issue under

---

[144] Canada's appellee's submission, para. 77 (referring to Panel Reports, paras. 6.110-6.113).

[145] Canada's appellee's submission, para. 79 (referring to Canada's comments on the United States' comments on the Canada Interim Report, para. 40; Canada's oral statement at the first Panel meeting, para. 37; Canada's second written submission to the Panel, p. 47, heading C, and para. 118; and Canada's oral statement at the second Panel meeting, p. 12, heading B, and para. 40).

[146] Canada's appellee's submission, para. 80 (referring to United States' appellant's submission, para. 139). See also *supra*, footnote 90.

[147] See *infra*, paras. 115-124.

[148] Canada's appellee's submission, para. 122 (quoting Panel Reports, para. 7.719).

Article 2.2, Canada considers that the United States' appeal must fail because the Panel's findings with respect to whether a measure must fulfil its objective and whether the COOL measure does so were correct.

(i) The Panel's Legal Framework

73. Canada disagrees that the Panel adopted an erroneous legal approach under the third step of its analysis under Article 2.2. Having correctly found that the COOL measure does not fulfil its objective because it fails to convey meaningful information, it was appropriate for the Panel to have stopped its analysis there. However, if the Appellate Body disagrees that, as a separate step, an assessment of whether a challenged measure fulfils its objective is required, then Canada agrees that the level of fulfilment found by the Panel is relevant for comparing the COOL measure with the proposed alternatives.

74. Canada submits, as a preliminary matter, that the United States' attempt to revise the position it took before the Panel—namely, that it is "appropriate to analyse whether the measure in question fulfils a legitimate objective first"[149]—should be rejected. Canada cautions that the Appellate Body "should be particularly wary"[150] of reversing the Panel's finding based on a new legal argument raised by the United States for the first time on appeal. Canada argues that this new argument is in any event not supported by the text of Article 2.2. According to the Panel's test, since a technical regulation will already have been found to be trade restrictive under the first step of its test, it will by definition be more trade restrictive than necessary if it does not actually fulfil its objective. Canada does not agree that this is an assessment of whether a measure is "necessary", in the abstract. Rather, it is an assessment of whether the measure does enough to achieve the objective to constitute "fulfilment".

75. Canada notes that the ordinary meaning of the word "fulfil" used in Article 2.2, as well as its French and Spanish equivalents ("*réaliser*" and "*alcanzar*", respectively), suggests that a measure must achieve its objective at 100%. Canada submits, however, that, when read in its context, and, in the light of the relevant object and purpose, a showing of something less than complete fulfilment may be sufficient. In support, Canada argues that the Appellate Body has recognized, in an assessment under Article XX of the GATT 1994, that measures may operate together to address a policy objective, implying that a single measure need not fully achieve a particular objective by itself.[151]

[149] Canada's appellee's submission, para. 83 (referring to Panel Reports, para. 7.556 and footnote 743 thereto).

[150] Canada's appellee's submission, para. 85.

[151] Canada's appellee's submission, para. 95 (referring to Appellate Body Report, *Brazil – Retreaded Tyres*, para. 151).

76. Canada also sees a useful analogy in the term "necessary" in Article XX(d) of the GATT 1994, which has been interpreted to encompass something less than 100% achievement of the objective.[152] Canada disagrees with the United States that Article XX of the GATT 1994 is not useful to interpret Article 2.2, and, in particular, to assess the COOL measure's fulfilment of its objective. Canada agrees with the Panel that a close connection between Article 2.2 of the *TBT Agreement* and Article XX of the GATT 1994 is evidenced by the second and sixth recitals of the preamble of the *TBT Agreement*; that the texts and structure of Article 2.2 and Article XX are similar; and that the text of the sixth recital is similar to the chapeau of Article XX. The United States is therefore incorrect that all that the two provisions have in common is the word "necessary".[153]

77. Canada notes that, while acknowledging a "close connection" between Article XX of the GATT 1994 and the *TBT Agreement*, the United States confines this connection to the recitals of the *TBT Agreement*, and suggests a "closer" connection "with Article 5.6 of the *SPS Agreement*".[154] However, the United States' reliance on Article 5.6 ignores the fact that the three-part test under that provision is derived from the text of footnote 3 thereto. Canada asserts that omissions must have meaning[155], and the fact that Article 2.2 of the *TBT Agreement* does not contain a footnote similar to footnote 3 of the *SPS Agreement* indicates that "significantly" should not be read into the "less trade-restrictive" test of Article 2.2.[156] Moreover, the United States ignores that the *SPS Agreement* addresses a more limited category of objectives.

78. Further, in response to the other arguments of the United States—that the two provisions ask different questions; that Article 2.2 is concerned with the necessity of the *trade-restrictiveness* rather than the measure *itself*; that Article XX is an exception; and that the allocation of the burden of proof is different—Canada submits that, while there are some distinctions between the provisions, they do not detract from the fact that there are common elements in Article XX of the GATT 1994, Article 2.2 of the *TBT Agreement*, and Article 5.6 of the *SPS Agreement* (excluding footnote 3 thereto). Moreover, any distinctions do not displace the similarity between the concept of "fulfilment" in Article 2.2 and the

---

[152] Canada's appellee's submission, para. 96 (referring to Appellate Body Report, *Korea – Various Measures on Beef*, paras. 160 and 161).

[153] Canada's appellee's submission, para. 100 (referring to United States' appellant's submission, para. 160).

[154] Canada's appellee's submission, para. 99 (referring to United States' appellant's submission, paras. 164-166).

[155] Canada's appellee's submission, para. 89 (referring to Appellate Body Report, *Japan – Alcoholic Beverages II*, p. 18, DSR 1996:I, 97, at 111).

[156] Canada's appellee's submission, para. 89 (referring to Panel Report, *US – Tuna II (Mexico)*, para. 7.464).

related concepts in Article XX of the GATT 1994. Canada also disputes the United States' invocation of the sixth recital of the preamble of the *TBT Agreement* as somehow providing to WTO Members a right to assert the level of fulfilment that a technical regulation "seeks" to achieve, rather than to establish their desired level through the level that the technical regulation actually achieves.

79. Canada further asserts that the level of achievement necessary to fulfil an objective depends on the "risks that non-fulfilment would create", as provided for in Article 2.2. Relying on the "necessity" case law developed under Article XX of the GATT 1994, Canada submits that a measure will be easier to justify if it pursues an objective that is "vital" or "important".[157] The same analysis applies under Article 5.6 of the *SPS Agreement*, although by definition SPS measures concern vital and important matters (human and animal life and health) where the risk of harm is greater. Canada considers that a similar approach of ranking objectives would be appropriate under Article 2.2, since the range of potential objectives provided for under that provision is broad, and includes objectives of less importance, such as those potentially covered in Article XX(d) of the GATT 1994 (necessary to secure compliance with laws or regulations not inconsistent with that Agreement), and those vital and important in the highest degree, such as the protection of human life and health.

80. In Canada's view, it is unnecessary to speculate about or determine in the abstract the level of fulfilment a WTO Member might have been striving to achieve, and, to the extent that it suggests otherwise, the United States errs. What is necessary is to determine the extent to which the challenged measure itself fulfils its objective. The determination of the actual, as opposed to theoretical, level of fulfilment of an objective is relevant for two reasons: first, in determining whether the level of contribution meets the minimum level necessary for "fulfilment"; and second, if it does meet or exceed that minimum level, the extent to which it does so is relevant for a comparison with proposed less trade-restrictive alternative measures. Canada reiterates that the level of fulfilment of a measure must be objectively determined by a panel, based on the relevant facts, including the structure and design of the measure, as well as other relevant evidence. Such an assessment can be made quantitatively and qualitatively. This approach is supported by case law developed in similar

---

[157] Canada's appellee's submission, para. 103 (quoting Appellate Body Report, *Korea – Various Measures on Beef*, para. 162). See also para. 104 (referring to Appellate Body Report, *Brazil – Retreaded Tyres*, paras. 150 and 179; Appellate Body Report, *EC – Asbestos*, para. 172; Appellate Body Report, *US – Gambling*, paras. 301, 306, and 326; Appellate Body Report, *China – Publications and Audiovisual Products*, paras. 251 and 255; and Panel Report, *Colombia – Ports of Entry*, para. 7.566).

contexts.[158] A determination of a level of fulfilment that is not objective, and is instead based on the statements of the defending Member, would give a Member every incentive to assert a high "level of fulfilment" of a challenged measure, both to meet the requirement that the measure itself "fulfil" its objective, and to make it impossible for proposed alternative measures to compare favourably with that level of fulfilment.

81. Canada notes that, while the United States agrees that the Panel's conclusion regarding the information that the COOL measure provides is relevant to the analysis of the United States' level of fulfilment in terms of comparison with alternative measures, it does not consider this to be a separate step in a correct analysis under Article 2.2. Canada disagrees and submits that in this dispute, consistent with a proper approach to applying Article 2.2, the Panel carefully reviewed the operation of the measure and related evidence and assessed the extent to which the COOL measure contributed to the fulfilment of the objective of providing information to consumers about origin. Canada notes that the risks non-fulfilment would create in this case are minimal—a few consumers who want to know particular origin information about a select group of products might not be able to find that information in the limited retail outlets covered by the COOL measure—and that the COOL measure restricts trade to a very significant extent. Therefore, in Canada's view, the level of fulfilment required of the COOL measure is much higher than it would be if the objective were of vital importance—for instance, the protection of human life. In this regard, Canada submits that, in order to "fulfil" the objective, the COOL measure must do more than provide an "insignificant" contribution. Rather, something closer to "very material", or "very significant" achievement of the objective should be required.[159] Based on the above, Canada considers that the Panel properly interpreted and applied Article 2.2 to the COOL measure.

82. If, however, the Appellate Body disagrees and considers that a separate finding with respect to the level of fulfilment is not required or provided for under Article 2.2, then Canada agrees with the United States that the level of fulfilment assessed by the Panel is relevant for comparing the COOL measure with the proposed alternative measures.

---

[158] Canada's appellee's submission, para. 115 (referring to Panel Report, *EC – Tariff Preferences*, paras. 7.210 and 7.211-7.218; Appellate Body Report, *US – Gambling*, para. 323; Panel Report, *US – Gambling*, paras. 6.494, 6.500-6.504, 6.507, 6.508, 6.511, and 6.516-6.518; Panel Report, *US – Shrimp (Thailand)*, paras. 7.190-7.192; Panel Report, *Mexico – Taxes on Soft Drinks*, para. 8.189; and Appellate Body Report, *China – Publications and Audiovisual Products*, paras. 252, 253, and 255-269).

[159] Canada's appellee's submission, para. 107.

(ii) The Level of Fulfilment Achieved by the COOL Measure

83. Canada disagrees with the United States that the Panel erred in its assessment of the level of fulfilment achieved by the COOL measure. First, with respect to the United States' argument that Label A "completely fulfils" the COOL measure's objective and that the Panel failed properly to take this into account[160], Canada notes that the United States "considerably overstates" the limited Panel finding, namely, that the COOL measure "appears to fulfil" its objective to a certain extent by preventing certain confusion created under the USDA grade labelling.[161] First, this finding applies only to beef, not pork, since, as the Panel noted, pork does not carry USDA grade labelling.[162] Second, even with respect to beef, the finding is much more limited than suggested by the United States. Canada recalls the Panel's finding that through the COOL measure the United States "aims to prevent meat derived from animals of non-US origin from carrying a US-origin label under any circumstances. *To that extent*, the COOL measure *appears* to fulfil the objective".[163] In Canada's view, the Panel found only that the COOL measure fulfils an objective that not even the United States suggested it did: to prevent meat from imported animals from ever carrying a US-origin label. The Panel did not find, as the United States suggests, that the COOL measure provides "'clear and accurate' consumer information" on Label A meat.[164]

84. Second, Canada refers to the United States' argument that less information is provided for cost reasons, and that this lowers costs to Canadian and Mexican producers. Canada responds that the United States points to no factual findings, or evidence, to support this claim. The argument is flawed because the major factor adding cost is the necessity to segregate, which remains. Moreover, even if it is assumed, contrary to the facts accepted by the Panel, that there were lower costs for producers of imported products, unless the objective is modified to include a cost component (as Canada argues above it should not), that does not affect a determination of whether the measure fulfils its objective. There is nothing in Article 2.2 that suggests that cost should be a factor in assessing whether the challenged measure fulfils its objective. By analogy with Article XX of the GATT 1994 and Article 5.6 of the *SPS*

[160] Canada's appellee's submission, para. 120 (quoting United States' appellant's submission, para. 172).

[161] Canada's appellee's submission, para. 120 (quoting Panel Reports, para. 7.713).

[162] Canada's appellee's submission, para. 120 (referring to Panel Reports, paras. 7.272 and 7.656).

[163] Canada's appellee's submission, para. 120 (quoting Panel Reports, para. 7.713). (emphasis added by Canada)

[164] Canada's appellee's submission, para. 120 (quoting United States' appellant submission, para. 177).

Agreement, it may be that a proposed alternative measure is disqualified because it is "not reasonably available" for being too costly[165]; however, in Canada's view, that is a different determination.

C. Arguments of Mexico – Appellee

1. Article 2.1 of the TBT Agreement

85. Mexico requests the Appellate Body to reject the United States' appeal of the Panel's finding that the COOL measure is inconsistent with Article 2.1 of the *TBT Agreement*. According to Mexico, the Panel's finding is consistent with the well-established body of WTO and GATT 1947 jurisprudence on the meaning of "treatment no less favourable" and with the Appellate Body's interpretation and application of Article 2.1 of the *TBT Agreement* in *US – Clove Cigarettes*. Furthermore, Mexico requests the Appellate Body to dismiss the United States' claims under Article 11 of the DSU, arguing that the Panel's finding was well supported by the evidence and reflected an objective analysis.

(a) The Interpretation and Application of Article 2.1 of the *TBT Agreement*

86. Mexico contends that the United States proposes a new test for "treatment no less favourable" that has no basis in law, that fails to distinguish between *de jure* and *de facto* discrimination, and that seeks to restrict the scope of the legal analysis under Article 2.1. Although the United States refers to various Appellate Body reports in support of its test, it misinterprets and misapplies the findings of the Appellate Body, and the various elements of the United States' test find no support in those reports. The United States asserts, for example, that, in order to accord less favourable treatment, "the measure *itself*"[166] must treat imported products less favourably than domestic products. Although it references various Appellate Body findings in setting out this requirement, the United States inserts the word "itself" and thereby seeks to shift the focus of the examination to the measure and away from the conditions of competition in the relevant market. In so doing, the United States significantly alters the analysis articulated by the Appellate Body in disputes such as *Korea – Various Measures on Beef*, and its emphasis on the conditions of competition in the relevant market. With regard to the United States' contention that differential treatment must be "based on origin", Mexico argues that the Appellate Body has recently

[165] Canada's appellee's submission, para. 121 (referring to Appellate Body Report, *US – Gambling*, para. 308).

[166] Mexico's appellee's submission, para. 63 (quoting United States' appellant's submission, paras. 71 and 75 (original emphasis)).

rejected such an argument by finding that, once a detrimental impact on imports has been established, a panel need not inquire further to determine whether that impact is unrelated to the foreign origin of the product.[167]

87. Mexico recalls the United States' argument that the Panel erred in finding that the COOL measure treats meat derived from imported and domestic livestock differently based on the definitions of origin provided in the labelling requirements. Mexico contends that the United States' argument that the COOL measure does not treat imported livestock differently than domestic livestock focuses on *de jure* discrimination. This is confirmed by the United States' argument that, "as a matter of logic, treatment that is identical cannot be less favourable".[168] In this respect, Mexico emphasizes the Appellate Body's findings in *Korea – Various Measures on Beef* that a formal difference in treatment between imported and domestic products is "neither necessary, nor sufficient" to demonstrate less favourable treatment.[169] In any event, Mexico acknowledges that the COOL measure does not discriminate against Mexican products on its face, and emphasizes that the Panel did not rely on its statement that certain labelling requirements reflect *de jure* different treatment for its finding on less favourable treatment under Article 2.1 of the *TBT Agreement*. Rather, the Panel rightly found that the complainants alleged that the COOL measure *de facto* discriminated against imported livestock, and went on to perform a *de facto* analysis.

88. Turning to the United States' allegations regarding the Panel's *de facto* analysis under Article 2.1, Mexico submits that the Panel's legal approach was correct. The United States misrepresents the Panel's findings when it suggests that the Panel in effect required the COOL measure to "ensure that imported products are placed on an equal footing in terms of their *ability* to compete".[170] Rather, consistent with relevant jurisprudence under the *TBT Agreement* and the GATT 1994, the Panel determined whether the COOL measure modified the conditions of competition within the US market to the detriment of imported cattle. Moreover, Mexico recalls the United States' contention that "[t]he question for purposes of Article 2.1 of the *TBT Agreement* is whether the technical regulation alters the *conditions* of competition so as to deny imported products the ability to compete under the same conditions as like domestic

[167] Mexico's appellee's submission, para. 76 (referring to Appellate Body Report, *US – Clove Cigarettes*, footnote 372 to para. 179).

[168] Mexico's appellee's submission, para. 73 (quoting United States' appellant's submission, para. 69).

[169] Mexico's appellee's submission, para. 68 (quoting Appellate Body Report, *Korea – Various Measures on Beef*, para. 137).

[170] Mexico's appellee's submission, para. 85 (quoting United States' appellant's submission, para. 62 (original underlining)).

products."[171] In Mexico's view, such a formulation changes the standard from a test of whether the measure *modifies* the conditions of competition to the detriment of imported products, to a test of whether the measure *denies* imported products the *ability* to compete under the *same* conditions as like domestic products. The United States' proposed standard would create a narrower scope of application at a higher threshold than that contemplated by the Appellate Body under Article 2.1. Thus, according to Mexico, the United States' proposed approach must be rejected because it has no basis in law and is inconsistent with the well-established principle of equality of competitive conditions.

89. Mexico submits that, in evaluating the conditions of competition in the US market, the Panel correctly found that costs resulting from technical regulations may qualify as a competitive disadvantage if they are incurred only by imported and not like domestic products. The Panel undertook a detailed examination of the costs of compliance of the COOL measure, including whether the COOL measure required segregation and whether segregation entailed higher costs for imported livestock. The Panel properly took a broad view of the costs that might be entailed by the measure, and found that the costs incurred by imported livestock included "discriminatory price discounts, loss of processing opportunities, increased logistical costs, prejudicial contractual treatment and notice requirements, increased financing costs and hurdles, and loss of premium market opportunities".[172] In Mexico's view, the Panel's analysis on this basis clearly demonstrates a modification of conditions of competition to the detriment of imported livestock. Mexico maintains that this conclusion becomes even more evident when the situation under the COOL measure is compared to the highly integrated nature of the North American livestock and meat market prior to the measure.

90. Mexico contends that, as part of its argument that the measure *itself* must modify the conditions of competition, the United States asserts that the Panel erred by basing its finding of less favourable treatment on "external factors"[173] "not under the Member's control, such as the market share of imports or the independent actions of private market actors".[174] However, contrary to the United States' argument, the Panel did not find that market effects that are "solely" the result of independent decisions of private market participants would

[171] Mexico's appellee's submission, para. 87 (quoting United States' appellant's submission, para. 63 (original emphasis)).

[172] Mexico's appellee's submission, para. 47 (referring to Panel Reports, paras. 7.373-7.381). See also para. 34.

[173] Mexico's appellee's submission, para. 77 (quoting United States' appellant's submission, para. 75).

[174] Mexico's appellee's submission, para. 77 (quoting United States' appellant's submission, para. 71).

give rise to a violation of Article 2.1 of the *TBT Agreement*. Rather, the Panel was correct to find that a measure creating a sufficiently strong incentive for private market participants to act in a particular way can properly be found to be inconsistent with Article 2.1. In reaching this finding, the Panel properly relied on findings in *Korea – Various Measures on Beef* and correctly found that, similar to the situation in that dispute, "any decisions by private market participants are not 'solely' the result of their independent business calculations, but are attributable in large part to the economic incentive and disincentive created by the provisions of the COOL measure."[175] Thus, Mexico submits, the Panel's finding, that "[i]t is the result of the COOL measure" that US producers "opted predominantly" to process exclusively US-origin livestock, was properly based on the Panel's determination that the COOL measure creates an incentive to do so.[176] As the Panel correctly found, without the effects of the measure, "market participants would not have opted this way".[177]

91. Mexico further argues that, by alleging that the adverse effects of the COOL measure are the result of external factors not related to the measure, the United States attempts to restrict the scope of the legal analysis to exclude the indirect effects of the measure on the conditions of competition in the US market, such as the measure's impact on market forces and market participants. Given that the Panel was performing a *de facto* analysis, however, it was appropriate for it to take into consideration all the relevant facts and circumstances in the market and to determine how the imposition of the challenged measure affects competitive conditions in the light of those facts and circumstances, including factors such as the smaller market share of imports and their longer distance from the market. In Mexico's view, it is part of the character of *de facto* discrimination that the pre-existing market factors play a role in the modification of the conditions of competition. In this case, the COOL measure disrupts the facts and circumstances that normally occur in the marketplace.

92. Mexico adds that the United States' position is not supported by the Appellate Body's finding, in *Thailand – Cigarettes (Philippines)*, that "there must be in every case a genuine relationship between the measure at issue and its adverse impact on competitive opportunities for imported versus like domestic products to support a finding that imported products are treated less favourably".[178] Mexico points out that this finding related to a discussion of "the degree of likelihood that an adverse impact on competitive opportunities would

---

175 Mexico's appellee's submission, para. 80 (quoting Panel Reports, para. 7.391).

176 Mexico's appellee's submission, para. 67 (quoting Panel Reports, para. 7.403). See also para. 80 (quoting Panel Reports, para. 7.390).

177 Mexico's appellee's submission, para. 67 (quoting Panel Reports, para. 7.403).

178 Mexico's appellee's submission, para. 70 (quoting Appellate Body Report, *Thailand – Cigarettes (Philippines)*, para. 134; and United States' appellant's submission, paras. 72 and 89).

materialize", and not, as in this case, to an evaluation of a modification of competitive opportunities that has already occurred.[179] In any event, Mexico argues, there clearly is a genuine relationship between the COOL measure and the reduced competitive opportunities for imported products. But for the COOL measure, the North American Free Trade Agreement ("NAFTA") market would be fully integrated, with market participants acting purely on the basis of competitive considerations of price and quality.

93. Finally, with regard to the United States' contention that the Panel's findings would jeopardize country of origin labelling regimes in other WTO Members, Mexico points out that it has not challenged the validity of general country of origin labelling requirements. Furthermore, none of the relevant labelling regimes in other WTO Members is similar to the United States' measure. Under Australia's, Japan's, and Korea's regimes, meat derived from Mexican-born cattle would be labelled as domestic meat; and "trace-back" systems, such as that applied in the European Union, impose equal burdens on all products regardless of origin.

(b) Article 11 of the DSU

94. Mexico emphasizes the high legal threshold established by the Appellate Body under Article 11 of the DSU, and contends that the United States' claims of error do not meet this standard. The United States makes the same arguments on appeal as it made before the Panel with respect to segregation, commingling, and the price differential, and essentially requests the Appellate Body to make a *de novo* review of the facts.

95. As an initial matter, Mexico highlights that the United States assumes that a finding of less favourable treatment must be evaluated based on the actual trade effects of the measure, which disregards the findings of both the Panel and the Appellate Body in this respect. The Panel specifically stated that it had already reached its conclusions on less favourable treatment under Article 2.1 before examining the actual trade effects resulting from the measure. Furthermore, the United States focuses on evidence of commingling, and "leaps to the conclusion" that if commingling were occurring on a widespread basis, there could not be less favourable treatment.[180] However, the Panel's finding of less favourable treatment was based on a number of factors and not on a finding that all imported cattle are segregated from all domestic cattle. In any event, Mexico recalls that, even in instances where commingling could be present, segregation is still necessary in order to comply with the COOL measure.

---

[179] Mexico's appellee's submission, para. 70 (referring to Appellate Body Report, *Thailand – Cigarettes (Philippines)*, para. 134).

[180] Mexico's appellee's submission, para. 99.

96. Notwithstanding the above deficiency underlying the United States' claim, Mexico responds to the United States' arguments concerning the Panel's treatment of the specific evidence on the record. Mexico claims that the United States acknowledges that the USDA survey of the use of the different labels is not statistically reliable, and that, considering how much is not known about the methodology of that survey, the Panel was not required to either discuss it or rely on it. Similarly, the Panel's finding on the limited evidentiary value of photographs of labels submitted by the United States showing labels for meat stating "U.S., Canadian, Mexican Origin" was justified, because the flexibilities in labelling rules mean that a label indicating multiple origins cannot be understood as demonstrating that the labelled products have been commingled. The two remaining pieces of evidence both contain information indicating how some producers are complying with the COOL requirements, but neither clearly demonstrates that commingling is occurring, and the Panel's conclusion that they did not provide compelling evidence of the occurrence or extent of commingling therefore is "entirely reasonable".[181] Mexico further asserts that the United States attempts to obfuscate the effects of the COOL measure on the livestock market by claiming that the Panel wrongly found that the COOL measure requires every muscle cut of meat to be traceable to a specific origin. In fact, the Panel correctly found that compliance with the COOL measure requires that suppliers and processors have information on the country of birth of each animal, and that this information must be passed on to retailers.

97. With respect to the United States' argument that the Panel erred in its findings regarding an increase in the price differential between imported and domestic livestock, Mexico points out that it presented direct evidence of a COOL discount being applied to imported cattle, including invoices, statements of US processors, and other data showing the price differential between Mexican and US feeder cattle. The Panel's finding was therefore well supported by the evidence, and reflected an objective analysis.

(c) The Relevance of the Appellate Body Report in *US – Clove Cigarettes* in this Appeal

98. Mexico recalls that the Appellate Body recently interpreted Article 2.1 of the *TBT Agreement* in *US – Clove Cigarettes*. In Mexico's view, although the Panel did not have the benefit of the Appellate Body Report in *US – Clove Cigarettes*, the Panel's finding of inconsistency under Article 2.1 of the *TBT Agreement* is consistent with the Appellate Body's test and is legally correct. This is because it is evident from the Panel's findings that the United States' technical regulation is not even-handed and that the detrimental impact on imported livestock does not stem exclusively from a legitimate regulatory

---

181 Mexico's appellee's submission, paras. 110 and 114.

distinction. Rather, the loss of competitive opportunities resulting from the COOL measure clearly reflects discrimination against the group of imported products.

99. Mexico observes that, in determining whether the detrimental impact stemmed from a legitimate regulatory distinction, the Appellate Body in *US – Clove Cigarettes* looked at: (i) the proportion of imported and like domestic products adversely affected by the measure; and (ii) other factors that indicated whether the detrimental impact on competitive opportunities for imported products stemmed from a legitimate regulatory distinction. Regarding the first element, Mexico alleges that the COOL measure adversely affects all or almost all imported products and does *not* adversely affect all or almost all like domestic products, and that there is an incentive to use domestic cattle inputs and a disincentive to use imported cattle inputs. Mexico adds that a measure designed and structured in such a way is not even-handed.

100. As regards other indicating factors, Mexico cautions that considerable care must be taken when evaluating the COOL measure, because distinctions made under such a measure are inherently linked to origin. In Mexico's view, Article 2.1 would be open to substantial circumvention if the detrimental impact incurred by imported products could be justified solely because it could be linked to such a distinction. In any event, Mexico maintains that several factors establish that the detrimental impact of the COOL measure does *not* stem exclusively from a legitimate regulatory distinction and is not even-handed, but, rather, it reflects discrimination against imported livestock. These factors are: (i) that the COOL measure is mandatory despite low consumer demand for such information; (ii) that the COOL measure is designed so that the least costly and most commercially desirable method of compliance is to exclude imported livestock; (iii) that the COOL measure is designed to distinguish between meat made from US-born cattle and meat made from foreign cattle rather than to give information on origin, as is clear from the fact that only Label A provides meaningful information; (iv) that the COOL measure includes "completely arbitrary" flexibility allowing Label B to be used for Category A meat when Category A and Category B meat are processed "on the same production day"[182]; and (v) that the COOL measure is not effective at achieving its objective, because very little meat in the US market is accurately labelled under the COOL measure. Finally, Mexico asserts that the sixth recital of the preamble of the *TBT Agreement* provides "an exhaustive list of the justifications" that are available for measures that otherwise would violate Article 2.1 because they qualify as

[182] Mexico's appellee's submission, para. 58.

legitimate regulatory distinctions, and none of those justifications are applicable to the COOL measure.[183]

2. *Article 2.2 of the TBT Agreement*

101. Mexico asserts that the legal test adopted by the Panel under Article 2.2 of the *TBT Agreement* was "appropriate"[184] in this dispute, and submits that the United States' appeal of the Panel's reasoning and findings under Article 2.2 is "without merit and should be rejected".[185]

(a) Trade-Restrictiveness

102. In response to the United States' appeal of the Panel's finding that the COOL measure is trade restrictive within the meaning of Article 2.2, Mexico acknowledges that Articles 2.1 and 2.2 of the *TBT Agreement* are two separate obligations that contain different legal tests. Nonetheless, evidence demonstrating the inconsistency of a measure with one obligation may be relevant for the analysis of the same measure under the other obligation. In this case, Mexico considers the Panel's finding under Article 2.1 that the COOL measure negatively affects the conditions of competition of imported livestock to be legally and factually sound, and, for the same reason, submits that the Panel did not err in finding the COOL measure to be trade restrictive under Article 2.2.

(b) The Objective Pursued and the Level at which the United States Considers It Appropriate to Fulfil Its Objective

103. Mexico disagrees with the United States that an analysis of the objective pursued under Article 2.2 should include a determination of "the level at which the United States considers it appropriate to fulfil the objective".[186] In Mexico's view, the absence of the words "at the level a Member considers appropriate" in Article 2.2 reinforces the view that there is no need to determine a desired theoretical "level of fulfilment" for the legitimate objective. To the contrary, the level a Member considers appropriate will be reflected in the technical regulation actually applied. This is to be objectively determined by a panel and, if the measure at issue does not fulfil the legitimate objective, it is not necessary to continue the analysis and examine an alternative measure. If, however, the

[183] Mexico's appellee's submission, para. 59.

[184] Mexico's appellee's submission, para. 127.

[185] Mexico's appellee's submission, para. 124.

[186] Mexico's appellee's submission, para. 140 (quoting United States' appellant's submission, para. 124).

interpretation of the United States were accepted, then the legal test under Article 2.2 would mean that, while a measure fails to achieve the desired theoretical level of fulfilment of the legitimate objective, an alternative measure must reach that theoretical level. Moreover, if a determination of "the level of fulfilment" were based on the statements of the defending Member, it would give that Member every incentive to inflate the desired theoretical "level of fulfilment" so that a proposed alternative measure would never achieve it, which could not possibly have been the intention of the negotiators or a reasonable interpretation.

104. In any event, Mexico submits that, contrary to the United States' contention, the Panel's identification of the objective pursued—namely, to provide as much clear and accurate origin information as possible to consumers—was based on a complete and coherent assessment of the relevant facts and arguments, including the United States' indication of the level at which it aimed to achieve the identified objective. Mexico argues that the statements relating to costs alleged by the United States to have been selectively quoted by the Panel refer to explanations of *why* and *how* the United States set its objectives and appropriate level, but not to the objectives and appropriate level themselves.

105. Mexico disagrees with the United States' assertion that the Panel wilfully distorted and misrepresented the United States' position as to its level of fulfilment and thus acted inconsistently with Article 11 of the DSU, and highlights that panels enjoy discretion in their assessment of the facts. Mexico recalls the argument of the United States that the Panel failed to take into account evidence regarding the "true balance between costs and consumer information".[187] Mexico responds that the Panel examined a similar argument by the United States and correctly concluded that "[t]he act of balancing conflicting interests cannot ... justify any inconsistency found in the impugned measure with the obligations of the respondent under the covered agreements."[188] In this dispute, the Panel considered the United States' arguments, explained why it did not accept them, and, thereby, satisfied its obligations under Article 11 of the DSU.

---

[187] Mexico's appellee's submission, para. 156 (quoting United States' appellant's submission, para. 143).

[188] Mexico's appellee's submission, para. 156 (quoting Panel Reports, para. 7.711).

(c) Whether the COOL Measure Is "More Trade-Restrictive than Necessary to Fulfil a Legitimate Objective"

(i) The Panel's Legal Framework

106. Mexico submits that the Panel did not err in adopting the legal framework for its analysis of the trade-restrictiveness of the COOL measure. First, Mexico disagrees with the United States that a technical regulation's conformity with the first sentence of Article 2.2 of the *TBT Agreement* must be established based on the elements of the second sentence.[189] As Mexico sees it, the second sentence elaborates on the meaning of the first sentence, but does not define it exhaustively. By focusing only on whether there is a less trade-restrictive alternative measure, the United States' interpretation of the test under Article 2.2 attempts to "unilaterally modify the language" of that provision.[190] In accordance with a proper interpretation, a panel should consider first whether a technical regulation *fulfils* the legitimate objective, based on a consideration of the risks at issue, the interests at stake, the Member's policy objective, and whether the government's interference in the market is unavoidable. Once the technical regulation at issue is fully assessed, and only if the technical regulation fulfils the legitimate objective, should the focus of the analysis shift to potential alternative measures. Mexico considers the first step of this analysis essential because it is impossible to assess whether there is a less trade-restrictive alternative if the measure does not fulfil the objective. Moreover, it would be impossible to take account of the risks non-fulfilment would create if, in fact, non-fulfilment already exists with the challenged measure. It follows that a measure that does not fulfil the legitimate objective is an unnecessary obstacle to international trade that is inconsistent with Article 2.2.

107. Mexico disagrees that a "material contribution" to fulfilling the legitimate objective is enough to satisfy the strict test of Article 2.2 of the *TBT Agreement*. The standard "to fulfil" is close in its degree to the standard "necessary", so the term "to fulfil" in the context of Article 2.2 requires that a technical regulation be located significantly closer to the pole of 100% fulfilment of the legitimate objective.[191] Mexico agrees that, consistent with the Appellate Body's Article XX "necessity" case law, "[t]he more vital or important those common

---

[189] Mexico's appellee's submission, para. 128 (referring to United States' appellant's submission, para. 122).

[190] Mexico's appellee's submission, para. 129.

[191] Mexico's appellee's submission, paras. 177 and 178 (referring to Appellate Body Report, *Korea – Various Measures on Beef*, para. 161 and footnote 104 thereto).

interests or values are, the easier it would be to accept" a measure as "necessary" for purposes of Article 2.2.[192]

108. Mexico notes the United States' argument that the "necessity" jurisprudence developed under Article XX of the GATT 1994 is inapplicable to Article 2.2 of the *TBT Agreement*. For Mexico, irrespective of whether the second sentence of Article 2.2 defines the first sentence (the interpretation of the Panel and the United States) or whether the first sentence could have a meaning that is independent of the second sentence (a possibility foreseen by Mexico), what is clear from the context provided by the first sentence is that, under Article 2.2, a technical regulation must not create an unnecessary obstacle to trade. Therefore, the United States' argument that Article 2.2 does not ask the question of "whether the measure *itself* is 'necessary'"[193] is incorrect. The concept of necessity is used in both the first and second sentences and must be given meaning in both sentences, that is, in the context of the creation of an obstacle to trade and in the context of a less trade-restrictive alternative. Thus, whether the technical regulation at issue is more trade restrictive than necessary is a "two-step" analysis. Mexico considers this approach to be in line with the Appellate Body's clarification in *US – Gambling* and in *Brazil – Retreaded Tyres* that weighing and balancing involves two steps: first, a preliminary analysis of the necessity of the challenged measure on the basis of all relevant factors and, second, the conclusion of the preliminary analysis must be confirmed by comparing the measure with possible alternatives.

109. Mexico considers the "one-step" approach developed for claims under Article 5.6 of the *SPS Agreement*, and advocated by the United States, to be inappropriate. First, a comparative analysis of the *SPS Agreement* and the *TBT Agreement* highlights that they provide different regimes and rules, their scope of application is mutually exclusive, and provisions of one Agreement should not be automatically incorporated in the provisions of the other, because that was not intended by Members.[194] Mexico notes that the United States seeks to incorporate footnote 3 to Article 5.6 of the *SPS Agreement* into Article 2.2 of the *TBT Agreement* by referring to a letter from GATT Director-General Sutherland to the US Chief Negotiator in 1993 as a supplementary means of interpretation under Article 32 of the *Vienna Convention*.[195] Mexico contests the need to

---

[192] Mexico's appellee's submission, para. 179 (quoting Appellate Body Report, *Korea – Various Measures on Beef*, para. 162).

[193] Mexico's appellee's submission, para. 162 (quoting United States' appellant's submission, para. 161 (original emphasis)).

[194] Mexico's appellee's submission, para. 166 (highlighting the contents of Articles 1.4, 2.2, 3.3, 5, and 5.6, and Annex A.1 to the *SPS Agreement*).

[195] Mexico's appellee's submission, paras. 184 and 185 (referring to United States' appellant's submission, footnote 269 to para. 179).

employ supplementary means of interpretation given that the text of Article 2.2 and the application of Article 31 of the *Vienna Convention* make clear that, unlike in Article 5.6 of the *SPS Agreement*, in Article 2.2 of the *TBT Agreement*, there is no footnote providing clarification on the meaning of the phrase "more trade-restrictive than necessary". The absence of such a footnote must have meaning. Indeed, even the letter relied upon by the United States indicates that it was not the common intention of Members to incorporate such a footnote in the *TBT Agreement*. Therefore, in Mexico's view, there is no legal basis for incorporating into Article 2.2 of the *TBT Agreement* the test in footnote 3 to Article 5.6 of the *SPS Agreement*.

110. For these reasons, Mexico requests the Appellate Body to reject the United States' incorrect interpretation of Article 2.2, and its attempt to shift the focus of the inquiry from the COOL measure and its consistency with Article 2.2 to the "*key* legal question [of] whether the importing Member could have adopted a less trade-restrictive measure", and to whether the proposed alternative measures would themselves be consistent with Article 2.2.[196] Instead, the Appellate Body should recognize that an analysis of whether a measure is more trade restrictive than necessary involves a two-step analysis: the first step is focused on the technical regulation at issue and the second step is focused on an alternative measure. Only if a panel determines that a measure fulfils the legitimate objective should it examine an alternative measure. Otherwise, submits Mexico, the legal test under Article 2.2 would mean "do as I *say*, not as I *do*".[197]

(ii) The Level of Fulfilment Achieved by the COOL Measure

111. Mexico argues that, having made an objective assessment of the facts, arguments, and evidence, the Panel correctly found that the COOL measure does not make a material contribution to or fulfil the objective of providing clear and accurate information on the places where animals were born, raised, and slaughtered.

112. Regarding the United States' contention that the Panel itself agreed that the COOL measure conveys clear and accurate information, and its further assertion that "it is an uncontested fact that meat carrying the A label constitutes at least 71% of the meat sold in the United States"[198], Mexico responds that the

---

196 Mexico's appellee's submission, paras. 192 (quoting United States' appellant's submission, para. 181 (original emphasis)) and 194.

197 Mexico's appellee's submission, para. 130. (original emphasis)

198 Mexico's appellee's submission, paras. 168 (referring to United States' appellant's submission, para. 173) and 169 (quoting United States' appellant's submission, para. 172).

United States "exaggerates or otherwise takes liberties with the Panel's findings and the evidence".[199] What is uncontested is that, given that the COOL measure covers only about 55% of the meat sold in the United States, the meat carrying Label A constitutes less than 39% (71% of 55%) of the meat sold in the United States.[200]

113. Mexico further observes that, contrary to the suggestion of the United States, the Panel did not make a clear finding endorsing the effectiveness of Label A. Although the United States quotes the statement of the Panel that "the COOL measure appears to fulfil the objective because the measure prohibits such meat from carrying a Label A even though the same meat may still carry a USDA grade label"[201], Mexico refers to other conclusions of the Panel indicating that the information provided through "all the labels" (that is, Labels A, B, C, and D), collectively, is confusing to consumers.[202] Moreover, although the Panel did find that origin information conveyed by Label A may be meaningful, Mexico understands this to refer to the fact that Label A, unlike Labels B and C, is defined in an unambiguous manner. However, this does not amount to a finding that, when Label A is used, the COOL measure overall is effective to any particular degree in fulfilling the United States' objective. Finally, Mexico considers that, through its statement that the COOL measure does not provide perfect information on origin in every conceivable scenario, the United States itself "concedes that the COOL measure is unreliable even for the products to which it applies".[203]

114. Mexico disagrees with the United States' argument that the ineffectiveness of the COOL measure can be justified as an effort to avoid imposing excessive costs.[204] Mexico notes the Panel's finding that the United States designed and implemented the COOL measure in a manner that imposed discriminatory higher costs on the use of imported livestock.[205] Mexico submits that Article 2.2 does not suggest that cost should be a factor in assessing whether a challenged measure fulfils its objective, and that the Panel therefore correctly

---

[199] Mexico's appellee's submission, para. 169.

[200] Mexico's appellee's submission, para. 169 (referring to, *inter alia*, United States' response to Panel Question 92, para. 15 and footnote 22 thereto).

[201] Panel Reports, para. 7.713.

[202] Mexico's appellee's submission, paras. 170 and 171 (referring to Panel Reports, paras. 7.715 and 7.702).

[203] Mexico's appellee's submission, para. 173 (referring to United States' appellant's submission, para. 144).

[204] Mexico's appellee's submission, para. 174 (referring to United States' appellant's submission, paras. 139, 140, and 142-144).

[205] Mexico's appellee's submission, para. 174 (referring to Panel Reports, paras. 7.347, 7.351, and 7.372).

concluded that the pertinent question for its analysis was whether the COOL measure is fulfilling the identified objective in accordance with Article 2.2 of the *TBT Agreement*. Moreover, if the arguments of the United States were accepted, it would imply that the United States' objective would have been redefined as to provide accurate information regarding whether meat was produced from US-born cattle only, and not to provide accurate information regarding meat from cattle of non-US origin. Such an objective would be inherently arbitrary and not even-handed. Having accepted the United States' characterization of its objective—to provide as much clear and accurate origin information as possible to consumers—the Panel was correct to find that the COOL measure does not fulfil that objective.

D. *Claims of Error by Canada – Other Appellant*

1. *"Legitimate Objective" under Article 2.2 of the TBT Agreement*

115. In its other appellant's submission, Canada supports the Panel's ultimate conclusion that the COOL measure is inconsistent with Articles 2.1 and 2.2 of the *TBT Agreement*, and, in addition, requests the Appellate Body: (i) to modify the reasoning of the Panel with respect to Article 2.2 while upholding the Panel's finding of a violation of that provision; (ii) in the event that the Appellate Body reverses the Panel's finding under Article 2.2, to complete the analysis and find, based on the evidence on the record regarding less trade-restrictive alternative measures, that the COOL measure is inconsistent with Article 2.2; (iii) to find that the COOL measure and the Vilsack letter are inconsistent with Article III:4 of the GATT 1994; and (iv) in the event that the Appellate Body neither upholds the Panel's finding under Article 2.1 of the *TBT Agreement*, nor finds that the COOL measure violates Article III:4 of the GATT 1994, to find that the COOL measure and the Vilsack letter nullify and impair benefits accruing to Canada within the meaning of Article XXIII:1(b) of the GATT 1994. Canada clarified the scope of the last two of these grounds of appeal at the oral hearing. First, Canada explained that its appeal of the Panel's exercise of judicial economy under Article III:4 and its request for a finding under that provision are conditional upon the Appellate Body reversing the Panel's finding of inconsistency under Article 2.1 of the *TBT Agreement*. Second, in the light of the apparent withdrawal of the Vilsack letter by the United States, Canada no longer seeks findings with respect to the Vilsack letter, although Canada maintains that the Appellate Body should take the Vilsack letter into account in the event that it makes a ruling with regard to the COOL measure under Article III:4 or Article XXIII:1(b) of the GATT 1994.

116. Canada claims that the Panel correctly found that the substantive obligation in Article 2.2 is found in the second sentence of that provision, and that the following five-step test that it adopted for its analysis under Article 2.2

was appropriate: (i) determine if the technical regulation restricts international trade; (ii) identify the objective pursued by the technical regulation in question; (iii) determine if the objective of the technical regulation is legitimate; (iv) determine if the technical regulation fulfils the legitimate objective; and (v) assess alternative measures that would fulfil the legitimate objective in a less trade-restrictive way, "taking account of the risks non-fulfilment would create".[206] Canada maintains, however, that the Panel erred in applying the second and third steps of the above test in its analysis, in identifying the objective pursued by the COOL measure, and in finding that the objective pursued by the COOL measure is legitimate.

(a) The Identification of the Objective

(i) The Focus on a General Policy Objective

117. Canada argues that, in identifying the objective of the COOL measure, the Panel erred in focusing its analysis on a general policy objective that the COOL measure might pursue, as stated by the United States, rather than the actual objective pursued by the measure. In so doing, the Panel also erred in analyzing evidence relating to the design, architecture, structure, and legislative history of the COOL measure only "as a secondary matter [and] as an alternative to the 'identified objective'".[207]

118. Canada considers that the Panel identified the objective "pursued by" the technical regulation as "something different and more abstract" than the objective related to the technical regulation itself.[208] In Canada's view, however, the text of Article 2.2 directly links the objective of a technical regulation with the legitimacy of that objective, and hence the focus of the inquiry is on the conduct of a Member when it prepares, adopts, or applies a technical regulation. Canada further argues that the Panel's approach is "an unnecessary and unhelpful addition to the analysis"[209], because it is still necessary to determine the objective of a particular technical regulation under the fourth step of the test articulated by the Panel, namely, whether the measure fulfils a legitimate objective. Therefore, "the separate step of assessing whether a theoretical objective is legitimate serves no purpose".[210]

---

206 Canada's other appellant's submission, para. 19 (referring to Panel Reports, paras. 7.554-7.556).

207 Canada's other appellant's submission, para. 29 (quoting Panel Reports, para. 7.677).

208 Canada's other appellant's submission, para. 21.

209 *Ibid.*

210 Canada's other appellant's submission, para. 24.

119. Canada asserts that, contrary to the Panel's suggestion, the Appellate Body's decision in *Australia – Salmon* does not support the Panel's approach to determining an abstract objective for purposes of an analysis under Article 2.2 of the *TBT Agreement*.[211] In that dispute, the Appellate Body relied on the words "when establishing or maintaining" in Article 5.6 of the *SPS Agreement* to find that the determination of the level of protection "is an element in the decision-making process which logically *precedes* and is *separate* from the establishment or maintenance of the SPS measure".[212] There is no similar language in Article 2.2 of the *TBT Agreement* to suggest that the objective that a technical regulation pursues should be divorced from the objective of that technical regulation itself. Moreover, whereas the concept of "appropriate level of protection" in the *SPS Agreement* refers to a "prerogative of the Member concerned"[213], the qualifier "legitimate" in the term "legitimate objective" under Article 2.2 of the *TBT Agreement* does not refer to an objective deemed legitimate by the Member. Rather, whether an objective pursued by a technical regulation is legitimate within the meaning of Article 2.2 is a legal question to be answered by a panel following an objective assessment of the evidence before it.

120. Canada further submits that a more fitting analogy in the *SPS Agreement* can be found in the phrase "applied to protect" in Annex A(1)(a) to that Agreement. In interpreting the meaning of that phrase, the Appellate Body found that "[w]hether a measure is 'applied ... to protect' in the sense of Annex A(1)(a) must be ascertained not only from the objectives of the measure as expressed by the responding party, but also from the text and structure of the relevant measure, its surrounding regulatory context, and the way in which it is designed and applied."[214]

(ii) Article 11 of the DSU

121. Canada claims that, in examining evidence concerning the design, architecture, and structure of the COOL measure, as well as its legislative history, the Panel failed to find that the objective of the COOL measure is protectionism and thereby acted inconsistently with Article 11 of the DSU. Canada maintains that, although it provided extensive evidence and arguments to the Panel concerning the design, architecture, structure, and legislative history

---

211 Canada's other appellant's submission, para. 25 (referring to Panel Reports, paras. 7.604 and 7.611).

212 Canada's other appellant's submission, para. 25 (quoting Appellate Body Report, *Australia – Salmon*, para. 203 (original emphasis)).

213 Canada's other appellant's submission, para. 26 (quoting Appellate Body Report, *Australia – Salmon*, para. 199). (original emphasis omitted by Canada)

214 Canada's other appellant's submission, para. 27 (quoting Appellate Body Report, *Australia – Apples*, para. 173).

showing that the objective of the COOL measure is the protection of domestic livestock producers, the Panel did not reach the appropriate conclusion based on that evidence and arguments. Canada highlights the following three categories of evidence and arguments.

122. First, asserts Canada, the evidence concerning the scope of the COOL measure shows that the measure includes and excludes products in a way that demonstrates its protectionist objective. More specifically, products that have little import competition are excluded from the scope of the measure, including products carrying USDA grade labels, even though the United States alleged that the COOL measure was designed to address the confusion caused by the USDA grade labels. The Panel, however, set out the evidence "in a cursory manner" and "made no attempt to objectively assess" such evidence.[215] Moreover, the Panel failed to "clearly mention" Canada's argument that, except for meat produced from certain livestock, almost all products that undergo a significant change in the United States are excluded from the scope of the COOL measure, and that such "singling out of livestock" demonstrates protectionist intent.[216]

123. Second, according to Canada, in identifying the objective, the Panel "did not appear to consider" the evidence showing the COOL measure's inability to provide useful information to consumers regarding meat derived from foreign-born livestock.[217] Third, the evidence regarding the legislative history of the COOL measure, including the fact that the measure was introduced as part of the 2002 Farm Bill, rather than with consumer information measures and statements by key legislators, as well as the fact that producers rather than consumer groups supported the legislation, show the "protectionist purpose" of the COOL measure.[218] Yet, the Panel failed to consider the probative value of this evidence that reveals the true objective of the COOL measure.

(iii) The Level of Detail of the Objective Identified

124. As an alternative to its claim that the Panel acted inconsistently with Article 11 of the DSU, Canada submits that the Panel erred in failing to characterize the objective of the COOL measure with a sufficient level of detail for purposes of determining its legitimacy. Canada submits that the Panel identified the objective of the COOL measure as providing "as much clear and accurate origin information as possible to consumers"[219], but erred in failing to

215 Canada's other appellant's submission, para. 36.

216 Canada's other appellant's submission, para. 37.

217 Canada's other appellant's submission, para. 38.

218 Canada's other appellant's submission, para. 41.

219 Canada's other appellant's submission, para. 44 (quoting Panel Reports, para. 7.620).

define the purpose for which this information is provided. In order to examine whether a government measure that requires the provision of certain information to consumers pursues a legitimate objective, it is necessary to know the purpose for which the government requires this information to be provided. This is because information can be required to support a wide range of objectives, including legitimate ones, such as allowing consumers to make informed decisions about health, and illegitimate ones, such as furthering racial discrimination or favouring domestic producers.

(b) The Legitimacy of the COOL Measure's Objective

125. Canada claims that the Panel erred in finding that the objective of the COOL measure is legitimate within the meaning of Article 2.2 of the *TBT Agreement*. The Panel failed to articulate the correct legal test for determining legitimacy, and the application of the correct legal test to the facts of the case shows, in Canada's view, that the COOL measure's objective is not legitimate within the meaning of Article 2.2.

126. Canada contends that the Panel discussed the meaning of the word "legitimate" without developing any principles that could guide its determination of whether an objective is legitimate. The Panel referred to the dictionary definition of the word in English, but that definition has "no practical meaning" and is unhelpful for assessing legitimacy under Article 2.2 of the *TBT Agreement*.[220] The Panel also referred to the finding of the panel in *Canada – Pharmaceutical Patents* regarding the term "legitimate interests" in Article 30 of the *Agreement on Trade-Related Aspects of Intellectual Property Rights* (the "*TRIPS Agreement*"). However, the legitimacy being assessed in that dispute concerned the interests of certain private parties, whereas the legitimacy in Article 2.2 of the *TBT Agreement* concerns a social value. Moreover, the term "legitimate" has a different context in Article 30 of the *TRIPS Agreement* than in Article 2.2 of the *TBT Agreement*, because the former contains general language rather than an illustrative list, but the latter contains an illustrative list. Although the Panel noted that the illustrative list of legitimate objectives in Article 2.2 of the *TBT Agreement* has interpretative value, the Panel did not conduct any further analysis in this regard.

127. According to Canada, the Panel wrongly concluded that any objective can be legitimate as long as it has a genuine link to a public policy or social norm. Contrary to this conclusion, what can be considered a "legitimate objective" should be informed by the importance of the objectives listed under Article 2.2 and should be linked to common interests or values. Canada further submits that the Panel erroneously rejected the relevance of the *ejusdem generis* principle to

[220] Canada's other appellant's submission, para. 49.

the interpretation of the word "legitimate" in Article 2.2, stating that "all of the listed examples are expressed at a high level of generality."[221] In Canada's view, specific terms following a general term "provide[] a measure" of the scope of the general term[222], and there are significant elements of commonality of the explicitly listed objectives that can helpfully inform whether a particular objective is "legitimate".

128. Canada maintains that the *TBT Agreement* prioritizes the listed objectives by providing them with a rebuttable presumption in Article 2.5, whereby a measure will not be an unnecessary obstacle to international trade if it is "prepared, adopted or applied" for one of the objectives listed in Article 2.2, and by referencing them in the closed list of legitimate objectives in the sixth recital of its preamble. Therefore, Canada contends that the correct test for determining the legitimacy of an objective requires assessing, first, whether the objective is directly related to one of the listed objectives in Article 2.2 and, if not, whether the objective is of the same type as the listed objectives. This second step involves some difficulty, because it requires determining the legitimacy of an unlisted objective. In this respect, Canada recalls that each of the listed objectives is also protected in Articles XX and XXI of the GATT 1994, which, in Canada's view, indicates that they are among the social values that WTO Members agreed can outweigh their obligations. Thus, objectives included in Articles XX and XXI of the GATT 1994 could also be considered as "legitimate" within the meaning of Article 2.2 of the *TBT Agreement*. Canada emphasizes, however, that it does not consider that the scope of legitimacy within the meaning of Article 2.2 of the *TBT Agreement* is exhausted by objectives explicitly included in exception provisions of the covered agreements. Other objectives can also be shown to be legitimate, but that requires greater specificity and "clear and compelling evidence" of legitimacy.[223]

129. Canada asserts that, even if the objective of the COOL measure is not protectionism but is, as the Panel found, to provide as much clear and accurate origin information to consumers as possible, application of the two-step test described above shows that the objective is not legitimate. First, the objective does not directly relate to any of the listed objectives in Article 2.2. Second, the objective does not fall within the type of objectives that are legitimate, because the general purpose of providing consumers with information is not an objective "privileged" in any of the covered agreements, and because the United States did

---

[221] Canada's other appellant's submission, para. 52 (quoting Panel Reports, para. 7.636).

[222] Canada's other appellant's submission, para. 52 (quoting Appellate Body Reports, *China – Raw Materials*, para. 326).

[223] Canada's other appellant's submission, para. 59 (quoting New Zealand's oral statement at the first Panel meeting, p. 3).

not provide "clear and convincing evidence that indicates why [the] objective is legitimate".[224]

130. Canada additionally alleges that the Panel's finding that the COOL measure's objective is legitimate is flawed for the following two reasons. First, the Panel referred to the existence of other country of origin labelling measures that purport to provide consumer information on origin of food products, even though these measures are not analogous to the COOL measure and the Panel never examined the purposes for which information is provided under those measures. Second, the Panel erred in relying on a reference to "protection of consumers" in *Accountancy Disciplines*, adopted in accordance with Article VI:4 of the *General Agreement on Trade in Services* (the "GATS"), and, in doing so, erroneously equated consumer protection with providing consumers with information generally. Canada adds in this regard that the United States has not presented evidence of consumer confusion with respect to the USDA grade labels and pre-COOL voluntary labelling programmes and that, in any event, USDA grade labels apply only to beef, and not to pork.

2. *Less Trade-Restrictive Alternative Measures*

131. Canada submits that, in the event that the Appellate Body reverses the Panel's finding that the COOL measure does not fulfil a legitimate objective, the Appellate Body should complete the analysis and find that the COOL measure is inconsistent with Article 2.2 of the *TBT Agreement* because there are less trade-restrictive alternative measures reasonably available.

132. Canada suggests that the appropriate elements of the test for assessing a challenged measure against an alternative measure are the following. First, the complaining party must propose one or more alternative measures. Second, each proposed alternative must be assessed against the challenged measure to determine the extent of trade-restrictiveness, that is, the extent to which a measure discriminates against, or denies any competitive opportunities to, imported products. Third, the assessment of alternative measures must be done taking account of the risks that non-fulfilment would create, that is, of the risks of harm that would arise from a failure to fulfil the legitimate objective. Fourth, it is appropriate to take into account the extent of fulfilment of the objective by both the challenged measure and the proposed alternative measure, even though the text of Article 2.2 does not explicitly envisage such a consideration. In Canada's view, the context provided by the *TBT Agreement* and by similar balancing tests in Article 5.6 of the *SPS Agreement* and Article XX of the GATT 1994 supports this approach.

---

[224] Canada's other appellant's submission, para. 62.

133. Canada further contends that determining the extent of fulfilment of the challenged and proposed alternative measures requires an assessment of the extent to which each measure carries out and performs its objective. That determination of fulfilment must be flexible and based on the circumstances of the measures at issue. In Canada's view, a regulation that restricts trade will be more or less justifiable depending in part on the risk of harm resulting from a failure to fulfil the objective it pursues. Thus, where the risk that would arise from the failure to fulfil an objective is extremely serious, a measure that restricts trade would be justifiable even if an alternative measure was much less trade restrictive, because the significant reduction in trade-restrictiveness would not justify a greater risk of non-fulfilment under the alternative measure. Canada notes that this is the approach taken in assessing proposed less trade-restrictive alternative measures under Article XX of the GATT 1994. In that context, the Appellate Body has found that, if a value is "vital and important in the highest degree", then the alternative measure must achieve the same end.[225] In so doing, Canada submits, the Appellate Body has implicitly acknowledged that, if the values are not vital and important in the highest degree, an alternative measure need not achieve precisely the same end if it is much less trade restrictive.

134. According to Canada, the application of this test to the COOL measure shows that it is extremely trade restrictive and, if it does fulfil the objective, it does so at the lowest level. Canada asserts that the lack of consumer interest in country of origin information and the measure's poor design show that the COOL measure provides little, if any, useful information that consumers want. By contrast, the application of the test to the proposed alternative measures shows that they are less trade restrictive and fulfil the objective at an equal or greater level than the COOL measure.

135. Canada proposes four alternative measures that are less trade restrictive than the COOL measure. First, voluntary labelling can provide a far more effective means to inform interested consumers where the objective pursued has no link to health and safety and the demand for the information required by the impugned measure is limited. Expanded as required to meet consumer interest, voluntary labelling can provide as much consumer information on origin to interested consumers as the COOL measure. Further, it could have a wider scope than the COOL measure and apply to points of sale not covered by the COOL measure, such as restaurants, small grocery stores, and speciality meat stores.

136. Second, Canada alleges that a mandatory labelling system based on substantial transformation is another alternative measure that avoids the trade-restrictiveness of the COOL measure because it does not impose differential

[225] Canada's other appellant's submission, para. 74 (quoting Appellate Body Report, *EC – Asbestos*, para. 172).

costs on the use of imported livestock. Under this form of labelling, where processing in a second country changes the nature of a product, the country of origin will be the second country. According to Canada, such a labelling system provides accurate and easy to understand information. Through labelling on the basis of substantial transformation, consumers are provided concise and meaningful information on origin without the confusion caused by the COOL regime. This is because it would be clear that meat that says "product of X country" was derived from livestock slaughtered in that country. This contrasts with the COOL measure, where "product of X country" means that slaughter took place in a foreign country if the meat is imported into the United States (Label D), but something else if the meat is obtained from an animal slaughtered within the United States.

137. Canada contends that a third alternative is a combination of the first two. Canada submits that this combined option is less trade restrictive than the COOL measure because it would not require segregation for the portion of the market that did not demand voluntary labels. Further, a combined system would ensure that all consumers have information about the origin of meat and would permit additional information for those that are interested. Canada adds that the greater flexibility of voluntary labelling could also encourage participation at points of sale currently not covered by the COOL measure.

138. Lastly, Canada asserts that a mandatory trace-back system could be instituted to provide extensive detailed information for each piece of meat. This information would not be restricted to country, but could indicate the precise location of each processing step by state/province and municipality. In Canada's view, if the objective of the COOL measure is to provide information to consumers on where the animals from which the meat is derived are born, raised, and processed, this alternative would contribute much more significantly to that objective. Canada acknowledges that this system could also increase costs, because there would need to be additional tracking throughout the supply chain, but argues that such costs would be balanced by a greater contribution to the objective of providing useful information to consumers. Canada stresses that, under this alternative, any additional costs would be distributed equally to all market participants, and that a trace-back system would be much less restrictive of international trade because it would impose the same obligation on producers and processors of both imported and domestic animals.

139. Canada further submits that, to the extent that the proposed alternative measures might fulfil the objective at a slightly lesser level than the COOL measure, they nevertheless demonstrate the COOL measure's inconsistency with Article 2.2 because they are much less trade restrictive, and because the risk that non-fulfilment of the COOL measure's objective would create is very low. Canada stresses that, in comparing the COOL measure with the proposed alternative measures, it is important to take account of the minimal contribution that the COOL measure makes to its objective, the vagueness of the information

it provides, the relative lack of harm caused by a failure to meet its goal, and the fact that labelling on the basis of the proposed alternative measures is significantly less restrictive on trade. The COOL measure is not concerned with food safety, environmental protection, or deceptive practices. The benefit that it theoretically provides is to give those few consumers who are interested more information on where the animals from which their meat is derived are born and raised. The USDA itself, however, acknowledges that consumer demand for this information is low. Thus, the risk non-fulfilment would create is that a few consumers who want to know about origin might not be able to find that information. Thus, according to Canada, when balancing the comparable contribution that the alternative measures could provide with the wide disparity in trade-restrictiveness between those alternatives and the COOL measure, and in the light of the minor consequences that non-fulfilment would create, the Appellate Body should find that the proposed alternative measures meet the test for a less trade-restrictive alternative under Article 2.2 of the *TBT Agreement*.

3. *Article III:4 of the GATT 1994*

140. Canada argues that the Panel erred in exercising judicial economy with respect to Canada's claim under Article III:4 of the GATT 1994. Canada notes that the Panel did not address Article III:4 of the GATT 1994 because its finding that the COOL measure is inconsistent with Article 2.1 of the *TBT Agreement* "necessarily means that it also violates GATT Article III:4".[226]

141. In Canada's view, because the relationship between Article 2.1 of the *TBT Agreement* and Article III:4 of the GATT 1994 "is not settled", the Panel's exercise of judicial economy in the circumstances of this case risked providing only a partial resolution of the matter at issue by failing to address Canada's claim of discrimination under Article III:4 of the GATT 1994.[227] Canada clarified, at the oral hearing, that this ground of its other appeal is conditional upon the Appellate Body reversing the Panel's finding that the COOL measure is inconsistent with Article 2.1 of the *TBT Agreement*. Should this condition be satisfied, Canada requests the Appellate Body to find, based on the evidence before the Panel, that the COOL measure is inconsistent with Article III:4 of the GATT 1994.[228]

---

[226] Canada's other appellant's submission, para. 93 (referring to Canada Panel Report, para. 8.4(a)).

[227] Canada's other appellant's submission, para. 96.

[228] In its other appellant's submission, Canada also requests the Appellate Body to find that the Vilsack letter is inconsistent with Article III:4 of the GATT 1994. (See Canada's other appellant's submission, para. 94) At the oral hearing, noting that the Vilsack letter has been withdrawn by the United States, Canada clarified that it is not requesting the Appellate Body to make a specific finding under Article III:4 of the GATT 1994 with respect to this measure. Canada, nonetheless, asked the Appellate Body to take the Vilsack letter into account in the event it were to make a ruling regarding

4. *Article XXIII:1(b) of the GATT 1994*

142. Should the Appellate Body reverse the Panel's finding of a violation of Article 2.1 of the *TBT Agreement* and not find a violation of Article III:4 of the GATT 1994, Canada "requests a finding by the Appellate Body, on the basis of the evidence presented by Canada to the Panel, of non-violation nullification or impairment under Article XXIII:1(b) of the GATT 1994".[229] Canada argues that it presented evidence before the Panel showing that the application of the COOL measure nullifies or impairs benefits accruing to Canada under successive multilateral trade negotiations[230] by "upsetting the competitive relationship and frustrating Canada's legitimate market access expectations" regarding its exports of cattle and hogs to the United States.[231]

143. Canada further notes that the Panel stated, without further explanation, that compliance by the United States with the Panel's findings of violation of Article 2.2 of the *TBT Agreement* and Article X:3(a) of the GATT 1994 would eliminate the basis of the non-violation nullification or impairment claim. In Canada's view, the Panel's statement was erroneous because compliance with Article 2.2 of the *TBT Agreement* or removal of the Vilsack letter would not necessarily remove the non-violation nullification or impairment.

E. *Claims of Error by Mexico – Other Appellant*

144. In its other appeal, Mexico advances a number of grounds of appeal, each of which is conditional upon the Appellate Body reversing the Panel's findings that the COOL measure is inconsistent with Article 2.1 and/or Article 2.2 of the *TBT Agreement*. More specifically, should the Appellate Body reverse the Panel's finding that the COOL measure is inconsistent with Article 2.2, then Mexico: (i) appeals the Panel's findings regarding the objective of the COOL measure, and requests the Appellate Body properly to identify the true objective of the COOL measure — namely, trade protectionism, which is not a legitimate

---

the COOL measure under Article III:4 of the GATT 1994. (Canada's response to questioning at the oral hearing)

[229] Canada's other appellant's submission, para. 98. In its other appellant's submission, Canada also requests the Appellate Body to find that the Vilsack letter nullifies and impairs benefits accruing to Canada within the meaning of Article XXIII:1(b) of the GATT 1994. (See *ibid.*, paras. 7 and 99) At the oral hearing, noting that the Vilsack letter has been withdrawn by the United States, Canada clarified that it is not requesting the Appellate Body to make a finding under Article XXIII:1(b) of the GATT 1994 with respect to this measure. Canada, nonetheless, asked the Appellate Body to take the Vilsack letter into account in the event it were to make a ruling regarding the COOL measure under Article XXIII:1(b) of the GATT 1994. (Canada's response to questioning at the oral hearing)

[230] Canada's other appellant's submission, para. 97 (referring to Panel Reports, paras. 7.889-7.891, 7.894, 7.896, and 7.897).

[231] Canada's other appellant's submission, para. 97.

objective — and to find, therefore, that the COOL measure is inconsistent with Article 2.2; and (ii) if the Appellate Body confirms the Panel's findings regarding the objective of the COOL measure and its legitimacy, requests the Appellate Body to complete the analysis and find that the COOL measure is inconsistent with Article 2.2 of the *TBT Agreement* because there are alternative measures that are less trade restrictive and that fulfil the legitimate objective taking into account the risks non-fulfilment would create. In addition, should the Appellate Body reverse the Panel's finding that the COOL measure is inconsistent with Article 2.1, then Mexico: (i) appeals the Panel's decision to exercise judicial economy in respect of Mexico's claim under Article III:4 of the GATT 1994 and requests the Appellate Body to complete the analysis and find that the COOL measure is inconsistent with Article III:4; and (ii) in the event that the Appellate Body does not find a violation of Article III:4, appeals the Panel's decision to exercise judicial economy with respect to Mexico's claim of non-violation nullification or impairment and requests the Appellate Body to complete the analysis and find that the COOL measure nullifies or impairs benefits accruing to Mexico under the GATT 1994 within the meaning of Article XXIII:1(b) of that Agreement.

1. "Legitimate Objective" under Article 2.2 of the TBT Agreement

145. Should the Appellate Body reverse the Panel's finding that the COOL measure is inconsistent with Article 2.2 of the *TBT Agreement*, Mexico appeals the Panel's finding that the objective of the COOL measure is to "provide as much clear and accurate origin information as possible to consumers"[232] and that "providing consumer information on origin is a legitimate objective within the meaning of Article 2.2" of the *TBT Agreement*.[233] In Mexico's view, the Panel committed legal error and failed to make an objective assessment of the matter as required by Article 11 of the DSU in identifying the objective of the COOL measure. Mexico, thus, requests the Appellate Body to reverse the Panel's finding in this regard and to complete the analysis and find that the objective of the COOL measure is not legitimate.

(a) The Identification of the Objective

(i) The Focus on a General Policy Objective

146. Mexico submits that the Panel erred in its approach to identifying the objective pursued by the United States through the COOL measure, because the

---

[232] Mexico's other appellant's submission, para. 28 (quoting Panel Reports, para. 7.620).

[233] Mexico's other appellant's submission, para. 28 (quoting Panel Reports, para. 7.651).

Panel relied solely on the United States' characterization of that objective. Mexico generally agrees that the identification of the objective of a technical regulation is the prerogative of the Member establishing the measure, and that there is a presumption of good faith in favour of a Member as regards the objective identified in a notification to the TBT Committee. However, determining the objective of a measure solely on the basis of a Member's characterization could undermine the effectiveness of the disciplines in Article 2.2 and open them to circumvention. Mexico further submits that, as recognized by the Panel, the presumption of good faith is rebuttable. Thus, the Panel should have verified the objective identified by the United States and ensured that it was congruent with the design, structure, and architecture of the COOL measure, as well as its legislative history and surrounding circumstances.

147. Mexico maintains that its view is supported by the findings of the panels in certain recent disputes. The panel in *US – Tuna II (Mexico)* stated that its determination regarding the objectives of the measures at issue was "guided by the description of the objectives of the measures by both parties, as well as by the structure and design of the U.S. dolphin-safe provisions".[234] In *US – Clove Cigarettes*, notwithstanding the parties' agreement on the objective of the measure at issue, the panel examined relevant evidence to confirm the objective identified by the parties.[235] Furthermore, Mexico notes that, in this dispute, the Panel relied in part on Article 5.6 of the *SPS Agreement* and the Appellate Body report in *Australia – Salmon* to support its view that the objective should be determined by the Member and cannot necessarily be implied from that technical regulation itself.[236] However, the Appellate Body's finding in *Australia – Salmon* concerns Article 5.6 of the *SPS Agreement* which, unlike Article 2.2 of the *TBT Agreement*, entails a specific requirement for Members to determine their appropriate level of sanitary and phytosanitary protection with sufficient precision. Moreover, even in the context of Article 5.6 of the *SPS Agreement*, the Appellate Body has found that the appropriate level of protection may be established by panels on the basis of the level of protection reflected in the SPS measure actually applied.[237]

---

[234] Mexico's other appellant's submission, para. 36 (quoting Panel Report, *US – Tuna II (Mexico)*, para. 7.406).

[235] Mexico's other appellant's submission, para. 36 (referring to Panel Report, *US – Clove Cigarettes*, paras. 7.336-7.343).

[236] Mexico's other appellant's submission, para. 37 (referring to Panel Reports, para. 7.604).

[237] Mexico's other appellant's submission, para. 37 (referring to Appellate Body Report, *Australia – Salmon*, para. 207).

(ii) Article 11 of the DSU

148. Mexico further submits that, due to the legal errors in the Panel's approach to identifying the COOL measure's objective, the Panel failed to take into account the facts presented by Mexico regarding the protectionist objective of the COOL measure, and thereby failed to comply with its duty to conduct an objective assessment of the matter before it, as required under Article 11 of the DSU. Instead, the Panel focused on the objective as described by the United States and "deliberately disregarded and excluded" Mexico's arguments and evidence relating to the design and architecture of the COOL measure, as well as its legislative history and surrounding circumstances.[238]

149. Mexico contends that the evidence it presented to the Panel shows that the COOL measure arbitrarily targets certain commodities, retailers, and meat products, and prohibits the creation of any tracing system for US cattle.[239] The evidence also demonstrates that US cattle producers wanted country of origin labelling as a means to regain market share taken by Mexican producers and to discourage use of foreign cattle.[240] Had the Panel properly examined such evidence, it would have found that the COOL measure's objective is protectionism. Consequently, the Panel would have also found that the COOL measure's objective is not legitimate within the meaning of Article 2.2 of the *TBT Agreement*.

150. On this basis, Mexico requests the Appellate Body to find that the Panel erred in its "refusal" to consider relevant evidence.[241] Mexico further requests the Appellate Body to complete the analysis by considering the relevant evidence and by concluding that the real policy objective of the COOL measure was not to provide consumer information, but to protect the US cattle industry.

(b) The Legitimacy of the COOL Measure's Objective

151. Mexico submits that, if the Appellate Body agrees with Mexico that the objective of the COOL measure is protectionism, it would automatically follow that trade protectionism cannot be a legitimate objective.

---

[238] Mexico's other appellant's submission, para. 40.

[239] Mexico's other appellant's submission, para. 43 (referring to Mexico's first written submission to the Panel, paras. 279, 280, and 296-302; Mexico's second written submission to the Panel, paras. 70-78; and Panel Exhibits MEX-87 and MEX-88).

[240] Mexico's other appellant's submission, para. 43 (referring to Mexico's first written submission to the Panel, paras. 168-191 and 280-283; Mexico's second written submission to the Panel, paras. 79-83; and Panel Exhibits MEX-49 through MEX-51, MEX-89, and MEX-91 through MEX-96).

[241] Mexico's other appellant's submission, para. 44.

2. *Less Trade-Restrictive Alternative Measures*

152. Should the Appellate Body reverse the Panel's finding that the COOL measure is inconsistent with Article 2.2 of the *TBT Agreement* and confirm the Panel's finding that the objective of the COOL measure is legitimate, then Mexico appeals the Panel's decision to exercise judicial economy in respect of the existence of a less trade-restrictive alternative. Mexico further requests the Appellate Body to complete the analysis and find that the COOL measure is inconsistent with Article 2.2 of the *TBT Agreement*.

153. Mexico submits that the "necessity test" in Article 2.2 of the *TBT Agreement* reflects a balance between the freedom of Members to set and achieve their legitimate objectives through technical regulations and the goal of discouraging Members from preparing, adopting, and applying technical regulations that create unnecessary obstacles to international trade. A technical regulation that restricts trade is permissible only if it is "necessary" to fulfil the Member's legitimate objective, taking account of the risks non-fulfilment would create. In Mexico's view, jurisprudence on the term "necessary" in the context of Article XX(b) and (d) of the GATT 1994 and Article XIV of the GATS is useful for the interpretation of the same term in Article 2.2 of the *TBT Agreement*. In the light of such jurisprudence, in order to determine whether the COOL measure is more trade restrictive than necessary to fulfil the legitimate objective, the following factors must be examined: (i) the importance of the interests or values at stake; (ii) the extent of the contribution of the measure to the achievement of the measure's objective; (iii) the trade-restrictiveness of the measure; and (iv) whether there are reasonably available alternative measures that may be less trade restrictive while providing an equivalent contribution to the achievement of the objective. Mexico stresses that Article 2.2 of the *TBT Agreement* "has an additional requirement", namely, "to take into account the risks of non-fulfilment of the legitimate objective".[242]

154. With respect to the trade-restrictiveness of a measure, Mexico points out that the Panel accepted that measures that are trade restrictive are those that deny competitive opportunities to imports and that a complaining party need not prove actual trade effects. As for the "risks non-fulfilment would create", Mexico emphasizes that the risks of non-fulfilment of technical regulations applied with the goal of protecting human, animal, or plant life or health will be different from the risks of non-fulfilment of technical regulations applied with the goal of providing consumer information. In assessing such risks, the Appellate Body should consider, in particular, available scientific and technical information. In addition, Mexico notes that Article 2.3 of the *TBT Agreement* requires periodical re-assessment of the necessity of technical regulations, and submits that

[242] Mexico's other appellant's submission, para. 51.

consideration of whether the circumstances giving rise to the adoption of the COOL measure still exist, or have changed and could be addressed in a less trade-restrictive manner, should be part of a process of weighing and balancing a series of factors.

155. On the basis of the foregoing, Mexico contends that the value of the information provided by the COOL measure and its contribution to the needs of US consumers is minimal. The possibility of adverse consequences arising should the objective not be fulfilled is low, and, to the extent that these consequences arise, they will be restricted to a limited subset of US consumers. Furthermore, Mexico argues, the COOL measure is highly trade restrictive, as evidenced, for example, by its adverse effect on imports of Mexican feeder cattle.

156. Moreover, Mexico submits that there are at least four alternative measures that are reasonably available and provide an equivalent contribution to the objective. The first alternative is a voluntary country of origin labelling scheme, which, in Mexico's view, could maintain the same labelling criteria on origin as the COOL measure—that is, born, raised, and slaughtered—and would allow market forces to fill consumer demand for this additional information to the extent such demand exists.

157. The second alternative is a labelling regime based on substantial transformation or a change in nature. According to Mexico, this option would eliminate the discrimination and trade restrictions affecting imports of Mexican feeder cattle. It would also be consistent with the origin rules applied to imported meat products under the COOL measure and thus would avoid confusion.

158. A third alternative would be a combination of the previous two. Mexico contends that such a combined system would ensure that consumers are provided with information on the origin of meat products in accordance with the traditional standard while allowing retailers to provide additional information if consumers indicated an interest.

159. Mexico submits as a fourth alternative a trace-back regime. Referring to a paper presented to the Panel[243], Mexico notes that two alternative compliance mechanisms could have been employed by the COOL measure, namely, "certification and audit" or "trace back".[244] The United States chose the certification and audit mechanism, which involves costs being disproportionately

[243] Mexico's other appellant's submission, para. 65 (referring to Dermot J. Hayes and Steve R. Meyer, "Impact of Mandatory Country of Origin Labeling on U.S. Pork Exports" (Panel Exhibit MEX-88)).

[244] Mexico's other appellant's submission, para. 65 (referring to Panel Exhibit MEX-88, p. 7).

born by Mexican animals, because the easiest way to comply with it is by excluding all non-US animals or by maintaining strict segregation of foreign-produced animals.[245] However, a trace-back system, which Mexico argues is technically and economically feasible in the United States, would impose the same requirements on both domestic and imported animals and, therefore, the economic incentive to discriminate against Mexican cattle would likely be eliminated. Mexico adds that, under a trace-back scheme, consumers would be provided with much more precise information than is possible under the COOL measure.

160. In view of these four alternative measures that are less trade restrictive while fulfilling the objective of providing consumer information, Mexico submits that the COOL measure is more trade restrictive than necessary within the meaning of Article 2.2 of the *TBT Agreement* and hence inconsistent with this provision.

3. *Article III:4 of the GATT 1994*

161. Should the Appellate Body reverse the Panel's finding that the COOL measure is inconsistent with Article 2.1 of the *TBT Agreement*, then Mexico appeals the Panel's exercise of judicial economy regarding Mexico's claim under Article III:4 of the GATT 1994 and requests the Appellate Body to complete the analysis and find that the COOL measure is inconsistent with that provision.

162. In Mexico's view, since the Panel's decision not to address Mexico's claim under Article III:4 of the GATT 1994 was contingent upon its finding that the COOL measure is inconsistent with Article 2.1 of the *TBT Agreement*, if this finding is reversed, the Panel's legal basis for exercising judicial economy will no longer exist. Accordingly, Mexico contends, completion of the analysis by the Appellate Body under Article III:4 of the GATT 1994 would be necessary to facilitate the prompt settlement of this dispute pursuant to Article 3.3 of the DSU. Mexico further asserts that there are sufficient factual findings by the Panel and undisputed facts on the record to enable the Appellate Body to complete the legal analysis.

163. Mexico argues that the COOL measure is inconsistent with Article III:4 of the GATT 1994 because it accords Mexican feeder cattle treatment less favourable than that accorded to US feeder cattle. Mexico notes, in this regard, the Appellate Body's statement in *Japan – Alcoholic Beverages II* that "Article III obliges Members of the WTO to provide equality of competitive conditions

---

[245] Mexico's other appellant's submission, para. 66 (referring to Panel Exhibit MEX-88, p. 7).

for imported products in relation to domestic products."[246] Moreover, Article III:4 is informed by the general principle in Article III:1 that internal measures should not be applied so as to afford protection to domestic production. According to Mexico, the COOL measure is "fundamentally incompatible" with this general principle because it has "both the purpose and effect" of affording protection to US cattle producers.[247]

164. In Mexico's view, the three elements that must be established in order for a Member's measure to be inconsistent with Article III:4 are met in the present case. First, Mexico argues that the Panel's finding under Article 2.1 of the *TBT Agreement* that Mexican and US feeder cattle are "like products"[248] is equally applicable to the determination of "like products" within the meaning of Article III:4 of the GATT 1994. Second, Mexico contends that the COOL measure falls within the category of laws, regulations, and requirements covered by Article III:4 and affects the internal sale, offering for sale, purchase, transportation, distribution, or use of feeder cattle. Mexico notes that the term "affecting" has been interpreted as having a broad scope of application. Accordingly, despite the fact that the COOL measure does not directly apply to feeder cattle, Mexico argues that it affects the internal sale, offering for sale, purchase, transportation, distribution or use of feeder cattle by means of regulating the retail beef that is derived from those cattle. In this regard, Mexico points to the Panel's finding that, although the labels at issue must be affixed on muscle cuts of meat and ground meat, these labels are "difficult to dissociate from upstream stages of meat production" since they are intended to convey information on the origin of the livestock from which the meat is derived.[249]

165. Third, Mexico submits that the COOL measure accords less favourable treatment to imports. Recalling the Appellate Body's findings in *Korea – Various Measures on Beef* and *Dominican Republic – Import and Sale of Cigarettes*, Mexico submits that the COOL measure denies competitive opportunities to Mexican feeder cattle.[250] Although the COOL measure does not *de jure* distinguish between Mexican and US feeder cattle, a formal difference in treatment is not necessary to show a violation of Article III:4 of the GATT 1994. Instead, the focus is on whether the measure modifies the conditions of

---

[246] Mexico's other appellant's submission, para. 75 (quoting Appellate Body Report, *Japan – Alcoholic Beverages II*, p. 16, DSR 1996:I, 97, at 109).

[247] Mexico's other appellant's submission, para. 76.

[248] Mexico's other appellant's submission, para. 79 (quoting Panel Reports, para. 7.256).

[249] Mexico's other appellant's submission, para. 88 (referring to Panel Reports, paras. 7.282 and 7.283).

[250] Mexico's other appellant's submission, para. 90 (referring to Appellate Body Report, *Korea – Various Measures on Beef*, para. 137; and Appellate Body Report, *Dominican Republic – Import and Sale of Cigarettes*, para. 93).

competition. In this regard, Mexico argues that several factual findings of the Panel "clearly demonstrate that the COOL measure denies competitive opportunities in such a manner".[251]

4. *Article XXIII:1(b) of the GATT 1994*

166. Should the Appellate Body decide that the Panel erred in finding that the COOL measure is inconsistent with Article 2.1 of the *TBT Agreement* and not make a finding that the COOL measure is inconsistent with Article III:4 of the GATT 1994, Mexico appeals the Panel's decision to exercise judicial economy in respect of Mexico's claim under Article XXIII:1(b) of the GATT 1994, and requests the Appellate Body to complete the analysis and find that the COOL measure nullifies and impairs benefits accruing to Mexico within the meaning of Article XXIII:1(b). Mexico also recalls the Panel's statement that compliance by the United States with the Panel's findings of violation of Article 2.2 of the *TBT Agreement* and Article X:3(a) of the GATT 1994 would eliminate the basis of the non-violation nullification or impairment claim.[252] According to Mexico, this statement is erroneous since measures taken to comply with those findings would not necessarily eliminate all of the discrimination and resulting nullification and impairment of tariff concessions. Accordingly, regardless of the Appellate Body's decision under Article 2.2 of the *TBT Agreement*, if the Appellate Body does not uphold the Panel's finding under Article 2.1 of the *TBT Agreement*, Mexico requests a finding under Article XXIII:1(b) of the GATT 1994. Mexico highlights that the Appellate Body may, upon reversing a particular legal finding of a panel, proceed to examine and complete the analysis of a claim that was not specifically addressed by the panel in order to resolve the dispute.

167. Mexico submits that the COOL measure nullifies and impairs tariff concessions made by the United States and inscribed in its WTO tariff bindings. More specifically, the United States' bound tariff for live cattle is 1 cent per kilogram, which is about $1.36 to $1.81 per head of feeder cattle. However, the actual price discount created by the COOL measure "has been up to $60"[253] for such animals. Moreover, the COOL measure reduced the number of US plants processing Mexican cattle, limited the number of days on which other plants would accept Mexican cattle, and resulted in new requirements for advance notice of delivery. In Mexico's view, the competitive disadvantage reflected in the price discount and other restrictions "vastly exceeds Mexico's legitimate

[251] Mexico's other appellant's submission, para. 93 (referring to Panel Reports, paras. 7.357, 7.372, 7.374-7.380, and 7.420).

[252] Mexico's other appellant's submission, para. 100 (referring to Panel Reports, para. 7.907).

[253] Mexico's other appellant's submission, para. 97.

expectation of a $1.36 to $1.81 tariff disadvantage per animal".[254] Mexico emphasizes that its complaint does not concern origin marking requirements in general, but concerns the particular features of the COOL measure that are discriminatory and arbitrary and that could not reasonably have been anticipated at the time the tariff concessions were negotiated.

168. Mexico further contends that the Panel's findings that the COOL measure has the effect of discouraging the use of Mexican cattle provides a sufficient basis upon which the Appellate Body can complete the analysis and find that the COOL measure results in non-violation nullification or impairment within the meaning of Article XXIII:1(b) of the GATT 1994.

F. Arguments of the United States – Appellee

169. The United States requests the Appellate Body to reject all of the appeals and conditional appeals contained in Canada's and Mexico's other appellant's submissions. With respect to the claims that the Panel erred in its identification of the objective of the COOL measure and its assessment of the legitimacy of that objective, the United States asserts that Mexico's appeal overlooks the Panel's analysis of the text, design, architecture, and structure of the COOL measure, while Canada's rests solely on a contention that the Panel did not conduct its analysis in the correct order and on the mistaken suggestion that it was inappropriate for the Panel even to consider the objective as expressed by the United States. Moreover, the complaining parties have not established that the Panel failed to comply with Article 11 of the DSU, and their arguments in this regard simply reflect their disappointment that the Panel did not accord to their evidence the same weight that they do. The United States rejects Canada's proposed test of "legitimacy" under Article 2.2 of the *TBT Agreement*, asserts that there is no basis on the record for the Appellate Body to complete the analysis as to whether the COOL measure is more trade restrictive than necessary, and adds that, in any event, the tests proffered by Canada and Mexico as to how such an analysis should be undertaken are erroneous. With respect to Article III:4 of the GATT 1994, the United States asserts that neither Canada nor Mexico has explained why the Panel's exercise of judicial economy was erroneous or explained how an assessment under that provision would differ from an assessment under Article 2.1 of the *TBT Agreement*. With respect to the Vilsack letter, the United States also considers that, absent an appeal of the Panel's finding under Article X:3(a) of the GATT 1994, it is unnecessary for the Appellate Body to undertake an Article III:4 assessment and, in any event, there are insufficient factual findings or undisputed facts to enable it to do so. As for the conditional appeals with respect to Article XXIII:1(b) of the GATT 1994, the

[254] Mexico's other appellant's submission, para. 97 (referring to Panel Reports, para. 7.898).

United States considers that Canada and Mexico have failed to explain why it is necessary for the Appellate Body to make a non-violation nullification or impairment finding on the COOL measure, and have failed to make a *prima facie* case with regard to their claims. In any event, adds the United States, there are insufficient factual findings by the Panel or undisputed facts on the record to provide a basis for completion of the analysis.

1. "Legitimate Objective" under Article 2.2 of the TBT Agreement

170. The United States contends that the Appellate Body should reject the complainants' other appeals regarding the Panel's identification of the objective of the COOL measure and its finding that the objective is legitimate. The United States further alleges that the complainants' claims under Article 11 of the DSU are unfounded in the light of the Panel's proper evaluation of the evidence on the record, and should also be rejected.

(a) The Identification of the Objective

(i) The Focus on a General Policy Objective

171. The United States characterizes as "fundamentally in error"[255] Mexico's view that "the Panel should have verified [the] objective [stated by the United States] and ensured that it was congruent with the design, structure, and architecture of the COOL measure as well as its legislative history and surrounding circumstances".[256] The United States also disagrees with Mexico that the Panel's "failure to do this was a legal error and was inconsistent with its obligations under Article 11 of the *DSU*".[257] In the United States' view, Canada concedes that the Panel did in fact verify the "identified" objective on the basis of an analysis of the text, design, architecture, and structure of the COOL measure in the Panel Reports.[258] Accordingly, for the United States, "the *entirety* of Mexico's appeal" in this respect rests on an erroneous factual premise.[259]

---

[255] United States' appellee's submission, para. 17.

[256] United States' appellee's submission, para. 15 (quoting Mexico's other appellant's submission, para. 41).

[257] *Ibid.*

[258] United States' appellee's submission, para. 17 (referring to Canada's other appellant's submission, para. 19(2), footnote 43 to paragraph 20, heading III.A.2, and para. 29, in turn referring to Panel Reports, paras. 7.608 and 7.678-7.691).

[259] United States' appellee's submission, para. 17. (original emphasis)

172. The United States recalls Canada's argument that the Panel's consideration of a general policy objective as stated by the United States was "an unnecessary and unhelpful addition to the analysis".[260] The United States considers this argument "surprising"[261], given that Canada agrees that, in applying the phrase "applied ... to protect" in Annex A(1)(a) to the *SPS Agreement*, it is appropriate to take into account both the objective of a measure "as expressed by the responding party" and the text and structure of the measure to determine whether that measure is an SPS measure.[262] Moreover, noting that the Member maintaining a measure is well situated to express the objective of that measure, the United States contends that Canada fails to explain why a panel should disregard the responding party's expression of the objective of the measure at issue. The United States emphasizes that, before the Panel, it explained the COOL measure's objective in response to Canada's and Mexico's erroneous assertions that the measure's objective is protectionism, and that the Panel correctly assessed the merits of the competing assertions against evidence regarding the design, structure, and architecture of the measure.

173. The United States adds that Canada misunderstands the Panel's analysis insofar as Canada suggests that the Panel committed legal error by undertaking its analysis regarding the design, structure, and architecture of the measure "only as a secondary matter as an alternative to the 'identified objective'".[263] On the contrary, this was a significant element of the Panel's overall analysis as to whether the measure actually achieves its identified objective at its identified level of fulfilment.

(ii) Article 11 of the DSU

174. The United States maintains that, contrary to Canada's and Mexico's claims, the Panel objectively assessed the relevant evidence relating to the COOL measure, consistent with Article 11 of the DSU. The United States recalls the Appellate Body's articulation of the legal standard for identifying a breach of Article 11, and contends that Canada and Mexico have failed to show that the Panel deliberately disregarded or wilfully distorted their evidence, or failed to refer to evidence that was material to its conclusion. Rather, the Panel carefully considered, assessed, and weighed the evidence presented by all of the parties related to the COOL measure's text, its design, architecture, and structure, and its

260 United States' appellee's submission, para. 16 (quoting Canada's other appellant's submission, para. 21).

261 United States' appellee's submission, para. 19.

262 United States' appellee's submission, para. 19 (quoting Canada's other appellant's submission, para. 27, in turn quoting Appellate Body Report, *Australia – Apples*, para. 173).

263 United States' appellee's submission, para. 21 (quoting Canada's other appellant's submission, para. 29, in turn quoting Panel Reports, para. 7.677).

legislative history. The Panel found that the text of the COOL measure is "devoted exclusively to the labelling requirements on origin", and that the stated purpose of the 2009 Final Rule (AMS) is "to provide consumers with origin information".[264] Furthermore, the Panel examined the evidence and arguments by Canada and Mexico regarding the design, architecture, structure, and legislative history of the COOL measure, including the COOL measure's scope and exceptions and various statements by legislators, before rightly concluding that it was not persuaded that the COOL measure is designed for a protectionist purpose.

175. The United States contests Mexico's assertion that the Panel "deliberately disregarded and excluded Mexico's arguments and evidence based on the design, architecture, and structure of the COOL measure as well as its legislative history" and surrounding circumstances.[265] Contrary to Mexico's assertion, much of the argumentation and evidence that Mexico claims the Panel ignored, which relates to the scope of the measure and its legislative history, is explicitly cited in the Panel Reports.[266]

176. The United States further contends that Canada's claims under Article 11 of the DSU are also without merit and largely reflect dissatisfaction with the weight the Panel accorded to particular arguments and evidence submitted by Canada. First, with respect to Canada's argument that the Panel gave "cursory treatment" to the evidence and arguments regarding the protectionist scope of the COOL measure[267], the United States submits that, as the Panel correctly concluded, the fact that the COOL measure does not cover every possible product and point of sale is not necessarily evidence of protectionism, because it is not atypical for regulations to have exceptions. Consistent with the standard articulated by the Appellate Body under Article 11 of the DSU, the fact that the Panel may not have set out all of the evidence proffered by Canada would not constitute a breach of Article 11. The United States further asserts that Canada's claim that the COOL measure includes commodities with import competition and excludes those without such competition is incorrect in the light of relevant evidence.

177. Second, with regard to Canada's argument that all products that undergo a significant change, except for meat from foreign livestock, are excluded from the

[264] United States' appellee's submission, para. 28 (quoting Panel Reports, para. 7.680).

[265] United States' appellee's submission, para. 32 (quoting Mexico's other appellant's submission, para. 40).

[266] United States' appellee's submission, para. 33 (referring to Panel Reports, paras. 7.683, 7.687, and 7.689).

[267] United States' appellee's submission, para. 35 (quoting Canada's other appellant's submission, para. 36).

COOL measure's scope (the "processed food exception"), the United States maintains that the Panel correctly found that "merely because the COOL measure does not apply to all food products ... does not necessarily mean that the measure is designed for a protectionist purpose."[268] In the United States' view, Canada's concern with the Panel's finding appears to be that the Panel did not consider Canada's arguments in Canada's "desired order" and failed to "clearly mention" the argument in its analysis.[269] However, the Appellate Body has found that a panel has the discretion "to address only those arguments it deems necessary to resolve a particular claim".[270] The United States adds that Canada's argument reflects its fundamental misunderstanding of the COOL measure, because the processed food exception applies equally to meat derived from Canadian livestock.

178. Third, concerning Canada's argument that the Panel did not consider evidence showing the COOL measure's inability to provide useful information to consumers, the United States maintains that the Panel addressed such evidence when examining whether the COOL measure fulfils its objective.[271] In any event, Canada's argument in this respect is not persuasive, because "it overlooks undisputed facts on the record that at least 71 percent of U.S.-origin meat products are receiving an A label", and thus are carrying labels that provide clear consumer information.[272] The United States also "finds it ironic" that the aspect of the COOL measure that Canada claims to be evidence of the purported protectionist intent of the COOL measure—that is, the commingling provisions—was specifically requested by Canada during the legislative process.[273]

179. Fourth, with respect to Canada's and Mexico's argument that the Panel failed to examine properly evidence regarding the legislative history of the COOL measure, the United States submits that the Panel examined all of the statements by individual legislators, including those referenced by Canada and Mexico, and found that they did not affect its conclusion. The fact that the Panel did not attribute the same weight to these statements as did the complainants does not give rise to a breach of Article 11 of the DSU.

268 United States' appellee's submission, para. 39 (quoting Panel Reports, para. 7.684).

269 United States' appellee's submission, para. 39 (quoting Canada's other appellant's submission, para. 37).

270 United States' appellee's submission, para. 39 (quoting Appellate Body Report, *EC – Poultry*, para. 135). (original emphasis omitted by the United States)

271 United States' appellee's submission, para. 41 (referring to Panel Reports, paras. 7.695-7.719).

272 United States' appellee's submission, para. 42 (referring to United States' appellant's submission, para. 153).

273 United States' appellee's submission, para. 42.

180. Finally, the United States stresses that the Panel's finding that the COOL measure's objective is consumer information on origin and not protectionism is supported by the evidence on the Panel record, including the statements of legislators involved with the measure[274], comments submitted by individuals during the regulatory process[275], comments of support from leading consumer advocacy organizations[276], the evolution of the measure itself[277], and conference and committee reports accompanying the COOL statute.[278] The United States also disagrees with Canada's assertion that the fact that the COOL measure was originally introduced in the 2002 Farm Bill supports the conclusion that the measure's objective is protectionism. Rather, US farm bills are omnibus measures that include many items related to the production and sale of food products.

181. For these reasons, the United States requests the Appellate Body to reject the complainants' claims that the Panel acted inconsistently with Article 11 of the DSU when finding that the objective of the COOL measure is to provide consumers with information on origin.

(iii) The Level of Detail of the Objective Identified

182. The United States recalls that, as an "alternative" to its claim under Article 11 of the DSU, Canada contends that the Panel committed legal error in identifying the objective as providing "as much clear and accurate origin information as possible to consumers" without also "defin[ing] the purpose for which this information is provided".[279] The United States maintains that this alternative claim of Canada does not differ substantively from its claim under Article 11 of the DSU, and must fail for the same reasons. The United States further contends that nothing in the *TBT Agreement* requires the importing

274 United States' appellee's submission, para. 44 (referring to Panel Reports, para. 7.690; United States' second written submission to the Panel, para. 129; and Panel Exhibits US-13, US-14, US-48, and US-61).

275 United States' appellee's submission, para. 44 (referring to Panel Reports, para. 7.646; United States' second written submission to the Panel, paras. 133-136; and Panel Exhibits US-113 and US-119 through US-126).

276 United States' appellee's submission, para. 44 (referring to Panel Reports, para. 7.645; United States' second written submission to the Panel, paras. 131 and 132; and Panel Exhibits US-4, US-5, US-61, US-84, US-89, US-90, US-100, US-111, US-113, US-116, and US-119 through US-125).

277 United States' appellee's submission, para. 44 (referring to United States' second written submission to the Panel, para. 137).

278 United States' appellee's submission, para. 44 (referring to United States' second written submission to the Panel, para. 128; and Panel Exhibits US-11 and US-12).

279 United States' appellee's submission, para. 46 (quoting Canada's other appellant's submission, para. 44, in turn quoting Panel Reports, para. 7.620).

Member to define its objective in either a narrow or broad fashion. If anything, the fact that the legitimate objectives listed in Article 2.2 are expressed at a high level of generality supports a Member defining its objective in general terms, as the Panel recognized. Moreover, Canada's alternative claim suggests that the Panel should have examined *why* the government requires the provision of the information under the COOL measure. However, as the Appellate Body has found, speculation on the subjective intent of a Member is not an appropriate form of analysis.[280] On this basis, the United States requests the Appellate Body to reject Canada's alternative claim regarding the Panel's identification of the objective of the COOL measure.

(b) The Legitimacy of the COOL Measure's Objective

183. The United States asserts that Canada's test for determining whether an objective is legitimate within the meaning of Article 2.2 of the *TBT Agreement* lacks any basis in the text of Article 2.2, for the following reasons. First, Article 2.2 contains a non-exhaustive list of legitimate objectives, as indicated by the term "*inter alia*". Thus, objectives not explicitly listed may be legitimate. For example, the United States submits, the panel in *EC – Sardines* found that market transparency and consumer protection—which are objectives not listed in Article 2.2—were legitimate within the meaning of that provision.[281] Moreover, Article 2.2 does not rank various objectives and does not reference Articles XX and XXI of the GATT 1994. Thus, there is no basis in the text of Article 2.2 to infer that objectives not listed therein enjoy a higher presumption of legitimacy simply because they derive from Articles XX and XXI of the GATT 1994. Canada also fails to recognize that the COOL measure's objective—that is, to provide consumers with information on origin—has been recognized under Article IX of the GATT 1994 as legitimate, and that nearly 70 WTO Members have country of origin labelling requirements, including many that listed consumer information as the objective in notifying these measures to the TBT Committee.

184. Second, the United States maintains that Canada mistakenly purports to rely on the principle of *ejusdem generis* in proposing the test for "legitimacy" under Article 2.2. The United States asserts that this principle is not one of the customary rules of interpretation of public international law reflected in the *Vienna Convention*. Further, as the Panel correctly found, the principle is not "helpful for determining whether the objective pursued by the United States is legitimate", given that "all of the listed examples are expressed at a high level of

280 United States' appellee's submission, para. 48 (referring to Appellate Body Report, *Japan – Alcoholic Beverages II*, p. 27, DSR 1996:I, 97, at 119).

281 United States' appellee's submission, para. 51 (referring to Panel Report, *EC – Sardines*, para. 7.123).

generality".[282] Canada also fails to explain how the enumerated objectives admit of a particular classification by "type". Moreover, Canada's position is at odds with the applicable rule on burden of proof, which requires Canada, as the complainant, to prove that the COOL measure's objective is not legitimate. Yet, the United States submits, according to Canada, the burden would rest on the respondent to demonstrate with clear and compelling evidence that the objective is legitimate.[283]

185. Third, the United States maintains that, by arguing that the listed objectives are more important than unlisted ones, Canada's test is based on the false assumption that Article 2.2 prioritizes the listed objectives over the unlisted ones. Contrary to Canada's assertion, Article 2.2 requires technical regulations to pursue legitimate objectives, rather than "important" objectives, and panels are not in a position to judge and rank the importance of various objectives.

186. Fourth, the United States asserts that, even under Canada's flawed approach, providing consumers with information on origin would be a legitimate objective under Article 2.2 because it is closely connected to the prevention of deceptive practices, which is a legitimate objective listed in that provision. This is because, like the prevention of deceptive practices, provision of consumer information is also intended to ensure that consumers have correct information about the products they buy.

187. The United States maintains that the Panel properly based its finding regarding the legitimacy of the COOL measure's objective on the evidence on the record, including the evidence showing "the strong desire on the part of consumers to receive" the information required by the COOL measure, and the "strong trend" of WTO Members requiring such information.[284] Although Canada asserts that the Panel's approach would allow an illegitimate objective to be considered as "legitimate" under Article 2.2, Canada fails to provide any reasons as to why this would be so. The Panel was also correct that a determination of whether an objective is legitimate should not be made in a vacuum, but in the context of "the world in which we live"[285], and in taking account of evidence as to whether the objective is widely shared. On this basis, the United States requests the Appellate Body to uphold the Panel's finding that providing consumer information on origin is a legitimate objective under Article 2.2 of the *TBT Agreement*.

---

[282] United States' appellee's submission, para. 54 (quoting Panel Reports, para. 7.636).

[283] United States' appellee's submission, para. 55 (referring to Canada's other appellant's submission, para. 62).

[284] United States' appellee's submission, para. 59.

[285] United States' appellee's submission, para. 59 (quoting Panel Reports, para. 7.650).

2. *Less Trade-Restrictive Alternative Measures*

188. The United States maintains that the Panel record does not contain a sufficient factual basis for the Appellate Body to complete the analysis as to whether the COOL measure is "more trade-restrictive than necessary", and that the Appellate Body should reject the flawed legal frameworks proposed by Canada and Mexico for interpreting Article 2.2 of the *TBT Agreement*.

189. First, the United States notes that the Appellate Body may complete the Panel's analysis "only if the factual findings of the panel and the undisputed facts in the panel record provide [the Appellate Body] with a sufficient basis for [its] analysis".[286] Although Mexico acknowledges this legal standard, it "points to *no* factual findings by the Panel" or undisputed facts regarding the four proposed alternative measures.[287] As for Canada's arguments in this regard, they "*ignore*[] the legal standard, and its application to the basis of its own appeal, altogether".[288] The United States contends that, "[i]n essence", Canada and Mexico are asking the Appellate Body to weigh and assess the evidence "on a *de novo* basis", contrary to Articles 17.6 and 17.13 of the DSU.[289]

190. As regards the four alternative measures that Canada and Mexico both propose, the United States contends that it responded in full with arguments before the Panel demonstrating that none of the proposals is an acceptable alternative, and notes that there are no undisputed facts as to any of these proposed alternatives. The United States adds that the Panel made no findings of fact with regard to these alternatives and neither complaining party asserts otherwise. The United States further notes that, with regard to the second alternative proposed by Canada and by Mexico—that is, labelling on the basis of substantial transformation—the Panel found, in the context of Mexico's claim under Article 2.4 of the *TBT Agreement*, that a Codex standard incorporating substantial transformation is "an ineffective and inappropriate means for the fulfilment of the legitimate objectives of the United States".[290] This finding, which has not been appealed, demonstrates, in the United States' view, that labelling on the basis of substantial transformation is not an alternative measure that would fulfil the United States' legitimate objective at the level the United States considers appropriate.

---

286 United States' appellee's submission, para. 66 (quoting Appellate Body Report, *EC – Asbestos*, para. 78).

287 United States' appellee's submission, para. 66 (referring to Mexico's other appellant's submission, paras. 62-68). (original emphasis)

288 United States' appellee's submission, para. 66 (referring to Canada's other appellant's submission, paras. 77-90). (original emphasis)

289 United States' appellee's submission, para. 67.

290 United States' appellee's submission, para. 68 (referring to Panel Reports, paras. 7.734 and 7.735).

191. Accordingly, the United States contends, there is not an adequate basis on the record for the Appellate Body to complete the analysis as Canada and Mexico have requested. The Appellate Body should therefore reject these two conditional appeals which, in essence, request the Appellate Body to engage in an inappropriate weighing and assessing of evidence.

192. Turning to the differing legal frameworks proposed by Canada and Mexico to interpret Article 2.2 of the *TBT Agreement*, the United States contends that these seem to derive largely from the jurisprudence developed to interpret Article XX of the GATT 1994, which is not an appropriate guidepost for interpreting the meaning of Article 2.2 of the *TBT Agreement*. In the United States' view, Canada and Mexico contend that Article 2.2 calls for panels to conduct a wide-ranging, intrusive test to balance different elements, including the importance of the legitimate objective, the trade-restrictiveness of the challenged measure, and various aspects of the proposed alternative measures. Whereas Mexico styles its version of the balancing test as a "necessity test", Canada adduces that where the value at issue is "'vital and important in the highest degree', then the alternative measure must achieve the same end" as the challenged measure[291], but, where the value is "not vital and important in the highest degree, an alternative measure need not achieve precisely the same end".[292] The United States argues that nothing in Article 2.2 of the *TBT Agreement* provides a basis for such an approach.

193. According to the United States, there are "at least four reasons" why Canada's and Mexico's analyses are each "flawed".[293] First, both Canada and Mexico seek to define a "trade-restrictive" measure as one that denies competitive opportunities. In doing so, they appear to be attempting to import into Article 2.2 the analytical approach developed for purposes of Article 2.1, as well as for less favourable treatment more generally. In the absence of a definition of the term "trade-restrictive" in the *TBT Agreement*, however, the United States submits that the interpretation of this term should be grounded in its ordinary meaning. Accordingly, a measure that is trade restrictive could include one that limits, prevents, or confines trade, or restrains it by prohibition.

194. Second, the United States submits that the text of Article 2.2 of the *TBT Agreement* does not create a balancing test. In particular, there is no textual support for requiring a panel to balance the importance of the legitimate objective against the proposed alternative. According to the United States,

---

[291] United States' appellee's submission, para. 74 (quoting Canada's other appellant's submission, para. 74, in turn quoting Appellate Body Report, *EC – Asbestos*, para. 172).

[292] United States' appellee's submission, para. 74 (quoting Canada's other appellant's submission, para. 74). (original emphasis omitted by the United States)

[293] United States' appellee's submission, para. 75.

panels are not in a position to make subjective determinations that some legitimate objectives are more important than others. In its view, the inquiry under Article 2.2 of the *TBT Agreement* does not call for "balancing" at all, but rather calls for a determination of whether a less trade-restrictive alternative measure is available and fulfils the objective of the challenged measure at the level the importing Member considers appropriate.

195. Third, the United States contends that Canada misreads the clause "taking account of the risks that non-fulfilment would create". The United States objects to the notion that, in some circumstances, a complaining party can prove that the challenged measure is "more trade-restrictive than necessary" by proposing an alternative measure that does not contribute to the fulfilment of the objective at the same level the challenged measure does. Although Canada "claims support for its position" in the jurisprudence of Article XX of the GATT 1994 and Article 5.6 of the *SPS Agreement*, the United States contends that, in interpreting these provisions, the Appellate Body has never held that panels are to apply a higher degree of scrutiny to measures that pursue objectives that are less important.[294] The United States considers that the clause "taking account of the risks non-fulfilment would create" is better understood as an element that Members take into consideration in determining the level that is appropriate for the particular legitimate objective at issue. Lastly, the United States stresses that, despite the elaborate balancing tests put forward by Canada and by Mexico, neither party seems to use its respective test to analyze the proposed alternatives.

3. *Article III:4 of the GATT 1994*

196. The United States contends that the Panel acted within its discretion in exercising judicial economy with respect to Canada's and Mexico's claims under Article III:4 of the GATT 1994. In its view, regardless of how the Appellate Body disposes of the appeal under Article 2.1 of the *TBT Agreement*, findings by the Appellate Body under Article III:4 are unnecessary and will not help to secure a positive resolution to these disputes. Therefore, the Appellate Body need not complete the legal analysis under Article III:4 of the GATT 1994 with respect to either the COOL measure or the Vilsack letter. In any event, adds the United States, there is not a sufficient factual basis for it to do so.

197. With respect to the COOL measure, the United States argues that, given its recognition of the close connection between Article 2.1 of the *TBT Agreement* and Article III:4 of the GATT 1994, the Panel's decision to exercise judicial economy was appropriate. In its view, Canada fails to explain why that decision was in error, beyond an unclear assertion that "the relationship between [these

[294] United States' appellee's submission, para. 79.

provisions] is not settled".[295] As for Mexico's conditional appeal, the United States asserts that the facts cited by Mexico with respect to less favourable treatment are some of the very facts that the United States has contended are insufficient to support a finding of a breach of Article 2.1 of the *TBT Agreement*. Because the parties have all recognized that the less favourable treatment analysis under Article 2.1 and Article III:4 "is similar"[296], there would be no basis for the finding that Mexico seeks.

198. Regarding the Vilsack letter[297], the United States submits that, because the Panel found this measure to be in breach of Article X:3(a) of the GATT 1994, it appropriately determined that it is unnecessary to examine the Vilsack letter under Article III:4. The United States further asserts that findings on the Vilsack letter under Article III:4 will not help secure a positive resolution to these disputes for two reasons. First, since the United States has not appealed the Panel's findings on the Vilsack letter, an additional finding against the measure would contribute nothing to resolving these disputes. Second, the United States contends that it has already withdrawn the Vilsack letter by means of a letter to industry representatives dated 5 April 2012. In addition, the United States argues, the complaining parties have failed to establish that Article III:4 applies to the Vilsack letter and that there are insufficient factual findings by the Panel or undisputed facts to provide a basis for finding that the Vilsack letter falls within the scope of Article III:4 of the GATT 1994.

4. *Article XXIII:1(b) of the GATT 1994*

199. The United States contends that Canada's and Mexico's conditional claims that the COOL measure nullifies or impairs their benefits under Article XXIII:1(b) of the GATT 1994 should be rejected in the light of the "cursory explanation" each provides as to how the measure at issue results in non-violation nullification or impairment.[298] The United States further contends that neither complainant explains why compliance with Article 2.2 of the *TBT Agreement* or removal of the Vilsack letter will not necessarily remove the non-violation nullification or impairment, contrary to the Panel's findings.

200. Moreover, the United States alleges that, even if Canada and Mexico could somehow explain why the Panel was required to make a non-violation

---

[295] United States' appellee's submission, para. 87 (quoting Canada's other appellant's submission, para. 96).

[296] United States' appellee's submission, para. 88 (referring to Panel Reports, para. 7.259).

[297] Canada clarified at the oral hearing that it is not seeking a finding against the Vilsack letter. (See *supra*, para. 115 and footnote 228 to para. 141) Mexico refers to only the COOL measure in its claims and argument regarding Article III:4 of the GATT 1994. (See *supra*, paras. 161-165)

[298] United States' appellee's submission, para. 93.

finding under the circumstances of this case, or the basis on which the Appellate Body could complete the analysis in the absence of such a finding, they have failed to make a *prima facie* case with regard to their claims. First, Canada and Mexico have failed to identify a relevant benefit accruing to them under the GATT 1994. Whereas Canada and Mexico identify the United States' WTO bound tariff rate for livestock as the benefit they are entitled to, they have admitted that they do not in fact pay any tariff when their livestock enters the United States because such products enjoy duty-free treatment under the NAFTA. Second, Canada and Mexico have also failed to demonstrate that they could not have reasonably anticipated the COOL measure, since the United States has long had some form of country of origin labelling requirements in place and has long been considering enhanced requirements like those included in the COOL measure. Third, Canada and Mexico have not demonstrated how the COOL requirements have nullified or impaired their tariff concessions because they have not shown a clear correlation between the harm they allege and the COOL measure.

201. Finally, the United States contends that there are insufficient factual findings by the Panel or undisputed facts on the Panel record to provide the basis for an analysis of the non-violation claims, because the Panel never directly assessed Canada's and Mexico's underdeveloped arguments as to why the COOL measure nullified or impaired their benefits under the covered agreements. Thus, even if the Appellate Body were to overturn the Panel's findings under Articles 2.1 and 2.2 of the *TBT Agreement* and decide that the Panel erred in exercising judicial economy with respect to Article XXIII:1(b) of the GATT 1994, it would not be appropriate for the Appellate Body to complete the analysis on this issue.

G. *Arguments of the Third Participants*

1. *Australia*

202. While recognizing the right of Members to maintain country of origin labelling requirements, Australia draws the attention of the Appellate Body to specific aspects of the phrase "more trade-restrictive than necessary to fulfill a legitimate objective" in Article 2.2 of the *TBT Agreement*. Australia submits that a complaining party would succeed in its claim under Article 2.2 of the *TBT Agreement* if it were able to demonstrate that the measure at issue is trade restrictive and any of the following elements: (i) the objective being pursued is not legitimate; (ii) the measure does not fulfil, or is not capable of fulfilling, the legitimate objective(s) at the level the Member considers appropriate; or (iii) less trade-restrictive alternatives are available and can fulfil, or are capable of fulfilling, the objective(s) being pursued at the level the Member considers appropriate, taking into account the risks that non-fulfilment would create.

203. Australia agrees with the Panel that, having decided that the measure does not fulfil, or is not capable of fulfilling, the stated objective, it was not necessary for the Panel to proceed with an examination of the third element described above. Australia disagrees with the United States' argument that a complaining party must prove that there is a reasonably available alternative measure that fulfils the Member's legitimate objective at the level the Member considers appropriate, and which is significantly less trade restrictive.[299] Accepting such an argument would lead to the "anomalous" consequence of requiring a complaining party to demonstrate the existence of reasonably available, less trade-restrictive alternative measures even if the challenged measure does not fulfil, or is not capable of fulfilling, the objective being pursued at the level the Member considers appropriate.[300] Moreover, while agreeing with the United States that it is the prerogative of WTO Members to decide which policy objectives they wish to pursue and the levels at which they wish to pursue them, Australia considers that the United States' argument "conflate[s]" the concept of "the levels [the Member] considers appropriate" in the sixth recital of the preamble of the *TBT Agreement* and the concept of "to fulfil" in Article 2.2 of that Agreement.[301]

204. Australia further submits that the interpretive framework developed in relation to Article XX of the GATT 1994 concerning whether a measure is "necessary" within the meaning of that provision provides useful guidance in understanding the term "more trade-restrictive than necessary" under Article 2.2 of the *TBT Agreement*. Australia highlights, in this regard, the Appellate Body's finding in *US – Clove Cigarettes* that "[t]he balance set out in the preamble of the *TBT Agreement* between, on the one hand, the desire to avoid creating unnecessary obstacles to international trade and, on the other hand, the recognition of Members' right to regulate, is not, in principle, different from the balance set out in the GATT 1994"[302], and observes that, although Article XX of the GATT 1994 and Article 2.2 of the *TBT Agreement* are independent provisions under two separate agreements, both provisions require a determination of whether the measure or its trade-restrictiveness is necessary to meet a particular objective.

205. With respect to a panel's assessment of the objective of a technical regulation, Australia observes that, as a starting point, WTO Members must

---

[299] Australia's third participant's submission, para. 9 (referring to United States' appellant's submission, para. 123).

[300] Australia's third participant's submission, para. 10 (referring to United States' appellant's submission, para. 123).

[301] Australia's third participant's submission, para. 12.

[302] Australia's third participant's submission, para. 14 (quoting Appellate Body Report, *US – Clove Cigarettes*, para. 96).

assume that other Members' characterizations of their measures are provided in good faith. Nonetheless, consistent with the Appellate Body's findings in prior disputes[303], a panel must make an objective assessment of the facts before it and is not bound by a Member's characterizations of its measure. Thus, a panel may examine the structure and operation of the measure, as well as evidence proffered by the complaining party, and it would be open to a panel to find that the actual objective of a measure is different from the stated objective(s). Australia maintains that the non-exhaustive list of objectives in Article 2.2 of the *TBT Agreement* informs what could be considered a legitimate objective. In Australia's view, enabling consumers to identify the source of a product by providing accurate information regarding its origin is a legitimate objective, because it is closely related to preventing deceptive practices, one of the listed objectives in Article 2.2. Nonetheless, in the context of the COOL measure, Australia submits that, if the measure results in the provision of information that is "misleading, inaccurate and/or confusing", it cannot be said to fulfil such a legitimate objective.[304] Finally, should the Appellate Body seek to complete the analysis under Article 2.2 of the *TBT Agreement* and examine whether there are less trade-restrictive alternatives to the COOL measure, Australia recalls the submissions that it made to the Panel in this regard.[305]

2. *Brazil*

206. With respect to Article 2.1 of the *TBT Agreement*, Brazil submits that the Panel properly recognized that, particularly in the context of a claim of *de facto* discrimination, the prevailing market conditions are relevant to the determination of whether an uneven distribution of compliance costs between imported and domestic like products constitutes less favourable treatment. Brazil rejects the apparent view of the United States that, if any factor other than the foreign origin of the product is found to be the basis for the discrimination, there will be no violation of Article 2.1. Brazil considers useful, in this regard, the guidance provided in the extensive WTO case law under Article III of the GATT 1994, and endorses the following definition provided by the panel in *Canada – Pharmaceutical Patents*: "*de facto* discrimination is a general term describing the legal conclusion that an ostensibly neutral measure transgresses a non-discrimination norm because its actual effect is to impose differentially disadvantageous consequences on certain parties, and because those differential

[303] Australia's third participant's submission, paras. 17 and 18 (referring to Appellate Body Report, *EC – Sardines*, paras. 276-278 and 280; Appellate Body Report, *US – Gambling*, para. 304; and Appellate Body Report, *US – Clove Cigarettes*, paras. 113 and 115).

[304] Australia's third participant's submission, para. 23.

[305] Australia's third participant's submission, paras. 24 and 25 (referring to Australia's third party submission to the Panel, paras. 79-83). See also Panel Reports, Annex C-1, para. 23.

effects are found to be wrong or unjustifiable."[306] For Brazil, differential effects imposed by a measure on imported and domestic like products can only be justified if they do not change the conditions of competition to the detriment of the imported like products. Assessing whether a measure modifies the conditions of competition requires "a comprehensive and objective analysis of the structure and application of the measure in question on domestic as compared to imported products".[307]

207. In Brazil's view, the Panel correctly found that "[a] cost resulting from a (technical) regulation may qualify as a competitive disadvantage if it is incurred only by imported and not like domestic products."[308] In reaching this finding, the Panel did not, as the United States asserts, adopt an "unprecedented" approach.[309] Brazil explains that, in *Dominican Republic – Import and Sale of Cigarettes*, the Appellate Body found that a difference in compliance costs was not sufficient in itself to establish a violation of Article III:4 of the GATT 1994, as long as such a difference does not alter the conditions of competition in the relevant market.[310] Moreover, in *Korea – Various Measures on Beef*, the Appellate Body found that a dual distribution system "that is *not* imposed directly or indirectly by law or governmental regulation, but is rather *solely* the result of private entrepreneurs acting on their own calculations of comparative costs and benefits", is not inconsistent with Article III:4 of the GATT 1994.[311] The Appellate Body, however, also emphasized that "the intervention of some element of private choice does not relieve [the Member] of responsibility under the GATT 1994 for the resulting establishment of competitive conditions less favourable for the imported product than for the domestic product".[312]

208. Brazil submits that the Panel rightly found that "assessing whether a measure has actual discriminatory effects cannot be dissociated from the circumstances prevailing in the market at issue."[313] If account were not taken of

---

306 Brazil's third participant's submission, para. 9 (quoting Panel Report, *Canada – Pharmaceutical Patents*, para. 7.101).

307 Brazil's third participant's submission, para. 12 (quoting Appellate Body Report, *Japan – Alcoholic Beverages II*, p. 29, DSR 1996:I, 97, at 120).

308 Brazil's third participant's submission, para. 10 (quoting Panel Reports, para. 7.313).

309 Brazil's third participant's submission, para. 13 (quoting United States' appellant's submission, para. 62).

310 Brazil's third participant's submission, paras. 14-17 (referring to Appellate Body Report, *Dominican Republic – Import and Sale of Cigarettes*, paras. 96 and 98; and Panel Report, *Dominican Republic – Import and Sale of Cigarettes*, para. 7.301).

311 Brazil's third participant's submission, para. 18 (quoting Appellate Body Report, *Korea – Various Measures on Beef*, para. 149 (original emphasis)). (underlining added by Brazil)

312 Brazil's third participant's submission, para. 19 (quoting Appellate Body Report, *Korea – Various Measures on Beef*, para. 146).

313 Brazil's third participant's submission, para. 20 (quoting Panel Reports, para. 7.397).

the market conditions prevailing before the enactment of a technical regulation, a major loophole in the national treatment obligation would exist, because a Member with protectionist intent could simply exploit the prevailing conditions in the relevant market to design a technical regulation under which compliance costs would be low for the domestic industry, but high or even prohibitive for foreign producers. This does not mean that there must be an equal distribution of compliance costs of a technical regulation between domestic and imported like products in order for a technical regulation to be consistent with Article 2.1 of the *TBT Agreement*. Rather, as the Appellate Body stated in *US – Clove Cigarettes*, Article 2.1 of the *TBT Agreement* does not prohibit detrimental impacts on imports that stem exclusively from a legitimate regulatory distinction. For Brazil, this implies that Article 2.1 requires the distribution of compliance costs among domestic and imported like products to be "even-handed" and, if one of the effects of a measure is the imposition of disproportionately high costs on imported products, this should be regarded as a strong indication of a lack of even-handedness.[314] Furthermore, in Brazil's view, regulatory distinctions that comply with the requirements of Article 2.2 and the sixth recital of the preamble of the *TBT Agreement* could be considered legitimate, but a regulatory distinction is not legitimate if it constitutes a means of arbitrary or unjustifiable discrimination between countries where the same conditions prevail, or a disguised restriction on international trade.

209. Referring to the United States' argument that it is impossible for a Member to know, at the time of developing a technical regulation, the precise costs the measure will impose on each producer in every Member, or the unique circumstances of every Member's industry[315], Brazil expresses the view that it is irrelevant to the analysis of less favourable treatment whether the detrimental effects on imported products were intended or foreseen by the Member applying the measure. Rather, what matters for determining whether a measure is inconsistent with Article 2.1 of the *TBT Agreement* is the application of the measure.[316] Brazil adds that, in any event, the Member applying a technical regulation cannot evade its obligations under the *TBT Agreement* by simply stating that it did not intend or foresee the detrimental impacts of the measure on imports, or that it would be difficult to assess the potential detrimental effects of a technical regulation beforehand.

---

[314] Brazil's third participant's submission, para. 24 (quoting Appellate Body Report, *US – Clove Cigarettes*, para. 182).

[315] Brazil's third participant's submission, para. 25 (referring to United States' appellant's submission, para. 99).

[316] Brazil's third participant's submission, paras. 26-28 (referring to Appellate Body Report, *Japan – Alcoholic Beverages II*, p. 28, DSR 1996:I, 97, at 119).

3. *Colombia*

210. Colombia disagrees with the United States' argument that, in reaching its finding under Article 2.1 of the *TBT Agreement*, the Panel adopted "a radical and unprecedented test for less favorable treatment that does not focus on whether the measure *itself* modifies the *conditions* of competition to the detriment of imported livestock ... but instead examines whether imported livestock are equally competitive with domestic livestock".[317] In Colombia's view, the Panel's approach in using economic analysis to compare the different costs of processing domestic and imported livestock is neither new, nor erroneous.

211. Colombia submits that it is a long-standing rule that the national treatment provisions of the covered agreements, including Article 2.1 of the *TBT Agreement*, protect the equality of competitive opportunities.[318] Competitive opportunities in the marketplace refer to the economic, regulatory, social, and cultural parameters that determine the way in which market participants take their decisions. Scrutiny of a technical regulation's consistency with Article 2.1 is not limited to an assessment of the impact the measure may have in abstract terms, but includes an assessment of the potential consequences that can be expected from market participants as a result of changes to, in particular, the economic incentives in the marketplace that are introduced by such regulation. Colombia maintains that this was expressly recognized by the Appellate Body in *China – Auto Parts* when it found that the administrative procedures imposed by the measures at issue on automobile manufacturers using imported auto parts, but not on those manufacturers using domestic auto parts, were incentives that adversely affected the conditions of competition for imported auto parts. Colombia adds that an examination of the way market participants behave in response to a measure is relevant to an analysis of less favourable treatment even if a measure facially does not distinguish between imported and domestic products.

212. Colombia posits that the changes in economic incentives must be attributable to the impugned measure in order for that measure to be found to accord less favourable treatment to imports. Colombia recalls the Appellate Body's finding in *Korea – Various Measures on Beef* that what is addressed under a less favourable treatment analysis is "the *governmental* intervention" that affects the conditions of competition.[319] Moreover, the Appellate Body has found that "the existence of a detrimental effect" on imports "does not

---

[317] Colombia's third participant's submission, para. 4 (quoting United States' appellant's submission, para. 62 (original emphasis)).

[318] Colombia's third participant's submission, para. 10.

[319] Colombia's third participant's submission, para. 21 (quoting Appellate Body Report, *Korea – Various Measures on Beef*, para. 149 (original emphasis)).

necessarily imply that this measure accords less favourable treatment to imports if the detrimental effect is explained by factors or circumstances unrelated to the foreign origin of the product".[320] On this basis, Colombia argues, a finding of violation under Article 2.1 of the *TBT Agreement* requires: (i) a direct link between the measure and the detrimental modification of conditions of competition; and (ii) that the detrimental effects are not explained by factors or circumstances unrelated to the foreign origin of the product. Colombia submits that there was sufficient evidence in these disputes demonstrating these two elements with respect to the COOL measure. More specifically, the COOL measure imposes higher costs on the processing of imported livestock, thereby creating a disincentive to use such imported livestock, and these disincentives are related to the foreign origin of the livestock.

213. Turning to Article 2.2 of the *TBT Agreement*, Colombia contends that the Panel erroneously transposed the necessity test under Article XX(b) of the GATT 1994, in its entirety, into its analysis regarding whether the COOL measure is more trade restrictive than necessary to fulfil a legitimate objective. According to Colombia, the necessity tests in different covered agreements cannot be used interchangeably but must be read in their context and in the light of the object and purpose of the agreement concerned. Colombia notes that the Panel's approach is "diametrically different" from that taken by the panel in *US – Clove Cigarettes*.[321] The latter panel recognized that there were "important differences in the architecture of both provisions"[322] by stating that "[i]t may well be that there are certain aspects of Article XX(b) jurisprudence that are not applicable in the context of Article 2.2 of the *TBT Agreement*".[323] Colombia argues that key differences exist between Article XX of the GATT 1994 and Article 2.2 of the *TBT Agreement*, including: (i) the fact that the former provides for an exception, whereas the latter establishes an obligation; (ii) the different objectives of the GATT 1994 and the *TBT Agreement*; and (iii) the specialized subject matter of the *TBT Agreement*.

214. Colombia clarifies that it is not suggesting that determinations under Article 2.2 should be subject to a completely different standard with respect to the word "necessary". Rather, the same elements of the necessity test under Article XX of the GATT 1994 should be potentially applicable throughout the covered agreements. Nonetheless, "the threshold of compliance for each of the

---

[320] Colombia's third participant's submission, para. 22 (quoting Appellate Body Report, *Dominican Republic – Import and Sale of Cigarettes*, para. 96).

[321] Colombia's third participant's submission, para. 40.

[322] *Ibid.*

[323] Colombia's third participant's submission, para. 39 (quoting Panel Report, *US – Clove Cigarettes*, para. 7.369).

elements", or the "the degree of stringency"[324], should vary depending on the different objects and purposes of the legal provisions containing the term "necessity", as well as the fact that some of the provisions are obligations while other are exceptions. Colombia draws an analogy, in this respect, with the concept of the accordion of "likeness" as articulated by the Appellate Body in previous cases. In Colombia's view, the provisions that provide for exceptions, such as Article XX of the GATT 1994, should be interpreted as having the highest degree of stringency. For these reasons, Colombia agrees with the United States that the Panel erred in transposing the standard of a material contribution from the Article XX context into Article 2.2 of the *TBT Agreement*.

215. Colombia agrees with the Panel's finding that the use of the term "*inter alia*" in Article 2.2 of the *TBT Agreement* indicates that the objectives that can be deemed legitimate extend beyond the listed objectives in that provision.[325] Colombia disagrees with Canada's argument that a determination of whether an objective is legitimate within the meaning of Article 2.2 involves determining whether an objective is directly related to one of those explicitly listed in Article 2.2 and, if not, whether the measure is of the same type as those listed.[326] In Colombia's view, Canada's interpretation imports into Article 2.2 a requirement to establish a link between the objectives listed in that provision and the objectives pursued by the measure at issue, even though such a requirement has no textual basis in Article 2.2. In addition, Canada's interpretation deprives the term "*inter alia*" of any effective meaning, contrary to Article 31(1) of the *Vienna Convention* and the principle of effective treaty interpretation. In Colombia's view, the explicit inclusion of the term "*inter alia*" shows that the function of the list is to ensure beyond doubt the legitimacy of the listed objectives, rather than to limit the universe of different objectives that may be deemed legitimate. Moreover, Colombia argues that the Panel did not err in finding that the legitimacy of an objective must be determined by assessing whether the objective is justifiable and supported by relevant public policies or other social norms.[327] The Panel examined the issue of legitimacy through the prism of "the requirements of current social norms in a considerable part of the WTO Membership".[328] Thus, the Panel's approach would not lead to the result, as Canada argues, that a measure designed to enhance racial discrimination

[324] Colombia's third participant's submission, para. 53.

[325] Colombia's third participant's submission, para. 59 (referring to Panel Reports, paras. 7.632 and 7.634-7.636).

[326] Colombia's third participant's submission, para. 65 (referring to Canada's other appellant's submission, paras. 53-59).

[327] Colombia's third participant's submission, para. 77 (referring to Panel Reports, para. 7.632).

[328] Colombia's third participant's submission, para. 75 (quoting Panel Reports, para. 7.650).

would be legitimate simply because it has a genuine link to a public policy of racial discrimination.[329]

216. Finally, Colombia submits that the Panel erred in its exercise of judicial economy with regard to Canada's claim that the Vilsack letter is inconsistent with Article III:4 of the GATT 1994. Colombia recalls that the Panel excluded the Vilsack letter from its Article 2.1 analysis because it found that the Vilsack letter is not a technical regulation. Subsequently, having found the COOL measure to be inconsistent with Article 2.1 of the *TBT Agreement*, the Panel found it unnecessary to rule on the claims regarding the COOL measure under Article III:4 of the GATT 1994 due to the close connection between this provision and Article 2.1 of the *TBT Agreement*.[330] However, the Panel did not refer to the Vilsack letter in reaching this finding. Colombia contends that the Panel was required to assess whether the Vilsack letter falls under the purview of the term "regulation" in Article III:4 of the GATT 1994. This is because Article 2.1 of the *TBT Agreement* applies only to "technical regulations", whereas Article III:4 applies to a much broader range of instruments, encompassing all laws, regulations, and requirements affecting the internal sale, offering for sale, purchase, transportation, distribution, or use of the products at issue that might adversely modify the conditions of competition between domestic and imported products. Colombia adds that, by exercising judicial economy with regard to the Vilsack letter, the Panel did not secure a positive solution to the dispute, as required by Article 3.7 of the DSU, and potentially diminished rights and obligations of the complainants in these disputes.

4. *European Union*

217. The European Union notes that the requests by both complainants for consultations and for the establishment of a panel referenced Article IX of the GATT 1994 and certain provisions of the *Agreement on Rules of Origin*[331], but that these provisions were not referenced in the parties' arguments or the Panel's assessment. The European Union submits that there may be an interpretative question regarding the relationship between the *Agreement on Rules of Origin* and the *TBT Agreement*. Article 1.2 of the *Agreement on Rules of Origin* defines the coverage of the Agreement as "all rules of origin used in non-preferential

---

329 Colombia's third participant's submission, para. 74 (referring to Canada's other appellant's submission, para. 50).

330 Colombia's third participant's submission, para. 90 (referring to Panel Reports, para. 7.807).

331 European Union's third participant's submission, para. 6 (referring to Request for Consultations by Canada, WT/DS384/1, and Addendum, WT/DS384/1/Add.1; Request for Consultations by Mexico, WT/DS386/1, and Addendum, WT/DS386/1/Add.1; Request for the Establishment of a Panel by Canada, WT/DS384/8; and Request for the Establishment of a Panel by Mexico, WT/DS386/7, and Corrigendum, WT/DS386/7/Corr.1).

commercial policy instruments, such as in the application of", *inter alia*, Articles III and IX of the GATT 1994. Although Article 1.2 does not expressly reference the *TBT Agreement*, the list in Article 1.2 is not exhaustive and technical regulations within the scope of the *TBT Agreement* are not, *per se*, excluded. Moreover, there may also be a question regarding the relationship between the terms "mark" and "marking" in Article IX of the GATT 1994 and the terms "label" and "labelling" in the *TBT Agreement*. Noting that Article 3(a) of the *Agreement on Rules of Origin* requires Members to apply rules of origin equally for all purposes as set out in Article 1, the European Union also contends that there may be an interpretative issue as to whether it is impermissible to use different origin rules with respect to the same product for different purposes. The European Union submits that it may be appropriate to have recourse to the principle of *lex specialis derogat legi generali* in case of conflict between the *Agreement on Rules of Origin* and the *TBT Agreement*. In sum, the European Union maintains that the *TBT Agreement* should not be used as an instrument to achieve indirectly harmonization of origin rules before Members have completed the harmonization work pursuant to Part IV of the *Agreement on Rules of Origin*.

218. With respect to the interpretation of Article 2.1 of the *TBT Agreement*, the European Union recalls the Appellate Body's findings in *US – Clove Cigarettes* that the balance that the preamble of the *TBT Agreement* strikes between the pursuit of trade liberalization and Members' right to regulate is not, in principle, different from the balance that exists between the national treatment obligation of Article III and the general exceptions provided under Article XX of the GATT 1994, that the same balance is to be found in Article 2.1 of the *TBT Agreement*, and that Article 2.2 informs Article 2.1.[332] In the light of these findings, the European Union disagrees with Canada's submission that the list of potentially legitimate objectives is different for purposes of Article 2.1 than it is for Article 2.2 of the *TBT Agreement*.[333]

219. The European Union also disagrees with the United States' argument that, in finding that imported livestock are accorded less favourable treatment, the Panel erred in basing its analysis on how the commingling flexibility under the measure affects a product not at issue in these disputes, that is, meat.[334] In the European Union's view, if the facts demonstrate that regulation of the downstream product has effects that are transmitted to an upstream product not

---

[332] European Union's third participant's submission, para. 27 (referring to Appellate Body Report, *US – Clove Cigarettes*, paras. 96 and 109).

[333] European Union's third participant's submission, para. 28 (referring to Canada's appellee's submission, para. 56).

[334] European Union's third participant's submission, para. 32 (referring to United States' appellant's submission, paras. 58 and 79).

directly subject to the measure, the question of *de facto* discrimination against the upstream product can be analyzed on the basis of an assessment of the downstream product.

220. The European Union agrees with the United States that compliance costs of any new regulation may vary among different market actors with different sizes, structures, and operations, and hence different economies of scale. The fact that such costs are not evenly distributed does not in itself mean that there is a breach of the national treatment obligation, because this obligation concerns equal competitive opportunities rather than equal competition *per se*. Furthermore, the interpretation of the national treatment obligation should not lead to a result whereby large Members are more susceptible to a finding of violation simply because they have large markets in which indigenous production often has a relative large market share. The European Union adds that it would seem incongruous if a measure adopted in accordance with international standards, and thus consistent with Articles 2.2 and 2.5 of the *TBT Agreement*, would nevertheless be inconsistent with Article 2.1 simply because it entails compliance costs that are not evenly distributed among market actors. Contrary to the United States' argument, however, the Panel did not focus its "entire" less favourable treatment inquiry on how compliance costs may differ for market actors.[335] Rather, the Panel's conclusion "appears to have been that the measure does not seek to even-handedly inform consumers about origin, but rather to facilitate or incentivise the switching of demand towards US products, and/or the freezing of entrenched patterns of consumption".[336]

221. With regard to the interpretation of the second sentence of Article 2.2 of the *TBT Agreement*, the European Union maintains that the "objective" of a measure within the meaning of that sentence is to be discerned from an objective assessment of the terms of the measure and the surrounding circumstances. The "legitimacy" of the objective under the second sentence is a matter with respect to which WTO Members have considerable discretion, and the list of objectives in that sentence is not exhaustive. WTO Members' discretion in this regard is not unfettered, however. For example, an objective inconsistent with other provisions of the covered agreements would not be "legitimate". The European Union submits that the concept of "at the levels it considers appropriate" in the sixth recital of the preamble of the *TBT Agreement* is analogous to the concept of "appropriate level of protection" or "acceptable level of risk" under the *SPS Agreement*. Both Agreements make it clear that such levels are a matter for the importing Member to decide, subject to certain disciplines. More specifically, just as Article 5.5 of the *SPS Agreement* prohibits

[335] European Union's third participant's submission, para. 37 (quoting United States' appellant's submission, para. 88).

[336] European Union's third participant's submission, para. 37.

arbitrary or unjustifiable distinctions when setting the level, the second sentence of Article 2.2 of the *TBT Agreement* requires a measure to be no more trade restrictive than "necessary" to fulfil a legitimate objective. In the European Union's view, whether one approaches the issue of necessity by examining the *necessity of the measure* taking into account the objective, level, and trade-restrictiveness, or by examining the *necessity of the trade-restrictiveness* taking into account the objective and level of the measure, it is just two different ways of approaching the same balancing issue. Assuming that the measure fulfils a legitimate objective, the European Union agrees with the participants that an adjudicator must consider whether there is an alternative measure that is less trade restrictive.

222. Moreover, in the European Union's view, it is also necessary to examine whether there are less trade-restrictive alternatives even if a measure partially fulfils a legitimate objective, for the following reasons. First, the second sentence of Article 2.2 does not impose the obligation that the measure must fulfil 100% of its objective. Second, if the word "fulfil" in the second sentence of Article 2.2 meant 100% fulfilment, the phrase "taking account of the risks non-fulfilment would create" at the end of that sentence would be reduced to redundancy. This is because, once an adjudicator ascertains that the measure does not fulfil the objective 100%, this is the end of the inquiry and the "risks of non-fulfilment" need not be taken into account. Third, the word "risks" in the final phrase generally refers to a calibrated concept. Fourth, the relevant context of Article 2.2 of the *TBT Agreement*, including Articles 2.3, 2.4, and 2.7 of that Agreement, and footnote 3 of the *SPS Agreement* support the view that the word "fulfil" encompasses partial fulfilment. Fifth, the texts of several provisions in the covered agreements indicate that the concept of trade-restrictiveness is calibrated. These include the phrases "more trade-restrictive than necessary" in Article 2.2 of the *TBT Agreement*, "less trade-restrictive" in Article 2.3 of that Agreement, and "minimize their negative effects on trade" in the fourth recital of the preamble of the *SPS Agreement*. Because trade-restrictiveness and fulfilment of legitimate objectives are two sides of the same balancing equation, they must both be calibrated concepts. Finally, the object and purpose of the *TBT Agreement* calls upon a panel to strike a balance between competing interests by considering all relevant factors, including less trade-restrictive alternatives.

223. On this basis, the European Union considers that the Panel erred in not considering whether less trade-restrictive alternatives existed, in reaching its finding of inconsistency under Article 2.2, simply because it had found that the COOL measure did not fulfil a legitimate objective. In the European Union's view, the Panel's approach implies that a measure that is only slightly trade restrictive but fulfils 99% of a legitimate objective breaches Article 2.2, even if no less trade-restrictive alternative is available that achieves the same result. Such an approach could lead to the "perverse result" that the importing Member replaces the impugned measure with one that fully achieves the legitimate

objective but is much more restrictive of trade.[337] For the same reason, the European Union maintains that Mexico's argument that the term "fulfil" in Article 2.2 of the *TBT Agreement* means 100% fulfilment is also incorrect.[338] Furthermore, the European Union disagrees with Canada's approach to draw upon the Appellate Body's findings regarding the issue of necessity under Article XX of the GATT 1994 in arguing that the word "fulfil" refers to something between material contribution and indispensable. To the European Union, Canada's approach fails to take into account the particular wording of the various provisions of the *TBT Agreement*.[339]

224. Turning to the concept of "trade-restrictive" in Article 2.2 of the *TBT Agreement*, the European Union submits that it is not the same as the concept of "effect on trade" that is relevant to an inquiry under Article 2.9 of that Agreement or Article 1.1 of the *SPS Agreement*. There is a category of regulations that are not trade restrictive, and therefore consistent with the covered agreements, even if they affect trade.

225. With respect to the United States' claim that the Panel acted inconsistently with Article 11 of the DSU in its identification of the COOL measure's objective by mischaracterizing the United States' position regarding its level of fulfilment, the European Union submits that the United States confuses the concepts of "objective" and "level", which concern, respectively, what the importing Member cares about and the degree of care. The European Union considers that the thrust of the United States' argument relates to the concept of "fulfilment", that is, the extent to which the measure achieves the objective at the desired level. Moreover, the European Union disagrees with the United States' argument that the Panel should have framed the objectives of the COOL measure as both to provide consumer information about origin and to limit compliance costs for market participants.[340] The assessment of a measure under Article 2.2 of the *TBT Agreement* requires the balancing of, on the one hand, the non-trade interest reflected in the measure's objective and, on the other hand, the trade interest including the measure's impact on market participants. By conflating these competing interests into one objective, the United States' argument would defeat the need to strike a balance in the interpretation and application of Article 2.2, and would mean that the defending Member's measure would never be found inconsistent with that provision.

---

[337] European Union's third participant's submission, para. 55.

[338] European Union's third participant's submission, paras. 55-64 (referring to Mexico's appellee's submission, paras. 129, 130, and 132).

[339] European Union's third participant's submission, para. 65 (referring to Canada's appellee's submission, para. 90).

[340] European Union's third participant's submission, para. 51 (referring to United States' appellant's submission, paras. 139 and 140).

226. Turning to the other appeals, the European Union disagrees with Canada and Mexico's common claim that the Panel erred in finding that the COOL measure pursues a legitimate objective.[341] Noting the Panel's reluctance to question the objective as stated by the United States[342], the European Union expresses sympathy for Canada and Mexico's position that the text of the measure is the correct starting point for determining the measure's objective. Nonetheless, the European Union does not consider that the Panel committed legal error in its overall assessment and identification of the objective of the COOL measure. The European Union adds that the provision of information to consumers about origin may, in itself, be a legitimate objective within the meaning of Article 2.2 of the *TBT Agreement*. The European Union also disagrees with the other appellants' claim that the Panel should have determined that the objective of the measure is, at least in part, protectionism.[343] Whether a measure's trade-restrictiveness reflects protectionist intent or is inadvertent is not pertinent to a finding that the measure breaches the second sentence of Article 2.2 of the *TBT Agreement*. The other appellants' position seems to "effectively short-circuit the full legal framework of Article 2.2" because, where the objective of a measure is protectionism, such an objective is by definition illegitimate.[344] As a result, the measure would be found to be inconsistent with Article 2.2 without an inquiry into the more complex questions of whether the measure fulfils its objective, what the less trade-restrictive alternatives are, and whether such alternatives fulfil the objective at the same level.

227. Finally, the European Union recalls Canada and Mexico's common claim that, in the event the Appellate Body finds that the COOL measure fulfils a legitimate objective, at least four less trade-restrictive alternative measures exist that fulfil the same objective. These are: (i) voluntary labelling; (ii) labelling based on substantial transformation; (iii) a combination of (i) and (ii); and (iv) a trace-back system.[345] With respect to voluntary labelling, the European Union maintains that the essential difference between voluntary and mandatory labelling is that an individual consumer lacks the power to demand labelling with respect to particular information. Thus, the fact that a domestic political process leads to legislation on mandatory origin labelling may indicate that consumers indeed demand such labelling. Moreover, contrary to the

[341] European Union's third participant's submission, para. 67 (referring to Canada's other appellant's submission, section III; and Mexico's other appellant's submission, section III.A).

[342] European Union's third participant's submission, para. 66 (referring to Panel Reports, paras. 7.590-7.621).

[343] European Union's third participant's submission, para. 67 (referring to Canada's other appellant's submission, section III; and Mexico's other appellant's submission, section III.A).

[344] European Union's third participant's submission, para. 70.

[345] European Union's third participant's submission, para. 75 (referring to Canada's other appellant's submission, section IV; and Mexico's other appellant's submission, section III.B).

complainants' assertions, there is no obligation under the *TBT Agreement* on the defending Member to demonstrate that their consumers want a particular technical regulation. With respect to labelling based on substantial transformation, the European Union considers that this alternative concerns substantive rules of origin and refers to its observation above regarding Article IX of the GATT 1994 and the *Agreement on Rules of Origin*. As for the trace-back system, the European Union highlights the distinction made in Article 3(b) of the *Agreement on Rules of Origin* between "the country where the good has been wholly obtained" and the situation in which more than one country is concerned in the production of the good. The European Union adds that, under relevant EU law, where there is more than one country concerned, the law requires that labels contain information about the country of birth, the country of fattening, the country where slaughter occurred, and the place of cutting, but the law does not refer to "origin".[346]

5. *Guatemala*

228. At the oral hearing, Guatemala stated its view that the term "necessary" under the second sentence of Article 2.2 of the *TBT Agreement* must be assessed in the light of the importance of the "legitimate objective". The importance of the legitimate objective, in turn, is to be determined by the risks non-fulfilment of the objective would create. The higher the risks, the more important the objective and, hence, the higher the degree of trade-restrictiveness that could be justifiable. As for the identification of the objective of a measure, Guatemala agreed with Mexico that the Panel should not have relied solely on the responding party's description, but should have determined the objective in the light of the architecture and structure of a technical regulation, as well as its legislative history and surrounding circumstances. Guatemala did not consider, however, that protectionism could be properly identified as the objective, because doing so conflates the objective of the measure with the effects or the intent of that measure. Guatemala further submitted that the legitimacy of the objective could be decided by examining: first, whether the objective is included in the non-exhaustive list under Article 2.2; second, whether the objective is not inconsistent with the covered agreements; and, third, whether the objective can be "defended" or is "reasonable".[347] Finally, with respect to the term "fulfil", Guatemala did not consider that Article 2.2 imposes an obligation to fulfil a legitimate objective to a certain degree. Rather, the level of fulfilment has a

---

[346] European Union's third participant's submission, para. 81 (referring to Regulation (EC) No. 1760/2000 of the European Parliament and of the Council of 17 July 2000 establishing a system for the identification and registration of bovine animals and regarding the labelling of beef and beef products and repealing Council Regulation (EC) No 820/97, *Official Journal of the European Communities*, L Series, No. 204 (11 August 2000), 1 (Panel Exhibit EU-4)).

[347] Guatemala's opening statement at the oral hearing.

consequence for the permitted level of trade-restrictiveness, in that the poor fulfilment of a legitimate objective would not justify a high degree of trade-restrictiveness.

6. *Japan*

229. Japan agrees with the Panel that Article III:4 of the GATT 1994 provides relevant context for interpreting Article 2.1 of the *TBT Agreement*, in particular for interpreting the phrase "treatment no less favourable than that accorded to like products of national origin".[348] However, Article 2.1 of the *TBT Agreement* does not prohibit *a priori* any obstacle to international trade. As the Appellate Body recently found in *US – Clove Cigarettes*, "the existence of a detrimental impact on competitive opportunities for the group of imported [products] vis-à-vis the group of domestic like products is not dispositive of less favourable treatment under Article 2.1".[349] Rather, "a panel must further analyze whether the detrimental impact on imports stems *exclusively* from a legitimate regulatory distinction".[350] Japan maintains that the notion of "legitimacy" contained in the Appellate Body's above finding should not be confused with the concept of "a legitimate objective" under Article 2.2 of the *TBT Agreement*, in that the pursuit of a legitimate objective might result in the application of either legitimate or illegitimate regulatory distinctions. Moreover, Japan urges the Appellate Body to be cautious in applying its recent findings in *US – Clove Cigarettes* in this appeal, because these findings were not yet available to the Panel during its proceedings.

230. Japan argues that, in assessing whether the COOL measure accords less favourable treatment to imported livestock, the Panel should have examined whether "the objective, design and structure of the COOL measure *itself*" modifies the conditions of competition to the detriment of imported products.[351] Japan recalls that, in finding that the COOL measure accords less favourable treatment to imported livestock, the Panel examined five business scenarios for the processing of livestock, and concluded that the scenario that involved processing exclusively imported livestock was more costly than the one involving processing exclusively domestic livestock.[352] To Japan, the Panel "seemed to have relied heavily" on the small market share of imported livestock

---

[348] Japan's third participant's submission, para. 5 (referring to Panel Reports, para. 7.234).

[349] Japan's third participant's submission, para. 6 (quoting Appellate Body Report, *US – Clove Cigarettes*, para. 182).

[350] Japan's third participant's submission, para. 6 (quoting Appellate Body Report, *US – Clove Cigarettes*, para. 182). (emphasis added by Japan)

[351] Japan's third participant's submission, para. 6. (original emphasis)

[352] Japan's third participant's submission, para. 7 (referring to Panel Reports, paras. 7.333-7.336).

in the US market and the geographical closeness of domestic livestock to the US market.[353] In so doing, the Panel failed to distinguish the effects of the objective, design, and structure of the COOL measure from those of other factors, including pre-existing market conditions. Thus, Japan urges the Appellate Body to consider carefully whether the detrimental impact on imports stems exclusively from the legitimate regulatory distinction created by the COOL measure.

231. Turning to Article 2.2 of the *TBT Agreement*, Japan submits that, in order to assess the legitimacy of an objective, as well as whether a measure is more trade restrictive than necessary, a panel must identify the objective of the measure in a sufficiently specific way. This means that not only the general purpose, but also "the level of strictness" of the measure must be determined.[354] In Japan's view, the objective of the COOL measure identified by the Panel—that is, "to provide as much clear and accurate origin information as possible to consumers"[355]—does not specify how much country of origin information the United States intends to deliver to consumers through the measure. As the Panel's analysis reveals, a failure to identify the "level of strictness" of a regulation affords a panel much discretion in determining whether the legitimate objective is fulfilled. Moreover, the Panel's approach would have made it difficult for the Panel to have appropriately examined whether the COOL measure was more trade restrictive than necessary to fulfil a legitimate objective, including whether there were less trade-restrictive alternatives in comparison to the COOL measure. Finally, Japan submits that the Panel could have relied on the development and history of the United States' country of origin labelling scheme in order to determine the specific level that the United States pursues through the COOL measure, and urges the Appellate Body to identify the objective of the COOL measure more specifically than the Panel did.

7. *Korea*

232. At the oral hearing, Korea disagreed with the Panel's finding that, because processing meat from exclusively domestic livestock is less costly in view of the need to segregate livestock under the COOL measure, the measure reduced the competitive opportunities of imported livestock vis-à-vis domestic livestock.[356] In Korea's view, how compliance costs are distributed may have been prompted by a wide spectrum of factors, such as consumer preference and choices by market participants, which a government usually cannot control or reasonably

[353] Japan's third participant's submission, para. 7 (referring to Panel Reports, para. 7.349).

[354] Japan's third participant's submission, para. 10.

[355] Japan's third participant's submission, para. 11 (quoting Panel Reports, para. 7.620).

[356] Korea's opening statement at the oral hearing (referring to Panel Reports, para. 7.357).

predict. Thus, the Panel failed to determine whether there was a causal link between the COOL measure and the detrimental impact on imported livestock. Furthermore, Korea recalled that the Panel found that the level at which the United States aims to achieve the identified objective is "to provide as much clear and accurate origin information as possible to consumers". Korea submitted that, in reaching this finding, the Panel should not have relied solely on the United States' description, but should have considered various provisions of the COOL measure, the legislative history, and the stakeholders' statements.

III. ISSUES RAISED IN THIS APPEAL

233. With respect to the Panel's findings that the COOL measure is inconsistent with Article 2.1 of the *TBT Agreement*, the following issues are raised by the United States:

(a) whether the Panel erred in finding that the COOL measure treats imported livestock differently than domestic livestock;

(b) whether the Panel erred in finding that the COOL measure accords less favourable treatment to imported livestock than to like domestic livestock; and

(c) whether the Panel acted inconsistently with its obligation under Article 11 of the DSU to make an objective assessment of the facts in its findings with respect to segregation, commingling, and the price differential between imported and domestic livestock in the US market.

234. With respect to the Panel's findings under Article 2.2 of the *TBT Agreement*, the following issues are raised by the participants:

(a) whether the Panel erred in finding that the COOL measure is "trade-restrictive" within the meaning of Article 2.2 (raised by the United States);

(b) whether the Panel failed to identify correctly the objective pursued by the United States through the COOL measure (raised by Canada and by Mexico);

(c) whether, in identifying the objective pursued by the United States through the COOL measure, the Panel:

    (i) acted inconsistently with its obligation under Article 11 of the DSU to make an objective assessment of the facts:

- in failing to find that the objective of the COOL measure is trade protectionism (raised by Canada and by Mexico); or

- in wilfully distorting and misrepresenting the United States' position as to the level at which the United States considers it appropriate to fulfil its objective (raised by the United States); or

(ii) failed to consider all relevant information concerning the United States' chosen level of fulfilment of its objective (raised by the United States);

(d) in the event that the Appellate Body does not find that the Panel acted inconsistently with its obligations under Article 11 of the DSU in failing to find that the objective of the COOL measure is trade protectionism, then whether the Panel erred in failing to characterize the objective of the COOL measure in sufficient detail (raised by Canada);

(e) whether the Panel erred in finding that the provision of consumer information on origin is a legitimate objective within the meaning of Article 2.2 (raised by Canada);

(f) whether, in its analysis of whether the COOL measure is "more trade-restrictive than necessary to fulfil a legitimate objective", the Panel:

(i) employed an erroneous legal framework by separately analyzing whether the COOL measure fulfils its objective and by relieving the complaining parties of their burden of proof with respect to the availability of less trade-restrictive alternative measures (raised by the United States); or

(ii) erred in finding that the COOL measure does not fulfil the objective of providing consumer information on origin with respect to meat (raised by the United States); and

(g) in the event that the Appellate Body reverses the Panel's finding that the COOL measure is inconsistent with Article 2.2 because it does not fulfil the objective of providing consumer information on origin with respect to meat products, then whether the COOL measure is more trade restrictive than necessary to fulfil a legitimate objective because there are less trade-restrictive alternative measures available to the United States (raised by Canada and by Mexico).

235. In the event that the Appellate Body reverses the Panel's finding that the COOL measure is inconsistent with Article 2.1 of the *TBT Agreement*, then the following issues are raised by Canada and by Mexico:

(a) whether the Panel erred in exercising judicial economy with respect to Canada's and Mexico's claims that the COOL measure is inconsistent with Article III:4 of the GATT 1994; and

(b) whether the COOL measure is inconsistent with Article III:4 of the GATT 1994.

236. In the event that the Appellate Body reverses the Panel's finding that the COOL measure is inconsistent with Article 2.1 of the *TBT Agreement*, and does not find that the COOL measure is inconsistent with Article III:4 of the GATT 1994, then the following issues are raised by Canada and by Mexico:

(a) whether the Panel erred in exercising judicial economy with respect to Canada's and Mexico's claims under Article XXIII:1(b) of the GATT 1994; and,

(b) whether the application of the COOL measure nullifies or impairs benefits accruing to Canada and to Mexico, within the meaning of Article XXIII:1(b) of the GATT 1994.

IV. BACKGROUND AND OVERVIEW OF THE MEASURES AT ISSUE

237. Before commencing our analysis of the issues of law and legal interpretations raised in this appeal, we provide an overview of the measures at issue and briefly outline certain pertinent facts and background information, as identified by the Panel. For additional details in this regard, recourse should be had to the Panel Reports.[357]

[357] See, in particular, Panel Reports, paras. 7.75-7.142.

238. Before the Panel, Canada and Mexico challenged the following five measures: (i) the "COOL statute"[358]; (ii) the "2009 Final Rule (AMS)"[359]; (iii) the "Vilsack letter"[360]; (iv) the "Interim Final Rule (AMS)"[361], and (v) the "Interim Final Rule (FSIS)".[362] The Panel assessed the first two of these instruments—the COOL statute and its implementing regulations, that is, the 2009 Final Rule (AMS)—together as the "COOL measure".[363] The Panel determined, however, "that the Vilsack letter should be considered as a separate measure distinguishable from the COOL statute and the 2009 Final Rule (AMS)"[364], and the complainants have not appealed such finding. The Panel decided not to make findings or recommendations on the Interim Final Rule (AMS) or the Interim Final Rule (FSIS), because they had expired prior to the establishment of the Panel.[365] This is also not appealed. The principal measure at issue in this appeal is the COOL measure. As explained further below, the Vilsack letter also has some relevance in the context of Canada's appeal regarding Articles III:4 and XXIII:1(b) of the GATT 1994 even though,

[358] The Agricultural Marketing Act of 1946 (60 Stat. 1087, *United States Code*, Title 7, section 1621 *et seq.*) (see Panel Exhibits MEX-1 and MEX-9), as amended by the Farm Security and Rural Investment Act of 2002, Public Law No. 107-171, section 10816, 116 Stat. 134, 533-535 (Panel Exhibits CDA-1 and MEX-2) (the "2002 Farm Bill") and the Food, Conservation, and Energy Act of 2008, Public Law No. 110-234, section 11002, 122 Stat. 923, 1351-1354 (Panel Exhibits CDA-2 and MEX-3) (the "2008 Farm Bill"). Through the enactment of the 2002 and 2008 Farm Bills, the COOL requirements were inserted into the Agricultural Marketing Act of 1946 as section 1638, and in turn codified as *United States Code*, Title 7, section 1638. (Panel Reports, paras. 7.12, 7.13, and 7.77)

[359] Final Rule on Mandatory Country of Origin Labeling of Beef, Pork, Lamb, Chicken, Goat Meat, Wild and Farm-Raised Fish and Shellfish, Perishable Agricultural Commodities, Peanuts, Pecans, Ginseng, and Macadamia Nuts, published in *United States Federal Register*, Vol. 74, No. 10 (15 January 2009) 2704-2707, codified as *United States Code of Federal Regulations*, Title 7, Part 65—Country of Origin Labeling of Beef, Pork, Lamb, Chicken, Goat Meat, Perishable Agricultural Commodities, Macadamia Nuts, Pecans, Peanuts, and Ginseng (Panel Exhibits CDA-5 and MEX-7).

[360] A letter dated 20 February 2009 from the US Secretary of Agriculture, Thomas J. Vilsack, to "Industry Representative[s]" (Panel Exhibits CDA-6 and MEX-8).

[361] Interim Final Rule on Mandatory Country of Origin Labeling of Beef, Pork, Lamb, Chicken, Goat Meat, Perishable Agricultural Commodities, Peanuts, Pecans, Ginseng, and Macadamia Nuts, published in *United States Federal Register*, Vol. 73, No. 149 (1 August 2008) 45106 (Panel Exhibits CDA-3 and MEX-4).

[362] *Supra*, para. 2 and footnote 13 thereto.

[363] Panel Reports, para. 7.61. The Panel explained that it did not consider the "COOL measure" to constitute a measure itself, but used the term to reflect "the collective effect of the operation of the COOL statute and the 2009 Final Rule (AMS) in respect of the country of origin labelling requirements contained in those instruments". (*Ibid.*)

[364] Panel Reports, para. 7.63.

[365] Panel Reports, paras. 7.30, 7.33, and 7.34. The Panel nevertheless noted the "legal and substantive connection between the Interim Final Rule (AMS) and the 2009 Final Rule (AMS)", which are both regulations implementing the COOL statute, and stated that it would take account of the Interim Final Rule (AMS) in its examination of the measures at issue. (*Ibid.*, para. 7.31. See also paras. 7.32, 7.34, 7.84, and 7.85) Pursuant to the US rulemaking process, an interim rule is issued for comments, and then subsequently superseded by a final rule. (*Ibid.*, paras. 7.84 and 7.85)

according to the United States, this measure was "withdrawn" in the course of these appellate proceedings.[366]

A. The COOL Measure

1. Introduction

239. The COOL measure comprises the COOL statute, passed by the US Congress, and its implementing regulations, promulgated by the Secretary of Agriculture through the US Department of Agriculture's (the "USDA") Agricultural Marketing Service ("AMS") (the 2009 Final Rule (AMS)). The COOL measure is a US internal measure, as opposed to a customs or border measure. It imposes an obligation on retailers selling specific products in the United States to label those products with their country of origin. This obligation applies irrespective of whether the products are imported or domestically produced. Specifically, the COOL statute provides that "a retailer of a covered commodity shall inform consumers, at the final point of sale of the covered commodity to consumers, of the country of origin of the covered commodity."[367] Both beef and pork are covered by the COOL measure.[368] The products at issue in these disputes are livestock, that is, cattle and hogs.[369] Although "livestock" are not formally covered by the COOL measure, the Panel found that the COOL measure "applies not only to beef and pork but also to cattle and hogs".[370] The Panel found that the COOL measure is a technical regulation subject to the requirements of Article 2 of the *TBT Agreement*.[371] This finding is not appealed.

---

[366] See *infra*, para. 251.

[367] Panel Reports, para. 7.87 (quoting COOL statute, section 1638a(a)(1)).

[368] In addition to beef and pork, the COOL measure also applies to lamb, chicken, goat meat, wild and farm-raised fish and shellfish, perishable agricultural commodities, peanuts, pecans, ginseng and macadamia nuts. (Panel Reports, para. 7.78 (referring to COOL statute, sections 1638(2)(A) and 1638a(a)(1)))

[369] Panel Reports, para. 7.64.

[370] Panel Reports, para. 7.246. The Panel noted that, "[f]ormally speaking, the category of 'covered commodities' under the COOL measure includes only beef and pork, not livestock." However, "without upstream livestock producers and processors providing the necessary information on origin as defined by the COOL measure, [the] retail labelling requirements are impossible to fulfil". (*Ibid.*) The United States acknowledges that the recordkeeping requirements under the COOL measure affect livestock directly. (United States' appellant's submission, para. 78) Hogs and pork are relevant only to the dispute initiated by Canada. (See Panel Reports, footnote 196 to heading VII.C.3(a)(ii) at p. 52, and para. 7.140)

[371] Based on the three-pronged test articulated by the Appellate Body in *EC – Sardines* to establish whether a document qualifies as a technical regulation, the Panel found that the COOL measure is a technical regulation within the meaning of Annex 1.1 to the *TBT Agreement* because: (i) compliance with the COOL measure is mandatory; (ii) the COOL measure applies to an identifiable product or group of products, namely beef and pork, and livestock (that is, cattle and hogs); and (iii) the COOL

240. The COOL measure is concerned with "country of origin" labelling, and specifically defines "origin" for purposes of this measure.[372] In the case of meat, including beef and pork[373], "origin" is defined as a function of the country(ies) in which the production steps involving the animals from which that meat is derived took place.[374] There are three relevant production steps for this purpose: birth, raising, and slaughter.[375] Meat labelled under the COOL measure may, therefore, have one or more countries of origin depending on where these steps took place.[376] For other covered commodities, such as perishable agricultural commodities, origin is defined as the single country in which they have been "produced", which is defined as "harvested".[377] Throughout these Reports, and except where the context clearly indicates otherwise, the term "origin" refers to origin as defined by the COOL measure for beef and pork, that is, the country(ies) where the cattle and hogs from which beef and pork are derived were born, raised, and slaughtered.

241. The definition of the "origin" of meat under the COOL measure differs from the conceptions of "origin" generally employed by the United States and other Members for customs purposes. For customs purposes, the United States relies on the rules of substantial transformation for determining the origin of

---

measure lays down one or more product characteristics by imposing a country of origin labelling requirement. (Panel Reports, paras. 7.162, 7.207, and 7.214) See also Appellate Body Report, *EC – Sardines*, para. 176.

[372] The 2009 Final Rule (AMS) expressly refers to "origin ... as defined by this law (e.g., born, raised, and slaughtered or produced)". (2009 Final Rule (AMS), section 65.300(f))

[373] This definition of "origin" also applies to lamb, chicken, and goat meat. (2009 Final Rule (AMS), section 65.260(a)) Furthermore, as explained further below, there are four different origin categories for muscle cuts of meat under the COOL measure: (i) United States country of origin; (ii) multiple countries of origin; (iii) imported for immediate slaughter; and (iv) foreign country of origin.

[374] Panel Reports, para. 7.89 (quoting *United States Code*, Title 7, section 1638a(2)(A)-(D)). Similarly, in the case of farm-raised fish and shellfish, "origin" is defined as a function of the country(ies) in which fish or shellfish were "hatched, raised, harvested, and processed". (Final Rule on Mandatory Country of Origin Labeling of Beef, Pork, Lamb, Goat Meat, Wild and Farm-Raised Fish and Shellfish, Perishable Agricultural Commodities, Peanuts, Pecans, Ginseng, and Macadamia Nuts, published in *United States Federal Register*, Vol. 74, No. 10 (15 January 2009) 2701-2704, codified as *United States Code of Federal Regulations*, Title 7, Part 60—Country of Origin Labeling for Fish and Shellfish (Panel Exhibits CDA-5 and MEX-7), section 60.128(c))

[375] See *infra*, footnote 390.

[376] If, for example, an animal is born and raised in Canada, and then slaughtered in the United States, according to the COOL measure, the countries of origin of the meat derived from that animal are Canada and the United States.

[377] 2009 Final Rule (AMS), section 65.225. For these covered commodities, there is in principle a single country of origin (that is, the country of harvesting) under the COOL measure. However, even for these commodities a label may indicate multiple countries of origin when products of the same type but with different origins are combined. (2009 Final Rule (AMS), section 65.300(g))

products imported into the United States.[378] The substantial transformation criterion confers origin exclusively to the country where the processing of food took place, which, in the case of meat, is the country where the animal is slaughtered. Accordingly, for customs purposes, meat can have no more than one country of origin.[379]

242. In addition to requiring retailers to provide information on the origin of the beef and pork that they sell, the COOL measure requires upstream suppliers to provide retailers with information on the origin of the meat supplied.[380] The measure also imposes certain obligations with respect to the manner in which information on origin is to be conveyed to consumers.[381] Furthermore, the COOL measure imposes recordkeeping requirements on producers along the livestock and meat production chain as part of its "audit verification system"[382], and grants auditing authority and enforcement powers to the Secretary of Agriculture.[383] The retailers subject to the COOL requirements are defined as those entities selling in excess of $230,000 worth of fruit and vegetables per year.[384] "Food service establishments", such as restaurants, cafeterias, and enterprises providing ready-to-eat foods are expressly exempted from the scope of the COOL requirements.[385] Any covered commodities that are an "ingredient

---

378 Panel Reports, para. 7.674 (referring to Canada's and Mexico's responses to Panel Question 59). The Panel also noted that for imports from a North American Free Trade Agreement ("NAFTA") country there are two sets of rules regarding NAFTA qualification: one set for preference purposes and another for marking purposes. Usually they have the same outcome. The NAFTA Marking Rules are based on the tariff-shift principle, according to which the tariff classification of the imported product is compared to the tariff classification of the finished product to determine whether a sufficient shift has occurred to warrant a change of origin. (*Ibid.*)

379 If, for example, an animal is born and raised in Brazil, and then slaughtered in Argentina, according to the substantial transformation rules, the country of origin of the meat derived from that animal is exclusively Argentina. (See Panel Reports, para. 7.734)

380 The COOL measure seeks to ensure that retailers are in possession of the information that they need to convey to their customers, and therefore establishes that "[a]ny person engaged in the business of supplying a covered commodity to a retailer shall provide information to the retailer indicating the country of origin of the covered commodity". (Panel Reports, paras. 7.205, 7.212, and 7.316; COOL statute, section 1638a(e))

381 The 2009 Final Rule (AMS) states that notification can be made in "the form of a placard, sign, label, sticker, band, twist tie, pin tag, or other format that allows consumers to identify the country of origin", and "must be legible and placed in a conspicuous location, so as to render it likely to be read and understood by a customer under normal conditions of purchase". (Panel Reports, paras. 7.110 and 7.111; 2009 Final Rule (AMS), section 65.400(a)-(b)) The Rule further states that the declaration of the country of origin may be made in the form of a statement, such as "Product of USA", or may contain the name of the country only, such as "USA" or "Mexico". (Panel Reports, para. 7.112; 2009 Final Rule (AMS), section 65.400(a))

382 Panel Reports, para. 7.116.

383 Panel Reports, paras. 7.116-7.122.

384 Panel Reports, para. 7.101 (referring to 2009 Final Rule (AMS), section 65.205).

385 Panel Reports, paras. 7.106, 7.107 (quoting COOL statute, section 1638(4)), and 7.108 (quoting 2009 Final Rule (AMS), section 65.140).

in a processed food item" are excluded from the scope of the COOL measure.[386] Origin information is not required to be provided in respect of such processed food items and, for beef and pork, this exclusion encompasses processing resulting in a change of their character—such as cooking, curing, smoking, and restructuring.[387]

2. *Categories of Origin for Meat*

243. The COOL statute establishes four categories of origin for muscle cuts of meat.[388]

- **Category A – United States country of origin**: meat derived from animals that are "exclusively born, raised, and slaughtered in the United States"[389];
- **Category B – Multiple countries of origin**: meat derived from animals:
    (1) "not exclusively born, raised, and slaughtered in the United States"; or
    (2) "born, raised, or slaughtered in the United States"; and
    (3) "not imported into the United States for immediate slaughter".
- **Category C – Imported for immediate slaughter**: meat derived from animals "imported into the United States for immediate slaughter"; and

[386] Panel Reports, para. 7.104 and footnote 159 thereto (referring to 2009 Final Rule (AMS), section 65.220)). See also 2009 Final Rule (AMS), section 65.135(b).

[387] Panel Reports, para. 7.105 (referring to 2009 Final Rule (AMS), section 65.220).

[388] See Panel Reports, para. 7.89; and COOL statute, section 1638a(2)(A)-(D). We do not address the additional category for ground meat (Category E) and the associated labelling rules since the Panel concluded that the complainants had not established that these result in less favourable treatment for imported livestock, and no participant appeals this finding. (See Panel Reports, para. 7.437)

[389] The COOL statute also defines meat as qualifying for US origin when it is derived from animals that were: (i) "born and raised in Alaska or Hawaii and transported for a period of not more than 60 days through Canada to the United States and slaughtered in the United States"; or (ii) "present in the United States on or before July 15, 2008, and once present in the United States, remained continuously in the United States". (Panel Reports, para. 7.89; COOL statute, section 1638a(a)(2)(A)(ii) and (iii))

- **Category D – Foreign country of origin**: meat derived from animals "not born, raised, or slaughtered in the United States".

244. Category A is therefore reserved for meat derived from animals for which all production steps (birth, raising, and slaughter) took place in the United States. Both Categories B and C involve meat of mixed origin, in the sense that they have more than one country of origin. For each of these categories, at least one production step has taken place outside the United States, and at least one production step has taken place within the United States. They are distinguished based on whether the animals were born in a foreign country and then raised and slaughtered in the United States (Category B), or raised outside the United States and then imported into the United States for immediate slaughter, that is, to be slaughtered within two weeks of the date the animal enters the United States (Category C).[390] Category D is reserved for meat produced from animals that are slaughtered outside the United States and imported into the United States in the form of meat.

3. *Labelling*

245. The COOL statute requires US retailers to provide consumers with country or countries of origin information for the meat they sell within the US market. The details as to how retailers are to comply with this obligation are elaborated in the 2009 Final Rule (AMS). Category D meat must be labelled according to the country of origin declared on import documentation for customs purposes.[391] Except where the flexibilities described in the next paragraph apply, Category A meat must be labelled as US origin[392], and the labels for Category B and Category C meat must reflect all of the countries in which relevant production steps occurred. For both Category B meat and Category C meat, *at least one* production step will have occurred in the United States, meaning that the United States is one of the countries of origin that must be indicated on the relevant label. Meat derived from animals born outside the United States but raised and slaughtered in the United States (Category B meat) must be labelled as a product of the United States and the foreign country in which the animal

[390] Panel Reports, para. 7.92. The term "raised" is considered to be "[the] period of time from birth until slaughter" or, in the case of animals imported for immediate slaughter, "the period of time from birth until date of entry into the United States". (*Ibid.*, para. 7.92; 2009 Final Rule (AMS), section 65.235) The term "imported for immediate slaughter" refers to "consignment directly from the port of entry to a recognized slaughtering establishment and slaughtered within 2 weeks from the date of entry". (Panel Reports, para. 7.92; 2009 Final Rule (AMS), section 65.180)

[391] Panel Reports, para. 7.119. As explained above, this means that the label will specify the country in which the animal from which the meat was derived was slaughtered.

[392] See Panel Reports, footnote 140 to para. 7.92.

was born, and the countries of origin may be listed in any order.[393] For meat derived from animals imported into the United States for immediate slaughter (Category C meat), labels must indicate all of the countries of origin of the animal, but cannot list the United States first.[394] Because the countries of origin for Category B meat can be listed in any order, the labels for Categories B and C meat could look the same in practice.[395]

246. The 2009 Final Rule (AMS) includes certain flexibilities regarding the permitted origin labelling of "commingled" meat. The implementing regulations do not define the term "commingle". They do, however, define "commingled covered commodities" as "covered commodities (of the same type) presented for retail sale in a consumer package that have been prepared from raw material sources having different origins".[396] Under the 2009 Final Rule (AMS), additional labelling rules apply in respect of meat that is commingled on a single production day.[397] Under these rules, when commingling occurs, the resulting meat may bear a different label from the one it should in principle bear under the above rules.[398] More specifically, when Category A and Category B meat is commingled during a single production day, all of the resulting meat may be labelled as if it were Category B meat[399], even though a particular piece of meat may have been derived from a Category A animal.[400] Further, when Category B and Category C meat is commingled during a single production day, all of the

---

[393] 2009 Final Rule (AMS), section 65.300(e)(1) and (4). Labels on Category B meat could state, for example, "Product of the US and Mexico" or "Product of Mexico and the US".

[394] 2009 Final Rule (AMS), section 65.300(e)(3). Labels following this rule would indicate "Product of Canada and the US", for example.

[395] See Panel Reports, para. 7.97 and footnote 148 thereto (referring to 2009 Final Rule (AMS), section 65.300(e)(4)) and footnote 929 to para. 7.702.

[396] 2009 Final Rule (AMS), section 65.125.

[397] Panel Reports, paras. 7.93-7.95 (referring to 2009 Final Rule (AMS), sections 65.300(e)(2) and 65.300(e)(4)). In response to Panel Question 29, the United States explained that US meat processors tend to operate one or two production shifts each day followed by a clean-up shift and, thus, "a single production day" is generally understood in the industry as the period of production between the two clean-up shifts. (Panel Reports, footnote 143 to para. 7.93)

[398] Panel Reports, para. 7.96.

[399] The Panel found that, under the Interim Final Rule (AMS)—not at issue in this appeal—there was a "major flexibility", because it was possible to label Category A meat as if it were Category B meat, *even without commingling*. (Panel Reports, para. 7.290 (quoting Interim Final Rule (AMS), section 65.300(e)(1)(i))) This flexibility, however, ended with the 2009 Final Rule (AMS). (*Ibid.*, para. 7.293)

[400] Panel Reports, para. 7.96. Section 65.300(e)(2) of the 2009 Final Rule (AMS) provides the following with regard to the commingling of Category A and Category B meat:

> For muscle cut covered commodities derived from animals born, raised, and slaughtered in the U.S. that are commingled during a production day with muscle cut covered commodities described in § 65.300(e)(1), the origin may be designated as Product of the United States, Country X, and (as applicable) Country Y.

resulting meat may be labelled as if it were Category B meat, even though a particular piece of meat may have been derived from a Category C animal.[401] In both cases, since the resulting meat may be labelled as if it were Category B meat, the declared countries of origin for all commingled meat may be listed *in any order*.[402]

247. The Panel understood the different labelling possibilities for muscle cuts of meat to be as follows[403]:

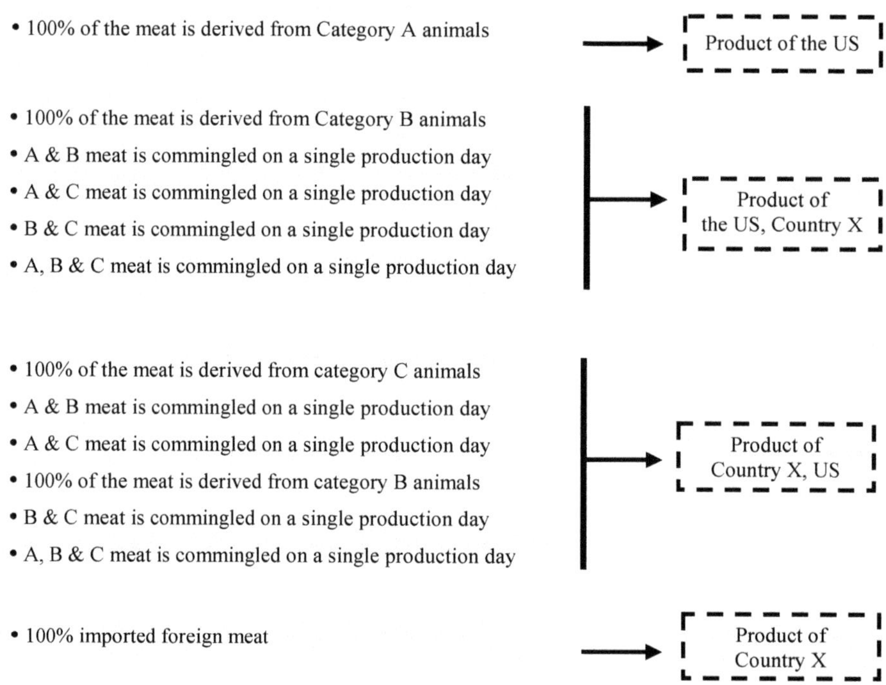

[401] Panel Reports, para. 7.96. Section 65.300(e)(4) of the 2009 Final Rule (AMS) states, *inter alia*:

> For muscle cut covered commodities derived from animals that are born in Country X or Country Y, raised and slaughtered in the United States, that are commingled during a production day with muscle cut covered commodities that are derived from animals that are imported into the United States for immediate slaughter as defined in § 65.180, the origin may be designated as Product of the United States, Country X, and (as applicable) Country Y.

[402] Panel Reports, para. 7.97; 2009 Final Rule (AMS), section 65.300(e)(4).

[403] See Panel Reports, para. 7.100. We note that, although the COOL measure applies the same labelling rules to meat that has three countries of origin, this simplified table only presents the labelling possibilities for meat that has one or two countries of origin.

248. The Panel included in its Reports some photographs submitted by the parties showing samples of Labels A, B, and C.

Figure 1. Samples of Label A submitted by Mexico and by the United States

Figure 2. Samples of Label B submitted by Canada and by the United States[404]

[404] Panel Reports, paras. 7.114 and 7.115; Panel Exhibits CDA-161 and US-67.

Figure 3. Sample of Label C submitted by the United States[405]

249. To label accurately muscle cuts of beef and pork under the COOL measure, a covered retailer needs to possess information on where the relevant production steps have taken place. This information can be obtained only from the upstream livestock and meat supply chain.[406] Accordingly, the COOL measure requires "[a]ny person engaged in the business of supplying a covered commodity to a retailer [to] provide information to the retailer indicating the country of origin of the covered commodity".[407] The COOL measure thus prescribes an "unbroken chain of reliable country of origin information" with regard to every animal and muscle cut.[408] In order to comply with the COOL requirements, livestock and meat producers need to possess, at each and every stage of the supply and distribution chain, information on origin, as defined by the COOL measure, and they need to transmit such information to the next processing stage.[409] To verify compliance, the COOL measure imposes certain recordkeeping requirements on producers along the meat production chain as part of its "audit verification system"[410], and grants authority to the Secretary of

---

405 Panel Reports, para. 7.115; Panel Exhibit US-67.

406 Panel Reports, para. 7.316.

407 Panel Reports, para. 7.316 (quoting COOL statute, section 1638a(e)).

408 Panel Reports, para. 7.317.

409 *Ibid.*

410 Panel Reports, para. 7.117. The 2009 Final Rule (AMS) specifies that any person engaged in the business of supplying a covered commodity to a retailer, whether directly or indirectly, must maintain records to establish and identify the immediate previous source (if applicable) and immediate subsequent recipient of a covered commodity for a period of one year from the date of transaction. (*Ibid.*, para. 7.118 (referring to 2009 Final Rule (AMS), section 65.500(b)(3))) In the case of beef and pork, the COOL measure provides that the slaughterhouse is the supplier responsible for "initiating a country(ies) of origin claim", and must therefore possess records to substantiate that claim for one

Agriculture to "conduct an audit of any person that prepares, stores, handles, or distributes a covered commodity for retail sale".[411] The Secretary is prohibited, however, from requiring any records other than those maintained in the course of the normal conduct of business of the audited person[412], or from using a mandatory identification system to verify the origin of meat.[413] The COOL measure also prescribes certain enforcement procedures and sanctions for non-compliance.[414]

B. *The Vilsack Letter*

250. The Vilsack letter was distributed to industry representatives on 20 February 2009 by the newly appointed US Secretary of Agriculture, Thomas J. Vilsack. At the time, the 2009 Final Rule (AMS) had been issued but had not yet entered into force. In the letter, Secretary Vilsack expressed concerns about certain aspects of the 2009 Final Rule (AMS), which had been promulgated by the prior Administration. Accordingly, he suggested "that the industry *voluntarily* adopt" certain practices in their implementation of the COOL requirements "to ensure that consumers are adequately informed about the source of food products".[415] Among the three specific suggestions made were: (i) "processors should voluntarily include information about what production step occurred in each country when multiple countries appear on the label"; and (ii) given that "[t]he definition of processed foods contained in the Final Rule may be too broadly drafted", "voluntary labeling would be appropriate" for covered commodities processed by "curing, smoking, broiling, grilling, or steaming".[416] The letter concludes with the following statement regarding compliance with the Secretary's suggestions:

---

year from the date of the transaction. (*Ibid.*, para. 7.118 (referring to 2009 Final Rule (AMS), section 65.500(b)(1))) With respect to imported commodities that fall under Category D, the 2009 Final Rule (AMS) requires that records provide clear product tracking from the port of entry into the United States to the immediate subsequent recipient, and accurately reflect the country of origin as identified in relevant Customs and Border Protection entry documents. (*Ibid.*, para. 7.119 (referring to 2009 Final Rule (AMS), section 65.500(b)(4)))

411 Panel Reports, para. 7.116; COOL statute, section 1638a(d)(1).

412 Panel Reports, para. 7.117; COOL statute, section 1638a(d)(2)(B).

413 Panel Reports, paras. 7.117 and 7.121; COOL statute, section 1638a(f)(1).

414 If retailers or suppliers fail to comply with the COOL requirements, they are first given notice that they have 30 days to remedy the non-compliance, after which, if they have not made a good faith effort to comply with the COOL requirements and continue wilfully to violate them, the Secretary may impose a fine of up to $1,000 per violation. (Panel Reports, para. 7.122; COOL statute, sections 1638b(a) and 1638b(b)) As of October 2010, no fines for failure to comply had been imposed. (Panel Reports, para. 7.122 (referring to United States' response to Panel Question 27))

415 Panel Reports, para. 7.123 (quoting Vilsack letter, p. 1). (emphasis added by the Panel)

416 Vilsack letter, p. 1. See also Panel Reports, paras. 7.125 and 7.126. Secretary Vilsack further suggested that, because the 60-day rule applicable to the labelling of ground meat "allows for labels

> The Department of Agriculture will be closely reviewing industry compliance with the regulation and its performance in relation to these suggestions for voluntary action. Depending on this performance, I will carefully consider whether modifications to the rule will be necessary to achieve the intent of Congress.[417]

251. According to the United States, the Vilsack letter was "withdrawn" on 5 April 2012.[418] This measure was implicated only in Canada's appeal regarding Articles III:4 and XXIII:1(b) of the GATT 1994. At the oral hearing, Canada stated that it was no longer seeking specific rulings from the Appellate Body on this measure, but requested us to take the Vilsack letter into account in the event that we rule on Canada's claims regarding the COOL measure under Articles III:4 and XXIII:1(b) of the GATT 1994.

C. *Background Information*

252. The market for livestock and meat in Canada, Mexico, and the United States is highly integrated, which means that different stages of livestock and meat production are often performed in more than one of these countries.[419] Canada and Mexico export cattle, and Canada also exports hogs, to the United States.[420] The vast majority of Canada's and Mexico's livestock exports are destined for the United States to be processed into meat.[421] However, Canadian and Mexican exports of cattle and hogs account for only a small percentage of total livestock slaughter in the United States.[422] Livestock are classified as "fed"

---

to be used in a way that does not clearly indicate the product's country of origin", producers should "[r]educ[e] the time allowance to ten days" to "enhance the credibility of the label". (Vilsack letter, pp. 1-2; Panel Reports, para. 7.127) For additional information on labelling rules for ground meat (Category E), see Panel Reports, paras. 7.421-7.437.

417 Vilsack letter, p. 2.

418 United States' appellee's submission, para. 90 and footnote 193 thereto (referring to a USDA letter to industry representatives, available at: <http://www.ams.usda.gov/AMSv1.0/cool>).

419 Panel Reports, para. 7.140. In general, the production process from cattle to beef consists of four stages: (i) the cow/calf stage; (ii) the backgrounding stage; (iii) the feeding stage; and (iv) the slaughtering, cutting, and packing stage. (*Ibid.*, para. 7.129) The production process from hogs to pork also involves four stages: (i) the farrowing stage; (ii) the nursery stage; (iii) the feeding stage; and (iv) the slaughtering, cutting, and packing stage. (*Ibid.*, para. 7.135)

420 Panel Reports, para. 7.140.

421 Panel Reports, para. 7.142.

422 Panel Reports, para. 7.142. The Panel found that, over the period 2005-2010, Canadian cattle imports as a share of US cattle slaughter, and Mexican cattle imports as a share of US feed placements, were both below 5%. It also found that Canadian hogs imported into the United States never exceeded a 10% share of US hog slaughter between 2005 and 2009. (*Ibid.*, para. 7.474)

or "feeder" depending on whether they are ready for slaughter ("fed"), or are still at the backgrounding or feeding operations stage ("feeder").[423] Most of the Canadian cattle exported to the United States are *fed cattle*, which are born and raised in Canada and exported to the United States for immediate slaughter.[424] Mexico, on the other hand, generally exports *feeder cattle* to US backgrounding and feeding operations, where they are raised to be subsequently slaughtered.[425] The products at issue in these disputes are imported Canadian cattle and hogs and imported Mexican cattle, which are used in the United States to produce beef and pork.[426] Muscle cuts of meat produced from such cattle and hogs may fall into Category B or C, but can never fall into Category A (exclusively US origin meat) or D (imported meat).

253. In addition to the COOL measure, the United States has maintained several voluntary labelling programmes for beef, such as the USDA grade labels, private premium label programmes, and animal production and raising label programmes.[427] None of these labelling programmes relates to hogs or pork.[428] USDA grade labels relate to the quality of meat and are affixed on the majority of beef derived from cattle slaughtered in the United States.[429] Other voluntary labelling programmes affect a smaller proportion of beef marketed in the United States.[430] These include private premium labelling programmes–such as the one for Certified Angus Beef.[431] Prior to the enactment of the COOL measure, the

---

423 Panel Reports, para. 7.141. "Fed" cattle and hogs are also referred to as "slaughter cattle" and "slaughter hogs". (See *supra*, footnote 419)

424 Panel Reports, para. 7.141. A smaller but considerable portion of Canadian cattle are *feeder cattle*, which are exported to the United States directly after the backgrounding stage. (*Ibid.*) Canadian hog exports to the United States involve a larger proportion of *feeder* than *fed hogs*. (*Ibid.*)

425 Because of a lack of sufficient grasslands in Mexico and the general lack of well-developed feed grains and cattle-feedlot sectors, Mexican cattle is generally exported to the United States immediately after the cow/calf stage. (Panel Reports, para. 7.141)

426 Panel Reports, para. 7.64.

427 See Panel Reports, paras. 7.405-7.412. The Panel noted that these voluntary programmes "exist to the extent that they meet consumer demand, i.e. they are also contingent upon consumers' willingness to pay for the type and quality of beef covered by such programmes". (*Ibid.*, para. 7.411)

428 Panel Reports, para. 7.412.

429 Panel Reports, para. 7.406. According to the United States, under the USDA's quality grading programme, the AMS assesses the quality and yield attributes of beef carcasses, and assigns them quality grades, such as "USDA Prime", "USDA Choice", or "USDA Select". (United States' response to Panel Question 43, para. 77) The United States noted that, although the USDA grading programme is voluntary, nearly 95% of the federally inspected meat is graded by the USDA, and the majority of this meat graded as USDA Choice or Prime is subsequently labelled with its grade at the retail level. (United States' second written submission to the Panel, para. 59; United States' response to Panel Question 43, para. 78)

430 Panel Reports, para. 7.406.

431 See Panel Reports, para. 7.410. The United States explained that, in addition to the USDA grading programme, US meat packers have also established their own private "value added" or "premium" programmes for higher quality meat, such as the Certified Angus Beef programme.

USDA's Food Safety Inspection Service ("FSIS") regulations also allowed certain animal production and raising labels to be approved for use on beef.[432] Thus, for example, meat could be labelled "Fresh American Beef" when all relevant production steps took place in the United States.[433] Furthermore, under FSIS rules concerning export requirements, producers were permitted to label beef "Product of the U.S.A." even when the meat products received only minimal processing in the United States.[434] The Panel did not make specific findings with respect to the operation of these voluntary labelling programmes. However, it repeatedly took note of the United States' argument that one of the objectives of the COOL measure is to prevent consumer confusion with regard to USDA grade labels and the previous FSIS "Product of the U.S.A." labelling system.[435]

(United States' response to Panel Question 43, para. 79 (referring to Panel Exhibit CDA-36); United States' second written submission to the Panel, para. 59)

[432] According to Mexico, this FSIS policy on "Product of the U.S.A." label has been cancelled to ensure conformity with the COOL regulations. (Mexico's first written submission to the Panel, para. 103) While the Panel made no specific finding in this regard, it did refer to this labelling programme as part of the "previous COOL regime", and to the United States' arguments about the "previous FSIS voluntary 'Product of the U.S.A.' labelling system". (Panel Reports, paras. 7.713 and 7.712, respectively)

[433] With respect to animal production and raising labelling programmes, the United States explained that the USDA's FSIS—which had the authority to approve meat product labels before the products could enter commerce—evaluated label claims that highlighted certain aspects of the way in which animals used as the source for meat products are raised. (United States' response to Panel Question 43, para. 83) The FSIS regulations permitted fresh beef to be labelled with terms such as "U.S. (Species)", "U.S.A. Beef", and "Fresh American Beef" when cattle from which the final product derived were born, raised, slaughtered, and prepared in the United States. (United States' first written submission to the Panel, para. 30; Mexico's first written submission to the Panel, paras. 101 and 102 (referring to Panel Exhibit MEX-32))

[434] Panel Reports, para. 7.589 (referring to United States' first written submission to the Panel, paras. 30 and 31; United States' response to Panel Question 56; and Panel Exhibits US-17 and MEX-32). Mexico noted that, according to FSIS regulations, meat satisfying the requirements for export from the United States labelled as "Product of the U.S.A." could also bear this label when sold within the US market. In order to qualify for the "Product of the U.S.A." label, the meat must have been "prepared" in the United States. (Mexico's first written submission to the Panel, para. 101 (referring to Panel Exhibit MEX-32)) The United States also noted that the FSIS permitted a "Product of the U.S.A." designation to be placed on any meat product as long as the animal from which the meat was derived was prepared in some form in the United States. (United States first written submission to the Panel, para. 30 and footnote 35 thereto (referring to Panel Exhibit MEX-32); United States' response to Panel Question 56)

[435] The Panel explained that the United States pointed to the following two types of confusion prior to the COOL measure:

> First, many consumers in the United States mistakenly believed that meat products affixed with a USDA grade label were derived from animals born, raised, and slaughtered in the United States when this was not the case. Second, many US consumers may also have been misled by the FSIS "Product of the U.S.A." labelling system, which allowed producers to voluntarily use this label if the meat products received minimal processing in the United States. (footnotes omitted)

V. ARTICLE 2.1 OF THE *TBT AGREEMENT*

A. Introduction

254. Canada and Mexico claimed before the Panel that the COOL measure is inconsistent with the United States' national treatment obligation under Article 2.1 of the *TBT Agreement*. The Panel found that "the COOL measure, [particularly] in regard to the muscle cut meat labels, violates Article 2.1 because it affords imported livestock treatment less favourable than that accorded to like domestic livestock."[436] The United States appeals this finding, as well as the Panel's intermediate conclusion that "the COOL measure on its face accords different treatment to imported livestock".[437] The United States also asserts that the Panel acted inconsistently with its duties under Article 11 of the DSU in reaching certain factual findings on which, according to the United States, the Panel's legal conclusions under Article 2.1 are based.

255. In addressing the United States' appeal, we first briefly describe the Panel's findings under Article 2.1, followed by a summary of the United States' claims on appeal. We then provide an interpretation of the "treatment no less favourable" requirement of Article 2.1 of the *TBT Agreement*, followed by a review of the Panel's findings, in the light of the participants' arguments.

B. Summary of the Panel's Findings

256. In examining the consistency of the COOL measure with Article 2.1 of the *TBT Agreement*, the Panel first found that the COOL measure is a "technical regulation" within the meaning of Annex 1.1 to the *TBT Agreement*[438], because it is "mandatory"[439], applies to an identifiable product or group of products[440], and, by imposing a country of origin labelling requirement, lays down one or more product characteristics.[441] Subsequently, the Panel found that Canadian cattle and US cattle, and Mexican cattle and US cattle, are "like products", and that

(Panel Reports, para. 7.589. See also, paras. 7.618, 7.642, 7.671, and 7.712)

[436] Canada Panel Report, para. 8.3(b); Mexico Panel Report, para. 8.3(b). See also Panel Reports, paras. 7.420 and 7.548.

[437] United States' appellant's submission, para. 84. See also paras. 78 and 81 (referring to Panel Reports, paras. 7.295 and 7.296).

[438] Panel Reports, para. 7.216.

[439] Panel Reports, para. 7.162.

[440] Panel Reports, para. 7.207.

[441] Panel Reports, para. 7.214.

Canadian hogs and US hogs are also "like products" for purposes of Article 2.1.[442] These findings have not been appealed.

257. The Panel then identified three issues that it would address in its analysis of whether the COOL measure affords less favourable treatment to imported livestock: (i) whether the different categories of labels under the COOL measure accord different treatment to imported livestock; (ii) whether the COOL measure involves segregation and, consequently, differential costs for imported livestock; and (iii) whether, through the compliance costs involved, the COOL measure creates any incentive to process domestic livestock, thus reducing the competitive opportunities of imported livestock.[443]

258. With regard to whether the different categories of labels under the COOL measure accord different treatment to imported livestock, the Panel first considered the flexibilities that the measure allows with respect to the use of the different labels.[444] The Panel focused on "the distinction between Label A, defined as 'United States Country of Origin' in the COOL statute, and the rest of the labels, which all involve livestock with an imported element".[445] The Panel found that meat eligible for Label A—that is, derived exclusively from livestock born, raised, and slaughtered in the United States—may, under the commingling flexibilities, carry Label B or C, which usually would indicate meat derived from mixed-origin livestock, including livestock imported into the United States for immediate slaughter. Meat derived from imported livestock, by contrast, can use only Label B or C, even under the commingling flexibilities, and is never eligible for Label A.[446] The Panel considered this "difference" in treatment, however, to be only "the starting point" for its analysis of less favourable treatment.[447]

259. The Panel then found that Article 2.1 of the *TBT Agreement*, like Article III:4 of the GATT 1994, prohibits not only *de jure* but also *de facto* less favourable treatment for imported like products, and proceeded to analyze whether the measure accords *de facto* less favourable treatment to imported

---

442 Panel Reports, para. 7.256.

443 Panel Reports, para. 7.279.

444 For a full summary of the operation of the COOL measure, see section IV.A of these Reports.

445 Panel Reports, para. 7.289.

446 Panel Reports, para. 7.295.

447 Panel Reports, para. 7.296 (quoting Panel Report, *EC – Trademarks and Geographical Indications (Australia)*, para. 7.464). The Panel further observed that formally different treatment of imported products does not necessarily amount to less favourable treatment of such imports, and that, in any event, the complainants were not challenging any formal difference in treatment under the COOL measure but instead raised claims of *de facto* less favourable treatment. (*Ibid.*, para. 7.296)

livestock.[448] In this respect, the Panel analyzed the complainants' arguments that the COOL measure modifies the conditions of competition in the US market to the detriment of imported livestock because it entails higher costs for handling imported livestock than for handling domestic livestock.

260. With respect to the operation of the COOL measure, the Panel found that, "[t]o accurately label muscle cuts under the COOL measure, a covered retailer needs to possess information on where livestock processing steps determining origin under the COOL measure have taken place with regard to each muscle cut", and observed that "[t]his information can be obtained only from the upstream livestock and meat supply chain."[449] Therefore, "as a matter of principle, the COOL measure prescribes an unbroken chain of reliable country of origin information with regard to every animal and muscle cut."[450] The Panel further reasoned that, although the COOL measure "does not explicitly require segregation"[451], "a practical way to ensure that the chain of reliable information on country of origin required by the COOL measure remains unbroken is the segregation of meat and livestock according to origin as defined by the COOL measure."[452] The Panel noted in this regard that the COOL measure does not require traceability of livestock or impose any particular livestock identification system, and prohibits USDA auditors from requesting of producers any records not maintained in the normal course of business.[453]

261. Regarding the costs associated with segregation, the Panel preliminarily found that, if imported and domestic livestock are both being processed, in principle, they both equally necessitate segregation, and therefore incur the same resulting implementation costs. At the same time, however, the Panel also considered it "evident that the more origins and ... labels involved, the more intensive the need for segregation throughout the livestock and meat supply and distribution chain", which "leads to higher compliance costs".[454]

262. The Panel then analyzed five possible business scenarios for market participants subject to the COOL measure[455]: (i) processing domestic and imported livestock and meat irrespective of origin and solely according to price and quality; (ii) processing meat exclusively from domestic livestock;

---

[448] Panel Reports, paras. 7.296, 7.299, and 7.302.

[449] Panel Reports, para. 7.316.

[450] Panel Reports, para. 7.317.

[451] Panel Reports, para. 7.315.

[452] Panel Reports, para. 7.320.

[453] Panel Reports, para. 7.319.

[454] Panel Reports, para. 7.331. See also para. 7.346.

[455] Panel Reports, para. 7.333.

(iii) processing meat exclusively from imported livestock; (iv) processing exclusively domestic and exclusively imported livestock at different times; and (v) processing both domestic and imported meat by commingling the two on the same production day. Based on its review of these scenarios, the Panel found the least costly scenarios to be those involving either exclusively domestic livestock or exclusively imported livestock. Comparing these two scenarios more closely, the Panel reasoned that "it seems logical" that processing exclusively domestic livestock is in general less costly and more viable than processing exclusively imported livestock.[456] The Panel considered this to be so because livestock imports are small in comparison to domestic livestock production, such that US demand cannot be satisfied with exclusively foreign livestock, and because US livestock is often geographically closer to US domestic markets than imported livestock.[457]

263. In addition, the Panel found that the costs of compliance with the COOL measure "cannot be fully passed on to consumers"[458], citing evidence that consumers are unwilling to bear such costs[459], as well as "direct evidence of major slaughterhouses applying a considerable COOL discount of USD 40-60 per head for imported livestock".[460] With regard to the United States' arguments that producers are avoiding compliance costs by taking advantage of the commingling flexibilities built into the COOL measure, the Panel recognized that some commingling appears to be taking place, but found it difficult to ascertain its precise extent.[461] The Panel also noted additional evidence demonstrating that: (i) fewer processing plants are accepting imported livestock, and those that do, do so at specific, limited times[462]; (ii) contractual terms for suppliers of imported livestock have changed as a result of the COOL measure[463]; (iii) certain suppliers of imported livestock have suffered significant financial disadvantages resulting from the COOL measure, including an increased price difference between imported and domestic livestock and the refusal of financial institutions to provide credits and loans[464]; and (iv) imported cattle have been excluded from "particularly profitable" premium beef programmes, such as the Certified Angus Beef programme.[465] Based on all of the

---

456 Panel Reports, para. 7.349.

457 *Ibid.*

458 Panel Reports, para. 7.353.

459 Panel Reports, paras. 7.354 and 7.355.

460 Panel Reports, para. 7.356. See also para. 7.379.

461 Panel Reports, paras. 7.364-7.370.

462 Panel Reports, paras. 7.376 and 7.377.

463 Panel Reports, para. 7.378.

464 Panel Reports, para. 7.379.

465 Panel Reports, para. 7.380.

above findings, the Panel concluded that "the COOL measure creates an incentive to use domestic livestock—and a disincentive to handle imported livestock—by imposing higher segregation costs on imported livestock than on domestic livestock", thereby "affect[ing] competitive conditions in the US market to the detriment of imported livestock".[466]

264. Having reached this conclusion, the Panel went on to examine the evidence of actual trade effects submitted by the parties. It did so while stating that it already had reached its conclusions under Article 2.1, and that an analysis of the actual trade effects was not "indispensable" to its disposition of the complainants' Article 2.1 claims.[467] The Panel deemed the trade effects of the COOL measure to be an "important factual matter" linked to its conclusions with respect to the violation of Article 2.1[468], and reviewed a substantial amount of data regarding the level and prices of cattle and hog imports, including econometric studies submitted by both the United States and Canada. The Panel concluded that the data, and in particular the "Sumner Econometric Study"[469] submitted by Canada, "concurs with our finding that the COOL measure ... accords less favourable treatment within the meaning of Article 2.1 of the *TBT Agreement*".[470]

C. *Overview of the Issues Raised on Appeal*

265. The United States requests us to reverse the Panel's finding that the COOL measure is inconsistent with Article 2.1 of the *TBT Agreement*. According to the United States, in reaching its findings under Article 2.1, the Panel relied upon a flawed legal interpretation of that provision and failed to make an objective assessment of the facts as required by Article 11 of the DSU. Specifically, the United States argues that the Panel erred in finding that: (i) the COOL measure treats imported livestock differently than domestic livestock; and (ii) the COOL measure accords less favourable treatment to imported livestock than to like domestic livestock by modifying the conditions of competition to the detriment of imported livestock. The United States also identifies several findings as having been made in a manner inconsistent with the Panel's duties under Article 11 of the DSU, namely, its findings that: (i) the segregation of livestock is "necessitated" by the COOL measure; (ii) "commingling" is not occurring on a widespread basis; and (iii) the COOL measure had a negative and significant impact on the prices of imported

466 Panel Reports, para. 7.372. See also paras. 7.381, 7.420, and 7.548.

467 Panel Reports, para. 7.445.

468 Panel Reports, para. 7.444.

469 *Supra*, footnote 82 (Panel Exhibit CDA-79).

470 Panel Reports, para. 7.546.

livestock and resulted in an increased "price differential" between domestic and imported livestock.[471] The United States further argues that the COOL measure is "even-handed", and does not discriminate against imported livestock in violation of Article 2.1. After setting out our interpretation of Article 2.1 of the *TBT Agreement*, we address each of the United States' claims on appeal in the order discussed above.

D. *Interpretation of Article 2.1 of the TBT Agreement*

266. Article 2 of the *TBT Agreement* governs the "Preparation, Adoption and Application of Technical Regulations by Central Government Bodies", and its first paragraph provides that, "[w]ith respect to their central government bodies":

> 2.1 Members shall ensure that in respect of technical regulations, products imported from the territory of any Member shall be accorded treatment no less favourable than that accorded to like products of national origin and to like products originating in any other country.

267. Article 2.1 contains both a national treatment obligation and a most-favoured nation ("MFN") treatment obligation. The MFN treatment obligation prohibits discrimination through technical regulations among like products imported from different countries, while the national treatment obligation prohibits discrimination between domestic and imported like products. In order to establish a violation of the national treatment obligation in Article 2.1, a complainant must demonstrate three elements: (i) that the measure at issue is a "technical regulation" as that term is defined in Annex 1.1 to the *TBT Agreement*; (ii) that the imported and domestic products at issue are "like products"; and (iii) that the measure at issue accords less favourable treatment to imported products than to like domestic products.[472] The first two of these elements have previously been addressed by the Appellate Body[473], and are not at issue in this appeal.[474]

---

[471] United States' appellant's submission, paras. 103-116 (referring to Panel Reports, paras. 7.316, 7.327, 7.336, 7.352, 7.353, 7.356, 7.364, 7.366-7.368, 7.379, 7.487, and 7.542).

[472] Appellate Body Report, *US – Clove Cigarettes*, para. 87. The elements required to establish an MFN violation are identified in paragraph 202 of the Appellate Body report in *US – Tuna II (Mexico)*.

[473] The Appellate Body examined the first element, whether a measure is a technical regulation, in its reports in *US – Tuna II (Mexico)* (paras. 183-188); *EC – Asbestos* (paras. 63-70); and *EC – Sardines* (paras. 175 and 176). It examined the second element, whether the products at issue are "like", in its report in *US – Clove Cigarettes* (paras. 108-120).

[474] See Panel Reports, paras. 7.216 and 7.256; and United States' appellant's submission, para. 54.

268. With regard to the national treatment obligation, which is the particular obligation before us in these disputes, an analysis of less favourable treatment involves an assessment of whether the technical regulation at issue modifies the conditions of competition in the relevant market to the detriment of the group of imported products vis-à-vis the group of like domestic products.[475] At the same time, the specific context of Article 2.1 of the *TBT Agreement*—which includes Annex 1.1; Article 2.2; and the second, fifth, and sixth recitals of the preamble—supports a reading that Article 2.1 does not operate to prohibit *a priori* any restriction on international trade.[476] As the Appellate Body has already observed, technical regulations are measures that, by their very nature, establish distinctions between products according to their characteristics, or related processes and production methods, as reflected in Annex 1.1 to the *TBT Agreement*.[477] Therefore, Article 2.1 should not be read to mean that any distinctions, in particular ones that are based *exclusively* on such particular product characteristics or on particular processes and production methods, would *per se* constitute less favourable treatment within the meaning of Article 2.1.[478]

269. The Appellate Body recognized in *US – Clove Cigarettes* and *US – Tuna II (Mexico)* that relevant guidance for interpreting the term "treatment no less favourable" in Article 2.1 may be found in the jurisprudence relating to Article III:4 of the GATT 1994.[479] As under Article III:4, the national treatment obligation of Article 2.1 prohibits both *de jure* and *de facto* less favourable treatment.[480] That is, "a measure may be *de facto* inconsistent with Article 2.1 even when it is origin-neutral on its face."[481] In such a case, the panel must take into consideration "the totality of facts and circumstances before it"[482], and assess any "implications" for competitive conditions "discernible from the design, structure, and expected operation of the measure".[483] Such an examination must take account of all the relevant features of the market, which

[475] Appellate Body Report, *US – Clove Cigarettes*, para. 180; Appellate Body Report, *US – Tuna II (Mexico)*, para. 215.

[476] Appellate Body Report, *US – Tuna II (Mexico)*, para. 212.

[477] Appellate Body Report, *US – Tuna II (Mexico)*, para. 211.

[478] Appellate Body Report, *US – Tuna II (Mexico)*, para. 211; Appellate Body Report, *US – Clove Cigarettes*, para. 169. See also Appellate Body Report, *EC – Asbestos*, para. 100 (where the Appellate Body found, in the context of Article III:4 of the GATT 1994, that a measure drawing distinctions between like products will not, "for this reason alone", accord imported products less favourable treatment than that accorded to the group of like domestic products).

[479] Appellate Body Report, *US – Clove Cigarettes*, paras. 100 and 176-180; Appellate Body Report, *US – Tuna II (Mexico)*, paras. 214, 215, and 236-239.

[480] Appellate Body Report, *US – Clove Cigarettes*, para. 175.

[481] Appellate Body Report, *US – Tuna II (Mexico)*, para. 225.

[482] Appellate Body Report, *US – Clove Cigarettes*, para. 206.

[483] Appellate Body Report, *Thailand – Cigarettes (Philippines)*, para. 130.

may include the particular characteristics of the industry at issue[484], the relative market shares in a given industry[485], consumer preferences[486], and historical trade patterns.[487] That is, a panel must examine the operation of the particular technical regulation at issue in the particular market in which it is applied.

270. In the context of both Article III:4 of the GATT 1994 and Article 2.1 of the *TBT Agreement*, for a measure to be found to modify the conditions of competition in the relevant market to the detriment of imported products, there must be a "genuine relationship" between the measure at issue and the adverse impact on competitive opportunities for imported products.[488] In each case, the relevant question is whether it is the governmental measure at issue that "affects the conditions under which like goods, domestic and imported, compete in the market within a Member's territory".[489] While a measure may not require certain treatment of imports, it may nevertheless create incentives for market participants to behave in certain ways, and thereby treat imported products less favourably.[490] However, changes in the competitive conditions in a marketplace that are "*not* imposed directly or indirectly by law or governmental regulation, but [are] rather solely the result of private entrepreneurs acting on their own calculations of comparative costs and benefits", cannot be the basis for a finding that a measure treats imported products less favourably than domestic like products.[491] In every case, it is *the effect of the measure on the competitive opportunities in the market* that is relevant to an assessment of whether a challenged measure has a detrimental impact on imported products.

271. If a panel determines that a measure has such an impact on imported products, however, this will not be dispositive of a violation of Article 2.1. This is because not every instance of a detrimental impact amounts to the less favourable treatment of imports that is prohibited under that provision. Rather, some technical regulations that have a *de facto* detrimental impact on imports may not be inconsistent with Article 2.1 when such impact stems exclusively

---

484 Appellate Body Report, *US – Tuna II (Mexico)*, para. 234.

485 Panel Report, *Mexico – Taxes on Soft Drinks*, para. 8.119.

486 Appellate Body Report, *US – Tuna II (Mexico)*, para. 233.

487 See, for example, Appellate Body Report, *Korea – Various Measures on Beef*, para. 145.

488 Appellate Body Report, *US – Tuna II (Mexico)*, footnote 457 to para. 214 (referring to Appellate Body Report, *Thailand – Cigarettes (Philippines)*, para. 134). See also Appellate Body Report, *Korea – Various Measures on Beef*, para. 137.

489 Appellate Body Report, *Korea – Various Measures on Beef*, para. 149.

490 Appellate Body Reports, *China – Auto Parts*, paras. 195 and 196; Appellate Body Report, *US – FSC (Article 21.5 – EC)*, para. 212.

491 Appellate Body Report, *Korea – Various Measures on Beef*, para. 149. (original emphasis) See also Appellate Body Report, *US – Tuna II (Mexico)*, para. 236.

from a legitimate regulatory distinction.[492] In contrast, where a regulatory distinction is not designed and applied in an even-handed manner[493]—because, for example, it is designed or applied in a manner that constitutes a means of arbitrary or unjustifiable discrimination—that distinction cannot be considered "legitimate", and thus the detrimental impact will reflect discrimination prohibited under Article 2.1. In assessing even-handedness, a panel must "carefully scrutinize the particular circumstances of the case, that is, the design, architecture, revealing structure, operation, and application of the technical regulation at issue".[494]

272. With respect to the burden of proof under Article 2.1, the Appellate Body found in *US – Tuna II (Mexico)* that, as with all affirmative claims, it is for the complaining party to show that the treatment accorded to imported products is less favourable than that accorded to like domestic products.[495] Where the complaining party has met the burden of making its *prima facie* case, it is then for the responding party to rebut that showing. If, for example, the complainant adduces evidence and arguments showing that the measure is designed and/or applied in a manner that constitutes a means of arbitrary or unjustifiable discrimination of the group of imported products and thus is not even-handed, this would suggest that the measure is inconsistent with Article 2.1. If, however, the respondent shows that the detrimental impact on imported products stems exclusively from a legitimate regulatory distinction, it follows that the challenged measure is not inconsistent with Article 2.1.[496]

E. Application of Article 2.1 of the TBT Agreement: "Treatment No Less Favourable"

273. In analyzing the Panel's findings under Article 2.1 of the *TBT Agreement* with respect to "treatment no less favourable", we first address the two claims of the United States relating to the detrimental impact that the Panel found was caused by the COOL measure, which challenge: (i) the Panel's intermediate conclusion that the labelling requirements under the COOL measure provide for different treatment of meat derived from imported livestock and meat derived from domestic livestock; and (ii) the Panel's finding that the COOL measure has a detrimental impact on imported livestock. We then examine the United States'

---

492 Appellate Body Report, *US – Clove Cigarettes*, para. 182; Appellate Body Report, *US – Tuna II (Mexico)*, para. 215.

493 Appellate Body Report, *US – Clove Cigarettes*, para. 182; Appellate Body Report, *US – Tuna II (Mexico)*, para. 216.

494 Appellate Body Report, *US – Clove Cigarettes*, para. 182.

495 Appellate Body Report, *US – Tuna II (Mexico)*, para. 216.

496 *Ibid.*

claims under Article 11 of the DSU. Finally, we review the Panel's factual findings as they relate to an assessment of whether any detrimental impact caused by the COOL measure reflects discrimination in violation of Article 2.1 of the *TBT Agreement*.

1. Detrimental Impact

(a) "Different Treatment"

274. At the outset of its analysis of less favourable treatment, the Panel explained the relationship among the muscle cut labels under the COOL measure. At the end of this short subsection, and before turning to assess Canada's and Mexico's claims that the COOL measure accords *de facto* less favourable treatment to imported livestock, the Panel observed that:

> ... under the COOL measure, in particular the 2009 Final Rule (AMS), Label B may be used for Label A meat but only in the case of commingling on a single production day. Under the COOL measure, therefore, imported livestock is ineligible for the label reserved for meat from exclusively US-origin livestock, whereas in certain circumstances meat from domestic livestock is eligible for a label that involves imported livestock.[497]

The Panel cautioned, however, that "this difference" was just "the starting point" for its analysis of the complainants' claims of less favourable treatment, and noted that the complainants were not alleging there to be "any formal difference in the treatment accorded to domestic and imported livestock *per se*".[498]

275. The United States argues on appeal that the Panel was wrong to conclude that "the COOL measure on its face accords different treatment to imported livestock".[499] The United States emphasizes that the COOL measure applies the same recordkeeping requirements to all US livestock producers regardless of the origin of their livestock, and requires retailers to label meat derived from both domestic and imported livestock "in the exact same set of conditions (i.e., retailers must affix a label to all categories of meat unless one of the origin-neutral exceptions applies)".[500] The United States adds that the COOL

[497] Panel Reports, para. 7.295.

[498] Panel Reports, paras. 7.296 and 7.297.

[499] United States' appellant's submission, para. 84.

[500] United States' appellant's submission, para. 90.

measure also does not treat muscle cuts of meat differently based on whether they are derived from imported or from domestic livestock. On the contrary, all meat derived from both domestic and imported livestock must be labelled with the same relevant information. Even in the circumstance where the Panel suggested that there is different treatment — that is, where commingling occurs — domestic and imported livestock are still being treated in the same way, because the same label, that is, a B or C Label, is affixed to all meat derived from commingled animals.

276. Canada and Mexico point out that the Panel did not rely upon its "initial finding of *de jure* different treatment"[501] in coming to its conclusion that the COOL measure is inconsistent with Article 2.1. Rather, the Panel recognized that different treatment on the face of a measure does not necessarily constitute less favourable treatment, as indicated by the Appellate Body's findings in *Korea – Various Measures on Beef*.[502] The Panel was correct, therefore, in going on to analyze whether, on the specific facts of this case, the COOL measure creates an incentive in favour of processing exclusively domestic livestock and a disincentive against handling imported livestock. Canada additionally contends that the United States "distorts the finding by the Panel" when it asserts that the Panel relied on "the commingling flexibility provided with regard to the labelling of meat" in reaching its conclusion that the COOL measure, on its face, provides different treatment to imported and domestic livestock.[503] Rather, the Panel found that the definitions of the four muscle cut labels under the measure are mutually exclusive, and went on to describe the limited flexibility, provided for under the measure, between the use of Label A and the rest of the labels when commingling is involved.

277. As discussed above, a finding of formal different treatment is not required for a finding of *de facto* less favourable treatment to be made. In the context of Article III:4 of the GATT 1994, the Appellate Body has expressly found that "[a] formal difference in treatment between imported and like domestic products is ... neither necessary, nor sufficient, to show a violation" of the national treatment obligation.[504]

278. In any event, we do not consider that the Panel in this case relied on any instance of different treatment explicitly provided for under the COOL measure to support its ultimate finding that the COOL measure accords less favourable

[501] Mexico's appellee's submission, para. 73. See also Canada's appellee's submission, paras. 61-63.

[502] See Mexico's appellee's submission, para. 68 (referring to Appellate Body Report, *Korea – Various Measures on Beef*, para. 137); and Canada's appellee's submission, para. 63.

[503] Canada's appellee's submission, para. 62 (quoting United States' appellant's submission, para. 57).

[504] Appellate Body Report, *Korea – Various Measures on Beef*, para. 137.

treatment to imported livestock than to like domestic livestock. As described above, the statement challenged by the United States was made as part of the Panel's explanation of the terms and requirements of the COOL measure, and the Panel itself did not characterize it as a finding or a legal conclusion. Indeed, the Panel expressly recognized that the formally different treatment of imported and like domestic products does not necessarily constitute less favourable treatment.[505] Moreover, the Panel stated that "this difference" under the COOL measure was only "the starting point" of its analysis, and highlighted that the claims before it were claims of *de facto* less favourable treatment.[506]

279. The statement challenged by the United States thus forms part of an introductory section setting out the Panel's understanding of the measure's *de jure* structure and operation, and precedes its indepth analysis of *de facto* discrimination. We view the statement, made at this initial stage of the Panel's reasoning, merely as a passing observation regarding the extent to which the COOL measure *de jure* treats imported livestock differently than domestic livestock. Furthermore, the Panel's later conclusions with regard to the COOL measure's *de facto* inconsistency with Article 2.1 are not based on this statement, or even directly connected to it. We also note that the United States does not challenge under Article 11 of the DSU any of the explanations or assessments made by the Panel in this initial section of its analysis setting out its understanding of the relationships among muscle cut labels under the COOL measure. For these reasons, we *find* that the Panel did not err, in paragraph 7.295 of the Panel Reports, in stating that the COOL measure treats imported livestock differently than domestic livestock.

(b) Did the Panel Err in Finding that the COOL Measure Has a Detrimental Impact on Imported Livestock?

(i) Arguments on Appeal

280. In appealing the Panel's ultimate finding of inconsistency under Article 2.1 of the *TBT Agreement*, the United States submits that, in order to determine whether the COOL measure accords less favourable treatment to imported products than to like domestic products, the Panel should have followed past Appellate Body reports in *Thailand – Cigarettes (Philippines)*, *Korea – Various Measures on Beef*, and *Dominican Republic – Import and Sale of Cigarettes*. According to the United States, these reports generally focused on: (i) whether the measure *itself* treats imported products differently and less favourably than

[505] Panel Reports, para. 7.296 (referring to Appellate Body Report, *Korea – Various Measures on Beef*, paras. 135-137).

[506] Panel Reports, paras. 7.296 and 7.297.

like domestic products *on the basis of their origin*; and (ii) to the extent that there are adverse effects on imported products, whether these effects are attributable to the measure *itself* or are based on external non-origin-related factors, such as pre-existing market conditions and the independent actions of private market actors.[507] The United States argues that the Panel, however, wrongfully assessed "whether imported livestock are equally competitive with domestic livestock".[508] This "fundamental misunderstanding" led the Panel to focus its entire analysis of less favourable treatment on "how compliance costs may differ for market participants depending on their business models and sourcing patterns and how the independent actions of these market participants in response to potential costs might hypothetically affect imported livestock in light of pre-existing market conditions".[509]

281. The United States asserts that, under Article 2.1, where imported products suffer detrimental impact because of the decisions of private market actors, and not because of the challenged measure itself, the measure cannot be found to accord less favourable treatment to imported products. Furthermore, where a measure does not treat imported products less favourably than like domestic products *on the basis of origin*, the measure cannot be found to violate the national treatment obligation. The United States claims that, in promulgating the COOL requirements, it included the commingling provisions "to help mitigate the need [for private actors] to ever make any choices that could potentially have an adverse effect on imports".[510] It insists, therefore, that any market participant's choice to segregate livestock instead of taking advantage of the commingling provisions is not legally required by the measure. Similarly, "any choice to pass the costs of segregation on to domestic or imported livestock instead of distributing them equally is not a choice required by the measure."[511] The United States also notes that, if segregation does occur, it will equally affect both imported and domestic livestock since the act of segregation inherently involves separating one type of animal from another.

282. The United States suggests that the Panel acknowledged that the measure itself did not lead to the detrimental impact on imports when the Panel found that the incentive to process exclusively domestic livestock was related to the fact

[507] United States' appellant's submission, para. 68 (referring to Appellate Body Report, *Korea – Various Measures on Beef*, paras. 137 and 143-148; Appellate Body Report, *Thailand – Cigarettes (Philippines)*, paras. 128-140; Appellate Body Report, *Dominican Republic – Import and Sale of Cigarettes*, para. 96; Panel Report, *US – Tuna II (Mexico)*, para. 7.334; and Panel Report, *Japan – Film*, paras. 10.381 and 10.382).

[508] United States' appellant's submission, para. 62. See also paras. 63-65.

[509] United States' appellant's submission, para. 88. See also paras. 87 and 92.

[510] United States' appellant's submission, para. 94.

[511] United States' appellant's submission, para. 91.

that "[l]ivestock imports have been and remain small compared to overall livestock production and demand", such that demand in the US market cannot be fulfilled with exclusively foreign livestock[512]; and that, because "US livestock is often geographically closer to most if not all US domestic markets, ... processing exclusively imported livestock and meat remains a relatively less competitive option".[513] In the United States' view, these facts demonstrate that the Panel relied on factors external to the COOL measure to determine the existence of a detrimental impact on imported livestock, instead of finding that the COOL measure itself had such a detrimental impact.

283. Canada and Mexico assert that the Panel's legal approach to interpreting and applying Article 2.1 was correct, and that the Panel rightly found that the COOL measure itself treats imported livestock less favourably than domestic livestock. Mexico argues that the United States' approach would restrict the scope of the legal analysis to exclude indirect effects of the measure on the conditions of competition in the market, such as the measure's impact on market forces and market participants. Canada and Mexico both contend that, given that the Panel was performing a *de facto* analysis, it was appropriate for the Panel to take into consideration "all relevant facts and circumstances in the market" to determine how the imposition of the COOL measure affects the equality of competitive opportunities.[514] In their view, the Panel was therefore correct in considering the low market share of imported livestock as part of its assessment under Article 2.1, as this factor has also been considered by panels and the Appellate Body in cases dealing with "treatment no less favourable" in the context of Article III:4 of the GATT 1994.[515]

284. Regarding the decisions of private market participants, Canada and Mexico further argue that, as the Panel found, any decisions made by private actors in order to comply with the COOL measure were not "solely" the result of their independent business calculations, but were attributable to the economic incentives and disincentives created by the COOL measure. Canada adds that there was "an abundance of uncontradicted specific evidence before the Panel" that the COOL measure "itself" caused private actors to change their behaviour to the detriment of imported cattle and hogs.[516]

---

[512] United States' appellant's submission, para. 92 (quoting Panel Reports, para. 7.349).

[513] *Ibid.*

[514] Mexico's appellee's submission, para. 82. See also Canada's appellee's submission, para. 39.

[515] See Canada's appellee's submission, para. 43 (referring to Appellate Body Report, *Korea – Various Measures on Beef*, para. 137; Panel Report, *Mexico – Taxes on Soft Drinks*, paras. 8.56, 8.119, and 8.120; and Appellate Body Report, *US – Clove Cigarettes*, para. 222).

[516] Canada's appellee's submission, para. 48 (referring to Panel Reports, paras. 7.374-7.380 and 7.420).

285. Finally, Canada and Mexico assert that Article 2.1 does not require complainants to show that the less favourable treatment accorded to imported products is expressly, or effectively, based on origin. The United States' arguments in this respect are based on its reading of the Appellate Body's findings in *Dominican Republic – Import and Sale of Cigarettes*, and in Canada and Mexico's view, the United States' understanding of that case was rejected by the more recent findings of the Appellate Body in *US – Clove Cigarettes*.[517]

(ii) Analysis

286. We first recall that, as explained above, Article 2.1 of the *TBT Agreement* prohibits both *de jure* and *de facto* discrimination between domestic and like imported products. Therefore, where a technical regulation does not discriminate *de jure*, a panel must determine whether the evidence and arguments adduced by the complainant in a specific case nevertheless demonstrate that the operation of that measure, in the relevant market, has a *de facto* detrimental impact on the group of like imported products. A panel's analysis must take into consideration the totality of the facts and circumstances before it, including any implications for competitive conditions discernible from the design and structure of the measure itself, as well as all features of the particular market at issue that are relevant to the measure's operation within that market. In this regard, "*any* adverse impact on competitive opportunities for imported products vis-à-vis like domestic products that is caused by a particular measure may potentially be relevant" to a panel's assessment of less favourable treatment under Article 2.1.[518]

287. The United States is correct to point out that, as the Panel found, the COOL measure does not legally compel market participants to choose between processing either exclusively domestic or exclusively imported livestock. However, the Panel also found that the design of the COOL measure and its operation within the US market meant that segregation of livestock was "a practical way to ensure [compliance]".[519] In examining the various possible methods of compliance with the COOL measure, the Panel found that the less costly methods would include an "absolute form of segregation"[520], whereby producers choose to process either exclusively domestic or exclusively imported livestock. Given the particular circumstances of the US livestock market—including the fact that "[l]ivestock imports have been and remain small compared to overall US livestock production and demand, and US livestock

[517] Canada's appellee's submission, para. 41; Mexico's appellee's submission, para. 76.

[518] Appellate Body Report, *US – Tuna II (Mexico)*, para. 225. (original emphasis)

[519] Panel Reports, para. 7.320.

[520] Panel Reports, para. 7.337.

demand cannot be fulfilled with exclusively foreign livestock"[521]—the Panel concluded that the least costly way of complying with the COOL measure is to rely exclusively on domestic livestock.[522] The Panel then relied on this finding, together with its finding that the costs of compliance cannot fully be passed on to consumers, to find that the COOL measure creates an incentive for US market participants to process exclusively domestic livestock and reduces the competitive opportunities of imported livestock as compared to domestic livestock.[523]

288. In our view, the circumstances of these disputes are similar to those in *Korea – Various Measures on Beef*. In that case, Korea established a "dual retail system" that required small retailers to sell either exclusively domestic beef or exclusively imported beef. The Appellate Body held that "the treatment accorded to imported beef, as a consequence of the dual retail system established for beef by Korean law and regulation, is less favourable than the treatment given to like domestic beef".[524] The Appellate Body did not find a detrimental impact on imported beef due only to "[t]he legal necessity of making a choice" that the measure itself imposed.[525] Rather, it held that the adoption of a measure requiring such a choice to be made had the "direct practical effect", in that market, of denying competitive opportunities to imports.[526] Such an effect was not "solely the result of private entrepreneurs acting on their own calculations of comparative costs and benefits", but was the result of the governmental intervention that affected the conditions of competition for beef in Korea.[527] Thus, contrary to the United States' arguments in this respect, the findings in *Korea – Various Measures on Beef* do not stand for the proposition that private market participants must be legally required to make a choice in order for the incentives that determine how such choice will be exercised to be attributed to a governmental measure. The relevant question is whether it is the governmental measure at issue that affects the conditions under which like goods, domestic and imported, compete in the market. While a measure may not legally require certain treatment of imports, it may nevertheless create incentives for market participants to behave in certain ways, and thereby have the "practical effect"[528] of treating imported products less favourably.[529] Thus, the findings in *Korea –*

---

[521] Panel Reports, para. 7.349.

[522] Panel Reports, para. 7.350.

[523] Panel Reports, para. 7.357.

[524] Appellate Body Report, *Korea – Various Measures on Beef*, para. 148.

[525] Appellate Body Report, *Korea – Various Measures on Beef*, para. 146.

[526] Appellate Body Report, *Korea – Various Measures on Beef*, para. 145.

[527] Appellate Body Report, *Korea – Various Measures on Beef*, para. 149.

[528] Appellate Body Report, *Korea – Various Measures on Beef*, para. 145.

[529] See, for example, Appellate Body Reports, *China – Auto Parts*, paras. 195 and 196; and Appellate Body Report, *US – FSC (Article 21.5 – EC)*, para. 212.

Various Measures on Beef are consistent with, and support the proposition that, whenever the operation of a measure in the market creates incentives for private actors systematically to make choices in ways that benefit domestic products to the detriment of like imported products, then such a measure may be found to treat imported products less favourably.

289. We furthermore agree with Canada and Mexico that the Panel's findings indicate that the COOL measure itself, as applied in the US livestock and meat market, creates an incentive for US producers to segregate livestock according to origin, in particular by processing exclusively US-origin livestock.[530] We thus reject the United States' contention that the Panel wrongly attributed to the COOL measure a detrimental impact on imports caused exclusively by factors "external" to that measure.[531] A market's response to the application of a governmental measure is always relevant to an assessment of whether the operation of that measure accords *de facto* less favourable treatment to imported products. That is, if a specific technical regulation adopted by a Member gives rise to adverse effects in the market, which disparately impact imported products, such effects will be attributable to the technical regulation for purposes of examining less favourable treatment under Article 2.1.

290. We understand the Panel to have considered that, in this case, the small market share held by Canadian and Mexican livestock imports exacerbates the effects of the COOL measure. In making its finding under Article 2.1, the Panel acknowledged that the incentive created by the COOL measure is "partly due to the relatively small market share of imported livestock".[532] Such reasoning is not inconsistent with a finding that it was the COOL measure that caused the detrimental impact. Indeed, the opportunity for a technical regulation to discriminate may well derive from its operation within a given market that exhibits particular characteristics. In some instances, the market share held by imported products may be one such relevant characteristic.

291. We further emphasize that, while detrimental effects caused *solely* by the decisions of private actors cannot support a finding of inconsistency with Article 2.1, the fact that private actors are free to make various decisions in order to comply with a measure does not preclude a finding of inconsistency. Rather, where private actors are induced or encouraged to take certain decisions *because*

---

[530] The Panel found that US producers can also segregate livestock according to origin by processing foreign and domestic livestock on different days or at different times. (Panel Reports, paras. 7.333 and 7.339)

[531] We note that, in *US – Clove Cigarettes*, the Appellate Body "eschewed an additional enquiry" as to whether detrimental impact was "related to the foreign origin of the products or explained by other factors or circumstances". (Appellate Body Report, *US – Clove Cigarettes*, footnote 372 to para. 179)

[532] Panel Reports, para. 7.395.

of the incentives created by a measure, those decisions are not "independent" of that measure. As the Appellate Body noted, the "intervention of some element of private choice does not relieve [a Member] of responsibility ... for the resulting establishment of competitive conditions less favourable for the imported product than for the domestic product", and thus does not preclude a finding that the measure provides less favourable treatment.[533] In this case, the Panel expressly found that "[i]t is the result of the COOL measure ... that in the circumstances of the US market, market participants, when faced with the choice between a scenario involving exclusively domestic livestock and a scenario involving both domestic and imported livestock, opted predominantly for the former."[534] Had it not been for the COOL measure, the Panel reasoned, "market participants would not have opted this way".[535] We therefore find that the Panel properly examined whether the COOL measure modifies the conditions of competition in the US market to the detriment of imported livestock. We also disagree with the United States' characterization of the Panel's legal approach as requiring that imported livestock be "equally competitive" with domestic livestock.

292. Based on the foregoing, we *find* that the Panel did not err, in paragraphs 7.372, 7.381, and 7.420 of the Panel Reports, in finding that the COOL measure modifies the conditions of competition in the US market to the detriment of imported livestock by creating an incentive in favour of processing exclusively domestic livestock and a disincentive against handling imported livestock.

293. Although the Panel's legal approach to assessing detrimental impact was correct, the Panel ended its analysis under Article 2.1 of the *TBT Agreement* there. The Panel seems to have considered its finding that the COOL measure alters the conditions of competition to the detriment of imported livestock to be dispositive, and to lead, without more, to a finding of violation of the national treatment obligation in Article 2.1. In this sense, the Panel's legal analysis under Article 2.1 is incomplete. The Panel should have continued its examination and determined whether the circumstances of this case indicate that the detrimental impact stems exclusively from a legitimate regulatory distinction, or whether the COOL measure lacks even-handedness. As noted above, where a regulatory distinction is not designed and applied in an even-handed manner—for example, because it is designed or applied in a manner that constitutes a means of arbitrary or unjustifiable discrimination—that distinction cannot be considered legitimate and, thus, the detrimental impact will reflect discrimination prohibited under Article 2.1. Therefore, we consider it appropriate to review the Panel's findings as they relate to the design, architecture, revealing structure, operation, and

[533] Appellate Body Report, *Korea – Various Measures on Beef*, para. 146.

[534] Panel Reports, para. 7.403.

[535] *Ibid.*

application of the COOL measure in order to determine whether we can reach a conclusion in this respect.

294. Before doing so, however, we will assess the United States' arguments as to whether the Panel erred under Article 11 of the DSU in making its factual findings relating to the necessity of segregation, the extent of commingling taking place in the US market, and the increase in the price differential between imported and domestic livestock. Based in part on this examination, we will then proceed to determine whether the detrimental impact occasioned by the COOL measure stems exclusively from a legitimate regulatory distinction, or whether it reflects discrimination in violation of Article 2.1 of the *TBT Agreeement*.

2. *Did the Panel Err under Article 11 of the DSU in Making Certain Factual Findings in the Course of Its Analysis under Article 2.1 of the TBT Agreement?*

(a) Segregation and Commingling

(i) Arguments on Appeal

295. The United States argues that the Panel acted inconsistently with its obligations under Article 11 of the DSU in finding that the COOL measure "necessitates" segregation, and in ignoring evidence showing that producers are taking advantage of the commingling flexibilities contained in the measure in order to avoid segregation "on a widespread basis".[536] The United States presents these claims as interconnected. That is, in its view, not only did the Panel err in finding that the COOL measure "necessitates" segregation, but, had the Panel properly assessed the evidence before it regarding the extent to which producers were taking advantage of the "commingling" flexibilities *as an alternative to segregation*, it could not have found that segregation was necessary.[537]

296. The United States emphasizes the Panel's own finding that "the COOL measure does not explicitly require segregation, let alone the segregation of domestic and imported livestock".[538] The United States points to evidence showing that a significant proportion of muscle cuts of beef and pork is labelled "Product of the United States, Canada and Mexico", to argue that US producers are choosing to commingle, instead of segregate, their livestock.[539] The United

---

[536] United States' appellant's submission, para. 106.

[537] See United States' appellant's submission, para. 107.

[538] Panel Reports, para. 7.315.

[539] The United States claims that, "[g]iven the negligible number of livestock that are born in either Canada or Mexico, raised in the other country, and then slaughtered in the United States (e.g., born in

States highlights, in this regard, its exhibits containing photographs of such meat labels[540], as well as a USDA survey indicating that "approximately 22 percent of beef sold and 4 percent of the pork sold in the United States is derived from commingled livestock or meat (i.e., some combination of Category A, B, and C meat processed together on the same production day)".[541] Finally, the United States refers to two producer affidavits that, in its view, provide further evidence of the occurrence of commingling on a widespread basis.[542]

297. Canada submits that the United States has not substantiated its claims under Article 11 of the DSU. According to Canada, the threshold for establishing a violation of Article 11 is high, and it is not enough "to simply note a few pieces of evidence that the panel considered, ignore evidence that the panel also considered, and ask the Appellate Body to come to a contrary conclusion".[543] Therefore, the Panel's factual findings must stand. Regarding the extent of commingling in the US market, Canada acknowledges that commingling is happening "to some extent", but points out that it did not argue otherwise before the Panel. It argues that, in any event, taking advantage of the commingling flexibility does not eliminate the need for segregation.

298. Mexico emphasizes the "high legal threshold" established by the Appellate Body under Article 11 of the DSU, and contends that the United States' claims of error do not meet this threshold.[544] Mexico argues that the United States' argument focuses on evidence of commingling, and leaps to the conclusion that because commingling is occurring there cannot be less favourable treatment. Mexico argues that there is a "defect in the underlying premise of the US claim".[545] This is because, even in instances where commingling can be taken advantage of by slaughterhouses, segregation is still necessary during the upstream stages of production in order to comply with the commingling provisions, which require that at least one foreign-born animal be commingled with at least one US-born animal on a single production day.[546]

Mexico, raised in Canada, slaughtered in the United States)", the use of a label indicating US, Canadian, and Mexican origin necessarily indicates that the sources of these meat products were commingled. (United States' appellant's submission, para. 106 (first bullet point))

540 United States' appellant's submission, para. 106 (second bullet point (referring to Panel Exhibits US-67, US-95, US-96, and US-98)).

541 United States' appellant's submission, para. 106 (first bullet point (referring to Panel Exhibit US-145)).

542 United States' appellant's submission, para. 106 (third bullet point (referring to Panel Exhibits US-101 (BCI) and US-102 (BCI))).

543 Canada's appellee's submission, para. 33.

544 Mexico's appellee's submission, para. 94.

545 Mexico's appellee's submission, para. 101.

546 Mexico's appellee's submission, para. 100 (referring to Mexico's oral statement at the second Panel meeting, para. 25; and Mexico's response to Panel Question 44, para. 98).

Regarding the specific evidence of commingling referred to by the United States, Mexico claims that the United States itself acknowledged that the USDA survey on the use of the different labels is not "statistically reliable", and that the Panel therefore was not required either to discuss it or to rely on it.[547] Similarly, the Panel's finding on the limited evidentiary value of photographs of labels submitted by the United States was "well justified"[548], because the flexibilities in the labelling rules mean that a label indicating multiple origins cannot be understood as demonstrating that livestock have been commingled. Other pieces of evidence referred to by the United States contain some information as to how producers are complying with the COOL requirements, but do not clearly demonstrate that they are commingling. According to Mexico, the Panel's conclusion that the evidence did not provide compelling proof of the occurrence or extent of commingling is, therefore, "entirely reasonable".[549]

(ii) Analysis

299. We recall that, in accordance with Article 11 of the DSU, a panel is required to "consider all the evidence presented to it, assess its credibility, determine its weight, and ensure that its factual findings have a proper basis in that evidence".[550] It must further provide in its report "reasoned and adequate explanations and coherent reasoning" to support its findings.[551] Within these parameters, "it is generally within the discretion of the [p]anel to decide which evidence it chooses to utilize in making findings."[552] Although a panel must consider evidence before it in its totality, and "evaluate the relevance and probative force" of all of the evidence[553], a panel is not required "to discuss, in

547 Mexico's appellee's submission, paras. 103-105.

548 Mexico's appellee's submission, para. 108.

549 Mexico's appellee's submission, paras. 110 and 114.

550 Appellate Body Report, *Brazil – Retreaded Tyres*, para. 185 (referring to, *inter alia*, Appellate Body Report, *EC – Hormones*, paras. 132 and 133). See also Appellate Body Reports in *Australia – Salmon*, para. 266; *EC – Asbestos*, para. 161; *EC – Bed Linen (Article 21.5 – India)*, paras. 170, 177, and 181; *EC – Sardines*, para. 299; *EC – Tube or Pipe Fittings*, para. 125; *Japan – Apples*, para. 221; *Japan – Agricultural Products II*, paras. 141 and 142; *Korea – Alcoholic Beverages*, paras. 161 and 162; *Korea – Dairy*, para. 138; *US – Carbon Steel*, para. 142; *US – Gambling*, paras. 330 and 363; *US – Oil Country Tubular Goods Sunset Reviews*, para. 313; and *EC – Selected Customs Matters*, para. 258.

551 Appellate Body Report, *US – Upland Cotton (Article 21.5 – Brazil)*, footnote 618 to para. 293.

552 Appellate Body Report, *EC – Hormones*, para. 135.

553 Appellate Body Report, *US – Continued Zeroing*, para. 331; Appellate Body Report, *Korea – Dairy*, para. 137.

its report, each and every piece of evidence" put before it[554], or "to accord to factual evidence of the parties the same meaning and weight as do the parties".[555]

300. Not every error committed by a panel in the appreciation of the evidence will amount to reversible legal error.[556] The Appellate Body will not "interfere lightly" with a panel's factual findings[557], and will find that a panel failed to comply with its duties under Article 11 of the DSU only if it is satisfied that the panel has exceeded its authority as the initial trier of the facts.[558] Thus, when a participant claims that a panel "ignored" or "disregarded" a particular piece of evidence, the mere fact that a panel did not explicitly refer to that evidence in its reasoning does not suffice to demonstrate that the panel acted inconsistently with Article 11. Rather, a participant must explain why such evidence is so material to its case that the panel's failure explicitly to address and rely upon it casts doubt on the objectivity of the panel's factual assessment.[559]

301. We further recall that an appellant cannot succeed in an Article 11 claim by simply "recast[ing]" its arguments before the panel "under the guise of an Article 11 claim" on appeal.[560] Rather, a claim that a panel failed to comply with its duties under Article 11 of the DSU must stand on its own, and should not be made merely as a "subsidiary argument" in support of a claim that the panel erred in its application of a WTO provision.[561]

302. The United States challenges the Panel's finding that the COOL measure "necessitates" segregation. Given the nature of the United States' arguments, we consider it useful, at the outset, to scrutinize the actual language used by the Panel in its reasoning to determine more precisely what the Panel found. The

---

554 Appellate Body Report, *Australia – Apples*, para. 271; Appellate Body Report, *Brazil – Retreaded Tyres*, para. 202.

555 Appellate Body Report, *Australia – Salmon*, para. 267.

556 Appellate Body Report, *EC – Fasteners (China)*, para. 442; Appellate Body Report, *EC and certain member States – Large Civil Aircraft*, para. 1318.

557 Appellate Body Report, *EC – Sardines*, para. 299; Appellate Body Report, *US – Carbon Steel*, para. 142; Appellate Body Report, *US – Wheat Gluten*, para. 151.

558 Appellate Body Report, *US – Wheat Gluten*, para. 151.

559 Appellate Body Report, *EC – Fasteners (China)*, paras. 442 and 499; Appellate Body Report, *US – Clove Cigarettes*, para. 154; Appellate Body Report, *EC and certain member States – Large Civil Aircraft*, para. 1318. See also paragraph 292 of the Appellate Body report in *US – Upland Cotton (Article 21.5 – Brazil)*, where the Appellate Body found that the panel erred in disregarding "the central piece of evidence relied on by the United States".

560 Appellate Body Report, *EC – Fasteners (China)*, para. 442; Appellate Body Report, *US – Clove Cigarettes*, para. 229.

561 Appellate Body Report, *EC – Fasteners (China)*, para. 442. See also Appellate Body Report, *US – Steel Safeguards*, para. 498; and Appellate Body Report, *Chile – Price Band System (Article 21.5 – Argentina)*, para. 238.

Panel stated that, "for all practical purposes, the COOL measure necessitates segregation of meat and livestock according to origin, *even though this segregation is subject to certain flexibilities*".[562] Thus, while the Panel found that the operation and application of the COOL measure "necessitates" segregation, it did not suggest that segregation is legally required, or is always required to the same extent. We further understand the Panel to have used the term "segregation" to encompass a broad range of activities, including physically segregating animals into different pens or fields or identifying each animal through the use of ear tags or other physical markings[563], temporally segregating animals by processing livestock of different origins on different days or at different times[564], and segregating animals completely in the sense of choosing to process only livestock of a single origin.[565]

303. In finding that the COOL measure "necessitates segregation", the Panel relied on several pieces of evidence. The Panel noted that the COOL measure itself does not impose any particular system of identification, such as a tracing system, and prohibits the USDA from requesting any documentation not kept in the normal course of business.[566] Given this lack of specific requirements as to how compliance must be achieved, the Panel found that "a *practical* way to ensure that the chain of reliable information on country of origin required by the COOL measure remains unbroken is the segregation of meat and livestock".[567] The Panel found confirmation that the COOL measure necessitates segregation in its review of the USDA's Country of Origin Labeling Compliance Guide[568] (the "Compliance Guide"). The Panel noted that the Compliance Guide mentions a "segregation plan" as one of the "examples of records and activities that may be useful" for compliance with the COOL measure.[569] The Compliance Guide further mentions "segregation" of meat and livestock as a "[r]esponsibility" of each type of market participant.[570] The Panel also referred to statements by other US entities indicating that segregation is either required or necessary.[571]

[562] Panel Reports, para. 7.327. (emphasis added)

[563] See, for example, Panel Reports, paras. 7.319 and 7.322-7.325.

[564] Panel Reports, paras. 7.339-7.342.

[565] Panel Reports, paras. 7.337 and 7.338.

[566] Panel Reports, para. 7.319.

[567] Panel Reports, para. 7.320. (emphasis added)

[568] Revised 12 May 2009 (Panel Exhibit CDA-65).

[569] Panel Reports, para. 7.321 (referring to Compliance Guide, p. 17; and Panel Exhibit MEX-41).

[570] Panel Reports, paras. 7.322 and 7.323 (referring to Compliance Guide, p. 17; and Panel Exhibit MEX-41).

[571] Panel Reports, para. 7.325 (referring to Panel Exhibits CDA-69 (BCI), CDA-75 (BCI), CDA-76 (BCI), CDA-81 (BCI), CDA-90 (BCI), CDA-117, CDA-192, CDA-199, MEX-33, MEX-37 (BCI), MEX-42 (BCI), MEX-53, MEX-55, and MEX-97 (BCI)).

304. We further note that the Panel qualified its finding that the COOL measure necessitates segregation somewhat, by recognizing that "segregation is subject to certain flexibilities".[572] This suggests that the Panel understood that commingling or other flexibilities might relieve, at least in part, the need for segregation. In fact, the Panel expressly acknowledged this when it found that "[m]arket participants might also benefit from the above-mentioned commingling flexibility", but that this flexibility "allows the reduction of segregation costs only to a certain extent".[573] The Panel also explained that:

> [e]ven at the stage where commingling takes place, it is limited to a single production day. Any commingled meat carrying, for instance, Label B still needs to be segregated at the processing stage and further downstream from Label A meat that was processed by the same slaughterhouse on another day. Also, commingling still requires keeping "accurate records" as well as maintaining the accuracy of country of origin information on mixed-origin labels.[574]

305. Regarding the extent of commingling occurring in the US market, the Panel discussed three pieces of evidence in its Reports. First, the Panel reviewed an affidavit from a person working in the US meat industry indicating that at least one major US processor is commingling Canadian, Mexican, and US origin meat at one of its facilities. About this affidavit the Panel stated:

> We accept this as showing that commingling has been taking place, although we note that this piece of evidence does not specify the extent of commingling either at the facility in question, let alone by the US processor concerned or in the US meat industry at large.[575]

---

572 Panel Reports, para. 7.327.

573 Panel Reports, para. 7.343.

574 Panel Reports, para. 7.344. The Panel also referred to the 2009 Final Rule (AMS), which explains that a processor making a claim as to the origin of its products "may elect to segregate and specifically classify each different category within a production day or mix different sources and provide a mixed label as long as accurate records are kept". (*Ibid.* (quoting Panel Exhibits CDA-5 and MEX-7, Agency response to comments on *Labeling Muscle Cut Covered Commodities of Multiple Countries of Origin That Include the United States*, at p. 2670))

575 Panel Reports, para. 7.364 (referring to Written statement of Larry R. Meadows, dated 28 October 2010 (Panel Exhibit US-102 (BCI))).

306. The Panel next reviewed a series of photographs submitted by the United States[576] portraying actual meat labels seen in the US market, each indicating mixed US, Canadian, and Mexican origin. Based on its review of these photographs, the Panel stated:

> The United States submitted photographs of Label B suggesting that these labels had been affixed on commingled meat. However, photographs of Label B merely demonstrate that there are muscle cuts carrying Label B. Label B, and in particular the photos of such labels submitted by the United States, provide no information on whether the muscle cuts in question result from commingling Label A and B meat on a single production day.[577] (footnote omitted)

307. Finally, the Panel looked at a producer affidavit declaring the origin of livestock supplied to a meat processor, which the Panel characterized as an affidavit that the livestock concerned were "eligible for Label B".[578] Despite the United States' claim that the origin indicated in the affidavit is evidence that commingling is taking place, the Panel found this affidavit to be "silent on whether such Label B livestock ends up being commingled, or whether livestock eligible for Labels A and B are being processed on separate production days".[579]

308. The United States does not directly dispute the Panel's interpretation of the various pieces of evidence, but seems to argue that, if they had been assessed properly, this would inevitably have led the Panel to the conclusion that widespread commingling is occurring in the US market. For example, the United States argues that the Panel "miss[ed] the fact that all of the photographs show muscle cuts labeled 'Product of the United States, Canada, and Mexico,' which is a label only used on commingled meat given the nature of the North American market".[580] It may well be that a muscle cut of meat will not often derive from an animal that has undergone different production steps in three different countries, but the United States does not point to any evidence submitted to the Panel or to Panel findings that would corroborate this assertion. Moreover, the United States

---

576 See Panel Exhibits US-67, US-95, US-96, and US-98.

577 Panel Reports, para. 7.366. One example of the Label B photographs referred to by the Panel is set out *supra*, in paragraph 248 of these Reports.

578 Panel Reports, para. 7.368 (referring to United States' second written submission to the Panel, para. 57; and Producer Affidavits: Continuous Country of Origin Affidavit/Declarations Provided to USDA in 2009/2010 (Panel Exhibit US-101 (BCI))).

579 Panel Reports, para. 7.368.

580 United States' appellant's submission, para. 106 (second bullet point).

itself seems to acknowledge that it is possible that a piece of meat could have three countries of origin under the COOL measure.[581] For these reasons, the Panel's conclusion—namely, that a Category B label displaying three countries of origin does not necessarily indicate that the package contains commingled meat—does not seem to us to be incompatible with an objective assessment of the evidence. Rather, because of its doubts as to the information that can meaningfully be gleaned from these photographs, the Panel did not accord to them substantial evidentiary weight.

309. Furthermore, it seems to us that, based on the totality of the evidence before it, the Panel drew, at least in part, the conclusion the United States desired, that is, that "commingling has been taking place".[582] However, the Panel did not find that the specific evidence relied upon by the United States demonstrated that commingling was taking place in the US market "on a widespread basis".[583] The fact that the Panel found this evidence not to be probative as to the *extent* of commingling occurring in the market as a whole, simply indicates that the Panel declined to attribute to the evidence the weight and significance that the United States considers it should have.

310. Based on the Article 11 standard articulated above, we do not believe that the Panel's determinations regarding segregation and commingling evince a failure to assess the facts objectively. While the United States argues that extensive commingling is taking place as an alternative to segregation, it points to no evidence that it submitted to the Panel demonstrating that the COOL measure's recordkeeping and verification requirements are being complied with by means other than segregation. Nor does the United States refer to any evidence that US producers, in particular upstream livestock producers, are not segregating their livestock according to the categories established under the COOL measure. Rather, the evidence to which the United States refers was expressly considered by the Panel and deemed inconclusive in this regard. Based on the foregoing, we *find* that the Panel did not act inconsistently with its duties under Article 11 of the DSU in finding that, "for all practical purposes, the COOL measure necessitates segregation of meat and livestock according to origin, even though this segregation is subject to certain flexibilities".[584]

[581] The United States argues that a "negligible number of livestock" are processed in three countries, and not that such livestock do not exist. (United States' appellant's submission, para. 106 (first bullet point))

[582] Panel Reports, para. 7.364.

[583] United States' appellant's submission, para. 106.

[584] Panel Reports, para. 7.327.

(b) The Existence of a Price Differential

(i) Arguments on Appeal

311. The United States also alleges that the Panel failed to make an objective assessment of the facts relating to the price differential between domestic and imported livestock in the US market. It contends that the Panel "failed to consider all the evidence before it, considered only the evidence submitted by the complainants, and failed to evaluate the relevance and probative force of the US evidence related to the existence of a COOL discount being applied in the marketplace".[585] The United States points to the Panel's statement that the United States did not respond to Canada's and Mexico's evidence as to the COOL discount[586], which the United States considers to be a mischaracterization.[587] In fact, stresses the United States, it provided a "detailed response"[588] to this evidence in its second written submission, and submitted evidence showing that the price differential between Canadian and US livestock has *narrowed* since the adoption of the COOL measure.[589] According to the United States, its evidence—Panel Exhibit US-108—directly contradicted Canada's and Mexico's claims that the COOL measure is responsible for the widespread price discounting of imported livestock. Even accepting the complainants' evidence, which shows only that selected individual slaughterhouses are imposing a COOL discount, the evidence that the United States submitted makes clear that overall prices in the US market did not show any such decrease in the price of imported livestock relative to the price of domestic livestock. Yet, the Panel ignored this evidence. The United States adds that the Panel also failed to make an objective assessment of the facts relating to prices in stating that the "Sumner Econometric Study"[590] "makes a prima facie case that the COOL measure negatively and significantly affected the import shares and *price basis* of Canadian livestock".[591] According to the United States, this finding lacks a factual basis since the

---

[585] United States' appellant's submission, para. 112.

[586] United States' appellant's submission, para. 113 (referring to Panel Reports, para. 7.356).

[587] United States' appellant's submission, para. 112.

[588] United States' appellant's submission, para. 114.

[589] United States' appellant's submission, para. 114 (referring to Data on North American cattle and hog prices (sourced from LMIC database for US and Canadian cattle, AMS data for Mexico feeder prices, ERS Exchange Rate database, and Statistics Canada (Panel Exhibit US-108)).

[590] Daniel A. Sumner, "Econometric Analysis of the Differential Effects of Mandatory Country of Origin Labeling in the United States on Canadian Cattle Prices and Imports of Canadian Cattle and Hogs into the United States" (16 June 2010) (Panel Exhibit CDA-79).

[591] Panel Reports, para. 7.542. (emphasis added)

Sumner Econometric Study did not find that the COOL measure had any effects on prices for feeder cattle, feeder hogs, or slaughter hogs.[592]

312. With respect to the price differential, Canada points out that the Sumner Econometric Study, relied on by the Panel, was expressly found by the Panel to account for non-COOL related variations in prices, such as those reflected in the one piece of evidence referred to by the United States. Canada also contests the probative value of the price data contained in Panel Exhibit US-108. Canada points out that the data show movements in the prices of imported and domestic livestock for a period that began only after the COOL measure had already "severely depressed the market for imports".[593] Furthermore, Canada argues that it is "to be expected" that there will be "a moderating of the negative effects of the COOL measure during periods of unusually tight supply", and evidence of such effects therefore does not mean that the negative impact of the COOL measure has been eliminated.[594]

313. For its part, Mexico argues that the Panel had direct evidence regarding the existence of a COOL discount being applied to imported livestock, including invoices, a letter from a US producer, and pricing charts.[595] In Mexico's view, the Panel's finding that such a discount existed was therefore well supported by the evidence. Furthermore, the United States' claims incorrectly assume that a finding of less favourable treatment must be evaluated based on the actual trade effects of the measure. Therefore, Mexico maintains, even if the Appellate Body considers that the Panel erred in making its factual findings in this respect, this would not lead to a reversal of the Panel's legal findings under Article 2.1 of the *TBT Agreement*.

(ii) Analysis

314. Before turning to assess this part of the United States' appeal, we briefly recall the parts of the Panel's analysis to which it pertains. The Panel discussed differences in the prices of imported Canadian and Mexican livestock in two distinct parts of its reasoning. The Panel's statements regarding the existence of a COOL discount being applied to imported livestock were first made in the context of its analysis of the consistency of the COOL measure with Article 2.1 of the *TBT Agreement*.[596] There, having found that "the least costly way of

---

[592] United States' appellant's submission, para. 115 (referring to Sumner Econometric Study (Panel Exhibit CDA-79); and Panel Exhibit CDA-206).

[593] Canada's appellee's submission, para. 27.

[594] *Ibid.*

[595] Mexico's appellee's submission, para. 120 (referring to Panel Exhibits MEX-37 (BCI), MEX-47, MEX-48, MEX-64 (BCI), and MEX-97 (BCI)).

[596] See Panel Reports, section VII.D.2(b).

complying with the COOL measure is to rely on exclusively domestic livestock"[597], the Panel cited to evidence demonstrating that slaughterhouses were passing the costs of processing *imported* livestock on to upstream producers, stating that:

> ... there is direct evidence of major slaughterhouses applying a considerable COOL discount of USD 40-60 per head for imported livestock.[*] This proves that major processors are passing on at least some of the additional costs of the COOL measure upstream to suppliers of imported livestock.[**] We have no evidence of a similar discount being applied to suppliers of domestic livestock, nor has the United States responded to the evidence submitted by Canada and Mexico in this respect.[598]
>
> [*original footnote 501] See Exhibits CDA-57 and 81 (both BCI), MEX-37, 46, 64, 97 and 105 (all BCI).
>
> [**original footnote 502] See Exhibits MEX-37, 46, 97 and 105 (all BCI). See also Exhibit MEX-101.

315. Later in that same section of its analysis, after finding that "the COOL measure creates an incentive to use domestic livestock—and a disincentive to handle imported livestock—by imposing higher segregation costs on imported livestock than on domestic livestock"[599], the Panel identified specific examples of a detrimental impact on the terms of trade offered to producers of imported livestock. One such example was that certain suppliers of imported livestock have suffered significant financial disadvantages resulting from the COOL measure, *including an increased price difference between imported and domestic livestock* and the refusal of financial institutions to provide credits and loans.[600]

316. After having concluded that the COOL measure "*de facto* discriminates against imported livestock by according less favourable treatment to Canadian cattle and hogs, and to Mexican cattle, especially Mexican feeder cattle, than to like domestic livestock", the Panel went on to analyze, in a separate subsection of its Reports[601], the actual trade effects of the COOL measure. It was undisputed by the parties that the Panel did not need to verify the actual trade

597 Panel Reports, para. 7.350.

598 Panel Reports, para. 7.356.

599 Panel Reports, para. 7.372.

600 Panel Reports, para. 7.379.

601 See Panel Reports, section VII.D.2(c).

effects of the COOL measure[602], and the Panel itself considered that findings in this respect were "not indispensable" for its analysis under Article 2.1.[603] The Panel nevertheless conducted an analysis of such effects, recognizing that the existence of "negative trade and economic effects is an important factual matter in this dispute".[604]

317. As part of its analysis, the Panel compared two econometric studies submitted by Canada and by the United States, each of which purported to demonstrate the effects—or lack thereof—of the COOL measure on import shares and prices of cattle and hogs. The Panel reviewed the methodologies and findings of each study, and found that the Sumner Econometric Study, submitted by Canada, was "sufficiently robust"[605] to provide reliable evidence of the effects of the COOL measure, and gave five specific reasons for this assessment.[606] It further found that the "USDA Econometric Study"[607] submitted by the United States "lack[ed] sufficient robustness both taken on its own and in comparison with the Sumner Econometric Study".[608] It therefore concluded that the Sumner Econometric Study made "a prima facie case that the COOL measure negatively and significantly affected the import shares and price basis of Canadian livestock"[609], which was "not refuted by the USDA Econometric Study".[610]

318. With respect to the existence of a COOL discount being applied to imported livestock, the United States does not dispute on appeal the content of the Canadian and Mexican exhibits upon which the Panel relied, but argues that other evidence that it put forward relating to prices contradicts the Panel's finding. The United States' arguments rely to a large extent on Panel Exhibit US-108. This exhibit contains data comparing the prices of US and Canadian feeder and slaughter cattle, of US and Mexican feeder cattle, and of US and Canadian hogs, during the first nine months of 2010. For each category, the data show a decrease in the price differential between imported and domestic livestock between January and September 2010.

---

602 Panel Reports, para. 7.442.

603 Panel Reports, para. 7.445.

604 Panel Reports, para. 7.444.

605 Panel Reports, para. 7.540.

606 Panel Reports, paras. 7.540 and 7.541.

607 *Supra*, footnote 132 (Panel Exhibit US-42).

608 Panel Reports, para. 7.543.

609 Panel Reports, para. 7.542.

610 Panel Reports, para. 7.546.

319. As described above, in finding that US producers were applying a COOL discount for imported livestock, the Panel relied on numerous exhibits submitted by Canada and by Mexico which, in its view, contained "direct evidence of major slaughterhouses applying a considerable COOL discount of USD 40-60 per head for imported livestock", and showed that "major processors are passing on at least some of the additional costs of the COOL measure upstream to suppliers of imported livestock."[611] These exhibits included: two affidavits submitted by Canada from exporters of fed cattle to the United States describing declines in cattle prices since the implementation of the COOL measure[612]; an affidavit from a Mexican industry group detailing the effects of the COOL provisions for Mexican producers[613]; procurement documents from a US processor showing the terms of trade for purchases of Mexican-born cattle[614]; a 2009 letter from a US processor informing sellers of the value differences between Mexican-born feeder cattle fed in the United States and US-born and -fed cattle due to the costs of compliance with the COOL measure, which ranged from a $45 to a $60 per head discount[615]; and several invoices indicating the sale prices of Mexican-born cattle sold in the US market.[616]

320. The evidence contained in Panel Exhibit US-108, on the other hand, charts overall pricing data. The figures that it contains, taken from several official US and Canadian sources, demonstrate an overall decrease in the price differential between imported and domestic livestock, with prices for Canadian cattle and hogs and for Mexican cattle increasing at a higher rate than prices for US cattle and hogs sold during the same period, that is, January through September 2010. The United States also argued before the Panel, in its second written submission, that the data in Panel Exhibit US-108 "confirm[] that US feed lots and slaughter houses are not as a general matter discounting the price that they pay for [Canadian and Mexican livestock] in response to the COOL measures".[617] The United States noted that, due to transportation costs and possible quality discounts, "the prices paid for Canadian and Mexican animals

---

[611] Panel Reports, para. 7.356.

[612] Witness Statement of Harvey Dann, dated 22 February 2010 (Panel Exhibit CDA-57 (BCI)); Witness Statement of John Lawton, dated 22 February 2010 (Panel Exhibit CDA-81 (BCI)).

[613] Affidavit of the Chairman of the Confederación Nacional de Organizaciones Ganaderas (CNOG), dated 17 May 2010 (Panel Exhibit MEX-37 (BCI)).

[614] Data on cattle procurement showing the terms of trade for Cargill's purchases of Mexican-born cattle (March 2009) (Panel Exhibit MEX-46 (BCI)).

[615] Letter from a Tyson Fresh Meats, Inc. executive to the President of the Confederación Nacional de Organizaciones Ganaderas (CNOG), dated 9 April 2009 (Panel Exhibit MEX-64 (BCI)).

[616] Affidavit of the Chairman of the Confederación Nacional de Organizaciones Ganaderas (CNOG), dated 25 October 2010 (Panel Exhibit MEX-97 (BCI)); Affidavit of the Chairman of the Confederación Nacional de Organizaciones Ganaderas (CNOG), dated 22 December 2010 (Panel Exhibit MEX-105 (BCI)).

[617] United States' second written submission to the Panel, para. 77.

have historically been discounted compared with the price paid for US cattle."[618] It also noted that, "[d]uring 2009, the price differential between US cattle and imported cattle widened slightly due to the economic downturn, but this price differential has returned to historic levels."[619]

321. We observe that the fact that the Panel did not refer to or discuss the evidence put forward by the United States in Panel Exhibit US-108 could suggest that the Panel did not take account of this evidence. The Panel did not explain why it did not consider this evidence to be relevant to its review of livestock prices. However, we recall that the Appellate Body has found that a panel need not refer to or discuss each and every piece of evidence put before it in order to comply with its obligations under Article 11 of the DSU.[620] Therefore, the mere fact that the Panel did not refer to one specific piece of evidence relating to prices is not dispositive of whether the Panel failed to make an objective assessment of the facts. Rather, when a panel makes no mention of a piece of evidence, the participant raising a claim under Article 11 of the DSU must demonstrate that the evidence is so material that the panel's failure to address it calls into question the objectivity of the panel's factual assessment.

322. Based on its submissions before the Panel, we agree with the United States that the Panel incorrectly stated that the United States had not responded to the evidence put forward by Canada and by Mexico. We also cannot exclude that the Panel may have ignored the evidence submitted by the United States in its second written submission and, in particular, Panel Exhibit US-108. Even if this is so, the United States does not explain in its submissions on appeal why these errors by the Panel rise to the level of a violation of Article 11 of the DSU. Instead, the United States argues that, despite evidence that selected individual slaughterhouses are imposing a COOL discount, Panel Exhibit US-108 makes clear that this has not impacted *overall* prices in the market. In our view, the evidence submitted by the United States was of a different nature than the evidence submitted by Canada and by Mexico, which referenced specific instances of the application of a COOL discount by US slaughterhouses. Furthermore, as Canada argues, the data submitted by the United States reflect changes in livestock prices during 2010, after the price effects of the COOL measure—implemented in March 2009—would already have been felt. The data do not, therefore, compare livestock prices before and after the implementation of the COOL measure, or otherwise speak to the effect of the COOL measure on prices of imported livestock.

---

[618] United States' second written submission to the Panel, para. 81.

[619] United States' second written submission to the Panel, para. 82.

[620] Appellate Body Report, *Brazil – Retreaded Tyres*, para. 202; Appellate Body Report, *Chile – Price Band System (Article 21.5 – Argentina)*, para. 240.

323. Therefore, it does not seem to us that, on its face, the evidence set out in Panel Exhibit US-108 vitiates the Panel's reliance on the evidence put forward by Canada and by Mexico. The Panel may simply not have been persuaded by that evidence. In any event, we recall that the Panel was not required under the proper interpretation of the national treatment obligation in Article 2.1 of the *TBT Agreement* to find actual negative effects on the prices of imported livestock, and that the Panel gave several other examples, in addition to the COOL discount, of the reduction in competitive opportunities for livestock resulting from the COOL measure.[621] We thus do not consider that the Panel's findings regarding a COOL discount were material to its overall legal findings under Article 2.1. Nor do we consider that the fact that the Panel did not specifically discuss Panel Exhibit US-108, or the corresponding arguments set out in the United States' second written submission, casts doubt on the objectivity of its factual findings regarding US livestock prices.

324. As for the Panel's findings regarding the Sumner Econometric Study, we recall that the Panel assessed the content of both Canada's and the United States' econometric studies, and determined that only the Sumner Econometric Study was "sufficiently robust" to account for price variations based on factors not related to the COOL measure.[622] The Panel provided reasons for this conclusion.[623] The United States argues that the study does not support the Panel's conclusion that the COOL measure affected the price basis of Canadian livestock, and that in fact the study "does not find any price effects on feeder cattle, feeder hogs, or slaughter hogs".[624] The United States acknowledges, however, that the study did show an impact on the prices for slaughter cattle, and we recall that the Panel found that the majority of the cattle imported into the United States from Canada are in fact slaughter cattle.[625]

325. In addition, as explained above, the Panel evaluated the Sumner Econometric Study as part of its examination of the actual trade effects of the COOL measure. The Panel made explicit that its finding of less favourable treatment was not dependent on its examination of the actual trade effects of the

---

[621] That is, the Panel found that: (i) fewer processing plants are accepting imported livestock, and those that do, do so at specific limited times; (ii) contractual terms for suppliers of imported livestock have changed as a result of the COOL measure; (iii) certain suppliers of imported livestock have suffered significant financial disadvantages resulting from the COOL measure, including an increased price differential between imported and domestic livestock and the refusal of financial institutions to provide credits and loans; and (iv) imported cattle have been excluded from profitable premium beef programmes. (See Panel Reports, paras. 7.376-7.380)

[622] Panel Reports, para. 7.540.

[623] Panel Reports, paras. 7.540 and 7.541.

[624] United States' appellant's submission, para. 115.

[625] Panel Reports, para. 7.141 (referring to United States' first written submission to the Panel, para. 89; Panel Exhibit US-28, Table 3; and Panel Exhibit CDA-196).

COOL measure and the evidence relating to such effects. Nor was the Panel required under Article 2.1 to confirm its legal conclusions based on the actual trade effects of the measure in the US market. We therefore consider that, even if the Panel were to have erred in its appreciation of the Sumner Econometric Study, such an error would not have materially affected its ultimate legal conclusion under Article 2.1 of the *TBT Agreement*.

326. We therefore *find* that the United States has not demonstrated that the Panel acted inconsistently with Article 11 of the DSU in its assessment of the evidence relating to the price differential between domestic and imported livestock.

3. *Does the Detrimental Impact on Imported Livestock Violate Article 2.1?*

327. Having evaluated and rejected the United States' challenge to the Panel's assessment of the facts with respect to segregation, commingling, and the price differential between domestic and imported livestock, we continue our analysis under Article 2.1 of the *TBT Agreement*. Only if we find that the detrimental impact reflects discrimination in violation of Article 2.1, can we uphold the Panel's finding that the COOL measure accords less favourable treatment to imported livestock than to like domestic livestock. We begin by summarizing the participants' arguments on appeal in this respect, and we then identify the relevant findings made by the Panel.

(a) Arguments on Appeal

328. With respect to *US – Clove Cigarettes*[626], the United States contends that the Appellate Body found that the measure at issue in that dispute had a detrimental impact on imported products, and then inquired as to whether the measure itself provided different treatment to imported products on the basis of origin. In the United States' view, this inquiry was not meant to provide an exception or to apply an additional test under Article 2.1. Rather, the inquiry performed in *US – Clove Cigarettes* is a way to illuminate whether a measure actually treats imports and like domestic products differently. Therefore, under Article 2.1, a panel should analyze whether a measure is even-handed to determine whether the measure has a detrimental impact, as well as to determine whether that impact stems exclusively from a legitimate regulatory distinction rather than reflecting discrimination. Ultimately, then, the question is whether

[626] The United States' appellant's submission was filed prior to the circulation of the Appellate Body report in *US – Clove Cigarettes* and therefore did not contain arguments relating to the Appellate Body's findings in that case. The United States addressed the relevance of the Appellate Body report in *US – Clove Cigarettes* in its oral statement and responses to questioning at the oral hearing.

the measure is even-handed. If it is even-handed, because it does not provide different treatment *in fact*, then it would not breach Article 2.1.

329. Regarding the "legitimate regulatory distinction", the United States points out that it is important not to confuse this notion with that of legitimate *objectives*. In its view, a Member could have a legitimate objective underlying its measure, but make illegitimate distinctions within that regulation. In applying this concept to the COOL measure, the United States argues that its measure does not contain a regulatory distinction, because there are no differential requirements imposed on products, or requirements that some products must be labelled and others not. In this respect, the United States emphasizes that the mere fact that the measure identifies the origins of products in order to label them accordingly at retail does not mean that there is a regulatory distinction made between domestic and imported products. Rather, the labels are simply conveying product information that is relevant to the consumer, and different information is conveyed depending on where the various production steps took place for the particular product.

330. Canada submits that, "[a]s a matter of logic", it would be incongruous for the United States to claim on appeal that the COOL measure implements a legitimate regulatory distinction, because, before the Panel, it never sought to defend the asserted violation of the parallel obligation in Article III:4 of the GATT 1994 on the grounds of a legitimate objective under Article XX of the GATT 1994.[627] Canada contends that the design, architecture, revealing structure, operation, and application of the COOL measure show that its objective is protectionism, and argues that a regulatory distinction based on such an objective is not legitimate. Canada further argues that the design, architecture, revealing structure, operation, and application of the COOL measure establish that the discrimination it causes is not consistent with an even-handed application of a legitimate regulatory distinction. The structure and design of the COOL measure are such that imported livestock can be used to produce only Label B or C meat, whereas meat derived from US-born and -raised animals has exclusive access to Label A, as well as limited access to Labels B and C. As a result, the segregation costs and reporting requirements create uneven costs that disproportionately fall on imported livestock. In addition, the detrimental impact incurred by imported livestock cannot be said to stem exclusively from legitimate regulatory distinctions, because the objective that the United States claims to be pursuing—that is, providing consumers with information on where the animal from which the meat is derived was born, raised, and slaughtered—is not reflected in the COOL measure. Nor is this objective "legitimate" for purposes of Article 2.1, because, in *US – Clove Cigarettes*, the Appellate Body's interpretation of legitimacy in this context was limited to those objectives

[627] Canada's appellee's submission, p. 25, heading IV.C.2.

contained in the "closed lists" of the sixth recital of the preamble of the *TBT Agreement* and of Article XX of the GATT 1994.[628]

331. In Mexico's view, although the Panel did not have the benefit of the Appellate Body report in *US – Clove Cigarettes*, the Panel's finding of inconsistency under Article 2.1 of the *TBT Agreement* is consistent with the Appellate Body's test and is legally correct. This is because it is evident from the Panel's findings that the COOL measure is not even-handed and that the detrimental impact on imported livestock does not stem exclusively from a legitimate regulatory distinction. Rather, the loss of competitive opportunities resulting from the COOL measure clearly reflects discrimination against the group of imported products. Mexico points to several factors in support of this argument, namely: (i) that the COOL measure is mandatory despite low consumer demand for such information; (ii) that the COOL measure is designed so that the least costly and most commercially desirable method of compliance is to exclude imported livestock; (iii) that the COOL measure is designed to distinguish between meat made from US-born cattle and meat made from foreign cattle rather than to give information on origin, as is clear from the fact that only Label A provides meaningful information; (iv) that the COOL measure includes "completely arbitrary" flexibility allowing Label B to be used for Category A meat when Category A and Category B meat are processed "on the same production day"; and (v) that the COOL measure "is not effective at achieving its objective", because "very little meat in the US market is accurately labelled for origin by the COOL measure".[629] Finally, Mexico asserts that the sixth recital of the preamble of the *TBT Agreement* provides "an exhaustive list of the justifications that are available for measures that otherwise would violate Article 2.1" because they qualify as legitimate regulatory distinctions, and none of those justifications are applicable to the COOL measure.[630]

(b) Relevant Panel Findings

332. We point out, as a preliminary matter, that the Panel identified the objective pursued by the United States through the COOL measure as being "to provide consumer information on origin"[631], and that the origin of beef and pork

[628] Canada's appellee's submission, para. 56 (referring to Appellate Body Report, *US – Clove Cigarettes*, paras. 96, 100, 101, and 173).

[629] Mexico's appellee's submission, para. 58.

[630] Mexico's appellee's submission, para. 59.

[631] Panel Reports, paras. 7.617, 7.620, 7.671, and 7.685. The Panel also referred several times to the additional objective of preventing consumer confusion. (See, for example, paras. 7.671 and 7.713) Each of the participants has appealed certain legal and factual aspects of the Panel's determination of the objective of the COOL measure and of whether such objective is "legitimate" within the meaning of Article 2.2 of the *TBT Agreement*. Those grounds of appeal are dealt with in section VI of these Reports.

is defined, under the COOL measure, as a function of the countries in which the cattle and hogs from which the meat is derived were born, raised, and slaughtered.

333. In our view, the Panel's findings regarding the various origin categories for muscle cuts of meat, and the labelling requirements applicable to each, are particularly relevant to an inquiry as to the COOL measure's even-handedness. The Panel found that Category A refers to US origin meat, derived from animals exclusively born, raised, and slaughtered in the United States.[632] Category B refers to mixed origin meat, derived from animals not exclusively born, raised, and slaughtered in the United States, and not imported into the United States for immediate slaughter—that is, to animals born outside, but raised and slaughtered in the United States.[633] Category C also denotes meat of mixed origin, but specifically refers to meat derived from animals born and raised in a foreign country and imported into the United States for immediate slaughter.[634] Category D meat derives from animals *not* born, raised, or slaughtered in the United States. This meat is considered to be of "foreign" origin.

334. With respect to labelling, the Panel also made a number of relevant findings. First, the Panel made findings regarding the products that must be labelled, and the retail entities that are required to label the covered commodities. The Panel found that the COOL measure applies to muscle cuts of, and ground, beef and pork sold at the retail level, but excludes certain products and entities from its coverage. By its terms, the COOL measure applies only to "retailers", which are defined as those entities selling in excess of $230,000 worth of fruit and vegetables per year.[635] Therefore, the COOL measure does not apply to smaller retail grocery stores, or to retailers who do not sell fruit and vegetables.[636] The Panel also found that "the COOL statute excludes from its scope any of the covered commodities that are an 'ingredient in a processed food item'".[637] Based on the 2009 Final Rule (AMS), such processing includes

[632] Panel Reports, para. 7.89 (referring to COOL statute, section 1638a(2)(A)); 2009 Final Rule (AMS), section 65.260.

[633] Panel Reports, para. 7.89 (referring to COOL statute, section 1638a(2)(B)); 2009 Final Rule (AMS), section 65.300(e)(1).

[634] Panel Reports, para. 7.89 (referring to COOL statute, section 1638a(2)(C)); 2009 Final Rule (AMS), section 65.300(e)(3).

[635] Panel Reports, para. 7.101 (referring to 2009 Final Rule (AMS), section 65.205). See also 2009 Final Rule (AMS), section 65.240.

[636] As Canada and Mexico point out in their submissions, by virtue of this definition of "retailer", the COOL measure does not apply to butcher shops—no matter how large—because they do not sell fruit and vegetables. (Canada's appellee's submission, para. 59 (fourth bullet point); Mexico's other appellant's submission, para. 15; Mexico's appellee's submission, paras. 58 (fifth bullet point) and 169 (second bullet point))

[637] Panel Reports, para. 7.104 (quoting COOL statute, section 1638(2)(B)).

"cooking, curing, smoking and restructuring".[638] Further, the COOL statute provides that it "shall not apply to food service establishments".[639] The COOL statute defines a "food service establishment" as "a restaurant, cafeteria, lunch room, food stand, saloon, tavern, bar, lounge, or other similar facility operated as an enterprise engaged in the business of selling food to the public".[640] The 2009 Final Rule (AMS) further specifies that "[s]imilar food service facilities include salad bars, delicatessens, and other food enterprises located within retail establishments that provide ready-to-eat foods that are consumed either on or outside of the retailer's premises".[641]

335. Given the above exemptions and exclusions, the Panel found that "a considerable proportion of beef and pork is exempted from the COOL measure".[642] Regarding the "relevance of these exceptions in terms of practical compliance with the COOL measure", the Panel noted the United States' response that:

> [it] is not aware of any evidence to suggest that meat producers in the distribution chain—feed lot operators and slaughterhouses—are systematically separating source animals or meat products depending on whether the ultimate meat products derived from those animals are subject to the 2009 Final Rule. This is due to the fact that the ultimate disposition of a meat product is often not known at any particular stage of the production chain.[643]

The Panel found that the "complainants' answers to the same question confirm that there is no systematic differentiation based on the ultimate destination of the meat produced".[644]

336. The Panel further observed that the COOL measure specifies how each of the origins of meat must be labelled in various circumstances. The COOL measure requires Category A meat to be labelled as US origin, except when it is commingled on a single production day with Category B and/or Category C meat, in which case it may be labelled as mixed origin, for example, "Product of

---

638 Panel Reports, para. 7.89 (referring to 2009 Final Rule (AMS), section 65.220).

639 Panel Reports, para. 7.106.

640 Panel Reports, para. 7.107 (quoting COOL statute, section 1638(4)).

641 Panel Reports, para. 7.108 (quoting 2009 Final Rule (AMS), section 65.140).

642 Panel Reports, para. 7.417.

643 Panel Reports, para. 7.417 (referring to United States' response to Panel Question 93).

644 Panel Reports, para. 7.418 (referring to Canada's and Mexico's responses to Panel Question 93).

Mexico and the United States".[645] Category B meat must always be labelled as having more than one country of origin, with the countries listed in any order, even when it is commingled with Category A and/or C meat.[646] Category C meat also must be labelled as mixed origin, and the United States cannot be listed first, except when it is commingled with Category A and/or B meat, in which case the countries may be listed in any order.[647] By contrast, Category D meat must be labelled with its "country of origin", as identified in the relevant customs entry documents[648], for example, "Product of Brazil".

337. The Panel found that, due to the commingling flexibilities under the COOL measure, "labelled countries may be listed *in any order* when the meat is derived from animals classified as category B, or when meat falling under categories A and B, as well as B and C, is commingled during a single production day".[649] It relied on this fact in reaching its later conclusion that "a B or C label affixed to a meat product may not necessarily correspond to the definition of origin under the measure".[650] It noted that this is the case even with meat derived from animals born, raised, and slaughtered in the United States (that is, Category A meat), as it may be carrying Label B or Label C rather than Label A, due to the commingling provisions.[651]

338. In terms of the information to be communicated to consumers through the COOL labels, the Panel considered that "several elements" were involved, based on "the US definition of origin [which] involves information on the places where animals from which meat is derived were born, raised, and slaughtered".[652] This being the case, the Panel considered a "Product of the United States" label, that is, Label A, to be the only label that provides "meaningful information for consumers", because *all* of the production steps in fact took place in the United States.[653] It found, however, that the descriptions of origin on Label B and Label C are "confusing"[654], and "do[] not, in fact, deliver origin information as defined under the measure or as the consumer might understand it".[655] A label stating "Product of the US, Mexico", for example, "does not describe what 'the US and

---

645 Panel Reports, paras. 7.94, 7.96-7.98, and 7.100.

646 Panel Reports, paras. 7.94-7.100.

647 Panel Reports, paras. 7.95-7.100.

648 Panel Reports, paras. 7.99, 7.100, and 7.119. See also para. 7.674.

649 Panel Reports, para. 7.97. (original emphasis)

650 Panel Reports, para. 7.703.

651 *Ibid.*

652 Panel Reports, para. 7.699.

653 Panel Reports, para. 7.718.

654 *Ibid.*

655 Panel Reports, para. 7.699.

Mexico' means as far as origin of the meat is concerned".[656] Furthermore, given "the interchangeable use of Label B and Label C allowed for commingled meat", the Panel found that even "a perfect consumer who is fully informed of the meaning of different categories of labels ... may never be assured that the label precisely reflects the origin of meat as defined under the COOL measure".[657]

339. Finally, with respect to the recordkeeping and verification requirements, the Panel found that, in order "to comply with the COOL measure, livestock and meat processors need to possess, at each and every stage of the supply and distribution chain, the kind of origin information required by the various COOL labels for which each animal or portion of meat is eligible, and they need to transmit such information to the next processing stage".[658] Based on this finding, the Panel noted that, where a producer chooses to purchase and process both domestic and imported livestock without regard to origin, it must nevertheless "identif[y] by origin ... each and every livestock and piece of meat throughout the supply and distribution chain".[659] The Panel further quoted the following from the AMS' analysis of the costs and benefits of the COOL measure:

> [T]his [Final R]ule directly regulates the activities of retailers (as defined by the law) and their suppliers. Retailers are required by the rule to provide country of origin information for the covered commodities that they sell, and firms that supply covered commodities to these retailers must provide them with this information. In addition, virtually all other firms in the supply chain for the covered commodities are potentially affected by the rule because country of origin information will need to be maintained and transferred along the entire supply chain.[660]

---

[656] Panel Reports, para. 7.700. The Panel explained that such a label could be understood as meaning products comprising meat originating in both the United States and Mexico. The Panel added that, where such a label is affixed to a package containing a single piece of meat, the meaning of the two country names listed on the label is not clear, and the average consumer would be unable to understand the meaning of a specific COOL label without also understanding the definition of each labelling category under the COOL measure. (*Ibid.*)

[657] Panel Reports, para. 7.702.

[658] Panel Reports, para. 7.317.

[659] Panel Reports, para. 7.336.

[660] Panel Reports, para. 7.318 (quoting Panel Exhibits CDA-5 and MEX-7, AMS' "Analysis of Benefits and Costs", at p. 2684).

340. In our view, these findings provide a sufficient basis for us to determine whether the detrimental impact on Canadian and Mexican livestock stems exclusively from a legitimate regulatory distinction. That is, these findings allow us to pronounce on whether the COOL measure is designed and applied in an even-handed manner, or whether it lacks even-handedness, for example, because it is designed or applied in a manner that constitutes a means of arbitrary or unjustifiable discrimination, and thus reflects discrimination in violation of Article 2.1 of the *TBT Agreement*. If we determine that the regulatory distinctions drawn by the COOL measure are designed or applied in a manner that constitutes arbitrary or unjustifiable discrimination, those distinctions cannot be considered "legitimate", and the COOL measure will be inconsistent with Article 2.1. In order to make this determination, we proceed to scrutinize "the particular circumstances" of this case, including "the design, architecture, revealing structure, operation, and application" of the COOL measure.

(c) Does the Detrimental Impact Reflect Discrimination?

341. We first identify the relevant regulatory distinction. The COOL measure defines the origin of beef and pork as a function of the countries in which certain steps of the production process (birth, raising, and slaughter) take place. The COOL measure also requires retailers of muscle cuts of beef and pork to label that meat with one of four mandatory labels. We consider that it is the distinctions between the three production steps, as well as between the four types of labels that must be affixed to muscle cuts of beef and pork, that constitute the relevant regulatory distinctions under the COOL measure. Accordingly, we must examine, based on the particular circumstances of this case, whether these distinctions are designed and applied in an even-handed manner, or whether they lack even-handedness, for example, because they are designed or applied in a manner that constitutes arbitrary or unjustifiable discrimination.

342. We start by considering the recordkeeping and verification requirements imposed by the COOL measure, which the Panel found to be the source of the incentive for US producers to process exclusively domestic livestock. As already explained, the Panel found that, at each and every stage of the supply and distribution chain, livestock and meat producers need to possess information sufficient to identify by origin each and every animal and piece of meat, and must transmit such information to the next processing stage.[661] Producers must maintain such records for a period of one year from the date of their purchase or sale of the livestock or meat[662], and be able to provide these records verifying

[661] Panel Reports, paras. 7.317 and 7.336.

[662] Panel Reports, para. 7.118. See also 2009 Final Rule (AMS), section 65.500(b)(1) and (3).

origin to the Secretary of Agriculture in the event of an audit.[663] In other words, the recordkeeping and verification requirements of the COOL measure require livestock and meat producers to track and transmit to their downstream buyers information regarding the countries in which each production step took place for the animals and/or meat that they process.[664] Thus, for example, a livestock producer must maintain and transmit information sufficient to enable its customers to differentiate between cattle born and raised in the United States, and cattle born in Mexico and raised in the United States. Similarly, a slaughterhouse must maintain information sufficient to enable it to differentiate between Canadian-born but US-raised hogs, and hogs imported from Canada for immediate slaughter in the United States, as these two types of hogs would fall within different origin categories under the COOL measure.

343. As designed and applied, however, the COOL measure does not impose labelling requirements for meat that provide consumers with origin information *commensurate* with the type of origin information that upstream livestock producers and processors are required to maintain and transmit. Rather, the origin information that must be conveyed to consumers is less detailed, and will often be less accurate. This is because the COOL measure requires the labels to list the country or countries of origin, but does not require the labels to mention production steps at all. If, for example, the relevant production steps took place in more than one country, the relevant label (B or C) will identify more than one country, but will not identify which production step took place in which of those countries.[665] Under the labelling rules, labels for Category B meat may also list countries of origin in any order[666], such that the order of countries listed on the labels cannot be relied upon to indicate where certain production steps took place. Furthermore, due to the additional labelling flexibilities allowed for commingled meat, a retail label may indicate that meat is of mixed origin when in fact it is of exclusively US origin, or that it has three countries of origin when in fact it has only one or two.[667] For Category D meat, the COOL measure

---

[663] Panel Reports, para. 7.117. See also COOL statute, section 1638a(d); and 2009 Final Rule (AMS), section 65.500(a).

[664] Specifically, the Panel found that, in principle:

> … to comply with the COOL measure, livestock and meat processors need to possess, at each and every stage of the supply and distribution chain, the kind of origin information required by the various COOL labels for which each animal or portion of meat is eligible, and they need to transmit such information to the next processing stage.

(Panel Reports, para. 7.317)

[665] See Panel Reports, paras. 7.89-7.100.

[666] Panel Reports, para. 7.97. See also 2009 Final Rule (AMS), section 65.300(e)(4).

[667] Panel Reports, paras. 7.93-7.100. See also 2009 Final Rule (AMS), section 65.300(e)(2) and (4).

requires only that the customs designation of origin be indicated.[668] Given that the United States does not use the same definition of "origin" for customs purposes as it does for the COOL measure[669], a D Label will not convey information on the countries of birth or raising of the livestock from which the imported meat was derived. Even Label A, indicating "Product of the USA", which the Panel found to be the only label that provides "meaningful information for consumers"[670], is not required to refer explicitly to the productions steps of birth, raising, and slaughter.[671]

344. In comparing the origin information requirements imposed on upstream producers with the origin information conveyed to consumers, we also consider relevant the fact that the COOL measure exempts from its labelling requirements muscle cuts of beef and pork that are "ingredient[s] in a processed food item", or are sold in a "food service establishment" or in an establishment that is not a "retailer".[672] As noted above, upstream producers do not, and likely could not, distinguish between livestock that will be used to produce a product exempt from the labelling requirements, and livestock that will be used to produce covered commodities that must be labelled when sold at retail. This is because "the ultimate disposition of a meat product is often not known at any particular stage of the production chain".[673] This means that, generally speaking, information regarding the origin of *all* livestock will have to be identified, tracked, and transmitted through the chain of production by upstream producers in accordance with the recordkeeping and verification requirements of the COOL measure, even though "a considerable proportion"[674] of the beef and pork derived from that livestock will ultimately be exempt from the COOL requirements and therefore carry no COOL label at all.

345. We also recall that the Panel considered that the burden of the recordkeeping and verification requirements, the consequent need for segregation, and the associated compliance costs, are all lower when a given producer processes single origin livestock only.[675] Conversely, the more origins

---

668 Panel Reports, para. 7.119 and footnote 179 thereto. See also 2009 Final Rule (AMS), section 65.300(f).

669 See Panel Reports, para. 7.674.

670 Panel Reports, para. 7.718.

671 Panel Reports, para. 7.100. See also 2009 Final Rule (AMS), section 65.300(d).

672 Panel Reports, paras. 7.103-7.108. See also COOL statute, sections 1638(2)(B) and 1638a(b); and 2009 Final Rule (AMS), sections 65.140, 65.220, and 65.240. As explained *supra*, at footnote 636, the definition of a "retailer" does not encompass butcher shops or small grocery stores.

673 Panel Reports, para. 7.417 (quoting United States' response to Panel Question 93, para. 16).

674 Panel Reports, para. 7.417.

675 Panel Reports, paras. 7.346 and 7.347.

involved, the higher the burden and the associated costs.[676] Given the particular circumstances of the US market[677], the least costly way of complying with the COOL measure is to rely exclusively on domestic livestock.[678] It follows from these findings that the least costly way of complying with the COOL measure is to process exclusively livestock that are eligible for an A Label, that is, for the only label that conveys meaningful information to consumers. When a producer nevertheless chooses to use livestock of different origins, compliance with the COOL measure will not only be more costly, it will also entail the subsequent use of Label B and/or C, which are labels that the Panel found to convey confusing information to consumers.

346. Taking account of the overall architecture of the COOL measure and the way in which it operates and is applied, we consider the detail and accuracy of the origin information that upstream producers are required to track and transmit to be significantly greater than the origin information that retailers of muscle cuts of beef and pork are required to convey to their customers. That is, the labels prescribed by the COOL measure reflect origin information in significantly less detail than the information regarding the countries in which the livestock were born, raised, and slaughtered, which upstream producers and processors are required to be able to identify in their records and transmit to their customers. Furthermore, upstream producers will be subject to the COOL measure's recordkeeping and verification requirements even when the meat derived from their animals is ultimately exempt from the labelling requirements of the COOL measure, for example, due to the type of establishment in which the meat is sold. Lastly, a processor's decision to use livestock of different origins rather than exclusively US origin livestock will not only be more costly, it will also lead to confusing information being conveyed to consumers.

347. For all of these reasons, the informational requirements imposed on upstream producers under the COOL measure are disproportionate as compared to the level of information communicated to consumers through the mandatory retail labels. That is, a large amount of information is tracked and transmitted by upstream producers for purposes of providing consumers with information on origin, but only a small amount of this information is actually communicated to

---

[676] The Panel considered it "evident that the more origins and the more types of muscle cut labels involved, the more intensive the need for segregation throughout the livestock and meat supply and distribution chain", which "leads to higher compliance costs". (Panel Reports, para. 7.331. See also para. 7.346)

[677] The Panel reasoned that processing exclusively domestic livestock is in general less costly and more viable than processing exclusively imported livestock, because livestock imports are small in comparison to domestic livestock production, such that US demand cannot be satisfied with exclusively foreign livestock, and because US livestock are often geographically closer to US domestic markets than imported livestock. (Panel Reports, para. 7.349)

[678] Panel Reports, para. 7.350.

consumers in an understandable manner, if it is communicated at all. Yet, nothing in the Panel's findings or on the Panel record explains or supplies a rational basis for this disconnect. Therefore, we consider the manner in which the COOL measure seeks to provide information to consumers on origin, through the regulatory distinctions described above, to be arbitrary, and the disproportionate burden imposed on upstream producers and processors to be unjustifiable.

348. We emphasize that this lack of correspondence between the recordkeeping and verification requirements, on the one hand, and the limited consumer information conveyed through the retail labelling requirements and exemptions therefrom, on the other hand, is of central importance to our overall analysis under Article 2.1 of the *TBT Agreement*. This is because, in reaching its finding of detrimental impact, the Panel found that it is the recordkeeping and verification requirements that "necessitate" segregation[679], and that create an incentive for US producers to process exclusively domestic livestock and a disincentive to process imported livestock. That is, the Panel found that the recordkeeping and verification requirements imposed under the COOL measure lead to the detrimental impact on imported livestock in the US market.[680] We have affirmed this finding above.

349. In sum, our examination of the COOL measure under Article 2.1 reveals that its recordkeeping and verification requirements impose a disproportionate burden on upstream producers and processors, because the level of information conveyed to consumers through the mandatory labelling requirements is far less detailed and accurate than the information required to be tracked and transmitted by these producers and processors. It is these same recordkeeping and verification requirements that "necessitate" segregation, meaning that their associated compliance costs are higher for entities that process livestock of different origins. Given that the least costly way of complying with these requirements is to rely exclusively on domestic livestock, the COOL measure creates an incentive for US producers to use exclusively domestic livestock and thus has a detrimental impact on the competitive opportunities of imported livestock. Furthermore, the recordkeeping and verification requirements imposed on upstream producers and processors cannot be explained by the need to convey to consumers information regarding the countries where livestock were born, raised, and slaughtered, because the detailed information required to be tracked and transmitted by those producers is not necessarily conveyed to consumers through the labels prescribed under the COOL measure. This is either because the prescribed labels do not expressly identify specific production steps and, in particular for Labels B and C, contain confusing or inaccurate origin

---

679 Panel Reports, para. 7.327.

680 Panel Reports, para. 7.372. See also paras. 7.381, 7.420, and 7.548.

information, or because the meat or meat products are exempt from the labelling requirements altogether. Therefore, the detrimental impact caused by the same recordkeeping and verification requirements under the COOL measure can also not be explained by the need to provide origin information to consumers. Based on these findings, we consider that the regulatory distinctions imposed by the COOL measure amount to arbitrary and unjustifiable discrimination against imported livestock, such that they cannot be said to be applied in an even-handed manner. Accordingly, we find that the detrimental impact on imported livestock does not stem exclusively from a legitimate regulatory distinction but, instead, reflects discrimination in violation of Article 2.1 of the *TBT Agreement*.

350. We therefore *uphold*, albeit for different reasons, the Panel's ultimate finding, in paragraph 7.548 of the Panel Reports, that the COOL measure, particularly in regard to the muscle cut meat labels, is inconsistent with Article 2.1 of the *TBT Agreement* because it accords less favourable treatment to imported livestock than to like domestic livestock.[681]

VI. ARTICLE 2.2 OF THE *TBT AGREEMENT*

A. Introduction

351. We turn now to the appeals relating to the Panel's finding that the COOL measure is inconsistent with Article 2.2 of the *TBT Agreement*. In ruling on the claims raised by Canada and by Mexico under Article 2.2 of the *TBT Agreement*, the Panel found that the COOL measure is "trade-restrictive"[682]; that the objective pursued by the United States through the COOL measure is "to provide consumer information on origin"[683]; and that this objective is "legitimate" within the meaning of Article 2.2.[684] Ultimately, the Panel sustained the claims of the complainants and found that "the COOL measure violates Article 2.2 because it does not fulfil the objective of providing consumer information on origin with respect to meat products".[685]

352. Each of the participants challenges aspects of the Panel's interpretation of Article 2.2 of the *TBT Agreement* and the application of its chosen legal

[681] See also Canada Panel Report, para. 8.3(b); Mexico Panel Report, para. 8.3(b).

[682] Panel Reports, para. 7.575.

[683] Panel Reports, para. 7.617. See also paras. 7.620 and 7.715. We recall in this respect that the COOL measure defines the "origin" of beef and pork as a function of the country or countries in which the livestock from which the meat is derived were born, raised, and slaughtered.

[684] Panel Reports, para. 7.651.

[685] Canada Panel Report, para. 8.3(c); Mexico Panel Report, para. 8.3(c). See also Panel Reports, para. 7.720.

framework to the COOL measure. The United States requests us to reverse the Panel's ultimate conclusion that the COOL measure is inconsistent with Article 2.2, whereas both Canada and Mexico request us to uphold this finding. In the event that we accept the United States' appeal and reverse the Panel's finding that "the COOL measure violates Article 2.2 because it does not fulfil the objective of providing consumer information on origin with respect to meat products"[686], both Canada and Mexico request us to complete the analysis and find that the COOL measure is inconsistent with Article 2.2 because it is more trade restrictive than necessary to fulfil a legitimate objective.

353. The United States seeks reversal of the Panel's ultimate conclusion that the COOL measure is inconsistent with Article 2.2 on three main grounds. First, the United States challenges the Panel's finding that the COOL measure is "trade-restrictive".[687] Second, the United States submits that the Panel wilfully distorted and misrepresented the United States' position as to its chosen "level of fulfilment" of the objective, contrary to Article 11 of the DSU, and further, failed to consider all the relevant information regarding that "level of fulfilment".[688] Third, the United States appeals the legal framework adopted by the Panel to determine whether a measure is more trade restrictive than necessary "to fulfil" a legitimate objective, as well as the Panel's application of that framework to the COOL measure.[689]

354. While supporting the Panel's overall conclusion that the COOL measure is inconsistent with Article 2.2 of the *TBT Agreement*, Canada seeks modification of certain elements of the Panel's analysis. Specifically, Canada challenges the Panel's approach to identifying the objective of the COOL measure.[690] Canada further argues that, in its assessment of Canada's arguments and evidence adduced to show that the objective of the COOL measure is trade protectionism, the Panel acted inconsistently with its duties under Article 11 of the DSU.[691] Canada further contests the Panel's finding that the objective of providing consumer information on origin is "legitimate", within the meaning of Article 2.2.[692] Finally, should the United States be successful in obtaining

686 Canada Panel Report, para. 8.3(c); Mexico Panel Report, para. 8.3(c). See also Panel Reports, para. 7.720.

687 United States' appellant's submission, para. 120 and footnote 187 to para. 124.

688 United States' appellant's submission, para. 136.

689 United States' appellant's submission, para. 171.

690 Canada alleges that the Panel erred in three ways: (i) by focusing on a general policy objective that the COOL measure might pursue, as articulated by the United States, rather than on the actual objective pursued by the COOL measure; (ii) by not considering the design, architecture, and structure of the COOL measure as relevant; and (iii) by failing to identify the objective in sufficient detail to determine its legitimacy. (Canada's other appellant's submission, para. 20)

691 Canada's other appellant's submission, paras. 32 and 33.

692 Canada's other appellant's submission, para. 47.

reversal of the Panel's finding that the COOL measure is inconsistent with Article 2.2 because it does not fulfil its objective, then Canada requests us to complete the analysis and find that the COOL measure does not comply with Article 2.2 because there are less trade-restrictive alternative measures available.[693]

355. Each of the grounds raised by Mexico in its other appeal is conditional upon our reversal of the Panel's finding that the COOL measure is inconsistent with Article 2.2.[694] In that event, Mexico seeks modification of certain aspects of the Panel's reasoning and an ultimate finding that the COOL measure is inconsistent with Article 2.2. Mexico challenges the Panel's approach to identifying the objective pursued through the COOL measure, and asserts that the "real" objective of the COOL measure is the protection of the US domestic cattle industry.[695] In the event that we reverse the Panel's Article 2.2 finding of inconsistency, but confirm the Panel's findings that the objective of the COOL measure is to provide consumer information on origin and that such objective is legitimate, then Mexico requests us to complete the analysis and find that the COOL measure is inconsistent with Article 2.2. In this regard, Mexico contends that there are less trade-restrictive alternative measures available to the United States to fulfil its objective, taking into account the risks non-fulfilment would create.[696] While we take note of the conditional nature of Mexico's other appeal, we will consider its arguments together with Canada's when we review the relevant portions of the Panel's analysis.

356. Below, we set out an overview of the Panel's findings before turning to assess the merits of the participants' arguments on appeal.

B. The Panel's Analysis

357. The Panel began by setting out the legal framework that it would apply in assessing the complainants' claims that the COOL measure is inconsistent with Article 2.2 of the *TBT Agreement*. The Panel understood that "the first sentence

---

693 Canada's other appellant's submission, para. 69. As discussed further below, Canada identifies four possible alternative measures that, in its view, demonstrate that the COOL measure is more trade restrictive than necessary to fulfil its objective.

694 Mexico's other appellant's submission, paras. 28 and 47. At the oral hearing, Mexico explained that, if the Appellate Body accepts the objective as defined by the Panel, and further accepts that it is legitimate, then its appeal should be considered as a conditional appeal. However, if the Appellate Body overturns either of these findings, then its arguments would be more akin to a request for completion of the analysis.

695 Mexico's other appellant's submission, para. 44. Mexico contends that, in concluding otherwise, the Panel committed legal error and, in addition, failed to conduct an objective assessment of the matter, as required under Article 11 of the DSU. (Mexico's other appellant's submission, para. 40)

696 Mexico's other appellant's submission, para. 47.

of Article 2.2 sets out a general principle", reflected in the fifth recital of the preamble of the *TBT Agreement*, as well as in Article 2.5 of the *TBT Agreement*, namely, that Members are not to create unnecessary obstacles to international trade through technical regulations.[697] The Panel explained that the conformity of a measure with that "general principle" must be ascertained based on the elements of the second sentence of Article 2.2, because, in its view, the second sentence explains what the first sentence means.[698]

358. The Panel observed that the second sentence of Article 2.2 comprises "several elements"[699], and that an analysis under that sentence could vary depending on the circumstances of a given dispute.[700] The Panel explained that its assessment of the Article 2.2 claims in these disputes would entail consideration of whether the complainants had established the following:

(i) that the COOL measure is trade restrictive within the meaning of Article 2.2;

(ii) that the objective pursued by the United States through the COOL measure is not legitimate; and

(iii) if the objective is legitimate, that the COOL measure is more trade restrictive than necessary to fulfil a legitimate objective.[701]

359. With respect to the first step, the Panel considered it unnecessary to define the exact scope of the term "trade-restrictive" under Article 2.2. Nonetheless, it did consider the scope of this term to be "broad".[702] For the Panel, a demonstration of a measure's trade-restrictiveness does not require a demonstration of any actual trade effects. Rather, the focus is on the competitive opportunities available to imported products.[703] The Panel declined to express a general view on the relationship between a technical regulation's non-conformity with Article 2.1 and the assessment of "trade-restrictiveness" under Article 2.2.[704] For purposes of these disputes, the Panel recalled its earlier finding that the COOL measure "negatively affects imported livestock's conditions of competition in the US market in relation to like domestic livestock

---

697 Panel Reports, para. 7.551.

698 Panel Reports, para. 7.552.

699 Panel Reports, para. 7.553.

700 *Ibid.*

701 Panel Reports, para. 7.558.

702 Panel Reports, para. 7.572.

703 *Ibid.*

704 Panel Reports, para. 7.573.

by imposing higher segregation costs on imported livestock".[705] On this basis, the Panel concluded that the complainants had demonstrated that the COOL measure is "trade-restrictive" within the meaning of Article 2.2. The Panel also explained that it was not making a finding on the *level* of trade-restrictiveness of the COOL measure, as this question would be addressed, if necessary, at the third step in its analysis of whether the COOL measure is more trade restrictive than necessary.[706]

360. Under the second step of its test, the Panel began by seeking to identify the objective pursued by the United States through the COOL measure. The Panel noted that, while Canada and Mexico argued that the "true objective of the COOL measure is to protect domestic industry", the United States responded that its objective is to provide consumer information on origin.[707] The Panel found the complainants' arguments to be "misplaced on several grounds".[708] On the basis of the information provided by the United States when it notified the COOL measure to the TBT Committee, as well as the United States' declared objective, as reflected in its submissions to the Panel during the course of the Panel proceedings, the Panel identified the objective pursued by the United States as being "to provide consumer information on origin"[709] and, further, as being "to provide as much clear and accurate origin information as possible to consumers".[710]

361. Turning to the question of whether the objective pursued by the United States is "legitimate", the Panel stated that Article 2.2 demonstrates that the legitimacy of a given objective must be found in the "*genuine nature*" of the objective, which is "justifiable" and "supported by relevant public policies or other social norms".[711] The Panel further stated that "providing consumers with information on the origin of the products they purchase is in keeping with the requirements of current social norms in a considerable part of the WTO Membership"[712], and concluded that "providing consumer information on origin is a legitimate objective within the meaning of Article 2.2".[713]

---

[705] Panel Reports, para. 7.574.

[706] Panel Reports, para. 7.575.

[707] Panel Reports, paras. 7.576 and 7.577.

[708] Panel Reports, para. 7.596.

[709] Panel Reports, para. 7.617.

[710] Panel Reports, para. 7.620.

[711] Panel Reports, para. 7.632. (original emphasis) See also para. 7.631 (referring to Panel Report, *EC – Sardines*, para. 7.121; and Panel Report, *Canada – Pharmaceutical Patents*, para. 7.69).

[712] Panel Reports, para. 7.650.

[713] Panel Reports, para. 7.651.

362. Under the third step of its test, the Panel considered whether the COOL measure is more trade restrictive than necessary to fulfil the legitimate objective of providing consumer information on origin. At the outset, the Panel found useful guidance in the legal tests established under Article XX of the GATT 1994 and Article 5.6 of the *SPS Agreement*[714], and rejected the United States' contention that Article XX is not relevant to the interpretation of Article 2.2 of the *TBT Agreement*.[715] The Panel began this part of its assessment by considering the objective of the COOL measure, as revealed in its text, design, architecture, and structure, as well as through various statements made by legislators during the legislative process leading to its enactment. The Panel concluded that these elements confirmed that the objective of the COOL measure "is consumer information on origin as declared by the United States".[716] The Panel then proceeded to examine whether the COOL measure fulfils this objective, explaining that this involved scrutiny of whether the COOL measure carries out and performs the objective of providing origin information to consumers.[717] The Panel found that the ability of a labelling regime to fulfil this objective will depend on the capability of labels to convey clear and accurate information on origin.[718] The Panel therefore stated that it would examine the specific labelling scheme under the COOL measure, "particularly the content and categorization of different categories of labels".[719]

363. The Panel noted that, under the COOL measure, the definition of "origin" involves information on the places where animals from which meat is derived were born, raised, and slaughtered, and that the labels identifying origin, therefore, refer to several elements. However, it found that Labels B and C did not deliver origin information as defined under the measure or as the consumer might understand it.[720] First, the Panel noted that, "in order for the average consumer to understand the meaning of a specific COOL label on meat products, he would also need to understand the definition of each category of labels as prescribed in the measure."[721] Second, while Labels B and C are differentiated

---

[714] Panel Reports, para. 7.667.

[715] Panel Reports, paras. 7.669 and 7.670.

[716] Panel Reports, para. 7.685.

[717] Panel Reports, para. 7.692 (referring to the dictionary definition of "fulfil"—"2. Provide fully with what is wished for; satisfy the appetite or desire of; 3. Make complete, supply with what is lacking; replace (something); ... 6. Carry out, perform, do (something prescribed)"—as provided in *Shorter Oxford English Dictionary*, 6th edn, A. Stevenson (ed.) (Oxford University Press, 2007), Vol. 1, p. 1053).

[718] Panel Reports, para. 7.695.

[719] *Ibid.*

[720] Panel Reports, para. 7.699.

[721] Panel Reports, para. 7.700. In this regard, the Panel observed that, with respect to mixed origin labels, that is, Labels B and C:

by the order in which the countries are listed on the label, it was not clear to the Panel that this information would be communicated to consumers or that they would be able to distinguish between these two labels in terms of origin.[722] The Panel also took note of the effect of the measure in respect of commingled meat, and observed that, even if there were "a perfect consumer who is fully informed of the meaning" of Labels B and C, "she may never be assured that the label precisely reflects the origin of meat as defined under the COOL measure" due to, *inter alia*, "the interchangeable use of Label B and Label C allowed for commingled meat".[723]

364. The Panel thus considered that the COOL measure "falls short" of fulfilling its objective.[724] While acknowledging that the COOL measure's labelling requirements provide some additional country of origin information, and may have reduced consumer confusion as compared to the situation prior to the COOL measure[725], the Panel nevertheless found that "origin information on labels as prescribed by the measure does not ensure meaningful information for consumers, except origin information on Label A."[726] Having determined that "the COOL measure does not fulfil the identified objective within the meaning of Article 2.2"[727], the Panel found it unnecessary to proceed to analyze whether the COOL measure is "more trade-restrictive than necessary" based on the alleged availability of less trade-restrictive alternative measures that could equally fulfil the identified objective.[728]

> ... a label "Product of the US, Mexico" does not describe what "the US and Mexico" means as far as origin of the meat is concerned. As Mexico suggests, on its face, these names could be understood as meaning products comprising meat originating in both the United States and Mexico. This may be the case particularly for meat sold in a bulk display. However, confusion is also likely in a case where a consumer-ready package contains only a single piece of meat, as the meaning of the two country names listed on the label is not clear.

(*Ibid.*)

722 Panel Reports, para. 7.701.

723 Panel Reports, para. 7.702.

724 Panel Reports, para. 7.716.

725 Panel Reports, para. 7.717 reads:

> We acknowledge that labels required to be affixed to meat products according to the requirements under the measure provide additional country of origin information that was not available prior to the COOL measure. We also agree that the labelling requirements under the COOL measure may have reduced consumer confusion that existed under the pre-COOL measure and USDA grade labelling system.

726 Panel Reports, para. 7.718.

727 Panel Reports, para. 7.719. See also para. 7.720.

728 Panel Reports, para. 7.719.

365. The Panel therefore concluded that:

> ... the complainants have demonstrated that the COOL measure does *not* fulfil the objective of providing consumer information on origin, particularly with respect to meat products, within the meaning of Article 2.2. We therefore find that the United States has acted inconsistently with Article 2.2.[729] (original emphasis)

C. Analysis

366. The participants' appeals relate to discrete aspects of the framework adopted by the Panel in its analysis of Article 2.2 of the *TBT Agreement* and require us to consider a number of issues relating to the interpretation of that provision. Accordingly, we begin with an overview of the elements involved in an Article 2.2 analysis, drawing in particular on the guidance provided in the recent report of the Appellate Body in *US – Tuna II (Mexico)*.

367. Thereafter, we address the specific arguments raised by the participants in their appeals. We consider first the United States' appeal of the Panel's finding that the COOL measure is trade restrictive, after which we assess the merits of the participants' arguments relating to the Panel's identification of the objective of the COOL measure and Canada's arguments relating to the Panel's finding that that objective is legitimate. We then proceed with an analysis of the appeal of the United States concerning the approach taken by the Panel in its examination of whether the COOL measure is more trade restrictive than necessary to fulfil its objective, including the Panel's decision to end its Article 2.2 analysis after having concluded that the COOL measure does not "fulfil" its objective.

1. Article 2.2 of the TBT Agreement

368. The text of Article 2.2 of the *TBT Agreement* reads as follows:

> Members shall ensure that technical regulations are not prepared, adopted or applied with a view to or with the effect of creating unnecessary obstacles to international trade. For this purpose, technical regulations shall not be more trade-restrictive than necessary to fulfil a legitimate objective, taking account of the risks non-fulfilment would create.

[729] Panel Reports, para. 7.720.

> Such legitimate objectives are, *inter alia:* national security requirements; the prevention of deceptive practices; protection of human health or safety, animal or plant life or health, or the environment. In assessing such risks, relevant elements of consideration are, *inter alia*: available scientific and technical information, related processing technology or intended end-uses of products.

369. The first two sentences of Article 2.2 establish certain obligations with which WTO Members must comply when preparing, adopting, and applying technical regulations. In accordance with the first sentence, they must ensure that such preparation, adoption, and application is not done "with a view to or with the effect of creating unnecessary obstacles to international trade"; and, in accordance with the second sentence, they must ensure that their technical regulations are "not ... more trade-restrictive than necessary to fulfil a legitimate objective, taking account of the risks non-fulfilment would create". The words "[f]or this purpose" linking the first and second sentences suggest that the second sentence informs the scope and meaning of the obligation contained in the first sentence.[730]

370. We begin with the meaning of the different elements set out in the text of Article 2.2. First, a "legitimate objective" refers to an aim or target that is lawful, justifiable, or proper.[731] Article 2.2 lists specific examples of such "legitimate objectives", namely: national security requirements; the prevention of deceptive practices; and the protection of human health or safety, animal or plant life or health, or the environment. The use of the words "*inter alia*" in Article 2.2 introducing that list, however, signifies that the list of legitimate objectives is not a closed one. In addition, the objectives expressly listed provide a reference point for other objectives that may be considered to be legitimate in the sense of Article 2.2.[732] The sixth and seventh recitals of the preamble of the *TBT Agreement* refer to several objectives, which to a large extent overlap with the objectives listed in Article 2.2.[733] As the Appellate Body has also noted, objectives recognized in the provisions of other covered agreements may provide guidance for, or may inform, the analysis of what might be considered to be a legitimate objective under Article 2.2.[734]

---

[730] Appellate Body Report, *US – Tuna II (Mexico)*, para. 318.

[731] Appellate Body Report, *US – Tuna II (Mexico)*, para. 313 (referring to *Shorter Oxford English Dictionary*, 6th edn, W.R. Trumble, A. Stevenson (eds) (Oxford University Press, 2007), Vol. 1, p. 1577; and Vol. 2, p. 1970).

[732] Appellate Body Report, *US – Tuna II (Mexico)*, para. 313.

[733] *Ibid.*

[734] *Ibid.*

371. A panel adjudicating a claim under Article 2.2 may face conflicting arguments by the parties as to the nature of the "objective" pursued by a responding party through its technical regulation. In identifying the objective pursued by a Member, a panel should take into account that Member's articulation of what objective(s) it pursues through its measure. However, a panel is not bound by a Member's characterizations of such objective(s).[735] Indeed, in order to make an objective and independent assessment of the objective that a Member seeks to achieve, the panel must take account of all the evidence put before it in this regard, including "the texts of statutes, legislative history, and other evidence regarding the structure and operation" of the technical regulation at issue.[736]

372. With respect to the determination of the "legitimacy" of the objective, we note first that a panel's finding that the objective is among those listed in Article 2.2 will end the inquiry into its legitimacy. If, however, the objective does not fall among those specifically listed, a panel must make a determination of legitimacy. It may be guided by considerations that we have set out above, including whether the identified objective is reflected in other provisions of the covered agreements.

373. We turn next to the phrase "fulfil a legitimate objective" in Article 2.2 of the *TBT Agreement*. The Appellate Body in *US – Tuna II (Mexico)* found that, while, read in isolation, the word "fulfil" could be understood to signify the *complete* achievement of something, as used in Article 2.2 this term is concerned with the *degree* of contribution that the technical regulation makes towards the achievement of the legitimate objective.[737] The Appellate Body found relevant contextual support for this reading in the sixth recital of the preamble of the *TBT Agreement*, which provides that, subject to certain qualifications[738], a Member shall not be prevented from taking measures necessary to achieve its legitimate objectives "at the levels it considers appropriate".[739] The degree or level of

---

[735] Appellate Body Report, *US – Tuna II (Mexico)*, para. 314 (referring to Appellate Body Report, *US – Gambling*, para. 304).

[736] Appellate Body Report, *US – Tuna II (Mexico)*, para. 314.

[737] Appellate Body Report, *US – Tuna II (Mexico)*, para. 315.

[738] The sixth recital reads:

> *Recognizing* that no country should be prevented from taking measures necessary to ensure the quality of its exports, or for the protection of human, animal or plant life or health, of the environment, or for the prevention of deceptive practices, at the levels it considers appropriate, subject to the requirement that they are not applied in a manner which would constitute a means of arbitrary or unjustifiable discrimination between countries where the same conditions prevail or a disguised restriction on international trade, and are otherwise in accordance with the provisions of this Agreement[.]

[739] Appellate Body Report, *US – Tuna II (Mexico)*, para. 316.

contribution of a technical regulation to its objective is not an abstract concept, but rather something that is revealed through the measure itself. In preparing, adopting, and applying a measure in order to pursue a legitimate objective, a WTO Member articulates, either implicitly or explicitly, the level at which it pursues that objective.[740] Thus, a panel adjudicating a claim under Article 2.2 must seek to ascertain—from the design, structure, and operation of the technical regulation, as well as from evidence relating to its application—to what degree, if at all[741], the challenged technical regulation, as written and applied, actually contributes to the achievement of the legitimate objective pursued by the Member.[742]

374. The notion of "necessity" is reflected in both the first and second sentences of Article 2.2, through the reference in the first sentence to "*unnecessary* obstacles to international trade", and in the second sentence to "not ... more trade-restrictive than *necessary*". As the Appellate Body observed in *US – Tuna II (Mexico)*, the assessment of "necessity", in the context of Article 2.2, involves a "relational analysis"[743] of the following factors: the trade-restrictiveness of the technical regulation; the degree of contribution that it makes to the achievement of a legitimate objective; and the risks non-fulfilment would create. In a particular case, a panel's determination of what is considered "necessary" will be based on a consideration of all these factors.[744]

375. By its terms, Article 2.2 requires an assessment of the necessity of the trade-restrictiveness of the measure at issue. In this regard, the Appellate Body in *US – Tuna II (Mexico)* defined "trade-restrictive" to mean "having a limiting

---

[740] *Ibid.*

[741] This may involve an assessment of whether the measure at issue is capable of achieving the legitimate objective. (Appellate Body Report, *US – Tuna II (Mexico)*, footnote 640 to para. 317)

[742] The Appellate Body explained that, as is the case when determining the contribution of a measure to the achievement of a particular objective in the context of Article XX of the GATT 1994, "a panel must assess the contribution to the legitimate objective actually achieved by the measure at issue." (Appellate Body Report, *US – Tuna II (Mexico)*, para. 317 (referring to Appellate Body Report, *China – Publications and Audiovisual Products*, para. 252))

[743] Appellate Body Report, *US – Tuna II (Mexico)*, para. 318.

[744] The Appellate Body noted that, similarly, in the context of Article XX of the GATT 1994 and Article XIV of the GATS, "necessity" is determined on the basis of "weighing and balancing" a number of factors. (Appellate Body Report, *US – Tuna II (Mexico)*, footnote 643 to para. 318 (referring to Appellate Body Report, *Brazil – Retreaded Tyres*, para. 178; and Appellate Body Report, *US – Gambling*, paras. 306-308)) The Appellate Body has also stated that the word "necessary" refers to a range of degrees of necessity, depending on the context in which it is used. At "one end of this continuum lies 'necessary' understood as 'indispensable'; at the other end, is 'necessary' taken to mean as 'making a contribution to'." (Appellate Body Report, *US – Tuna II (Mexico)*, footnote 642 to para. 318 (quoting Appellate Body Report, *Korea – Various Measures on Beef*, para. 161))

effect on trade".[745] Moreover, it found that the reference in Article 2.2 to "unnecessary obstacles" implies that "some" trade-restrictiveness is allowed and, further, that what is actually prohibited are those restrictions on international trade that "exceed what is necessary to achieve the degree of contribution that a technical regulation makes to the achievement of a legitimate objective".[746]

376. The Appellate Body considered that the use of the comparative "more ... than" in the second sentence of Article 2.2 suggests that the existence of an "unnecessary obstacle[] to international trade" in the first sentence may be established on the basis of a comparative analysis of the above-mentioned factors. In most cases[747], this will involve a comparison of the trade-restrictiveness of, and the degree of achievement of the objective by, the measure at issue, with that of possible alternative measures[748] that may be reasonably available *and* that are less trade restrictive than the challenged measure, taking account of the risks non-fulfilment would create.[749]

377. With respect to the requirement under Article 2.2 to consider "the risks non-fulfilment would create", the Appellate Body explained that this suggests that the comparison of the challenged measure with a possible alternative measure should be made "in the light of the nature of the risks at issue and the gravity of the consequences that would arise from non-fulfilment of the legitimate objective", which suggests a "further element of weighing and balancing" in the analysis under Article 2.2.[750]

378. In summary, the Appellate Body explained the elements of an analysis under Article 2.2 of the *TBT Agreement* as follows:

---

[745] Appellate Body Report, *US – Tuna II (Mexico)*, para. 319.

[746] *Ibid.*

[747] The Appellate Body observed that there are "at least two instances" when such a comparison might not be required, namely, when the measure is not trade restrictive at all, or when a trade-restrictive measure makes *no* contribution to the achievement of the relevant legitimate objective. (Appellate Body Report, *US – Tuna II (Mexico)*, footnote 647 to para. 322)

[748] The Appellate Body explained that the comparison with reasonably available alternative measures is a "conceptual tool" to be used for the purpose of ascertaining whether a challenged measure is more trade restrictive than necessary. (Appellate Body Report, *US – Tuna II (Mexico)*, para. 320)

[749] The Appellate Body drew an analogy with the analysis of "necessity" in the context of Article XX of the GATT 1994 and Article XIV of the GATS, in which a measure found to be inconsistent with a relevant obligation is to be compared with reasonably available less trade-restrictive alternative measures. (Appellate Body Report, *US – Tuna II (Mexico)*, footnote 645 to para. 320 (referring to Appellate Body Report, *Korea – Various Measures on Beef*, para. 166))

[750] Appellate Body Report, *US – Tuna II (Mexico)*, para. 321.

> [A]n assessment of whether a technical regulation is "more trade-restrictive than necessary" within the meaning of Article 2.2 of the *TBT Agreement* involves an evaluation of a number of factors. A panel should begin by considering factors that include: (i) the degree of contribution made by the measure to the legitimate objective at issue; (ii) the trade-restrictiveness of the measure; and (iii) the nature of the risks at issue and the gravity of consequences that would arise from non-fulfilment of the objective(s) pursued by the Member through the measure. In most cases, a comparison of the challenged measure and possible alternative measures should be undertaken. In particular, it may be relevant for the purpose of this comparison to consider whether the proposed alternative is less trade restrictive, whether it would make an equivalent contribution to the relevant legitimate objective, taking account of the risks non-fulfilment would create, and whether it is reasonably available.[751] (footnote omitted)

379. Finally, we recall the burden of proof under Article 2.2. In order to demonstrate that a technical regulation is inconsistent with Article 2.2, the complainant must make a *prima facie* case by presenting evidence and arguments sufficient to establish that the challenged measure is more trade restrictive than necessary to achieve the contribution it makes to the legitimate objective, taking account of the risks non-fulfilment would create. A complainant may, and in most cases will, also seek to identify a possible alternative measure that is less trade restrictive, makes an equivalent contribution to the relevant objective, and is reasonably available. It is then for the respondent to rebut the complainant's *prima facie* case by presenting evidence and arguments showing that the challenged measure is not more trade restrictive than necessary to achieve the contribution it makes toward the objective pursued, for example, by demonstrating that the alternative measure identified by the complainant is not, in fact, "reasonably available", is not less trade restrictive, or does not make an equivalent contribution to the achievement of the relevant legitimate objective.[752]

380. With these interpretations in mind, we turn now to the specific arguments on appeal.

---

[751] Appellate Body Report, *US – Tuna II (Mexico)*, para. 322.

[752] Appellate Body Report, *US – Tuna II (Mexico)*, para. 323.

2. *Did the Panel Err in Finding that the COOL Measure Is Trade Restrictive?*

381. The United States appeals the Panel's finding that the COOL measure is "trade-restrictive", within the meaning of Article 2.2.[753] The United States submits that, "[f]or the reasons" provided in its appeal of the Panel's analysis under Article 2.1 of the *TBT Agreement*, the Panel also erred in finding that the COOL measure is trade restrictive for purposes of its Article 2.2 analysis.[754] In response to questioning at the oral hearing, the United States clarified that its argument on appeal is simply that, because the Panel relied upon a finding that it had made in the course of its analysis under Article 2.1 to conclude that the COOL measure is trade restrictive for purposes of Article 2.2, the latter finding must be reversed once that Article 2.1 finding has been reversed.[755] The United States' appeal is therefore dependent on the success of its appeal under Article 2.1. As we have, however, upheld the Panel's finding that the COOL measure is inconsistent with Article 2.1[756], we need not further consider this ground of the United States' appeal.

3. *Did the Panel Err in Its Identification of the Objective Pursued?*

382. We begin by recalling the divergent positions taken by the parties as to the objective pursued by the United States through the COOL measure. Before the Panel, both Canada and Mexico asserted that, based on "the text as well as the design, architecture, and structure of the COOL measure", the objective of the COOL measure is trade protectionism.[757] The United States maintained that the objective of the COOL measure is to "provide consumer information about origin".[758]

---

[753] United States' appellant's submission, para. 120.

[754] United States' appellant's submission, footnote 187 to para. 124 (quoting Panel Reports, para. 7.574).

[755] Although the Panel expressed the view that "a technical regulation's non-conformity with Article 2.1 is not *per se* an issue for that technical regulation's conformity with Article 2.2 in general or the 'trade-restrictive' element in particular" (Panel Reports, para. 7.573), it nevertheless relied upon findings that it had made in its Article 2.1 analysis to find that the COOL measure is trade restrictive within the meaning of Article 2.2. The United States challenges, in particular, the Panel's reliance upon its finding that "the COOL measure negatively affects imported livestock's conditions of competition in the US market in relation to like domestic livestock by imposing higher segregation costs on imported livestock." (*Ibid.*, para. 7.574) We have rejected the United States' claims of error on appeal related to this finding at paragraph 292 of these Reports.

[756] *Supra*, para. 350.

[757] Panel Reports, para. 7.596. See also para. 7.580.

[758] Panel Reports, paras.7.581 and 7.587.

383. The Panel addressed the question of "what is the objective" in two separate places in its Reports. It did so, first, under the second step[759] of its analysis of the claims (when it considered whether the objective pursued by the United States is legitimate) at paragraphs 7.594-7.620, and again under the third step[760] of its analysis (whether the COOL measure is more trade restrictive than necessary to fulfil its objective) at paragraphs 7.678-7.691.

384. When it addressed the issue of the objective pursued by the COOL measure for the first time, the Panel considered it "inapposite" to address the complainants' arguments that trade protectionism is the objective of the COOL measure, and explained that it would defer its consideration of these arguments to the third step of its analysis.[761] Instead, the Panel decided "to accept the objective as identified by the United States"[762], which it sought to determine based on the United States' submissions during the Panel proceedings, as well as on the notification of the COOL measure provided by the United States to the TBT Committee. The Panel observed that the United States' formulation of the objective had "varied somewhat" throughout its written submissions[763], but that "the main element" consistently highlighted by the United States had been "to provide consumer information on origin".[764] Thus, the Panel stated that it would "proceed on the understanding that this is the objective pursued by the United States through the COOL measure".[765] The Panel further elaborated that "the objective pursued by the United States through the COOL measure is to provide as much clear and accurate origin information as possible to consumers."[766]

385. The second time the Panel considered the COOL measure's objective was in the context of its assessment of whether the COOL measure "fulfils" its objective under the third step of its three-part test.[767] At that juncture, the Panel specifically addressed the complainants' argument that the text, design, architecture, and structure of the COOL measure, as well as statements made during the legislative process for the COOL statute, demonstrated that the COOL measure was designed to protect the United States' domestic industry.[768] Having considered the relevant evidence and arguments of the parties in this regard, the

---

759 See Panel Reports, para. 7.558 (second bullet point).

760 See Panel Reports, para. 7.558 (third bullet point).

761 Panel Reports, para. 7.610.

762 Panel Reports, para. 7.615.

763 Panel Reports, para. 7.617.

764 *Ibid.*

765 *Ibid.*

766 Panel Reports, para. 7.620.

767 Panel Reports, paras. 7.678-7.691.

768 Panel Reports, para. 7.678.

Panel concluded that these additional factors did "not affect" its prior finding that "the objective of the COOL measure is to provide consumer information on origin".[769]

386. In this appeal, the participants raise a number of objections with respect to the approach taken by the Panel in identifying the "objective" pursued. Before addressing these arguments, we wish to express our own concerns with the manner in which the Panel referred to the objective of the COOL measure throughout the course of its analysis.

387. First, we observe that the Panel's formulation of the objective pursued by the United States varied over the course of its analysis. For instance, at times the Panel identified the objective as being "to provide consumer information on origin"[770]; at other times, the Panel referred to the objective as being "to provide as much clear and accurate origin information as possible to consumers".[771] Through these differing formulations of the objective, the Panel introduced a level of uncertainty in its reasoning.[772] It is of course self-evident that panels should seek to avoid using different language to denote the same concept. This is especially so in the context of an analysis under Article 2.2 of the *TBT Agreement*, given that the relevant objective is the benchmark against which a panel must assess the degree of contribution made by a challenged technical regulation, as well as by proposed alternative measures. For these reasons, the importance of a panel identifying with sufficient clarity and consistency the objective or objectives pursued by a Member through a technical regulation cannot be overemphasized.

---

[769] Panel Reports, para. 7.691.

[770] Panel Reports, paras. 7.617, 7.671, and 7.685.

[771] Panel Reports, para. 7.620. See also para. 7.715. The Panel also referred several times to the additional objective of preventing consumer confusion. For example, at paragraph 7.671 of its Reports, the Panel stated:

> Specifically with respect to meat products, the United States describes its objective in more detail as follows: (i) consumer information—the COOL measure purports "to provide consumers with as much clear and accurate information as possible about the country or countries of origin of meat products that they buy at the retail level", particularly "information on the countries, where the animal from which the meat was derived was born, raised, and slaughtered"; and (ii) prevention of consumer confusion—the COOL measure purports to prevent confusion relating to a USDA grade label and the previous FSIS "Product of the U.S.A." labelling system, which allowed this label if the meat products received minimal processes in the United States.

The Panel further paraphrased the second of these objectives as follows: "[T]he United States aims to prevent meat derived from animals of non-US origin from carrying a US-origin label under any circumstances." (*Ibid.*, para. 7.713)

[772] Such uncertainty was also reflected in the divergent formulations expressed by the participants at the oral hearing when asked what they understood the objective identified by the Panel to be.

388. In these disputes, it may be that the reason for the difference in the formulations used by the Panel lies in the fact that the Panel understood the more general formulation (that is, the provision of consumer information on origin) to reflect the objective pursued, and the more detailed formulation (that is, the provision of *as much clear and accurate* origin information *as possible* to consumers) to represent the level of fulfilment of that objective that the United States desired to achieve. Such a view is arguably implicit in the following statement by the Panel:

> [T]he United States aims to achieve its stated objective by providing as much *clear* and *accurate* origin information as possible. Considered *against this level of fulfilment* of its objective and in light of the nature of the objective (i.e. to provide *accurate* origin information), merely providing *more* information than under the previous labelling regime or fulfilling only a limited aspect of the identified objective does not contribute in a meaningful way to fulfilling the objective.[773]
>
> (original italics; underlining added)

389. We note that the United States also points to this statement as setting out the Panel's articulation of "the level at which the United States considers it appropriate to fulfill the objective".[774] In its appeal, the United States contends that it was appropriate for the Panel to include this step in its analysis[775], but that the Panel erred in the way in which it identified the level of fulfilment desired by the United States.[776]

---

[773] Panel Reports, para. 7.715. Read together, paras. 7.619 and 7.620 of the Panel Reports also suggest that the Panel may have been using such an approach.

[774] United States' appellant's submission, para. 124.

[775] The United States contends that Article 2.2 and the sixth recital of the preamble of the *TBT Agreement* make clear "that a Member is entitled to take measures 'at the level it considers appropriate,' in pursuance of a legitimate objective under the Agreement". (United States' appellant's submission, para. 124 (quoting Panel Report, *US – Tuna II (Mexico)*, para. 7.460)) For the United States, this "level", sometimes referred to as the "level of protection", is more accurately termed the "'level of fulfillment' (of the objective)", and this is how "the Panel refers to it". (United States' appellant's submission, para. 124 (referring to Panel Reports, para. 7.715))

[776] As discussed further below, the United States contends that the Panel wrongly understood the United States' "level of fulfilment" as being "to *completely* fulfill its objective of providing consumer information by providing 'clear and accurate' consumer information in every conceivable scenario". (United States' appellant's submission, para. 132 (original emphasis); see subsection VI.C.3(c) of these Reports) According to the United States, in so finding, the Panel acted inconsistently with Article 11 of the DSU because it mischaracterized the United States' position by relying on partial quotes from the United States' submissions. The United States further alleges that the Panel erred in

390. However, as we have explained above, in preparing, adopting, and applying a measure in order to pursue a legitimate objective, a Member articulates, either implicitly or explicitly, the level at which it seeks to pursue that particular objective.[777] Neither Article 2.2 in particular, nor the *TBT Agreement* in general, requires that, in its examination of the objective pursued, a panel must discern or identify, in the abstract, the level at which a responding Member wishes or aims to achieve that objective.[778] Rather, what a panel *is* required to do, under Article 2.2, is to assess the degree to which a Member's technical regulation, as adopted, written, and applied, contributes to the legitimate objective pursued by that Member.[779]

391. Having identified what we consider the Panel's understanding of the objective pursued through the COOL measure to be—that is, the provision of consumer information on origin—we proceed to discuss the participants' arguments on appeal.

(a) Canada's and Mexico's Other Appeals of the Panel's Approach to Identifying the Objective Pursued

392. Canada and Mexico both consider the Panel's reliance on the United States' articulation of the objective alone to be an erroneous basis on which to identify the objective pursued through the COOL measure for the purposes of an Article 2.2 analysis. Canada submits that the Panel erred in focusing its analysis on a general policy objective that the COOL measure might pursue, as stated by the United States, rather than on the actual objective pursued by the measure. In so doing, the Panel also erred in analyzing evidence relating to the design, architecture, structure, and legislative history of the COOL measure only "as a secondary matter [and] as an alternative to the 'identified objective'".[780] While Mexico generally agrees that the identification of the objective of a technical regulation is the prerogative of the Member establishing the measure, and that there is a presumption of good faith in favour of that Member's declared objective—for instance, through its notification of the measure to the TBT Committee—it submits that the Panel should have verified the objective identified by the United States to ensure that it was congruent with the design,

---

failing to consider all relevant information in its determination of the United States' chosen level of fulfilment. (United States' appellant's submission, paras. 136-144)

[777] See *supra*, para. 373.

[778] We have noted above that the sixth recital of the preamble of the *TBT Agreement* provides that a Member shall not be prevented from taking measures necessary to achieve a legitimate objective "at the levels it considers appropriate". (See *supra*, para. 373) This does not, however, require a separate assessment of a *desired* level of fulfilment.

[779] Appellate Body Report, *US – Tuna II (Mexico)*, para. 316.

[780] Canada's other appellant's submission, para. 29.

structure, and architecture of the COOL measure, as well as its legislative history and surrounding circumstances.[781]

393. For its part, the United States considers that the Panel took the United States' declared objective only as "a starting point"[782] for its analysis and did in fact verify the identified objective on the basis of an analysis of the text, design, architecture, and structure of the COOL measure.[783]

394. We explained above that the Panel addressed the question of "what is the objective" twice. The Panel appears to have first determined "the United States' objective" in the abstract, and then turned to consider the specific objective pursued by the COOL measure itself. The Panel also seems to have accorded considerably more deference to the United States' articulation of its objective in its initial consideration of the issue than in its subsequent consideration. In both instances, however, the Panel reached the same result: that the objective that the United States pursues through the COOL measure is the provision of consumer information on origin.

395. We have already set out the proper approach to be followed by a panel in determining the objective a Member seeks to achieve by means of a technical regulation. That analysis calls for an independent and objective assessment, based on an examination of the text of the measure, its design, architecture, structure, legislative history, as well as its operation. While a panel may take as a starting point the responding Member's characterization of the objective it pursues through the measure, a panel is not bound by such characterization. This is so especially where the objective of a measure is contested between the parties, and competing arguments have been raised on the basis of the text of the measure, its design, architecture, structure, legislative history, and evidence relating to its operation. Indeed, the United States itself accepts that the responding Member's declared objective is only a starting point in the panel's analysis of the objective pursued by a measure. Having said this, we note that, while the Panel, when it considered the objective for the first time, stopped once it had determined the declared objective of the United States, it did consider the evidence relating to the COOL measure's text, design, architecture, structure, operation, and legislative history, when it considered the objective for the second time.[784]

---

[781] Mexico's other appellant's submission, para. 35.

[782] United States' appellee's submission, para. 20.

[783] United States' appellee's submission, para. 17.

[784] During questioning at the oral hearing, Mexico and Canada both accepted that the Panel in fact did take into account these elements in its consideration of the objective pursued by the United States through the COOL measure.

396. We are somewhat puzzled by the Panel's segmentation of its analysis of the objective pursued by the COOL measure into two parts. Such segmentation strikes us as unnecessary. Moreover, we have concerns that, at least when it addressed the question of the objective for the first time, the Panel apparently considered itself bound to accept the objective as identified by the United States. Because, however, the Panel ultimately evaluated all relevant features relating to the COOL measure's objective, including evidence and arguments presented by the parties relating to the measure's text, design, architecture, structure, and legislative history, as well as its operation, we do not agree with Canada and Mexico that the Panel erred in its application of Article 2.2 of the *TBT Agreement* by determining the objective of the COOL measure in the "abstract", and solely on the basis of the United States' declared objective.

(b) Canada's and Mexico's Claims under Article 11 of the DSU with respect to the Panel's Identification of the Objective Pursued

(i) Introduction

397. Canada and Mexico each submits that the Panel failed to comply with its duties under Article 11 of the DSU when it assessed the evidence relating to the design, structure, architecture, and legislative history of the COOL measure. In their view, a proper assessment of that evidence would have yielded a conclusion that the true objective of the COOL measure is trade protectionism, that is, the protection of the United States' domestic producers of cattle and hogs.

398. As already explained, the Panel unnecessarily segmented its analysis of the objective of the COOL measure into two parts. To some extent, the complainants', and, in particular, Mexico's claims of error under Article 11 of the DSU relate to the first time that the Panel addressed the issue of the objective pursued by the United States, and consist of allegations that, *because* it committed legal error in identifying the objective "based *solely* on the descriptions, formulations and elaborations provided by the United States"[785], the Panel also ignored or failed to take account of evidence with respect to the design, architecture, and structure of the COOL measure, as well as its legislative history and surrounding circumstances.

399. As discussed above, however, the Panel did not identify the objective based solely on the submissions of the United States. Rather, the Panel undertook a bifurcated analysis of the objective of the COOL measure. Although it declined to take account of evidence relating to the text, design, and structure

[785] Mexico's other appellant's submission, para. 32. (original emphasis)

of the COOL measure, as well as to its legislative history, when it considered the objective for the first time, the Panel explained that it would do so at a subsequent stage of its analysis.[786] The Panel did, indeed, take such evidence into account when it considered the objective for the second time.[787] For this reason, we found above that the Panel did not commit legal error in applying Article 2.2 of the *TBT Agreement*. For the same reason, the Panel cannot be said to have refused to take *any* account of evidence relating to the text, design, and structure of the COOL measure, as well as its legislative history. It also follows that the merits of the claims raised under Article 11 of the DSU must be evaluated through an examination of *both* of the Panel's analyses of the objective pursued by the United States through the COOL measure. With these considerations in mind, we turn to the relevant claims of error raised by each other appellant under Article 11 of the DSU, beginning with Mexico.

(ii) Mexico's Other Appeal under Article 11 of the DSU

400. The bulk of Mexico's argumentation in support of its Article 11 claim is tied to and based on its claim that the Panel committed legal error in basing its finding as to the objective of the COOL measure exclusively on the United States' identification of that objective.[788] Since we have already found that the Panel did not err in this respect, this part of Mexico's appeal must fail. In this vein, we recall that, as the Appellate Body has previously observed, a claim that a panel failed to comply with its duties under Article 11 of the DSU must stand on its own, and should not be made merely as a "subsidiary argument" in support of a claim that the panel erred in its application of a WTO provision.[789]

401. In addition to those arguments in support of its Article 11 claim that are dependent upon its claim of error in the application of Article 2.2 of the *TBT Agreement*, Mexico contends that, "[h]ad the Panel taken into account the

[786] Panel Reports, para. 7.610.

[787] We recall that the Panel addressed this issue for the second time at the outset of its analysis of whether the COOL measure is more trade restrictive than necessary to fulfil its objective. (Panel Reports, paras. 7.678-7.691)

[788] Thus, Mexico contends that, "*because* the legal errors led to the exclusion of relevant facts, the approach is factually erroneous". (Mexico's other appellant's submission, para. 33 (emphasis added)) Mexico further argues that, "[a]s a consequence of this legal error [failing to take into account when assessing the objective of the measure the design, architecture, and structure of a technical regulation as well as its legislative history and surrounding circumstances], the Panel did not take into account the facts presented by Mexico regarding the protectionist character of the COOL measure", and, "[i]n this sense", failed to make an objective assessment of the matter before it and thereby acted inconsistently with Article 11 of the DSU". (*Ibid*, para. 40 (footnote omitted))

[789] Appellate Body Report, *EC – Fasteners (China)*, para. 442. See also Appellate Body Report, *US – Steel Safeguards*, para. 498; and Appellate Body Report, *Chile – Price Band System (Article 21.5 – Argentina)*, para. 238.

relevant evidence, it would have been able to identify the genuine objective of the COOL measure"[790], that is, trade protectionism. Mexico further requests us to complete the legal analysis and to find that the objective of the COOL measure is the protection of the US domestic cattle industry.[791] Mexico does not, however, identify any specific error that the Panel made, the second time that it considered the objective of the COOL measure, in its assessment of the evidence relating to the text, design, architecture, and structure of the COOL measure, as well as its legislative history. Nor does Mexico allege that, or explain why, the Panel's findings with respect to the objective of the COOL measure lack a factual basis in the record. For these reasons, the remainder of Mexico's arguments under Article 11 of the DSU—which are very brief[792]—must be understood either as mere disagreement with the way in which the Panel weighed the evidence, or as a request for us to conduct a *de novo* assessment of the facts. Neither type of argument can suffice to make out a claim that the Panel failed to comply with its duty, under Article 11 of the DSU, to conduct an objective assessment of the facts.

402. For these reasons, we do not consider that Mexico has demonstrated that the Panel failed to comply with its duties under Article 11 of the DSU in its assessment of the evidence relating to the design, structure, architecture, and legislative history of the COOL measure. We therefore proceed to the arguments made by Canada under this provision.

(iii) Canada's Other Appeal under Article 11 of the DSU

403. In evaluating this part of Canada's other appeal, we are mindful that our inquiry is limited to determining whether Canada has demonstrated that the Panel failed to assess objectively the evidence presented to it regarding the objective of the COOL measure. As the Appellate Body has previously noted, Article 11 of the DSU requires a panel to "consider all the evidence presented to it, assess its credibility, determine its weight, and ensure that its factual findings have a proper basis in that evidence".[793] Within these parameters, "it is generally within the discretion of the panel to decide which evidence it chooses to utilize

[790] Mexico's other appellant's submission, para. 42.

[791] Mexico's other appellant's submission, para. 44.

[792] Mexico's other appellant's submission, paras. 42 and 43.

[793] Appellate Body Report, *Brazil – Retreaded Tyres*, para. 185 (referring to Appellate Body Report, *EC – Hormones*, paras. 132 and 133).

in making findings"[794], and panels "are not required to accord to factual evidence of the parties the same meaning and weight as do the parties".[795]

404. In alleging that the Panel failed to make an objective assessment of the facts, Canada identifies four discrete groups of evidence. We deal with each of these in turn. Before doing so, we briefly recall how the Panel dealt with the relevant evidence and arguments in determining the objective of the COOL measure.

405. The Panel began by examining the text of the COOL measure, which it viewed as confirming "that the objective is to provide consumer information on origin".[796] The Panel then turned to the COOL measure's design and structure. The Panel set out the complainants' arguments regarding the scope of the commodities covered by, and excluded from, the requirements of the COOL measure. The Panel noted that Canada and Mexico asserted that products that face little or no competition from imports are not subject to the COOL measure[797], and also highlighted that the COOL measure excludes covered commodities that are an ingredient in a processed food item or that undergo processing. Moreover, they also pointed out that certain entities that sell meat are excluded from the measure's coverage, such as food service establishments and entities selling perishable agricultural commodities below a certain annual value.[798] The Panel also explained that, according to the complainants, these exemptions and exclusions are evidence that the objective of the COOL measure is trade protectionism because, if the objective of the COOL measure were really to provide origin information, "it would have to apply on a more widespread basis".[799]

406. The Panel dealt collectively with these arguments relating to the scope of the covered commodities, as well as to the exemptions and exclusions from the COOL measure's labelling requirements. In rejecting them, the Panel explained that:

> ... it is not atypical for any kind of regulation to have exceptions in terms of the products and entities that are subject to it. Some ... exceptions might be justifiable for practical reasons and simply facilitate

---

[794] Appellate Body Report, *EC – Hormones*, para. 135.

[795] Appellate Body Report, *Australia – Salmon*, para. 267.

[796] Panel Reports, para. 7.680.

[797] Panel Reports, para. 7.682.

[798] Panel Reports, para. 7.683.

[799] *Ibid.*

> the implementation of the measure at issue without necessarily involving protectionist intent. We also consider that the scope of the COOL measure is broad enough to cover a significant range of food products and entities handling these products.[800]

407. The Panel concluded, based on the text, design, and structure of the COOL measure, that the COOL measure's objective is to provide consumer information on origin.[801]

408. Finally, the Panel considered evidence of various statements made by legislators during the legislative process and observed that, "while the sentiment in some of them finds expression in the COOL measure, the sentiment in others does not."[802] On balance, therefore, the Panel did "not find this evidence of assistance" in its inquiry into the objective of the COOL measure, adding that "it is not inconceivable that parliaments and governments pursue more than one objective through a certain measure."[803] For this reason, the Panel concluded that the statements at issue "[did] not affect" its "conclusion that the objective of the COOL measure is to provide consumer information on origin".[804]

409. On appeal, Canada refers, first, to evidence that it presented to the Panel to demonstrate that the COOL measure "includes and excludes products in a way that makes no sense" from the perspective of providing information on origin but does make sense from the perspective of protecting the domestic industry.[805] As it did before the Panel, Canada argues that the COOL measure cannot be intended to clear up confusion caused by USDA grade labelling, because the COOL measure applies to many products that are not USDA graded—when such products are subject to competition from imports. Conversely, products that face little or no competition from imports in the US market are excluded from the COOL regime, even if they are USDA graded.[806] Canada argues that the Panel mentioned some, but not all, of the evidence that Canada had submitted in this regard, and provided only a brief conclusion as to why the exceptions from coverage under the COOL measure are justifiable. Canada emphasizes that both

---

800 Panel Reports, para. 7.684.

801 Panel Reports, para. 7.685.

802 Panel Reports, para. 7.691.

803 *Ibid.*

804 *Ibid.*

805 Canada's other appellant's submission, para. 34.

806 Canada's other appellant's submission, para. 35.

prohibitive and permissive elements are relevant to an evaluation of the measure as a whole.[807]

410. We observe that, while it may not have done so in as detailed a manner as Canada might have liked, the Panel did grapple with, and reject, most of Canada's arguments regarding the scope of coverage of the COOL measure and its relevance to the identification of its objective. The Panel explicitly referred to Canada's argument that products produced in the United States that face little competition from imports are excluded from the measure, and to the evidence adduced in support of that argument, namely, the percentage of the market share occupied by the domestic industry for certain products not covered under the COOL measure.[808] It is true that the Panel did not specifically reference Canada's additional argument relating to the products covered by the COOL measure—that, if the United States' objective were really to avoid the confusion engendered by USDA grade labelling, then the COOL measure should have applied to all products that have such USDA labelling and not to any products that are not USDA graded. Yet, this alone does not establish that the Panel breached its duties under Article 11 of the DSU. A panel is not obliged to discuss in its report every argument made, or each piece of evidence adduced, by a party.[809] Moreover, in this case, the Panel repeatedly emphasized that the objective of the COOL measure is to provide consumers with information on the origin of the meat they purchase. Although it also acknowledged the objective of preventing consumer confusion, the Panel appears to have considered this to be an additional, and secondary, objective of the COOL measure. Canada asserts that the fact that the COOL measure applies to some products that do not have USDA grade labelling, and does not apply to others that do, calls into question whether the measure really aims to prevent consumer confusion. Even if this were true, however, Canada has not explained why this would necessarily also vitiate the Panel's finding that the objective of the COOL measure is to provide consumers with information on origin.

411. In addition, the Panel did acknowledge limitations on the scope of coverage of the COOL measure. Moreover, it provided reasoning as to why it was not persuaded that the exclusion of certain products from the COOL measure necessarily means that the COOL measure was intended to protect

---

[807] Canada's other appellant's submission, para. 35 (referring to Appellate Body Report, *EC – Asbestos*, para. 64).

[808] We note that the Panel provided details of Canada's arguments in a footnote: "Canada argues that the products that face little or no import competition, include almonds (with a market share of 99.5%), walnuts (with a market share of 99.1%), pistachios (with a market share of 99%), and turkey (with a market share of 99.9%)". (Panel Reports, footnote 897 to para. 7.682) It also referred to the specific paragraphs in the submissions of Canada and Mexico where these figures, and supporting arguments, were presented.

[809] Appellate Body Report, *EC – Poultry*, para. 135.

domestic industry, including that such exclusions may reflect practical reasons and simply facilitate implementation of the COOL measure.[810] Canada does not take issue with this finding *per se*, but rather repeats arguments that it made before the Panel that the evidence it submitted reveals protectionist intent. Canada appears to request us to weigh this evidence differently on appeal.

412. A second argument raised by Canada relates to the Panel's treatment of an argument by Canada that the COOL measure applies "special rules" to imported livestock that it does not apply to other products. Before the Panel, Canada submitted that "the COOL regime excludes from coverage almost all products that undergo significant change after they pass a WTO Member's border" and that "the only exception is meat from livestock imported into the United States."[811] As we understand it, Canada highlighted that, while substantially transformed perishable agricultural products are removed from the scope of the COOL measure, meat is not so excluded, even though it has also been substantially transformed from its original state—livestock. This, argued Canada, shows that livestock have been "singled out" for different treatment and, therefore, that the objective of the COOL measure is protectionist. As additional support, Canada argued that the definition of a "processed food item" applies differently for meat and livestock than for other products, such as vegetables. These arguments were contained in part of one paragraph of Canada's second written submission to the Panel.[812]

413. On appeal, Canada reiterates that this singling out of livestock demonstrates the objective of protecting livestock producers in the United States and that the Panel erred since it did not "clearly mention" this in its analysis, "much less make an objective assessment of the fact and its relevance to the determination of the COOL measure's objective".[813]

414. We consider, however, that the Panel's statement that "[t]he complainants further submit that the true objective of the COOL measure is trade protectionism as demonstrated by the fact that the COOL measure excludes from its scope covered commodities that are an ingredient in a processed food item or that undergo processing"[814] may be understood as referring to, *inter alia*, this

---

[810] Panel Reports, para. 7.684.

[811] Canada's second written submission to the Panel, para. 57(a).

[812] *Ibid.*

[813] Canada's other appellant's submission, para. 37.

[814] Panel Reports, para. 7.683 (referring to 2009 Final Rule (AMS), section 65.220). That provision, in conjunction with section 65.135(b), excludes from the COOL measure labelling requirements those covered commodities that have undergone specific processing that results in a change in their character.

argument by Canada. Indeed, Canada itself recognizes this.[815] To the extent that the Panel's decision to deal with several arguments together may have resulted in the Panel not clearly mentioning each one separately, this alone does not establish that the Panel breached Article 11 of the DSU. As we have already noted, the fact that a panel does not explicitly reflect all of a party's arguments, or accord to specific evidence the weight that one party considers it should, does not, in and of itself, constitute error. The Appellate Body has also stated that a panel has the discretion "to address only those arguments it deems necessary to resolve a particular claim".[816]

415. Third, Canada contends that the Panel failed to consider Canada's arguments and evidence demonstrating the COOL measure's inability to provide useful information. Canada refers to arguments provided in its second written submission to the Panel regarding alleged deficiencies in the labels under the COOL measure in disclosing information about origin, especially in cases where mixed origin labels are used.[817] While acknowledging that the Panel considered this evidence elsewhere in its analysis[818], Canada considers that it was also relevant for determining the objective of the COOL measure. Such evidence reveals the protectionist intent of the COOL measure because, "if the objective had been truly to provide information, the measure would have been designed to do that."[819] Therefore, asserts Canada, the Panel should also have taken this evidence into account as part of that inquiry.

416. As we see it, however, a panel has a degree of discretion to assess and employ the evidence before it in the context in which the panel finds it most probative and useful.[820] The Panel clearly took account of evidence relating to the ability of the different COOL labels to convey meaningful information. It is unclear to us why, as Canada's arguments imply, the Panel was also bound to treat that evidence as not only relevant to, but highly probative of, the objective of that measure.

---

[815] Canada notes that the Panel "advert[ed]" to that argument in its analysis. (Canada's other appellant's submission, footnote 74 to para. 37 (referring to Panel Reports, para. 7.683))

[816] Appellate Body Report, *EC – Poultry*, para. 135.

[817] Canada's other appellant's submission, para. 38 (referring to Canada's second written submission to the Panel, para. 57(c)).

[818] Canada's other appellant's submission, para. 38 (referring to Panel Reports, para. 7.718).

[819] Canada's other appellant's submission, para. 38.

[820] The Appellate Body has said that:

> ... nothing in the DSU limits the faculty of a panel freely to use arguments submitted by any of the parties—or to develop its own legal reasoning—to support its own findings and conclusions on the matter under its consideration.

(Appellate Body Report, *EC – Hormones*, para. 156)

417. Finally, Canada refers to the Panel's treatment of evidence regarding the legislative process leading to the adoption of the COOL measure. Canada highlights the evidence that it adduced to this effect, including the fact that the COOL measure formed part of the 2002 Farm Bill, rather than being placed within a legislative package relating to consumer information.[821] Canada also refers to statements by key legislators, including Senator Johnson (allegedly a "key" architect of the COOL measure[822]), and Congressman Peterson (regarded by Canada as "pivotal" to the passage of the COOL measure).[823] Finally, Canada also points to evidence that it was "overwhelmingly"[824] US producers, rather than consumer groups, who intervened to support the COOL measure.

418. Canada observes that "the Panel correctly found that it was appropriate to consider evidence of legislators", and acknowledges that the Panel summarized some of the evidence put forward by Canada (and Mexico) on that point.[825] Canada faults the Panel, however, for failing to review *all* of the evidence on this point, and for failing to evaluate it. Instead, the Panel simply stated that, "while the sentiment in some of [the statements by legislators] finds expression in the COOL measure, the sentiment in others does not", and then concluded that "[o]n balance, [it did not] find this evidence of assistance".[826] Yet, the Panel did not consider the probative value of the statements that, in Canada's view, reveal the true objective of the COOL measure, and did not explain which statements "found expression" in the COOL measure and which did not. For Canada, such failure constitutes an error under Article 11 of the DSU.

419. We point out first that the Panel referred to evidence from a wide range of sources, including some of those specifically referred to by Canada on appeal, such as the statement by Congressman Peterson.[827] The Panel also noted

[821] Canada's other appellant's submission, para. 39.

[822] Canada's other appellant's submission, para. 40 (referring to Canada's second written submission to the Panel, para. 60; and 107th Congressional Record–Senate, Statement by Senator Tim Johnson (daily ed. 14 December 2001) S13270 (Panel Exhibit US-61), at S13271).

[823] Canada's other appellant's submission, para. 40 (referring to Panel Reports, para. 7.688; Canada's first written submission to the Panel, para. 174; and Country-of-Origin Meat Labeling Act, Hearing on HR 1144 before the Subcommittee on Livestock and Horticulture of the Committee on Agriculture, House of Representatives, 106th Congress, 2nd Session, 26 September 2000 (Panel Exhibit CDA-10)).

[824] Canada's other appellant's submission, para. 41 (referring to Canada's second written submission to the Panel, para. 62).

[825] Canada's other appellant's submission, para. 42 (referring to Panel Reports, para. 7.686).

[826] Panel Reports, para. 7.691.

[827] As Canada itself notes, the Panel referred specifically to the following statement by Congressman Collin Peterson: "I am perfectly willing to put barriers at the borders so I just want to clear that up". (Panel Reports, para. 7.688 (quoting Panel Exhibit CDA-10, *supra*, footnote 823, at p. 77 of the Subcommittee Report)

evidence adduced by Mexico[828], and by the United States.[829] It appears, therefore, that the Panel did consider the evidence relied upon by the parties. As we have already stated, the mere fact that the Panel did not refer explicitly to each and every statement or piece of evidence submitted by Canada (or accord to them the weight that Canada considers they deserve) does not mean that it erred or failed to comply with its duties under Article 11 of the DSU. Furthermore, although Canada does not consider the evidence to have been probative, Canada does acknowledge that the Panel also referred to two statements by members of Congress, which the United States had introduced as evidence of a non-protectionist purpose[830], and that the Panel record did contain one letter from consumer groups on the record, expressing support for origin labelling.[831]

420. It also seems to us that Canada's arguments fail to recognize that the Panel appears not to have considered evidence of legislative intent to be particularly probative of a measure's objective, in general. Before assessing the arguments of the parties—which were based primarily on statements of a number of persons and constituents involved in or related to the passage of the COOL measure—the Panel referred to earlier findings of the Appellate Body which, in its view, suggested that the subjective intent of legislators was not relevant to an inquiry into the objective of a measure[832], but which recognized that it was possible to have recourse to the purpose or objectives of the legislature "to the extent that they are given objective expression in the statute itself".[833] Having "examined all of the statements" submitted by the parties in these disputes, the Panel concluded that it did not find statements by individual legislators to be of assistance in its inquiry.[834] While Canada suggests that the Panel was required to explain further its finding, we do not consider this to have been necessary. The Panel explicitly and properly recognized the caution with which evidence of this nature should be treated. Moreover, the Panel was clearly of the view that the protective intent alleged by Canada did not clearly or consistently find "objective expression" in the COOL measure, a view that it was entitled to reach, in the exercise of its discretion, based on its appreciation of the evidence before it.

---

828 Panel Reports, para. 7.689.

829 Panel Reports, para. 7.690.

830 Canada's other appellant's submission, para. 42 (referring to Panel Reports, para. 7.690, in turn referring to Panel Exhibits US-13 and US-14).

831 Canada's other appellant's submission, para. 41 (referring to Panel Exhibit US-61).

832 Panel Reports, para. 7.686 (referring to Appellate Body Report, *Japan – Alcoholic Beverages II*, p. 27, DSR1996:I, 97, at 119; and Appellate Body Report, *Chile – Alcoholic Beverages*, para. 62).

833 Panel Reports, para. 7.686 (quoting Appellate Body Report, *Chile – Alcoholic Beverages*, para. 62).

834 Panel Reports, para. 7.691.

(iv) Overall Disposition of Canada's and Mexico's Claims under Article 11 of the DSU with respect to the Panel's Identification of the Objective Pursued

421. Overall, the arguments that Canada puts forward in support of its appeal under Article 11 of the DSU consist mainly of the identification of four groups of evidence that it put before the Panel, coupled with an assertion that "the Panel did not reach the appropriate conclusion based on that evidence."[835] Canada does not explain, specifically, *how* the Panel failed to comply with its duty to assess objectively the facts under Article 11 of the DSU. Nor does Canada make clear whether it is arguing that the Panel erred in its treatment of *each* of these four groups of evidence, or only in its collective assessment of all four groups of evidence, taken together. Moreover, Canada explicitly recognizes that the Panel did take some account of each such group of evidence.

422. It seems to us that, in arguing that the Panel did not reach the appropriate conclusion based on the evidence, Canada in effect seeks to have us conduct our own assessment of the facts, and to ascribe a different weight to the evidence than did the Panel. Yet, we are not called upon, on appeal, to re-weigh factual evidence, or to disturb the Panel's exercise of its discretion merely because we might have arrived at a different conclusion. We also consider that the lack of importance that the Panel attached to the evidence of statements made by legislators reflects not only its appreciation of the facts, but also its recognition that, as a matter of law, care should be exercised in relying upon this type of evidence in order to determine the objective pursued by a measure. Furthermore, apart from asserting that the Panel should have made a different finding, Canada does not contend that either the finding actually made by the Panel in rejecting its arguments regarding the protectionist intent of the COOL measure[836], or the Panel's finding as to the objective of the COOL measure, lacked a proper factual underpinning. It follows that we do not consider that Canada has demonstrated that the Panel failed to satisfy its duty to assess objectively the facts with respect to its analysis of the objective pursued by the United States through the COOL measure.

423. We recall that we have dismissed the arguments raised by Mexico in support of its Article 11 claim on appeal, either because these arguments are based on its claim that the Panel committed legal error in basing its finding as to the objective of the COOL measure exclusively on the United States'

[835] Canada's other appellant's submission, para. 33.

[836] The Panel found that "the scope of the COOL measure is broad enough to cover a significant range of food products and entities handling these products". (Panel Reports, para. 7.684)

identification of that objective, which we have rejected[837], or because they amount to mere disagreement with the way in which the Panel weighed the evidence or to a request for us to conduct a *de novo* assessment of the facts.[838]

424. Accordingly, we reject these grounds of appeal and *find* that Canada and Mexico have not established that the Panel acted inconsistently with its obligations under Article 11 of the DSU in assessing the evidence regarding the design, architecture, structure, and legislative history of the COOL measure in its analysis of the objective pursued by the United States through that measure.

(c) The United States' Appeal of the Panel's Finding concerning the COOL Measure's "Level of Fulfilment" of Its Objective

425. The United States alleges that the Panel committed two errors in its analysis of the level at which the United States considers it appropriate to fulfil its objective.[839] Specifically, in concluding that the United States "aimed to provide '*as much clear and accurate* origin information *as possible*'"[840], the Panel: (i) acted inconsistently with Article 11 of the DSU because it wilfully distorted and misrepresented the United States' position as to the level at which the United States considers it appropriate to fulfil that objective; and (ii) failed to consider all relevant information regarding the level at which the United States sought to achieve its objective.[841]

426. We note that these two allegations made by the United States relate to paragraphs 7.590-7.621 of the Panel Reports, that is, to the Panel's first analysis of the objective pursued by the United States.[842] The United States characterizes the Panel's finding that "the objective pursued by the United States through the COOL measure is to provide *as much clear and accurate* origin information *as possible* to consumers"[843] as the Panel's "determination of [the United States'] chosen level of fulfilment"[844] of its objective. The United States claims that, in so finding, the Panel erred in its application of Article 2.2 of the *TBT Agreement*,

---

837 See *supra*, para. 396.

838 See *supra*, paras. 401 and 402.

839 United States' appellant's submission, para. 136.

840 United States' appellant's submission, para. 138 (quoting Panel Reports, para. 7.620). (emphasis added by the United States)

841 United States' appellant's submission, para. 136.

842 United States' appellant's submission, para. 136 (referring to Panel Reports, paras. 7.590-7.621).

843 United States' appellant's submission, para. 138 (quoting Panel Reports, para. 7.620). (emphasis added by the United States)

844 United States' appellant's submission, para. 136 (referring to Panel Reports, paras. 7.590-7.620 and 7.715).

and also failed to make an objective assessment of the facts as required under Article 11 of the DSU. Both of these allegations are, however, misplaced, because they assume that, in identifying the objective, the Panel was also required to identify the desired "level of fulfilment". We have already explained in our analysis above why it was not necessary or appropriate for the Panel, in identifying the objective (that is, to provide consumer information on origin), to further identify the level at which the United States desired to fulfil its objective of providing consumer information on origin (that is, to provide *as much clear and accurate* origin information *as possible* to consumers).[845] As we noted, the fulfilment of an objective is a matter of degree, and what is relevant for the inquiry under Article 2.2 is the degree of contribution to the objective that a measure *actually* achieves.

427. The United States further argues that the Panel erred and acted inconsistently with Article 11 of the DSU by relying on partial quotes that omitted key elements of the United States' description of the desired level of fulfilment of its objective. In particular, the United States points to the complete versions of excerpts from its Panel submissions that, in its view, demonstrate that it intended to strike a balance between providing information to consumers, on the one hand, and minimizing the costs to market participants of implementing the measure, on the other hand.[846] The United States contends that, by "selectively editing" these statements, however, the Panel misrepresented the United States' objective as being "to provide 'as much clear and accurate origin information as possible' *without regard to ... cost*".[847] Thus, the Panel disregarded evidence that the COOL measure reflects a balance between the provision of information and the costs incurred, and wilfully distorted the United States' position.

428. We disagree that the Panel erred in its identification of the objective pursued in this case because it failed to take into account the fact that the COOL measure was implemented with a view to minimizing the costs to market participants. First, as Canada points out, the Panel rejected a similar attempt to introduce a consideration of costs into the formulation of the objective during the stage of interim review on the ground that the United States had not presented arguments during the Panel proceedings.[848] Moreover, and even if the

---

845 See *supra*, paras. 373 and 390.

846 United States' appellant's submission, paras. 136, 139, and 140.

847 United States' appellant's submission, para. 142. (original emphasis)

848 The Panel stated:

> Based on the United States' arguments in the panel proceedings, the Panel decided that the objective as identified by the United States was "to provide consumer information on origin". The Panel was not presented with the argument from the United States that the reduction of compliance costs for market participants also formed part of the objective pursued by the United States through the

United States had raised its argument in a timely manner, we fail to see how the balancing of cost considerations or the extent to which the United States otherwise sought to achieve its objective (with "as much clear and accurate ... information as possible") are properly considered as part of the relevant objective. Indeed, the Panel itself considered the issue of costs only when it came to assess whether the COOL measure fulfilled its objective.[849]

429. For all of these reasons, we reject the United States' claims that the Panel erred in its determination of the United States' "level of fulfilment" of its objective.

(d) Canada's Claim that the Panel Failed to Define the Objective of the COOL Measure at a "Sufficiently Detailed Level"

430. Finally, Canada argues that, should we disagree with its arguments under Article 11 of the DSU with respect to the Panel's identification of the objective pursued through the COOL measure, then we should find that the Panel erred in failing to define that objective at a "sufficiently detailed level".[850] Canada asserts that the Panel erred in not identifying the purpose for which origin information is provided to consumers.[851] Canada argues that, unlike a measure aimed at protecting human life or health, which can be used for only legitimate purposes, the provision of "consumer information" can be used for "illegitimate" purposes, such as to further racial discrimination or favour domestic producers over foreign competition.[852] Therefore, "[b]y vaguely framing the objective of the COOL measure without a description of its underlying rationale, the Panel puts itself in a position of having to test the legitimacy of an objective that can cover both legitimate and illegitimate purposes."[853]

431. We disagree with Canada that the Panel failed to identify the purpose for which the COOL measure seeks to provide information. The Panel did so, at least in part, by specifying the type of information to be provided (on "origin" as defined under the COOL measure), and the persons to whom that information is

---

> COOL measure. As Mexico points out, the United States submitted that reducing compliance costs was one of the factors that it considered in *implementing* the COOL measure to achieve the objective of providing consumer information on origin. Reducing compliance costs therefore cannot form part of the objective itself.

(Panel Reports, para. 6.113 (footnotes omitted; original emphasis))

849 See Panel Reports, para. 7.711.

850 Canada's other appellant's submission, p. 19, subheading III.(A).2(b).

851 Canada's other appellant's submission, para. 44.

852 Canada's other appellant's submission, paras. 45 and 46.

853 Canada's other appellant's submission, para. 46.

to be provided (consumers). In any event, we are not persuaded by Canada's argument that, because a variety of purposes, both legitimate and illegitimate, could in theory be served by a measure with the objective of providing consumer information on origin, this is not an objective that is defined at a "sufficiently detailed level". In our view, while framed as a matter relating to the precision with which the Panel identified the objective, Canada's arguments relate more to the Panel's analysis of the legitimacy of the objective, an issue we turn to in the next section. We therefore reject this ground of appeal.

(e) Summary of Conclusions

432. We have found above that, although the Panel unnecessarily conducted two analyses of the objective pursued by the United States through the COOL measure, it did not err under Article 2.2 of the *TBT Agreement*. We so found because the Panel's finding that the objective of the COOL measure is to provide to consumers information on origin was, ultimately, based on a global assessment of the United States' declared objective together with evidence relating to the text, design, structure, and legislative history of the COOL measure. We have rejected arguments by Canada and by Mexico that, in its treatment of the evidence relating to the COOL measure's design, structure, and legislative history, the Panel failed to make an objective assessment of the matter, as required under Article 11 of the DSU. We have also rejected the United States' argument that the Panel erred in applying Article 2.2 of the *TBT Agreement* and acted inconsistently with its obligations under Article 11 of the DSU in its characterization of the United States' chosen "level of fulfilment". Finally, we have rejected Canada's argument that the Panel erred by failing to define the objective of the COOL measure at a "sufficiently detailed level".

433. On the basis of the above, we *find* that the Panel did not err, in paragraphs 7.617, 7.620, and 7.685 of the Panel Reports, in identifying the objective pursued by the United States through the COOL measure as being to provide consumer information on origin.[854]

4. Did the Panel Err in Finding that the Objective of the COOL Measure Is "Legitimate"?

434. Canada also challenges the Panel's finding that "providing consumer information on origin is a legitimate objective within the meaning of Article 2.2" of the *TBT Agreement*.[855] Canada raises this ground of appeal in the event that

[854] We recall in this respect that the COOL measure defines the "origin" of beef and pork as a function of the country or countries in which the livestock from which the meat is derived were born, raised, and slaughtered.

[855] Panel Reports, para. 7.651. Mexico does not raise a separate ground of appeal in this regard.

we reject its claim that the objective pursued by the United States through the COOL measure is trade protectionism and that the Panel erred in finding otherwise.[856] As we have affirmed the Panel's finding regarding the objective pursued by the United States through the COOL measure, we turn to this part of Canada's appeal.

435. Canada asserts that the Panel: (i) failed to articulate a test for determining what constitutes a legitimate objective[857]; (ii) wrongly concluded that any objective that has a "genuine link" to a "public policy" or "social norm" is legitimate[858]; and (iii) erred in the two reasons that it gave for finding the objective of the COOL measure to be legitimate.[859] According to Canada, the correct "test" for determining whether an objective not explicitly listed in Article 2.2 is "legitimate" entails three elements. First, a panel should determine whether an objective is "directly related" to one of the objectives explicitly listed in Article 2.2.[860] Second, if it is not, then the panel should determine, in accordance with the principle of *ejusdem generis*[861], "if the measure is of the same type as the listed objectives".[862] In applying this principle, Canada contends that there are "significant elements of commonality" in the explicitly listed objectives that can helpfully inform whether a particular objective is legitimate.[863] In Canada's view, the objectives explicitly listed in the "General Exceptions" provisions of Article XX of the GATT 1994 and Article XIV of the GATS are of the same "type" as those listed in Article 2.2 of the *TBT Agreement*, and the fact that such objectives are "prioritized" in the covered agreements is one way to determine that they are "legitimate" for purposes of Article 2.2.[864] Third, Canada submits that other unlisted objectives may also be shown to be "legitimate" with "clear and compelling evidence", and provided that they are identified with an appropriately high level of specificity.[865] Canada stresses that the objective of providing consumers with information "is not an objective privileged in any of the covered agreements, nor has the United States provided clear and convincing

[856] Both Mexico and Canada submit that, if we accept that the "true" objective of the measure is to protect domestic industry, then it would automatically follow that such an objective is not "legitimate". (Mexico's other appellant's submission, para. 45; Canada's other appellant's submission, para. 60)

[857] Canada's other appellant's submission, paras. 48 and 50.

[858] Canada's other appellant's submission, para. 50.

[859] Canada's other appellant's submission, para. 63.

[860] Canada's other appellant's submission, para. 53.

[861] Canada's other appellant's submission, para. 52 and footnote 100 thereto.

[862] Canada's other appellant's submission, para. 53.

[863] Canada's other appellant's submission, para. 52.

[864] Canada's other appellant's submission, para. 58.

[865] Canada's other appellant's submission, para. 59 (quoting New Zealand's oral statement at the first Panel meeting).

evidence that indicates why that objective is legitimate in this case".[866] Moreover, argues Canada, the Panel erred in finding the objective pursued through the COOL measure to be legitimate on the basis only of the existence of other WTO Members' labelling measures that "purport" to provide consumer information on the origin of food products, and a reference to the "protection of consumers" as one of the legitimate objectives in the *Disciplines on Domestic Regulation in the Accountancy Sector*[867] (the "*Accountancy Disciplines*"), adopted in accordance with Article VI:4 of the GATS.[868]

436. The United States rejects Canada's "test" for determining the "legitimacy" of objectives on the ground that it lacks any basis in the text of Article 2.2.[869] First, according to the United States, nothing in Article 2.2 "ranks" or "prioritizes" various objectives or provides for an "ever-escalating presumption against the legitimacy of an objective depending on how closely related it is to the list in Article 2.2".[870] Second, Canada's reliance on the principle of *ejusdem generis* in creating its "test" to interpret Article 2.2 is mistaken.[871] Third, Canada's test is based on the false assumption that Article 2.2 "prioritizes" the listed objectives over the unlisted ones, such that the explicitly listed objectives are more "important" than the unlisted ones.[872] Fourth, even under Canada's approach, the legitimacy of providing consumer information as an objective finds support in the enumerated objectives themselves. Specifically, the United States considers the objective of the COOL measure to be closely connected to the prevention of deceptive practices, which is explicitly listed in Article 2.2.[873]

437. We recall that the Panel began its analysis of this issue by noting that the burden of proving that the relevant objective is not legitimate within the meaning of Article 2.2 rested on the complainants.[874] Turning to the meaning of "legitimate", the Panel referred to the dictionary definitions of this word, to the analysis of the panel in *EC – Sardines,* and to the objectives that are explicitly listed in Article 2.2. According to the Panel, these demonstrated that "the legitimacy of a given objective must be found in the '*genuine nature*' of the objective, which is 'justifiable' and 'supported by relevant public policies or other

---

[866] Canada's other appellant's submission, para. 62.

[867] S/L/64, adopted by the Council for Trade in Services on 14 December 1998.

[868] Canada's other appellant's submission, para. 63.

[869] United States' appellee's submission, para. 50.

[870] United States' appellee's submission, para. 52.

[871] United States' appellee's submission, para. 54.

[872] United States' appellee's submission, para. 56.

[873] United States' appellee's submission, para. 57.

[874] Panel Reports, para. 7.629.

social norms'."[875] The Panel underlined that Article 2.2 "provides a non-exhaustive, open list of legitimate objectives", "without any modifying language", which "indicates that a wide range of objectives could potentially fall within the scope of legitimate objectives under Article 2.2".[876] The Panel saw no explicit requirement, in the text of Article 2.2 or elsewhere in the *TBT Agreement*, "that a policy objective pursued by a technical regulation must be specifically linked in nature to those objectives explicitly listed in Article 2.2".[877] Turning to Canada's argument that Article 2.2 must be interpreted and applied according to the *ejusdem generis* principle, the Panel stated that it did not find that principle to be "helpful for determining whether the objective pursued by the United States is legitimate".[878] The Panel nevertheless added that, even assuming that the *ejusdem generis* principle were relevant, this would not assist Canada because all of the examples of legitimate objectives listed in Article 2.2 "are expressed at a high level of generality"[879], and thus would not clearly indicate any particular limitations on the class of "legitimate objectives" covered by that provision.

438. The Panel noted that, while Canada and Mexico did not contest that, at a general level, the provision of consumer information on country of origin can constitute a legitimate objective under Article 2.2, they emphasized that the legitimacy of the specific objectives pursued by the United States must be determined according to the factual circumstances of these disputes.[880] The Panel observed that nearly 70 other WTO Members maintain some form of mandatory country of origin labelling, and that many apply such requirements at the retail level. The Panel found that this constituted evidence that "consumer information on country of origin is considered by a considerable proportion of the WTO Membership to be a legitimate objective under the *TBT Agreement*."[881] The Panel found further support for its view in the fact that the "protection of consumers" is listed as an example of a legitimate objective in the *Accountancy Disciplines* developed in accordance with Article VI:4 of the GATS.[882] This suggested to the Panel that "objectives relating to consumer information or consumer protection can in principle constitute a legitimate objective under the WTO covered agreements".[883]

---

875 Panel Reports, para. 7.632. (original emphasis)

876 Panel Reports, para. 7.634.

877 *Ibid.*

878 Panel Reports, para. 7.636.

879 *Ibid.*

880 Panel Reports, paras. 7.633 and 7.641.

881 Panel Reports, para. 7.638.

882 Panel Reports, paras. 7.639 and 7.640.

883 Panel Reports, para. 7.640.

439. The Panel next referred to the complainants' argument that the United States' objective "should not be found legitimate unless the United States can prove that it is important for consumers to be provided with that information or why consumers need that information".[884] It also noted the United States' arguments that the origin information in question helps consumers make informed choices and prevents consumer confusion, and that there is strong consumer demand for such information.[885] The Panel expressed doubt as to the probative value of the United States' evidence of consumer demand for such information, which consisted of comments made during the legislative process. At the same time, the Panel did not consider that the absence of independent evidence of consumer desire for the particular kind of information on origin provided under the COOL measure demonstrated that the objective of providing it was not legitimate.[886] The Panel then expressed the view that:

> [c]learly, if consumers know the country of origin, they will be able to make informed choices with respect to origin of products, including meat. Some consumers may indeed have preferences for products produced by or originating in particular countries for a variety of reasons.[887]

440. The Panel further acknowledged that WTO Members enjoy certain "policy space" in pursuing their regulatory objectives, and may decide to adopt regulations even absent specific demand for them, provided that this is not done in order to shape consumer expectations through regulatory intervention.[888]

441. The Panel was persuaded, "based on the evidence before [it] regarding US consumer preferences as well as the practice in a considerable proportion of WTO Members, that consumers generally are interested in having information on the origin of the products they purchase."[889] The Panel further set out its view that "whether an objective is legitimate cannot be determined in a vacuum, but must be assessed in the context of the world in which we live. Social norms must be accorded due weight in considering whether a particular objective pursued by

---

[884] Panel Reports, para. 7.641.

[885] Panel Reports, paras. 7.642 and 7.645.

[886] Panel Reports, para. 7.647.

[887] Panel Reports, para. 7.648.

[888] Panel Reports, para. 7.649. See also paras. 7.643 and 7.644.

[889] Panel Reports, para. 7.650. The Panel further observed that "many WTO Members have responded to that interest by putting measures in place to require the provision of such information, *albeit with different definitions of 'origin'*". (*Ibid.* (emphasis added))

a government can be considered legitimate."[890] On that basis, the Panel concluded that "providing consumer information on origin is a legitimate objective within the meaning of Article 2.2."[891]

442. Returning to Canada's appeal, we first observe that Canada does not challenge the Panel's articulation of the burden of proof with respect to the issue of whether an objective is legitimate within the meaning of Article 2.2. Furthermore, we agree with the Panel that it is for the complainant raising an Article 2.2 claim to establish that the relevant objective falls outside the scope of the legitimate objectives covered by that provision. We also take note that there appears to be agreement among the participants that the relevant issue is whether the provision of consumer information on origin[892]—an objective not explicitly listed in Article 2.2—can be considered "legitimate".[893] Although the United States has to some extent linked the provision of consumer information on origin with the objective of "preventing deceptive practices"—which is listed in Article 2.2—its claim appears to be that these objectives are "closely connected", and not that they are the same thing.[894]

443. As we see it, the thrust of Canada's appeal is directed at the Panel's alleged failure to articulate a proper test for determining whether an objective that is not explicitly listed in Article 2.2 is "legitimate" within the meaning of that provision. More specifically, Canada considers that the Panel erred in not

---

[890] Panel Reports, para. 7.650. (footnote omitted) The Panel derived support for this statement from the Appellate Body's finding in *EC – Hormones* that:

> [i]t is essential to bear in mind that the risk that is to be evaluated in a risk assessment under Article 5.1 is not only risk ascertainable in a science laboratory operating under strictly controlled conditions, but also risk in human societies as they actually exist, in other words, the actual potential for adverse effects on human health in the real world where people live and work and die.

(Appellate Body Report, *EC – Hormones*, para. 187)

[891] Panel Reports, para. 7.651.

[892] As discussed above, Canada also argues that, because the provision of consumer information can seek to achieve both legitimate and illegitimate purposes, this objective is too broadly cast to assess its legitimacy under Article 2.2. For the reasons already discussed *supra*, at paragraph 431, however, we do not consider that the Panel failed to identify the objective pursued through the COOL measure with sufficient precision.

[893] The United States did not assert that it seeks to provide consumers with information on the origin of the meat they purchase through the COOL measure in furtherance of one of the listed objectives under Article 2.2, such as the protection of human health and safety, or the environment. (See Panel Reports, para. 7. 637)

[894] United States' appellant's submission, para. 57. In its responses to Panel Questions, the United States explained that it never asserted that the COOL measure was enacted in "direct response" to deceptive practices. However, the United States did note that its objectives—that is, providing consumer information and preventing consumer confusion—are *related* to preventing deceptive practices "in that they help ensure that consumers receive accurate and non-misleading information about the products that they buy". (United States' response to Panel Question 56(b))

adopting the test proposed by Canada in this regard, which relies upon the *ejusdem generis* principle to limit the class of "legitimate" objectives to those objectives that are of the same type or kind as the ones explicitly listed in that provision.

444. As we have explained above, and drawing upon the Appellate Body report in *US – Tuna II (Mexico)*, in determining whether an unlisted objective qualifies as legitimate, a panel may usefully have regard to those objectives that are expressly listed in Article 2.2, because these may provide an illustration and reference point for other objectives that may be considered "legitimate".[895] Thus, an objective that is linked or related to a specific listed objective may be more likely to be found to be legitimate. Yet, like the Panel, we do not see, and Canada does not elaborate, the alleged "significant elements of commonality of the explicitly listed objectives" that would illuminate the relevant *type* of objective and thus serve to delineate the class of legitimate objectives that fall within Article 2.2.[896] Indeed, it is difficult to discern such commonality amongst the disparate listed objectives that are, moreover, "expressed at a high level of generality".[897] In addition, it seems to us that any relevant "commonality" among explicitly listed objectives would have to relate to the nature and content of those objectives themselves, rather than, as Canada seems to suggest, to the fact that each objective in Article 2.2 is also listed in exceptions provisions in other covered agreements. For these reasons, we do not consider the Panel to have erred in failing to rely upon the *ejusdem generis* principle to identify the class of "legitimate objectives" under Article 2.2 of the *TBT Agreement*.

445. The Appellate Body also explained, in *US – Tuna II (Mexico),* that objectives listed in the recitals of the preamble of the *TBT Agreement* and provisions of other covered agreements may guide or usefully inform a panel's determination of which other objectives can be considered "legitimate" for purposes of Article 2.2.[898] We observe, in this regard, that the provision of information to consumers on origin bears some relation to the objective of prevention of deceptive practices reflected in both Article 2.2 itself and Article

---

[895] Appellate Body Report, *US – Tuna II (Mexico)*, para. 313.

[896] As the Appellate Body noted in *US – Large Civil Aircraft (2nd complaint)*, the principle of Latin canon of construction, "*ejusdem generis*", provides that, when a general word or phrase follows a list of specific persons or things, the general word or phrase will be interpreted to include only persons or things of the *same type* as those listed. (Appellate Body Report, *US – Large Civil Aircraft (2nd complaint)*, footnote 1290 to para. 615 (referring to *Black's Law Dictionary*, 7th edn (West Group, 1999), p. 535)) Canada does not explain what is the common feature across the range of specifically listed objectives of the protection of health, safety, environment, national security requirements, and the prevention of deceptive practices that would provide an indication of the *type* of objectives that might be considered legitimate.

[897] Panel Reports, para. 7.636.

[898] Appellate Body Report, *US – Tuna II (Mexico)*, para. 313.

XX(d) of the GATT 1994, insofar as consumers could be deceived as to the origin of products if labelling is inaccurate or misleading. In our view, support for the legitimate nature of the objective of providing information to consumers on origin is also found elsewhere in the covered agreements, in particular in Article IX of the GATT 1994. This provision, entitled "Marks of Origin", expressly recognizes the right of WTO Members to require that imported products carry a mark of origin. Although the applicability of this provision to the circumstances of these disputes has not been explored by the participants, and it is in any event not at issue[899], Article IX does indicate that requiring origin labelling for imported goods is, at least in some circumstances and for some definitions of "origin", considered under WTO law to be a permissible means of regulating trade in goods.

446. While Canada has accepted, at a general level, that the provision of consumer information on origin can constitute a legitimate objective[900], it appears to consider that the Panel erred in finding the objective of providing consumers with information on origin *as defined under the COOL measure* (that is, based on where the livestock from which meat is derived were born, raised, and slaughtered) to be legitimate. In this regard, we understand Canada to assert that the Panel's reasoning does not show that many Members require the provision of *that type* of consumer information on origin.[901] We further understand Canada to assert that, even if many Members do require the provision of consumer information on origin, generally, this would not suffice to show that the specific objective pursued by the United States is legitimate.

447. We observe in this regard that Canada's arguments seem to imply that, in assessing legitimacy, a distinction should be drawn between the provision of consumer information on origin, generally[902], and the provision of consumer information on origin based on the definition of "origin" under the COOL measure. Yet, Canada has not explained why it is *not* legitimate to define the origin of meat according to the countries in which the livestock from which it is derived were born, raised, and slaughtered. Indeed, in a separate section of its Reports, the Panel noted that the United States' definition of origin for purposes

---

[899] We note that, while both Canada and Mexico included claims under Article IX of the GATT 1994 in their requests for establishment of a panel (WT/DS/384/8 and WT/DS/386/7 and Corr. 1), neither pursued these claims in its submissions to the Panel.

[900] Panel Reports, para. 7.633.

[901] Canada argues, for instance, that in examining the COOL regime of other WTO Members, the Panel "did not examine them to consider whether they are analogous to the COOL measure, much less examine the purposes for which that information was provided in those cases". (Canada's other appellant's submission, para. 64)

[902] Panel Reports, paras. 7.623, 7.633, and 7.641.

of the COOL measure is different from that employed for customs purposes.[903] The Panel added that there was "no basis" for it to find that the United States is prohibited from adopting for labelling purposes an origin definition—based on the places where animals used to produce meat were born, raised, and slaughtered—which is different from that used for customs purposes.[904] Canada does not contest this statement by the Panel or argue, for example, that it is not legitimate for the United States to define "origin" differently for purposes of the labelling of meat for retail sale than it does for customs purposes. It is therefore unclear on what basis or to what extent, in the context of its arguments relating to legitimacy, Canada challenges the precise way in which the COOL measure defines "origin". We note, for example, that Canada's position appears to imply that it would accept the legitimacy of providing consumers with information on origin when such labelling is based on origin as defined by the principle of substantial transformation—that is, according to the country in which the last production step (slaughter) took place. Yet, Canada does not elaborate its implicit view that providing consumers with information on origin is *not* a legitimate objective when origin is defined based on *all* of the countries in which relevant production steps took place. Rather, as it did before the Panel, Canada simply links its approach to legitimacy to its arguments on the need to know the purpose for which information on origin is provided to consumers in order to determine whether the objective is legitimate.[905]

448. Furthermore, although Canada appears to consider that the Panel wrongly assumed that a widely held social norm is always legitimate, we do not see that the Panel made any such assumption. Indeed, as explained below, we find the Panel's statements regarding "social norms" to be somewhat opaque and, ultimately, of no consequence for its conclusion on legitimacy. In its arguments, Canada is also critical of the Panel's reference to the origin labelling practices of other WTO Members. We recall that the Panel took account of evidence that was put before it by the United States to show that many WTO Members maintain some form of mandatory origin labelling scheme. To the extent that Canada is arguing that, when there are differences among the "origin" information that different Members require be provided to consumers, the probative value of such evidence may be limited, we agree. Indeed, the Panel itself seems to have

---

[903] As the Panel noted, for customs purposes, the United States relies on the rules of substantial transformation for determining the origin of products imported into the United States. (Panel Reports, para. 7.674)

[904] Panel Reports, para. 7.675.

[905] In its other appellant's submission, Canada contends that its proposed approach to a determination of legitimacy "unlike the approach of the Panel, would also ensure that a measure providing information to consumers in order to discriminate on the basis of race or to advance protectionist interests could not be 'legitimate'". (Canada's other appellant's submission, para. 51) See also the Panel's summary of Canada's arguments with respect to legitimacy as set out in paragraph 7.633 of the Panel Reports.

recognized this since, when it referred to evidence that a "considerable proportion of the WTO Membership"[906] provides consumers with information on origin, the Panel explicitly acknowledged that such schemes use different definitions of "origin" than the one set out in the COOL measure.[907] In any event, Canada does not raise a claim under Article 11 of the DSU in this respect.

449. We are nevertheless troubled by certain aspects of the Panel's analysis of the legitimacy of the United States' objective. First, although the Panel recognized, at the outset of its analysis, that the burden of proving that an objective is *not* legitimate lay with the complainants, its reasoning at times suggests that it, instead, placed on the United States the burden of proving that its objective was legitimate. Thus, for example, the Panel referred to the complainants' position that "the United States' stated objectives in this dispute should not be found legitimate unless the United States can prove that it is important for consumers to be provided with that information or why consumers need that information"[908], and then proceeded to examine whether the United States had done so. Furthermore, in the paragraph summarizing its conclusions with respect to the legitimacy of the objective, the Panel stated: "We are persuaded, based on the evidence before us ..., that consumers generally are interested in having information on the origin of the products they purchase."[909] In the same paragraph, the Panel also observed that "whether an objective is legitimate cannot be determined in a vacuum, but must be assessed in the context of the world in which we live".[910]

450. Second, it is not clear upon what basis the Panel reached its finding "that consumers generally are interested in having information on the origin of the products they purchase"[911], given that the Panel itself cast doubt on the probative value of the evidence that the United States adduced to demonstrate such

---

906 Panel Reports, para. 7.638.

907 The Panel considered the mandatory labelling requirements maintained by the complainants and third parties in these disputes and found that they purported to provide consumer information on origin of food products. (Panel Reports, para. 7.638) Moreover, in its conclusion, the Panel found that:

> ... based on the evidence before us regarding US consumer preferences as well as the practice in a considerable proportion of WTO Members, ... consumers generally are interested in having information on the origin of the products they purchase. We also observe that many WTO Members have responded to that interest by putting measures in place to require the provision of such information, *albeit with different definitions of "origin"*.

(Panel Reports, para. 7. 650 (emphasis added))

908 Panel Reports, para. 7.641.

909 Panel Reports, para. 7.650.

910 *Ibid.*

911 *Ibid.*

demand.[912] Canada does not, however, challenge this finding under Article 11 of the DSU.

451. Third, we are uncertain as to the basis on which the Panel had recourse to the *Accountancy Disciplines* developed under the GATS, and to the objective of "the protection of consumers" set out in those Disciplines.[913] That being said, however, we do not agree with Canada that it was improper for the Panel to link the objective of consumer protection with the objective of providing consumers with information on origin. We have already explained that we view the objective of providing consumers with information on origin as related to the objective of preventing deceptive practices, which is in turn linked to the objective of consumer protection. Thus, like the Panel, we consider that providing accurate and reliable information may protect consumers from being misled or misinformed.[914]

452. Fourth, we have some difficulties understanding how the Panel viewed the relationship between "the practice in a considerable proportion of WTO Members" and "social norms", and the role that these considerations played in its analysis. Ultimately, however, while these ambiguities may detract from the overall clarity of the Panel's analysis, they do not taint its conclusion.

453. Based on all of the above, we see no reason to disturb the Panel's finding with respect to the legitimacy of the objective pursued by the United States through the COOL measure, namely, to provide consumers with information on the countries in which the livestock from which the meat they purchase is produced were born, raised, and slaughtered. The Panel's analysis reveals that the arguments and evidence submitted by the complainants failed to persuade the Panel that providing consumers with information on origin, as defined under the COOL measure, is *not* a legitimate objective. On appeal, Canada has not shown that the Panel erred in rejecting its arguments and evidence in this regard. We therefore dismiss this ground of Canada's appeal and *find* that the Panel did not err, in paragraph 7.651 of the Panel Reports, in finding the provision of

---

[912] Panel Reports, para. 7.647.

[913] None of the participants cited these Disciplines in support of their positions on the legitimacy of the United States' objective. The Panel might, for example, have considered these Disciplines to be a subsequent agreement between the parties, within the meaning of Article 31(3)(a) of the *Vienna Convention*. Even if this had been the case, however, it would have been helpful for the Panel to have explained why it considered that such an agreement, made in connection with the GATS, was also relevant to the interpretation or application of term "legitimate" in Article 2.2 of the *TBT Agreement*.

[914] We also recall, in this respect, that the Panel on several occasions recognized that the COOL measure has the additional objective of eliminating the consumer confusion that existed prior to the COOL measure as a result of the USDA grade labels and the voluntary FSIS labels. (See, for example, Panel Reports, paras. 7.671 and 7.713)

consumer information on origin is a legitimate objective within the meaning of Article 2.2 of the *TBT Agreement*.

5. *Did the Panel Err in Its Analysis of Whether the COOL Measure Is More Trade Restrictive than Necessary to Fulfil a Legitimate Objective, Taking Account of the Risks Non-Fulfilment Would Create?*

454. Having found that the Panel did not err in finding that the objective of the COOL measure is "legitimate", we turn now to address the United States' arguments on appeal relating to the third step of the Panel's analysis of the claims under Article 2.2 of the *TBT Agreement*, that is, to the Panel's assessment of whether the COOL measure is "more trade-restrictive than necessary to fulfil" a legitimate objective.[915]

455. The United States appeals the legal framework adopted by the Panel to determine whether a measure is "more trade-restrictive than necessary to fulfil a legitimate objective", including its failure to require the complaining parties to meet their burden of proving that the measure is "more trade-restrictive than necessary" based on the availability of a significantly less trade-restrictive alternative measure. With respect to the legal framework, the United States submits that the Panel erroneously employed a two-stage test that involved an initial inquiry into whether the measure fulfils the objective, and only if so, a separate and subsequent examination of whether the measure is more trade restrictive than necessary based on the existence of a reasonably available less trade-restrictive alternative measure. According to the United States, such a two-stage analysis is not required under Article 2.2. Rather, as with the "parallel provision" in Article 5.6 of the *SPS Agreement*, Article 2.2 of the *TBT Agreement* calls for a "single analysis, containing three elements that are to be judged cumulatively".[916] The three elements include an assessment of whether (i) there is a reasonably available alternative measure (ii) that fulfils the Member's legitimate objective at the level that the Member considers appropriate and (iii) is significantly less trade restrictive.[917]

---

[915] See Panel Reports, para. 7.558 (third bullet point).

[916] United States' appellant's submission, para. 156.

[917] The United States quotes, in this regard, the Appellate Body's statement, in *Australia – Salmon*, that an inconsistency with Article 5.6 of the *SPS Agreement* will be demonstrated when "there is an SPS measure which: (1) is reasonably available taking into account technical and economic feasibility; (2) achieves the Member's appropriate level of sanitary or phytosanitary protection; and (3) is significantly less restrictive to trade than the SPS measure contested." (United States' appellant's submission, para. 156 and footnote 241 thereto (quoting Appellate Body Report, *Australia – Salmon*, para. 194))

456. The United States explains that the Panel's improper use of the two-stage test led it to find that the United States acted inconsistently with Article 2.2 simply because the COOL measure does not contribute to the objective—or fulfil the objective—"*enough*".[918] Yet, the United States emphasizes, a measure cannot be found to be inconsistent with Article 2.2 "*solely* because it does not meet some minimum threshold of contribution to its objective".[919] The United States emphasizes that, while a panel's determinations of the objective and of the level at which a Member seeks to fulfil that objective are important for an Article 2.2 analysis, they are not an end in themselves. Rather, these determinations are relevant *in order to* assess whether the complaining party has met its burden of showing that the same level of fulfilment could be achieved by a significantly less trade-restrictive alternative measure.

457. In addition to the allegedly erroneous legal framework adopted by the Panel, the United States appeals what it characterizes as a finding by the Panel that the COOL measure does not fulfil its objective at the level the United States considers appropriate.[920] The United States argues that the Panel failed properly to take into account that the COOL measure "completely" fulfils its objective for meat that carries Label A.[921] Moreover, the United States asserts that, notwithstanding its various criticisms of the information that Labels B and C provide, even the Panel acknowledged that those labels made some contribution to the objective of providing consumers with information on the origin of meat.[922]

458. Both Canada and Mexico reject the United States' argument that the Panel adopted an erroneous legal approach to its analysis under the third stage of its test. Although neither Canada nor Mexico specifies the precise threshold that must be met for a technical regulation to be considered to "fulfil" its objective, both suggest that this threshold is fairly high.[923] Moreover, Canada and Mexico

---

918 United States' appellant's submission, para. 167. (original emphasis)

919 United States' appellant's submission, para. 167. (original emphasis) The United States further submits that whether a measure makes a "material contribution" to its objective, in the sense that the Appellate Body used the term in *Brazil – Retreaded Tyres*, is not the correct test for purposes of Article 2.2. (*Ibid.* (referring to Appellate Body Report, *Brazil – Retreaded Tyres*, para. 151))

920 United States' appellant's submission, paras. 171-177 (referring to Panel Reports, para. 7.719).

921 United States' appellant's submission, para. 172.

922 United States' appellant's submission, para. 172 (referring to Panel Reports, para. 7.717).

923 In this regard, Canada notes that, while the ordinary meaning of the word "fulfil" used in Article 2.2, as well as its French and Spanish equivalents ("*réaliser*" and "*alcanzar*", respectively), suggest that a measure must achieve its objective at 100%, when read in its context, and, in the light of the relevant object and purpose, the word "fulfil" requires a showing of something less than complete fulfilment. (Canada's appellee's submission, paras. 92-94) Mexico argues that the standard "to fulfil" is close in its degree to the standard "necessary", so the term "to fulfil" in the context of Article 2.2 of the *TBT Agreement* requires that a technical regulation be located significantly closer to the pole of 100% fulfilment of the legitimate objective. (Mexico's appellee's submission, paras. 177

disagree with the United States that the Panel erred in its assessment of the level of fulfilment achieved by the COOL measure, and submit that the Panel correctly found that the COOL measure does not fulfil its objective because it fails to convey meaningful information. For this reason, they consider that it was appropriate for the Panel to have stopped its analysis after having determined that the COOL measure does not fulfil its objective. If, however, the Appellate Body disagrees that there is a separate step for assessing whether a challenged measure fulfils its objective, then Canada and Mexico agree that the level of fulfilment found by the Panel is relevant for assessing the COOL measure against proposed alternatives.

459. Turning to the Panel's treatment of this issue, we recall that the Panel first articulated the approach it would take in determining the COOL measure's consistency with Article 2.2 in the introduction to its assessment of the complainants' claims under that provision. There, the Panel stated that, if it determined that the objective of the COOL measure is "legitimate" under the second step of its Article 2.2 analysis, then its inquiry under the third, and final, step would proceed as follows. First, it would determine whether the technical regulation fulfils the identified objective.[924] If that question were answered in the affirmative, the Panel stated that it would then consider whether the technical regulation is more trade restrictive than necessary to fulfil the objective. This would entail an analysis of the availability of less trade-restrictive alternative measures that can equally fulfil the objective, taking into account the risks that non-fulfilment would create.[925] When it came to applying this framework later in its analysis, however, the Panel never reached the stage of comparing the COOL measure against less trade-restrictive alternative measures because it found that the COOL measure "does not fulfil the identified objective within the meaning of Article 2.2 because it fails to convey meaningful origin information to consumers".[926]

---

and 178 (referring to Appellate Body Report, *Korea – Various Measures on Beef*, para. 161 and footnote 104 thereto))

[924] Panel Reports, para. 7.556. In this regard, the Panel noted the parties' agreement that such an inquiry was the "starting point" and "an analytical step" that is required in order to examine whether that technical regulation is more trade restrictive than necessary. (*Ibid.*, footnote 743 to para. 7.556) The Panel further noted the United States' argument that it is appropriate to analyze whether the measure in question fulfils a legitimate objective first because an analysis of "more trade-restrictive than necessary", which often includes a consideration of the existence of alternative measures, would not be possible without first establishing the responding party's objective. The Panel also noted that, according to the United States, "taking account of the risks non-fulfilment would create" in Article 2.2 is an element considered by Members in determining the appropriate level for the particular legitimate objective at issue. (*Ibid.*)

[925] Panel Reports, paras. 7.556 and 7.557. See also para. 7.558 (third bullet point).

[926] Panel Reports, para. 7.719.

460. This part of the United States' appeal comprises both a challenge to the Panel's interpretation of Article 2.2 and a challenge to the Panel's application of that interpretation to the COOL measure. In particular, the United States seeks reversal of the Panel's ultimate finding under Article 2.2 based on its view that Article 2.2 does not require a separate assessment of whether a technical regulation "fulfils" a legitimate objective, and does require a complainant to prove that there is a less trade-restrictive alternative measure available. The United States adds, in this regard, that, in finding that the COOL measure does not fulfil its objective, the Panel ignored its own findings about the extent of the contribution that the COOL measure makes to achieving its objective.

461. Many of the issues relating to the proper approach to be adopted and applied in determining whether a measure "fulfils" its objective were dealt with by the Appellate Body in *US – Tuna II (Mexico)*. There, the Appellate Body clarified that an analysis under Article 2.2 involves an assessment of a number of factors, and that one such factor is whether a technical regulation "fulfils" an objective. The Appellate Body explained that this factor is concerned with the degree of contribution that the technical regulation makes towards the achievement of the legitimate objective, and that a panel must seek to ascertain to what degree, or if at all[927], the challenged technical regulation, as written and applied, actually contributes to the legitimate objective pursued by the Member. The degree of achievement of a particular objective may be discerned from the design, structure, and operation of the technical regulation, as well as from evidence relating to the application of the measure. The Appellate Body did not find or imply that, in order for a measure to comply with Article 2.2, it must meet some minimum threshold of fulfilment. Rather, the contribution that the challenged measure makes to the achievement of its objective must be determined objectively, and then evaluated along with the other factors mentioned in Article 2.2, that is: (i) the trade-restrictiveness of the measure; and (ii) the nature of the risks at issue and the gravity of the consequences that would arise from non-fulfilment of the objective(s) pursued by the Member through the measure. In most cases, a comparison of the challenged measure and possible alternative measures will then also need to be undertaken.[928] Through such an analysis, a panel will be able to judge the "necessity" of the trade-restrictiveness of the measure at issue, that is, to discern whether the technical regulation at issue restricts international trade beyond what is necessary to achieve the degree of contribution that it makes to the achievement of a legitimate objective.

---

[927] This may involve an assessment of whether the measure at issue is capable of achieving the legitimate objective.

[928] Appellate Body Report, *US – Tuna II (Mexico)*, para. 322. The Appellate Body identified "at least two instances where a comparison of the challenged measure and possible alternative measures may not be required", namely, when the measure is not trade restrictive at all, or when a trade-restrictive measure makes *no* contribution to the achievement of the relevant legitimate objective. (Appellate Body Report, *US – Tuna II (Mexico)*, footnote 647 to para. 322)

462. In these disputes, the Panel attempted to articulate a standard of "fulfilment" at the beginning of its analysis. After referring to a number of dictionary definitions of the word "fulfil", the Panel found that "to meet the requirement in Article 2.2 of the *TBT Agreement*, the COOL measure must *carry out and perform* the objective of providing origin information to consumers."[929] The Panel also considered it "useful to recall" the Appellate Body's clarification in the context of Article XX(b) of the GATT 1994 that "a contribution exists when there is *a genuine relationship of ends and means* between the objective pursued and the measure at issue."[930]

463. When it came to actually applying a standard of "fulfilment" to the COOL measure, the Panel noted that, as the parties agreed, information on the origin of products must be clear and accurate for it to be able to convey *meaningful information* to consumers. Therefore, "[u]nder a labelling regime adopted for this purpose, the fulfilment of this objective will depend on the capability of labels to convey clear and accurate information on origin."[931] The Panel then referred to the argument of the complainants that the COOL measure did not fulfil its objective because the labels under that measure provide consumers with "inaccurate or misleading information".[932]

464. In the course of its analysis, the Panel confined itself largely to addressing the complainants' arguments as regards Labels B and C.[933] The Panel agreed with the complainants that the information provided through these labels was not accurate and was confusing. The Panel concluded, with respect to Labels B and C that:

> ... in light of the origin definition as determined by the United States for meat products, the description of origin for Label B and Label C is confusing in terms of the meaning of multiple country names listed in these labels. Moreover, the possibility of interchangeably using Label B and Label C for all categories of meat based on commingling does not contribute in a meaningful way to providing

[929] Panel Reports, para. 7.692. (emphasis added)

[930] Panel Reports, para. 7.693 (quoting Appellate Body Report, *Brazil – Retreaded Tyres*, para. 145). (emphasis added by the Panel)

[931] Panel Reports, para. 7.695.

[932] Panel Reports, para. 7.696.

[933] Panel Reports, paras. 7.697-7.705.

> consumers with accurate information on origin of meat products.[934]

465. In the next paragraph, the Panel found that the COOL measure "does not fulfil the identified objective within the meaning of Article 2.2 because it fails to convey meaningful origin information to consumers".[935]

466. Despite this overall finding, a number of findings and observations made by the Panel in the course of its analysis belie this conclusion and suggest that the COOL measure does *contribute* to the objective of providing information to consumers on the countries in which the livestock from which meat is derived were born, raised, and slaughtered. With respect to Label A, the Panel found that the COOL measure "appears to fulfil the objective because the measure prohibits [meat derived from animals of non-US origin] from carrying a Label A".[936] Even with respect to Labels B and C, the Panel found that these labels provide at least some origin information, namely, "information on meat with regard to the *possible* ... origin as defined by the measure".[937] Moreover, the Panel found that, on the whole, the COOL measure provides more information to consumers than was available to them prior to its enactment.[938] The Panel also noted that the "labels required to be affixed to meat products ... provide additional country of origin information that was not available prior to the COOL measure" and that this "may have reduced consumer confusion that existed under the pre-COOL measure and USDA grade labelling system".[939]

467. While recognizing these contributions, the Panel's concluding statements and ultimate finding suggest that the Panel considered that, in order for the COOL measure to fulfil its objective, either all of the labels had to provide 100% accurate and clear information, or that the COOL measure had to meet or surpass some minimum threshold. Whichever test it employed, the Panel was clearly of

---

934 Panel Reports, para. 7.718.

935 Panel Reports, para. 7.719.

936 Panel Reports, para. 7.713. The finding of the Panel in its entirety is as follows:

> In essence, the specific objective pursued by the United States through the COOL measure as explained above, namely the prevention of confusion caused by the previous COOL regime as well as USDA grade labelling, is that the United States aims to prevent meat derived from animals of non-US origin from carrying a US-origin label under any circumstances. To that extent, the COOL measure appears to fulfil the objective because the measure prohibits such meat from carrying a Label A even though the same meat may still carry a USDA grade label.

937 Panel Reports, para. 7.707.

938 According to the Panel, the COOL measure provides "*more* information than under the previous labelling regime". (Panel Reports, para. 7.715 (original emphasis))

939 Panel Reports, para. 7.717.

the view that the COOL measure did not meet that standard. For instance, the Panel found that the COOL measure "falls short"[940] of its objective, and that merely "providing *more* information than under the previous labelling regime or fulfilling only a limited aspect of the identified objective does not contribute in a meaningful way to fulfilling the objective".[941]

468. We have stated above that a panel's assessment of whether a measure fulfils its objective is concerned primarily with the actual contribution made by the measure towards achieving its objective. Thus, a panel's assessment should focus on ascertaining the degree of contribution achieved by the measure, rather than on answering the questions of whether the measure fulfils the objective completely or satisfies some minimum level of fulfilment of that objective.[942] Because the Panel seems to have considered it necessary for the COOL measure to have fulfilled the objective completely, or satisfied some minimum level of fulfilment to be consistent with Article 2.2, it erred in its interpretation of Article 2.2. Moreover, because the Panel ignored its own findings, which demonstrate that the labels under the COOL measure did contribute towards the objective of providing consumer information on origin, it also erred in its analysis under Article 2.2. For these reasons, we *find* that the Panel erred, in paragraph 7.719 of the Panel Reports, in finding that "the COOL measure does not fulfil the identified objective within the meaning of Article 2.2 because it fails to convey meaningful origin information to consumers", and we *reverse* the Panel's ultimate finding, in paragraph 7.720 of the Panel Reports, that, for this reason, the COOL measure is inconsistent with Article 2.2 of the *TBT Agreement*.[943]

469. We note that the United States further argues that the Panel erred by relieving the complaining parties of their burden to prove that the measure is "more trade-restrictive than necessary" based on the availability of less trade-restrictive alternative measures. We have reversed the Panel's finding, that the COOL measure is inconsistent with Article 2.2 because it does not fulfil its objective, on the basis that the Panel's own findings indicate that the COOL measure did contribute to its objective. It follows therefore that, as the Appellate Body explained in *US – Tuna II (Mexico)*, the Panel in this case was required also to evaluate the other factors referred to in Article 2.2, and to undertake a comparison with the alternative measures proposed by Mexico and by Canada. The Appellate Body has found, and the participants do not contest, that the burden of proof with respect to such alternative measures is on the complainants.[944] Accordingly, we agree with the United States that, by finding

---

[940] Panel Reports, para. 7.716.

[941] Panel Reports, para. 7.715. (original emphasis)

[942] See *supra*, para. 373.

[943] See also Canada Panel Report, para. 8.3(c); and Mexico Panel Report, para. 8.3(c).

[944] Appellate Body Report, *US – Tuna II (Mexico)*, para. 323.

the COOL measure to be inconsistent with Article 2.2 of the *TBT Agreement* without examining the proposed alternative measures, the Panel erred by relieving Mexico and Canada of this part of their burden of proof.

6. Completion of the Legal Analysis – Is the COOL Measure More Trade Restrictive than Necessary to Fulfil the Legitimate Objective, Bearing in Mind the Risks that Non-Fulfilment Would Create?

470. We have reversed the Panel's finding that the COOL measure is inconsistent with Article 2.2 of the *TBT Agreement* because it does not fulfil the objective of providing consumer information on origin.[945] Therefore, the condition that triggers Canada's and Mexico's requests for completion of the legal analysis under this provision has been met.[946] Accordingly, we proceed to consider whether we can rule on the complainants' claims that the COOL measure is inconsistent with Article 2.2 because it is more trade restrictive than necessary to fulfil a legitimate objective. To the extent possible, we shall seek to complete the legal analysis in order to foster resolution of these disputes. However, we can do so only to the extent that "the factual findings of the panel and the undisputed facts in the panel record provide … a sufficient basis" for our analysis.[947] With these considerations in mind, we turn to address the complainants' request for completion of the analysis under Article 2.2 of the *TBT Agreement*.

471. As we have already noted above, in *US – Tuna II (Mexico)*, the Appellate Body explained that an assessment of whether a technical regulation is "more trade-restrictive than necessary" within the meaning of Article 2.2 involves an evaluation of a number of factors, including: (i) the degree of contribution made by the measure to the legitimate objective at issue; (ii) the trade-restrictiveness of the measure; and (iii) the nature of the risks at issue as well as the gravity of the consequences that would arise from non-fulfilment of the objective pursued by the Member through the measure.[948] The Appellate Body further stated that, "[i]n most cases, a comparison of the challenged measure and possible alternative measures should be undertaken."[949] In making this comparison, it will

---

945 Panel Reports, para. 7.720. See also Canada Panel Report, para. 8.3(c); and Mexico Panel Report, para. 8.3(c).

946 Canada's other appellant's submission, para. 69; Mexico's other appellant's submission, para. 47.

947 Appellate Body Report, *EC – Asbestos*, para. 78.

948 Appellate Body Report, *US – Tuna II (Mexico)*, para. 322.

949 Appellate Body Report, *US – Tuna II (Mexico)*, para. 322. As noted above, the Appellate Body identified two instances where a comparison of the challenged measure with possible alternative measures may not be required, namely, when the measure is not trade restrictive at all, or when a

be relevant to consider whether the proposed alternative is less trade restrictive; whether it would make an equivalent contribution to the relevant legitimate objective, taking account of the risks non-fulfilment would create; and whether it is reasonably available.[950] For the reasons that led us to reverse the Panel's finding under Article 2.2, we consider the present case to be one that calls for an examination of the factors identified above for both the COOL measure and the alternatives proposed by the complainants in order to determine whether the COOL measure is more trade restrictive than "necessary" to fulfil its objective.

472. We start by examining the COOL measure. We recall that we have affirmed the Panel's findings on the objective pursued by the United States through the COOL measure and its legitimacy.[951]

473. With respect to the degree of contribution made by the COOL measure to its objective, we have already referred to a number of Panel findings suggesting that the COOL measure does contribute, at least to some degree, to providing consumers with information on origin. The Panel found, for example: that the labels required to be affixed to meat products "provide additional country of origin information that was not available prior to the COOL measure"[952]; that the labelling requirements under the COOL measure "may have reduced consumer confusion that existed under the pre-COOL measure and USDA grade labelling system"[953]; that Label A ensures "meaningful information for consumers"[954]; that, to the extent the United States aims to prevent meat derived from animals of non-US origin from carrying a US-origin label under any circumstances, "the COOL measure appears to fulfil the objective because the measure prohibits such meat from carrying a Label A"[955]; and that, even with respect to Labels B and C, the COOL measure contributes to providing information with regard to the *possible* countries in which the livestock from which meat is derived were born, raised, and slaughtered.[956]

474. On appeal, the participants disagree as to the implications of the Panel's findings for assessing the contribution made by Label A to the objective of the

---

trade-restrictive measure makes *no* contribution to the achievement of the relevant legitimate objective. (Appellate Body Report, *US – Tuna II (Mexico)*, footnote 647 to para. 322)

[950] Appellate Body Report, *US – Tuna II (Mexico)*, para. 322.

[951] See subsections VI.C.3 and VI.C.4 of these Reports.

[952] Panel Reports, para. 7.717.

[953] *Ibid.*

[954] Panel Reports, para. 7.718. We also note Canada's and Mexico's acceptance during the oral hearing that Labels B and C convey some information, namely, the fact that at least one stage of production took place in the United States.

[955] Panel Reports, para. 7.713.

[956] Panel Reports, para. 7.707.

COOL measure, both in terms of the proportion of meat sold in the United States that carries this label, and in terms of the clarity and accuracy of the information that Label A conveys.[957] We recall the Panel's finding that Label A ensures "meaningful information for consumers".[958] We also recall that the COOL measure does not apply to all beef and pork sold within the United States. Indeed, the COOL measure's labelling requirements do not apply to all entities that sell pork and beef[959], or to all beef and pork products.[960] The Panel found, in this regard, that, "as a result of these exceptions, a considerable proportion of beef and pork is exempted from the COOL measure."[961] Although the Panel did not identify the precise percentage of beef and pork sold in the United States that is subject to the COOL labelling requirements, according to the United States and Mexico, 55% of beef sold in the United States is subject to the COOL requirements.[962] With respect to the subset of beef and pork subject to the COOL

---

957 The United States asserts that the Panel found that Label A "completely" fulfils this objective, and points to the Panel's finding that the COOL measure provides clear and accurate consumer information for at least 71% of the meat sold in the United States. (United States' appellant's submission, para. 172 (referring to Panel Reports, paras. 7.713, 7.718, and footnote 941 to para. 7.715)) Canada argues that the Panel never found that Label A provides consumers with information that is "clear and accurate" and, moreover, that the United States ignores that the Panel's finding with respect to Label A applies only to beef, and not to pork. (Canada's appellee's submission, para. 120) Mexico argues that the United States' figure of 71% is exaggerated and that, in fact, only 39% (71% of 55%) of all meat sold in the United States carries Label A. (Mexico's appellee's submission, para. 58)

958 Panel Reports, para. 7.718.

959 As explained *supra*, at paragraphs 242 and 334, only entities selling in excess of $230,000 worth of fruit and vegetables per year are subject to the COOL measure, and "[f]ood service establishments", such as restaurants, cafeterias, and enterprises providing ready-to-eat foods are expressly exempted from the COOL requirements.

960 As explained *supra*, at paragraphs 242 and 334, covered commodities that are an "ingredient in a processed food item" are excluded from the scope of the COOL measure and, for beef and pork, this exclusion encompasses processing such as cooking, curing, smoking, and restructuring.

961 Panel Reports, para. 7.417.

962 Before the Panel, the United States stated that approximately 65% of beef purchased in retail stores is for home use, and, of this beef, approximately 85% is either muscle cuts or ground beef not subject to the processed foods exemption. Therefore, on the United States' own figures, slightly more than half of the beef consumed in the United States is covered by the COOL measure (85% of 65% is 55.25%). The United States also noted that the percentage is similar for pork products, but likely a bit lower, since a larger percentage of pork products is processed. (United States' response to Panel Question 92, para. 15 (referring to Panel Exhibit US-148, p. 9)) The United States confirmed these statistics at the oral hearing. Mexico also referred to the 55% figure in its appellee's submission when rejecting the United States' assertion that at least 71% of the meat sold in the United States carries Label A. Mexico contended that, "[a]ccording to uncontested facts, meat products carrying Label A constitute less than 39% (71% of 55%) of the meat products sold in the United States." (Mexico's appellee's submission, para. 58) See also *supra*, footnote 957.

measure, the Panel referred to evidence that 90% of this meat would be eligible for Label A[963] and that the "vast majority" of it in fact carries an A Label.[964]

475. At the same time, as already discussed, the Panel also identified multiple examples of ways in which the labelling scheme prescribed by the COOL measure provides unclear, imperfect, or inaccurate information to consumers, in particular with respect to Labels B and C. The Panel found, for instance, that "the description of origin on Label B and Label C does not, in fact, deliver origin information as defined under the measure or as the consumer might understand it."[965] The Panel noted that "confusion is also likely in a case where a consumer-ready package contains only a single piece of meat, as the meaning of the two country names listed on the label is not clear."[966] It also observed that "[i]t is far from clear ... that differentiation of origin based on the order of country names will indeed communicate accurate origin information."[967] Further, the Panel found that, due to the commingling flexibilities, not even a "perfect consumer who is fully informed of the meaning of different categories of labels under the COOL measure" could ever "be assured that the label precisely reflects the origin of meat as defined under the COOL measure".[968] In addition, since commingling can take place at multiple stages of the meat production process, including at the retail level, this "further diffuses the content and impact of origin labels as defined by the measure".[969] Finally, in observing that the labelling under the COOL measure provides information with regard to the *possible* origin(s) of meat, the Panel added that the information would not

---

[963] The Panel also referred, in this regard, to evidence submitted by the complainants to the effect that several major US meat processors had indicated that, with the entry into force of the 2009 Final Rule (AMS), "around 90 percent of all of the fresh, retail beef and pork cuts produced in the US would qualify for the Category A label." (Panel Reports, para. 7.370 (quoting Panel Exhibit CDA-38))

[964] The Panel stated that it was uncontested among the parties that "the use of Label A affects the *vast majority* of meat labelled under the COOL requirements." (Panel Reports, para. 7.370 (referring to United States' response to Panel Question 91) (emphasis added)) The Panel noted that, according to Canada, data collected during the first quarter of 2010 show that Label A was affixed to 78.6% of muscle cuts of beef supplied in major supermarkets, and that according to the United States, as of July 2009, Label A was affixed to 71% of muscle cuts of beef. (*Ibid.*, footnote 941 to para. 7.715 (referring to Panel Exhibits CDA-211 and US-145)) Canada and Mexico did not contest that the use of Label A affects the vast majority of meat *labelled under the COOL requirements*. (*Ibid.*, para. 7.370) However, as already mentioned, Mexico notes that, out of *all meat sold in the United States*, less than 39% carries a Label A (71% of 55%). (Mexico's appellee's submission, para. 58) See *supra*, footnotes 957 and 962.

[965] Panel Reports, para. 7.699.

[966] Panel Reports, para. 7.700.

[967] Panel Reports, para. 7.701.

[968] Panel Reports, para. 7.702.

[969] Panel Reports, para. 7.704.

necessarily convey the "actual, or for that matter accurate, origin as defined by the measure".[970]

476. Overall, the findings of the Panel and undisputed facts on the record indicate that the labelling requirements under the COOL measure make some contribution to the objective of that measure. Under the COOL measure, more meat will bear labels indicating some form of origin than was previously the case, despite the fact that not all beef and pork sold within the United States is required to carry a country of origin label.[971] Where that meat carries Label A, the label is capable of conveying to consumers that the livestock from which it is derived were born, raised, and slaughtered in the United States, and some of the risk of confusion that existed under the previous labelling regime is avoided.[972] With respect to meat bearing Labels B and C, however, any contribution made is much more limited because the information may be confusing and inaccurate. We observe that — even though they appear to be at odds with the Panel's ultimate conclusion[973] — the Panel's own findings indicate that the COOL measure *does* make some contribution to its objective, notably where Label A is used. Nevertheless, these Panel findings do not enable us to ascertain the *degree* of contribution made by the COOL measure to such an objective.

477. As for the trade-restrictiveness of the COOL measure, we recall the Panel's finding that the COOL measure is "'trade-restrictive' within the meaning of Article 2.2 by affecting the competitive conditions of imported livestock".[974] The Panel found that the scope of the term "trade-restrictive" is broad[975] and "does not require the demonstration of any actual trade effects, as the focus is on the competitive opportunities available to imported products".[976] In its analysis under Article 2.1 of the *TBT Agreement*, the Panel observed that "the United States does not contest the complainants' description of the situation preceding the COOL measure [in which] conditions of competition were the same for imported and domestic products".[977] It then found that "by imposing higher

[970] Panel Reports, para. 7.707.

[971] As already noted, according to the United States and Mexico, the COOL requirements apply to approximately 55% of beef sold in the United States. (See *supra*, para. 474 and footnote 962 thereto)

[972] See *supra*, para. 253 and footnote 435 thereto.

[973] We recall that the Panel found that "the COOL measure does not fulfil the identified objective within the meaning of Article 2.2 because it fails to convey meaningful origin information to consumers." (Panel Reports, para. 7.719. See also para. 7.720)

[974] Panel Reports, para. 7.575.

[975] The Panel noted that the ordinary meaning of the term "restrictive" is "[i]mplying, conveying, or expressing restriction or limitation" and "[h]aving the nature or effect of a restriction; imposing a restriction". (Panel Reports, para. 7.567 (quoting *Shorter Oxford English Dictionary*, 6th edn, A. Stevenson (ed.) (Oxford University Press, 2007), Vol. 2, p. 2553))

[976] Panel Reports, para. 7.572.

[977] Panel Reports, para. 7.387.

segregation costs on imported livestock" the COOL measure negatively affects the conditions of competition of imported livestock vis-à-vis like domestic livestock in the US market.[978] In our view, although the Panel declined to make a finding "on the level of trade-restrictiveness" of the COOL measure[979], its findings suggest it considered the measure to have a considerable degree of trade-restrictiveness insofar as it has a limiting effect on the competitive opportunities for imported livestock as compared to the situation prior to the enactment of the COOL measure.[980] This was confirmed by the Panel's analysis of the actual trade effects of the COOL measure.[981]

478. The Panel did not make findings regarding the risks that non-fulfilment of the objective pursued by the United States through the COOL measure would create. The Panel did, however, cast doubt on the probative value of evidence presented by the United States in order to show that consumers want information on the countries of birth, raising, and slaughter of livestock from which meat is derived.[982] The Panel also took note of US consumers' unwillingness to "bear all the costs of country of origin labelling of beef and pork".[983] That most US consumers are not prepared to pay to receive information on origin as defined in the COOL measure with respect to the meat products they purchase suggests that obtaining such information is not a high priority for such consumers. This in turn seems to indicate that the consequences that may arise from non-fulfilment of the objective would not be particularly grave.

---

978 Panel Reports, para. 7.574.

979 Panel Reports, para. 7.575.

980 The Panel found, for instance, that "there is direct evidence of major slaughterhouses applying a considerable COOL discount of USD 40-60 per head for imported livestock". (Panel Reports, para. 7.356) It noted that "some plants and companies are simply refusing to process any imported livestock any more". (*Ibid.*, para. 7.375) Moreover, the Panel found that, as a result of the COOL measure, "fewer US processing plants are accepting imported livestock than before." (*Ibid.*, para. 7.376) As a result of the reduction of available processing plants, certain suppliers "had to transport imported livestock longer distances than before the COOL measure"; several US plants process imported livestock only "at specific, limited times", which creates "congestion" that, in turn, increases "waiting time" and creates "delays"; and these have "increased the transportation costs of certain suppliers of imported livestock". (*Ibid.*, para. 7.377) The Panel further found that "[c]ontractual terms for suppliers of imported livestock have also changed", becoming less favourable, and that certain suppliers have suffered "significant financial disadvantages resulting from the COOL measure". (*Ibid.*, paras. 7.378 and 7.379) In addition, the Panel referred to undisputed evidence that imported cattle have been excluded from private premium programmes, such as the Certified Angus Beef programme, which are "particularly profitable for operators in the supply chain, including livestock suppliers". (*Ibid.*, para. 7.380)

981 The Panel found that "the Sumner Econometric Study makes a prima facie case that the COOL measure negatively and significantly affected the import shares and price basis of Canadian livestock." (Panel Reports, para. 7.542) The Panel also found that "[t]his significant and negative impact of the COOL measure" was not refuted by the USDA Econometric Study. (*Ibid.*, para. 7.546)

982 Panel Reports, para. 7.647.

983 Panel Reports, para. 7.354 and footnote 498 thereto.

479. Overall, in our view, the Panel's factual findings suggest that the COOL measure makes some contribution to the objective of providing consumers with information on origin; that it has a considerable degree of trade-restrictiveness; and that the consequences that may arise from non-fulfilment of the objective would not be particularly grave. We stress, however, that we lack clear and precise Panel findings with regard to these factors, and, in particular, findings that would enable us to identify the *degree* of contribution made by the COOL measure to the United States' objective. Against this preliminary assessment of the COOL measure, we proceed to examine the alternative measures proposed by Canada and by Mexico in order to see whether we are able to complete our assessment of whether the COOL measure is "more trade-restrictive than necessary to fulfil a legitimate objective".

480. As they did in their submissions to the Panel, Canada and Mexico point to four alternative measures, which, in their view, are reasonably available to the United States, are less trade restrictive, and fulfil the objective of providing consumers with information on origin at an equal or greater level than the COOL measure. These alternatives are: (i) a voluntary country of origin labelling requirement; (ii) a mandatory country of origin labelling requirement based on the criterion of substantial transformation; (iii) a voluntary country of origin labelling regime combined with a mandatory country of origin labelling requirement based on substantial transformation; and (iv) a trace-back regime.[984]

481. We note that the Panel made no factual findings with regard to these four proposed labelling schemes because, having found that the COOL measure does not fulfil its objective, it did "not consider it necessary to proceed with the next step of the analysis, namely whether the COOL measure is 'more trade-restrictive than necessary' based on the availability of less trade-restrictive alternative measures".[985] Therefore, to the extent that our analysis of the proposed alternative measures entails consideration of factual elements, we will be able to complete the analysis only if there are sufficient undisputed facts on the record, or factual findings made by the Panel elsewhere in its analysis, that are relevant to our evaluation of: (i) whether these alternative measures are less trade restrictive than the COOL measure; (ii) whether they would make an equivalent contribution to the relevant objective, taking account of the risks non-fulfilment would create; and (iii) whether they are reasonably available to the United States.[986] We note, at this juncture, that we are faced with a challenging exercise since, in its Article 2.2 analysis, the Panel made no findings with respect to any of the four proposed alternative measures, and made only limited

[984] Canada's other appellant's submission, paras. 77-90; Mexico's other appellant's submission, paras. 61-68.

[985] Panel Reports, para. 7.719.

[986] Appellate Body Report, *US – Tuna II (Mexico)*, para. 322.

findings with respect to the COOL measure itself, in particular with respect to its degree of contribution to the United States' objective.

482. With regard to *voluntary labelling*[987], Canada submits that such a scheme could contribute to the fulfilment of the objective of the COOL measure, while being "significantly less trade-restrictive", because segregation costs would be borne only by those livestock producers catering to interested consumers, and it would not impose a differential burden on the use of Canadian livestock.[988] Mexico adds that a voluntary labelling regime could maintain the same strict labelling criteria on origin as the COOL measure—namely, where the livestock were born, raised, and slaughtered—while allowing market forces to fill consumer demand for this information to the extent such a demand exists.[989] The United States responds that a system based on voluntary labelling would not fulfil its objective at the level it considers appropriate, and stresses that it did try a voluntary labelling system before adopting the COOL measure, but that such voluntary scheme "did not result in country of origin information routinely being provided to consumers".[990]

483. We observe that the trade-restrictiveness of this proposed alternative labelling regime would likely be a function of who would bear the costs associated with the labelling, that is, whether the costs would be incurred by producers or passed on to consumers. Its trade-restrictiveness would also depend on the extent to which such labels would be used. We observe, however, that there are no uncontested facts on the record, and the Panel made no findings, with regard to how a voluntary labelling requirement would operate in the market at issue in terms of trade-restrictiveness. At the same time, the contribution of a voluntary labelling requirement to the objective of providing consumers with information on where livestock were born, raised, and slaughtered would be a function of the accuracy with which labels reflect origin as the country or countries in which different production steps took place, the scope of the products covered by such a voluntary labelling scheme, and the extent to which labels would be used. We note that, in its analysis under Article 2.1 of the *TBT Agreement*, the Panel referred to evidence suggesting that US

---

[987] Voluntary country of origin labelling is a business-driven system contingent upon consumers' willingness to pay for the information on where livestock were born, raised, and slaughtered. This system allows "market forces to recognize and fill the consumer need for additional information". (Mexico's first written submission to the Panel, para. 316) Accordingly, if US consumers "were to express a demand for country-of-origin information", US industry could "use these voluntary programs to provide it". (Canada's first written submission to the Panel, para. 196)

[988] Canada's other appellant's submission, para. 78.

[989] Mexico's other appellant's submission, para. 62.

[990] United States' appellee's submission, footnote 139 to para. 68 (referring to United States' second written submission to the Panel, para. 161).

consumers are not generally willing to pay for information on origin[991], and that, prior to the introduction of the COOL measure, there was a lack of widespread participation in voluntary origin labelling programmes.[992] Overall, these findings do not enable us to determine to what extent a voluntary labelling scheme would contribute to the objective of providing consumers with information on where livestock were born, raised, and slaughtered, or how such a contribution would compare to the degree of contribution made by the COOL measure itself. We are faced with limited elaboration by the parties of their arguments, and we are unable to identify Panel findings or sufficient undisputed facts on the record that would enable us to complete the legal analysis.

484. Regarding the second alternative measure proposed by the complainants—namely, mandatory labelling of origin of beef and pork based on the criterion of *substantial transformation*[993]—Canada submits that such a system would provide "accurate and easy to understand information"[994], while avoiding the trade-restrictiveness of the COOL measure, "as it does not impose differential costs on the importation of livestock".[995] According to Mexico, this option would eliminate the discrimination and trade restrictions affecting imports of Mexican feeder cattle, and would also be consistent with the origin rules applied to imported meat products under the COOL measure (Label D), thereby avoiding confusion.[996] The United States argues that a system that defines origin on the basis of substantial transformation—that is, slaughter—would not fulfil the US objective at the level it considers appropriate because it would not

991 When referring to voluntary labelling programmes maintained by the United States, the Panel found, for instance, that animal production and raising labels, which relate to the place in which production steps took place, "affect a smaller proportion of beef marketed in the United States" than USDA grade labels, which relate to the quality of meat. (Panel Reports, para. 7.406)

992 Panel Reports, paras. 7.354 and 7.355. The Panel found that "[t]he fact that consumers are not ready to bear all the costs of country of origin labelling of beef and pork is also demonstrated by the lack of interest in a voluntary COOL regime." (*Ibid.*, para. 7.354) The Panel also noted the USDA Chief Economist's explanation on "the lack of consumer interest in voluntary country of origin labelling". (*Ibid.*, para. 7.355 (referring to Mandatory Country of Origin Labeling, Hearing before the Committee on Agriculture, House of Representatives, 108th Congress, 26 June 2003 (Panel Exhibit MEX-51)))

993 The substantial transformation system "considers that where processing in a second country changes the nature of a product, the country of origin is that of the second country". (Canada's first written submission to the Panel, para. 201; see also Mexico's first written submission to the Panel, para. 317) We note that a substantial transformation principle confers origin *exclusively* based on the country in which the relevant processing took place, and that this rule of origin is used by the United States for customs purposes. (Panel Reports, paras. 7.674 and 7.734)

994 Canada's other appellant's submission, para. 81.

995 Canada's other appellant's submission, para. 82.

996 Mexico's other appellant's submission, para. 63.

provide information about the countries where the animals were born and raised.[997]

485. We note that a mandatory labelling system according to which the country of origin is the one in which substantial transformation—that is, slaughter—took place would not entail costs of segregation of livestock for purposes of country of origin labelling. In practice, there would be no "restriction or limitation"[998] imposed on imported livestock since all meat products derived from cattle and hogs slaughtered in the United States would bear a "Product of the US" label. We also note that, under such a labelling scheme consumers would be provided with information on where livestock were slaughtered, but they would not be provided with any information as to where the livestock were born and raised. We recall the Panel's finding that the COOL measure's objective is to provide "consumer information on origin"[999], and that the United States "defines the origin of meat based on the place where an animal from which meat is derived was born, raised, and slaughtered".[1000] In this respect, we note that, in the context of Article 2.4 of the *TBT Agreement*, the Panel found that CODEX STAN 1-1985[1001], which is based on the principle of substantial transformation, "does not have the function or capacity of accomplishing the objective of providing information to consumers about the countries in which an animal was born, raised and slaughtered"[1002] and hence is "*ineffective* and *inappropriate* for the fulfilment of the specific objective as defined by the United States".[1003]

486. To the extent that these Panel findings are relevant for an analysis under Article 2.2 of the *TBT Agreement*, they suggest that a mandatory labelling regime based on substantial transformation would, at best, contribute only

---

997 United States' appellee's submission, footnote 142 to para. 68.

998 Panel Reports, para. 7.567 (quoting the definition of "restrictive", *Shorter Oxford English Dictionary*, 6th edn, A. Stevenson (ed.) (Oxford University Press, 2007), Vol. 2, p. 2553).

999 Panel Reports, para. 7.685.

1000 Panel Reports, para. 7.673. We also recall the Panel's findings that "[t]here is no basis ... to find that the United States is prohibited from adopting for labelling purposes an origin definition which is different from that for customs purposes." (*Ibid.*, para. 7.675)

1001 General Standard for the Labelling of Prepackaged Foods, as amended. (See Panel Reports, para. 7.722)

1002 Panel Reports, para. 7.734.

1003 Panel Reports, para. 7.735. (original emphasis) We also note that, in response to the complainants' argument that even if US consumers might be interested in the "origin" of their meat, this does not necessarily mean that they are interested in origin defined as the places in which every stage of production of the relevant livestock took place, the United States referred during the oral hearing to Panel Exhibit US-115. This exhibit is a letter to the USDA from a consumer explicitly expressing a preference for a definition of origin that states where livestock were born, raised, and slaughtered.

partially to the objective of providing information to consumers on where livestock from which meat is derived were born, raised, and slaughtered. In any event, as stated above, there are insufficient Panel findings to enable us to ascertain the degree of contribution made by the COOL measure to the United States' objective. Moreover, without knowing whether a mandatory labelling system based on substantial transformation would require *all* beef and pork sold in the United States to be labelled, we are unable to compare the degree of the COOL measure's contribution with that of this alternative measure proposed by the complainants.

487. Regarding the third alternative measure suggested by the complainants—namely a *combination* of the two schemes already discussed[1004]—Canada submits that this option would be less trade restrictive than the COOL measure because it "would not require segregation for the portion of the market that did not require voluntary labels".[1005] In addition, both Canada and Mexico argue that a combined system would ensure that all consumers are provided with information on the origin of the meat that they purchase on the same basis as they currently are for imported meat products (Label D), and would permit additional information to be conveyed to those who are interested.[1006] The United States rejects this alternative because, in its view, such a scheme would ultimately depend on the choice of the retailer, and not the consumer, as to whether meat will be labelled with additional information about where livestock were born and raised, and, without a recordkeeping infrastructure similar to that under the COOL measure in place, many retailers would not have the ability to provide this information even if they desired to do so.[1007]

488. We observe that this combined alternative measure would not require segregation of livestock for the portion of the market that does not voluntarily choose to provide consumer information on where livestock were born and raised. Moreover, no segregation costs would result from the compulsory labelling part of the measure based on substantial transformation. However, for the same reasons already discussed under the two previous alternatives, it is unclear whether a voluntary labelling scheme combined with a mandatory labelling requirement based on substantial transformation would make a contribution to the objective of providing consumers with information on where

[1004] This alternative is a combination of a mandatory labelling system based on the criterion of substantial transformation and a voluntary country of origin labelling regime. (See Canada's other appellant's submission, para. 85; and Mexico's other appellant's submission, para. 64)

[1005] Canada's other appellant's submission, para. 86.

[1006] Canada's other appellant's submission, para. 87; Mexico's other appellant's submission, para. 64.

[1007] United States' appellee's submission, footnote 147 to para. 68 (referring to United States' answer to Panel Question 37, paras. 69 and 70; and United States' second written submission to the Panel, para. 144).

livestock were born, raised, and slaughtered, at least equivalent to the contribution made by the COOL measure. Again, we are faced with limited elaboration by the parties of their arguments and we are unable to identify Panel findings or sufficient undisputed facts on the record that would enable us to complete the legal analysis.

489. Lastly, with respect to the fourth suggested alternative measure—namely, a *trace-back* system[1008]—Canada argues that such a regime could provide detailed information for each piece of meat. Although Canada acknowledges that a trace-back system could also increase costs because of the additional tracking throughout the supply chain, it stresses that "any additional cost would be distributed equally to all market participants."[1009] Mexico submits that this alternative is "technically and economically feasible in the United States"[1010] and that, since it would impose the same requirements on both domestic and imported animals, the economic incentive to discriminate against Mexican cattle would likely be eliminated. Mexico noted during the oral hearing that the United States already imposes a trace-back system for sanitary and phytosanitary reasons, pursuant to which all Mexican cattle are identified with ear tags and can be traced back to the farm. The United States replies that a trace-back system is not a reasonably available alternative because it is more trade restrictive than the COOL measure, since it would increase the costs on entities throughout the supply chain, including on Canadian and Mexican livestock producers.[1011]

490. All of the participants appear to accept that a trace-back system would entail additional costs.[1012] They also appear to accept that a trace-back system could require the provision of consumer information on the country(ies) where livestock were born, raised, and slaughtered, or of even more detailed information, such as the specific location of individual production steps within a country. However, the participants hold opposing views as to the trade-

---

[1008] A trace-back system requires "that a retailer be able to trace a piece of meat back to the original animal". (Mexico's second written submission to the Panel, para. 78 (referring to Panel Exhibit MEX-88, p. 7); see also Canada's opening statement at the second meeting of the Panel, para. 70) The information provided under this system can indicate "the precise location of each processing step (farm, feedlot, processing facility) by state/province, municipality, etc.". (Canada's other appellant's submission, para. 88)

[1009] Canada's other appellant's submission, para. 90.

[1010] Mexico's other appellant's submission, para. 67 (referring to Panel Exhibit MEX-88, p. 7).

[1011] United States' appellee's submission, footnote 150 to para. 68. In the United States' view, "a traceability system is significantly costly to implement and would increase overall compliance costs." (United States' answer to Panel Question 146, para. 103)

[1012] We note, however, that the mere fact that an alternative measure would entail some additional cost does not, alone, mean that such a measure is not reasonably available to a Member. (See Appellate Body Report, *China – Publications and Audiovisual Products,* para. 327 (referring to Appellate Body Report, *US – Gambling*, para. 308; and Appellate Body Report, *Korea – Various Measures on Beef*, para. 181))

restrictiveness of such a system. In the absence of specific information and argumentation regarding the relationship between costs, prices, and demand in the US market for livestock and meat, it is not clear to what extent an increase in costs would be trade restrictive, or would affect livestock from all sources equally. With regard to Mexico's argument that the United States already imposes a trace-back system on all Mexican cattle for sanitary and phytosanitary purposes, the Panel made no findings, and there are no undisputed facts on the record regarding how this trace-back scheme for Mexican cattle operates, or whether it would already satisfy the requirements of a trace-back regime imposed for labelling purposes. Therefore, we are not in a position to reach a conclusion as to how the trade-restrictiveness of a trace-back system would compare to the status quo.

491. Overall, due to the absence of relevant factual findings by the Panel, and of sufficient undisputed facts on the record, we are unable to complete the legal analysis under Article 2.2 of the *TBT Agreement* and determine whether the COOL measure is more trade restrictive than necessary to fulfil its legitimate objective.

VII. ARTICLE III:4 OF THE GATT 1994

492. Canada and Mexico each raises a conditional appeal[1013] with respect to Article III:4 of the GATT 1994. Both appeals are conditional upon our reversal of the Panel's finding of inconsistency under Article 2.1 of the *TBT Agreement.* In that event, Mexico appeals the Panel's exercise of judicial economy and requests us to complete the legal analysis and find the COOL measure to be inconsistent with Article III:4. In its other appellant's submission, Canada appeals the Panel's exercise of judicial economy with respect to its claims regarding both the COOL measure and the Vilsack letter under Article III:4 of the GATT 1994, and requests us to complete the legal analysis and find these measures to be inconsistent with the United States' obligations under that provision. At the oral hearing, however, Canada clarified that, in the light of the United States' asserted withdrawal of the Vilsack letter[1014], Canada was no longer seeking a discrete finding with respect to that measure.[1015]

[1013] In its other appellant's submission, Canada's appeal with respect to Article III:4 did not appear to be made on a conditional basis. However, at the oral hearing, Canada stated that this ground of its appeal is indeed conditional upon our reversal of the Panel's finding under Article 2.1 of the *TBT Agreement*.

[1014] In its appellee's submission, the United States asserts that the Vilsack letter was withdrawn on 5 April 2012. (United States' appellee's submission, para. 90 and footnote 193 thereto (referring to a USDA letter to industry representatives, available at: *<http://www.ams.usda.gov/AMSv1.0/cool>)).*

[1015] Canada did, however, request us to take the Vilsack letter into account insofar as it relates to our analysis of the COOL measure under Article III:4 of the GATT 1994.

493. Having upheld the Panel's finding that the COOL measure is inconsistent with Article 2.1 of the *TBT Agreement*, the condition upon which Canada's and Mexico's appeals under Article III:4 are made is not satisfied, and we therefore need not make any findings in respect of Article III:4 with regard to the COOL measure. It is also unnecessary for us to make any finding with regard to the Vilsack letter.

VIII. ARTICLE XXIII:1(B) OF THE GATT 1994

494. Canada and Mexico also each conditionally appeals the Panel's exercise of judicial economy with respect to whether the COOL measure nullifies and impairs benefits within the meaning of Article XXIII:1(b) of the GATT 1994. Canada further raises a conditional appeal with respect to the Vilsack letter. That is, should we reverse the Panel's finding of inconsistency under Article 2.1 of the *TBT Agreement*, and not find the COOL measure to be inconsistent with Article III:4 of the GATT 1994, then Canada requests us to complete the legal analysis under Article XXIII:1(b) and to find that both the COOL measure and the Vilsack letter nullify and impair benefits accruing to Canada under successive multilateral trade negotiations. Should those same conditions be satisfied, then Mexico requests us to complete the legal analysis under Article XXIII:1(b) and to find that the COOL measure nullifies and impairs benefits accruing to Mexico from the tariff concessions made by the United States in its tariff bindings.

495. Having upheld the Panel's finding that the COOL measure is inconsistent with Article 2.1 of the *TBT Agreement*, the first condition upon which Canada's and Mexico's appeals under Article XXIII:1(b) of the GATT 1994 are made is not met, and we therefore need not make any findings in respect of Article XXIII:1(b) with regard to the COOL measure. It is also unnecessary for us to make any finding with regard to the Vilsack letter.[1016]

[1016] As noted above, the United States stated in its appellee's submission that the Vilsack letter has been withdrawn. At the oral hearing, Canada stated that it was no longer seeking a specific finding under Article XXIII:1(b) of the GATT 1994 with regard to the Vilsack letter, although it encouraged us to take that measure into account insofar as it relates to our analysis of the COOL measure under Article XXIII:1(b) of the GATT 1994.

IX. FINDINGS AND CONCLUSIONS

496. In the appeal of the Panel Report, *United States – Certain Country of Origin Labelling (COOL) Requirements* (Complaint by Canada) (WT/DS384/R) (the "Canada Panel Report"), for the reasons set out in this Report, the Appellate Body:

(a) with respect to the Panel's findings under Article 2.1 of the *TBT Agreement*:

(i) *finds* that the Panel did not err, in paragraph 7.295 of the Canada Panel Report, in stating that the COOL measure treats imported livestock differently than domestic livestock;

(ii) *finds* that the Panel did not err, in paragraphs 7.372, 7.381, and 7.420 of the Canada Panel Report, in finding that the COOL measure modifies the conditions of competition in the US market to the detriment of imported livestock by creating an incentive in favour of processing exclusively domestic livestock and a disincentive against handling imported livestock;

(iii) *finds* that the Panel did not act inconsistently with its obligation under Article 11 of the DSU to make an objective assessment of the facts in its findings with respect to segregation, commingling, and the price differential between imported and domestic livestock in the US market; and

(iv) *upholds*, albeit for different reasons, the Panel's ultimate finding, in paragraphs 7.548 and 8.3(b) of the Canada Panel Report, that the COOL measure, particularly in regard to the muscle cut meat labels, is inconsistent with Article 2.1 of the *TBT Agreement* because it accords less favourable treatment to imported livestock than to like domestic livestock;

(b) with respect to the Panel's findings under Article 2.2 of the *TBT Agreement*:

(i) *makes no finding* with respect to the United States' claim that the Panel erred in finding that the COOL measure is "trade-restrictive" within the meaning of Article 2.2, because that claim of error is dependent upon the Appellate

Body's reversal of the Panel's finding under Article 2.1 of the *TBT Agreement*;

(ii) *finds* that the Panel did not err, in paragraphs 7.617 and 7.685 of the Canada Panel Report, in finding that the objective pursued by the United States through the COOL measure is the provision of consumer information on origin[1017];

(iii) *finds* that, in identifying the objective pursued by the United States through the COOL measure, the Panel did not act inconsistently with its obligation under Article 11 of the DSU to make an objective assessment of the facts, and did not fail to characterize the objective of the COOL measure in sufficient detail;

(iv) *finds* that the Panel did not err, in paragraph 7.651 of the Canada Panel Report, in finding that the provision of consumer information on origin is a legitimate objective within the meaning of Article 2.2 of the *TBT Agreement*;

(v) *finds* that the Panel erred in the interpretation and application of Article 2.2 of the *TBT Agreement* in its analysis of whether the COOL measure is "more trade-restrictive than necessary to fulfil a legitimate objective", and, consequently, *finds* that the Panel erred, in paragraph 7.719 of the Canada Panel Report, in finding that "the COOL measure does not fulfil the identified objective within the meaning of Article 2.2 because it fails to convey meaningful origin information to consumers"; and, therefore,

(vi) *reverses* the Panel's ultimate finding, in paragraphs 7.720 and 8.3(c) of the Canada Panel Report, that the COOL measure is inconsistent with Article 2.2 of the *TBT Agreement*; and

(vii) *finds* that, in the light of the lack of sufficient undisputed facts on the Panel record or factual findings by the Panel, the Appellate Body is unable to complete the legal analysis under Article 2.2 of the *TBT Agreement* and properly assess

[1017] We recall in this respect that the COOL measure defines the "origin" of meat as a function of the country or countries in which the livestock from which the meat is derived were born, raised, and slaughtered.

whether the COOL measure is more trade restrictive than necessary to fulfil its legitimate objective; and

(c) with respect to Canada's conditional appeals under Articles III:4 and XXIII:1(b) of the GATT 1994, *finds* that the conditions upon which these appeals are premised are not satisfied, and, consequently, *makes no finding* with respect to Canada's claims that the COOL measure is inconsistent with Article III:4 of the GATT 1994, or that the application of the COOL measure nullifies or impairs benefits accruing to Canada within the meaning of Article XXIII:1(b) of the GATT 1994.

497. The Appellate Body *recommends* that the DSB request the United States to bring its measures, found in this Report, and in the Canada Panel Report as modified by this Report, to be inconsistent with the GATT 1994 and the *TBT Agreement*, into conformity with its obligations under those Agreements.

IX. FINDINGS AND CONCLUSIONS

496. In the appeal of the Panel Report, *United States – Certain Country of Origin Labelling (COOL) Requirements* (Complaint by Mexico) (WT/DS386/R) (the "Mexico Panel Report"), for the reasons set out in this Report, the Appellate Body:

(a) with respect to the Panel's findings under Article 2.1 of the *TBT Agreement*:

(i) *finds* that the Panel did not err, in paragraph 7.295 of the Mexico Panel Report, in stating that the COOL measure treats imported livestock differently than domestic livestock;

(ii) *finds* that the Panel did not err, in paragraphs 7.372, 7.381, and 7.420 of the Mexico Panel Report, in finding that the COOL measure modifies the conditions of competition in the US market to the detriment of imported livestock by creating an incentive in favour of processing exclusively domestic livestock and a disincentive against handling imported livestock;

(iii) *finds* that the Panel did not act inconsistently with its obligation under Article 11 of the DSU to make an objective assessment of the facts in its findings with respect to segregation, commingling, and the price differential between imported and domestic livestock in the US market; and

(iv) *upholds*, albeit for different reasons, the Panel's ultimate finding, in paragraphs 7.548 and 8.3(b) of the Mexico Panel Report, that the COOL measure, in particular in regard to the muscle cut meat labels, is inconsistent with Article 2.1 of the *TBT Agreement* because it accords less favourable treatment to imported livestock than to like domestic livestock;

(b) with respect to the Panel's findings under Article 2.2 of the *TBT Agreement*:

(i) *makes no finding* with respect to the United States' claim that the Panel erred in finding that the COOL measure is "trade-restrictive" within the meaning of Article 2.2, because that claim of error is dependent upon the Appellate Body's reversal of the Panel's finding under Article 2.1 of the *TBT Agreement*;

(ii) *finds* that the Panel did not err, in paragraphs 7.617 and 7.685 of the Mexico Panel Report, in finding that the objective pursued by the United States through the COOL measure is the provision of consumer information on origin[1018];

(iii) *finds* that, in identifying the objective pursued by the United States through the COOL measure, the Panel did not act inconsistently with its obligation under Article 11 of the DSU to make an objective assessment of the facts;

(iv) *finds* that the Panel erred in the interpretation and application of Article 2.2 of the *TBT Agreement* in its analysis of whether the COOL measure is "more trade-restrictive than necessary to fulfil a legitimate objective", and, consequently, *finds* that the Panel erred, in paragraph 7.719 of the Mexico Panel Report, in finding that "the COOL measure does not fulfil the identified objective within the meaning of Article 2.2 because it fails to convey meaningful origin information to consumers"; and, therefore,

(v) *reverses* the Panel's ultimate finding, in paragraphs 7.720 and 8.3(c) of the Mexico Panel Report, that the COOL measure is inconsistent with Article 2.2 of the *TBT Agreement*; and

(vi) *finds* that, in the light of the lack of sufficient undisputed facts on the Panel record or factual findings by the Panel, the Appellate Body is unable to complete the legal analysis under Article 2.2 of the *TBT Agreement* and properly assess whether the COOL measure is more trade restrictive than necessary to fulfil its legitimate objective; and

(c) with respect to Mexico's conditional appeals under Articles III:4 and XXIII:1(b) of the GATT 1994, *finds* that the conditions upon which these appeals are premised are not satisfied, and, consequently, *makes no finding* with respect to Mexico's claims that the COOL measure is inconsistent with Article III:4 of the GATT 1994, or that the application of the COOL measure nullifies or impairs benefits accruing to Mexico within the meaning of Article XXIII:1(b) of the GATT 1994.

497. The Appellate Body *recommends* that the DSB request the United States to bring its measures, found in this Report, and in the Mexico Panel Report as modified by this Report, to be inconsistent with the GATT 1994 and the *TBT Agreement*, into conformity with its obligations under those Agreements.

ANNEX I

WORLD TRADE ORGANIZATION

WT/DS384/12
WT/DS386/11

28 March 2012

(12-1654)

Original: English

UNITED STATES – CERTAIN COUNTRY OF ORIGIN LABELLING (COOL) REQUIREMENTS

Notification of an Appeal by the United States under Article 16.4 and Article 17 of the Understanding on Rules and Procedures Governing the Settlement of Disputes (DSU), and under Rule 20(1) of the *Working Procedures for Appellate Review*

The following notification, dated 23 March 2012, from the Delegation of the United States, is being circulated to Members.

Pursuant to Article 16 of the *Understanding on Rules and Procedures Governing the Settlement of Disputes* ("DSU") and Rule 20 of the *Working Procedures for Appellate Review*, the United States hereby notifies its decision to appeal to the Appellate Body certain issues of law covered in the Reports of the Panel in *United States – Certain Country of Origin Labelling (COOL) Requirements* (WT/DS384/R and WT/DS386/R) ("Panel Reports") and certain legal interpretations developed by the Panel.

1. The United States seeks review by the Appellate Body of the Panel's findings and conclusion that U.S. country of origin labeling requirements[1] are

[1] The U.S. COOL requirements consist of the relevant sections of the Agricultural Marketing Act of 1946 (7 U.S.C. __ 1638-1638c) ("the COOL statute") and regulations promulgated by the United States Department of Agriculture's Agricultural Marketing Service on January 15, 2009, entitled

inconsistent with Article 2.1 of the *Agreement on Technical Barriers to Trade* (the "*TBT Agreement*").[2] This conclusion is in error and is based on erroneous findings on issues of law and legal interpretations including:

(a) the Panel's finding that the U.S. COOL requirements treat imported livestock differently than domestic livestock.[3]

(b) the Panel's finding that the U.S. COOL requirements accord less favorable treatment to imported livestock than that accorded to domestic livestock by modifying the conditions of competition to the detriment of imported products.[4]

2. The United States also requests the Appellate Body to find that the Panel acted inconsistently with Article 11 of the DSU by failing to make an objective assessment of the facts related to these issues, specifically that segregation of livestock is "necessitated" by the COOL requirements, that commingling is not occurring on a widespread basis, and that the COOL requirements resulted in a "price differential" between domestic and imported livestock,[5] and by using these faulty factual findings to support its conclusions with regard to different treatment and less favorable treatment.

3. The United States also seeks review of the Panel's findings and conclusion that the COOL requirements are inconsistent with Article 2.2 of the *TBT Agreement*.[6] This conclusion is in error and is based on erroneous findings on issues of law and legal interpretations including:

(a) with regard to section VII.D.3(b) of the Panel Reports, the Panel's finding that the COOL measure is "trade restrictive" for purposes of Article 2.2.[7]

"Mandatory Country of Origin Labeling of Beef, Pork, Lamb, Chicken, Goat Meat, Wild and Farm-Raised Fish and Shellfish, Perishable Agricultural Commodities, Peanuts, Pecans, Ginseng, and Macadamia Nuts, which are codified at 7 C.F.R. Parts 60 and 65 ("2009 Final Rule"). *See* Panel Reports, para. 7.61.

2 *See, e.g.*, Panel Reports, paras.7.420, 7.548, 8.3(b).

3 *See, e.g.*, Panel Reports, paras.7.295-7.296.

4 *See, e.g.*, Panel Reports, paras. 7.420, 7.548

5 *See, e.g.*, Panel Reports, paras. 7.316, 7.327, 7.336, 7.352-353, 7.356, 7.364, 7.366-368, 7.379. 7.487, and 7.542.

6 *See, e.g.*, Panel Reports, para. 8.3(c).

7 *See, e.g.*, Panel Reports, paras. 7.565-7.575.

(b) with regard to section VII.D.3(c) of the Panel Reports, the Panel's failure to consider all relevant information regarding the U.S. chosen level of fulfillment of the legitimate objective.[8]

(c) with regard to sections VII.D.3(d)-(e) of the Panel Reports: (1) the Panel's legal framework for determining whether a measure is "more trade-restrictive than necessary to fulfil a legitimate objective";[9] (2) the Panel's finding that the COOL requirements do not fulfill the legitimate objective at the level the United States considers appropriate;[10] and (3) the Panel's failure to require the complaining parties to meet their burden to prove that the measure is "more trade-restrictive than necessary" based on the availability of a significantly less trade-restrictive alternative measure that also fulfills the objective at the level the United States considers appropriate.[11]

4. The United States also requests the Appellate Body to find that the Panel acted inconsistently with Article 11 of the DSU by failing to make an objective assessment of the facts related to these issues, specifically the Panel's findings regarding the level at which the United States considers it appropriate to fulfill its objective.[12]

The United States is providing a copy of this letter directly to Canada, Mexico and to the third parties.

[8] *See, e.g.*, Panel Reports, paras. 7.590-7.620.

[9] *See* Panel Reports, paras. 7.652, 7.666-7.670, 7.692-7.720.

[10] *See, e.g.*, Panel Reports, paras. 7.692-7.720.

[11] *See* Panel Reports, para. 7.719.

[12] *See, e.g.*, Panel Reports, paras. 7.619-7.620, 7.715.

ANNEX II

WORLD TRADE ORGANIZATION

WT/DS384/13

2 April 2012

(12-1706)

Original: English

UNITED STATES – CERTAIN COUNTRY OF ORIGIN LABELLING (COOL) REQUIREMENTS

Notification of an Other Appeal by Canada under Article 16.4 and Article 17 of the Understanding on Rules and Procedures Governing the Settlement of Disputes (DSU), and under Rule 23(1) of the *Working Procedures for Appellate Review*

The following notification, dated 28 March 2012, from the Delegation of Canada, is being circulated to Members.

Pursuant to Article 16 of the *Understanding on Rules and Procedures Governing the Settlement of Disputes* (DSU) and Rule 23 of the *Working Procedures for Appellate Review*, Canada hereby notifies its decision to appeal to the Appellate Body certain issues of law covered in the Report of the Panel in *United States – Certain Country of Origin Labelling (COOL) Requirements* (WT/DS384/R) (Panel Report) and certain legal interpretations developed by the Panel.

1. Canada seeks review by the Appellate Body of the Panel's legal conclusions that:

   (a) Article 2.2 of the Agreement on Technical Barriers to Trade requires identifying a potential objective of a challenged measure rather than the actual objective of that measure; and

(b) the objective of the COOL measure[1] is legitimate within the meaning of Article 2.2 of the Agreement on Technical Barriers to Trade.

2. Canada also appeals the Panel's failure, in contravention of Article 11 of the DSU, to make an objective assessment of the facts demonstrating that the objective of the COOL measure is protectionism. In the alternative, if the objective of the COOL measure is not protectionism, the Panel erred by failing to define the objective at a sufficiently detailed level.

3. If the Appellate Body does not uphold the Panel's finding that the COOL measure fails to fulfil a legitimate objective, then Canada seeks a finding by the Appellate Body that there are less trade-restrictive alternative measures that fulfil that objective, and that therefore the COOL measure violates Article 2.2 of the Agreement on Technical Barriers to Trade.

4. Canada further seeks review by the Appellate Body of the Panel's exercise in judicial economy on Canada's GATT Article III:4 claim regarding the COOL measure and the Vilsack letter[2].

5. Finally, Canada seeks conditional review by the Appellate Body of the Panel's failure to find that the COOL measure and the Vilsack letter constitute an instance of non-violation nullification or impairment under GATT Article XXIII:1(b). That request for review is conditional on the Appellate Body not finding a violation of either Article 2.1 of the *TBT Agreement* or Article III:4 of the GATT.

---

[1] The COOL measure includes the COOL Statute and the Final Rule, as set out in the Panel Report, paras. 7.21, 7.34, and 7.63.

[2] Defined in the Table of Abbreviations of the Panel as "Letter to 'Industry Representative' from the United States Secretary of Agriculture, Thomas J. Vilsack, of 20 February 2009".

ANNEX III

WORLD TRADE ORGANIZATION

WT/DS386/12
2 April 2012
(12-1707)

Original: English

UNITED STATES – CERTAIN COUNTRY OF ORIGIN LABELLING (COOL) REQUIREMENTS

Notification of an Other Appeal by Mexico under Article 16.4 and Article 17 of the Understanding on Rules and Procedures Governing the Settlement of Disputes (DSU), and under Rule 23(1) of the *Working Procedures for Appellate Review*

The following notification, dated 28 March 2012, from the Delegation of Mexico, is being circulated to Members.

---

1. Pursuant to Articles 16.4 and 17 of the *Understanding on Rules and Procedures Governing the Settlement of Disputes* (DSU) and Rule 23(1) of the *Working Procedures for Appellate Review*, the United Mexican States ("Mexico") hereby notifies its decision to appeal to the Appellate Body certain issues of law and certain legal interpretations developed by the Panel in *United States – Certain Country of Origin Labelling (COOL) Requirements* (WT/DS386) ("Panel Report").

2. Pursuant to Rule 23(2)(c)(ii) of the *Working Procedures for Appellate Review*, this Notice of Other Appeal includes an indicative list of the paragraphs of the Panel Report containing the alleged errors, without prejudice to Mexico's ability to refer to other paragraphs of the Panel Report in the context of this appeal.

I. Conditional Appeal of the Panel's Decision to Exercise Judicial Economy with Respect to Mexico's Claims under Article III:4 of the GATT 1994

3. This appeal is conditional in the event that the Appellate Body overturns the Panel's finding that the COOL measure is inconsistent with Article 2.1 of the *TBT Agreement*.

4. If this condition is triggered, Mexico appeals the Panel's decision to exercise judicial economy in respect of Mexico's claim under Article III:4 of the GATT 1994.[1]

5. The Panel erred in its decision to exercise judicial economy with respect to Mexico's claims under Article III:4 of the GATT 1994, considering the particular circumstances of this case, where, if the Panel's finding on inconsistency of Article 2.1 of the *TBT Agreement* is overturned, the Panel's legal basis for exercising judicial economy will no longer exist and Mexico will be left with no positive solution to its discrimination claims under Article III:4 of the GATT 1994.

6. As a result of the foregoing error, Mexico requests the Appellate Body to modify the Panel's legal conclusions and findings in paragraph 8.4 (a) and paragraph 7.807 of the Panel Report, complete the analysis of Mexico's claims under Article III:4 of the GATT 1994, and find that the COOL Measure is inconsistent with Article III:4 of the GATT 1994.

II. Conditional Appeal of the Panel's Finding Regarding the Identification of the Objective Pursued by the COOL Measure and the Examination of Its Legitimacy

7. This appeal is conditional in the event that the Appellate Body overturns the Panel's finding that the COOL measure is inconsistent with Article 2.2.

8. If this condition is triggered, Mexico appeals the Panel's finding that the objective of the COOL measure is to "*provide as much clear and accurate information as possible to consumers*"[2] and that "*providing consumer*

---

[1] Panel Report, 7.807, 8.4(a).

[2] Panel Report, 7.620.

information on origin is a legitimate objective within the meaning of Article 2.2".[3]

9. The Panel applied an incorrect legal analysis to determine the objective and, by doing so, it incorrectly identified that objective. Having erred in identifying the objective, the Panel incorrectly found that the objective was legitimate.

10. Moreover, because the legal errors led to the exclusion of relevant facts, the approach is also factually erroneous. In this sense, the Panel failed to make an objective assessment of the matter before it and thereby acted inconsistently with Article 11 of the DSU.

11. As a result of the foregoing errors, Mexico requests the Appellate Body to modify the Panel's legal conclusions and findings in paragraphs 7.620, 7.651, *inter alia*, of the Panel Report, apply the correct analysis to identify the objective and examine its legitimacy, and find that the objective is inconsistent with Article 2.2 of the *TBT Agreement*.

III. Conditional Appeal of the Panel's Decision to Exercise Judicial Economy in Respect of the Existence of an Alternative Measure That is Less Trade Restrictive and That Fulfils the Legitimate Objective Taking Into Account the Risks Non-Fulfilment Would Create

12. This appeal is conditional in the event that the Appellate Body overturns the Panel's finding that the COOL measure is inconsistent with Article 2.2 of the *TBT Agreement*.

13. If this condition is triggered, Mexico appeals the Panel's decision to exercise judicial economy in respect of "whether the COOL measure is 'more trade-restrictive than necessary' based on the availability of less trade-restrictive alternative measure that can equally fulfil the identified objective".[4]

14. The Panel erred in its decision to exercise judicial economy in respect to Mexico's claims that the COOL measure is more trade restrictive than necessary. In particular, there are alternative measures that are less trade restrictive and that fulfil the legitimate objective taking into account the risks non-fulfilment would

---

3 Panel Report, 7.651.

4 Panel Report, 7.719.

create and, considering the particular circumstances of this case, if the Panel's finding on inconsistency of Article 2.2 of the TBT is overturned, the Panel's legal basis for exercising judicial economy will no longer exist and Mexico will be left with no positive solution to its claims under Article 2.2 of the *TBT Agreement*.

15. As a result of the foregoing error, Mexico requests that the Appellate Body modify the Panel's legal conclusions and findings in the second sentence of paragraph 7.719 of the Panel Report, complete the analysis and find that the COOL measure is inconsistent with Article 2.2 of the *TBT Agreement*.

IV. Conditional Appeal of the Panel's Decision to Exercise Judicial Economy with Respect to Mexico's Claim of Non-Violation Nullification or Impairment under Article XXIII:1(b) of the GATT 1994.

16. This appeal is conditional in the event that the Appellate Body overturns the Panel's findings that the COOL measure is inconsistent with Article 2.1 of the *TBT Agreement* and does not complete the analysis and find that the measure is inconsistent with Article III:4 of the GATT 1994.

17. If this condition is triggered, Mexico appeals the Panel's decision to exercise judicial economy with respect to Mexico's claim of non-violation nullification or impairment under Article XXIII:1(b) of the GATT 1994.[5]

18. The Panel erred in its decision to exercise judicial economy with respect to Mexico's claim of non-violation nullification or impairment under Article XXIII:1(b) of the GATT 1994, considering the particular circumstances of this case, where, if the Panel's finding on inconsistency of Article 2.1 is overturned and there is not a finding that the measure is inconsistent with Article III:4 of the GATT 1994, the Panel's legal basis for exercising judicial economy will no longer exist and Mexico will be left with no positive solution to its claim of non-violation nullification or impairment under Article XXIII:1(b) of the GATT 1994.

---

5 Panel Report, 7.907, 8.5.

19. As a result of the foregoing error, Mexico requests the Appellate Body to modify the Panel's legal conclusions and findings in paragraph 8.5 and paragraph 7.907, inter alia, of the Panel Report, complete the analysis of Mexico's claim, and find that the COOL measure nullifies or impairs benefits accruing to Mexico under the GATT 1994 within the meaning of Article XXIII:1(b) of the GATT 1994.

ANNEX IV

United States – Certain Country of Origin Labelling (COOL) Requirements

AB-2012-3

Procedural Ruling

1. On 5 April 2012, we received a joint communication from the participants in the above appellate proceedings. In that letter, Canada and the United States request that we allow observation by the public of the oral hearing. Mexico indicates that it does not object to allowing such public observation of the hearing, but requests that we reflect in our report that its position in these proceedings is without prejudice to its systemic views on the matter.[1]

2. Specifically, Canada and the United States jointly request that all WTO Members and the public be allowed to observe the statements and answers to questions of the participants and third participants that agree to make their statements and answers public. The participants observe that nothing in the *Understanding on Rules and Procedures Governing the Settlement of Disputes* (the "DSU") or the *Working Procedures for Appellate Review* (the "*Working Procedures*") precludes the Appellate Body from authorizing public observation of the oral hearing. The participants also rely on the rulings by the Appellate Body in eight previous proceedings authorizing public observation of the oral hearing.[2]

---

[1] Mexico pointed to a similar statement made by the Panel in paragraph 2.5 of its Reports.

[2] These proceedings are: *United States – Continued Suspension of Obligations in the EC – Hormones Dispute* (WT/DS320/AB/R) and *Canada – Continued Suspension of Obligations in the EC – Hormones Dispute* (WT/DS321/AB/R); *European Communities – Regime for the Importation, Sale and Distribution of Bananas – Second Recourse to Article 21.5 of the DSU by Ecuador* (WT/DS27/AB/RW2/ECU) and *European Communities – Regime for the Importation, Sale and Distribution of Bananas – Recourse to Article 21.5 of the DSU by the United States* (WT/DS27/AB/RW/USA); *United States – Continued Existence and Application of Zeroing Methodology* (WT/DS350/AB/R); *United States – Laws, Regulations and Methodology for Calculating Dumping Margins ("Zeroing") – Recourse to Article 21.5 of the DSU by the European Communities* (WT/DS294/AB/RW); *United States – Measures Relating to Zeroing and Sunset Reviews – Recourse to Article 21.5 of the DSU by Japan* (WT/DS322/AB/RW); *Australia – Measures Affecting the Importation of Apples from New Zealand* (WT/DS367/AB/R); *European Communities and Certain Member States – Measures Affecting Trade in Large Civil Aircraft* (WT/DS316/AB/R); and *United States – Measures Affecting Trade in Large Civil Aircraft (Second Complaint)* (WT/DS353/AB/R).

3. The participants recall that Article 18.2 of the DSU affirms the right of WTO Members to disclose statements of their positions to the public, and that this includes statements and answers to questions during an Appellate Body hearing. Thus, they maintain, when the parties to a dispute so request, it is appropriate to have such statements and answers made public at the time that they are uttered. The participants further observe that public observation has operated smoothly in previous appellate proceedings, and that the rights of those third participants that have not wanted their oral statements to be subject to public observation have been fully protected.

4. The participants add that the request is made on the understanding that any information that was designated as confidential in the documents filed in the Panel proceedings would be adequately protected in the course of the hearing. They propose that public observation be permitted via simultaneous closed-circuit television broadcasting, with the option for the transmission to be turned off should the participants find it necessary to discuss issues that involve confidential information, as well as for those third participants that do not wish to have their oral statements subject to public observation.

5. On the day that we received the communication from the participants, we invited the third participants to comment in writing on the request by noon on 12 April 2012. By that deadline, we received responses from Brazil, China, Colombia, and the European Union. Brazil and Colombia indicated that they do not object to allowing public observation of the hearing, but requested that the Appellate Body reflect in its report that their acceptance of an open hearing in these proceedings is without prejudice to their systemic views on the matter. China indicated that it had no comments on the request to allow public observation of the hearing, but that it reserved the right to make an oral statement in closed session. The European Union indicated that it had no objection to the request by Canada and the United States for public observation of the oral hearing, or to the specific logistical arrangements proposed, and expressed its intent to make its submissions during the public hearing.[3]

---

[3] We also received a number of responses after the deadline of noon on 12 April 2012. Australia and New Zealand stated that they have no objection to the request for public observation of the oral hearing, or to the logistical arrangements proposed, and added that any oral statement that they may make will be made in the open session. Guatemala stated that, although it does not oppose the request for public observation of the oral hearing in these proceedings, this is without prejudice to Guatemala's position on this matter within the framework of the DSU review, and does not prejudge Guatemala's position in future cases. India recalled that it has consistently taken the view that the DSU does not permit open hearings. India stipulated that, should the Appellate Body agree to the request from the United States and Canada, it would make its oral statement, if any, in the session closed to public, and further requested the Appellate Body to reflect in its report India's systemic concerns on this issue. It was not compulsory for the third participants to submit comments on the

6. We recall that requests to allow public observation of the oral hearing have been made, and have been authorized, in eight previous appeals.[4] In its rulings, the Appellate Body has held that it has the power to authorize such requests by the participants, provided that this does not affect the confidentiality in the relationship between the third participants and the Appellate Body, or impair the integrity of the appellate process. We concur with the reasons previously expressed by the Appellate Body, and its interpretation of Article 17.10 of the DSU, in this regard, and consider that it applies equally in circumstances such as those prevailing in these appellate proceedings.

7. In this appeal, Canada and the United States have suggested that the Appellate Body allow observation by the public of the oral hearing by means of simultaneous closed-circuit television broadcasting. They have further suggested that provision be made for transmission to be turned off should the participants find it necessary to discuss issues that involve information that was designated as confidential by any participant in the documents filed with the Panel, as well as for the oral statements and responses to questions by those third participants who have indicated that they do not wish to have such statements and responses subject to public observation. We agree that such modalities would operate to protect confidential information in the context of a hearing that is open to public observation, and would not have an adverse impact on the integrity of the adjudicative function performed by the Appellate Body. We also consider that during public observation in previous appeals, the rights of those third participants that did not wish to have their oral statements made subject to public observation have been fully protected.

8. For these reasons, the Appellate Body Division in these appellate proceedings authorizes the public observation of the oral hearing on the terms set out below. Accordingly, pursuant to Rule 16(1) of the *Working Procedures*, we adopt the following additional procedures for the purpose of this appeal:

(a) The oral hearing will be open to public observation by means of simultaneous closed-circuit television broadcast, shown in a separate room to which duly registered delegates of WTO Members and members of the general public will have access.

(b) Oral statements and responses to questions by the third participants that have indicated their wish to maintain the

joint communication from the participants. Yet, for those that chose to do so, we recall the importance of the timely filing of documents in appeals.

4 See *supra*, footnote 2.

confidentiality of their submissions, as well as —at the request of any participant—any discussion of information that the participants designated as confidential in documents submitted to the Panel, will not be subject to public observation.

(c) Any request by a third participant wishing to maintain the confidentiality of its oral statements and responses to questions should be received by the Appellate Body Secretariat *no later than 17:00 p.m. Geneva time on Wednesday, 25 April 2012*.

(d) An appropriate number of seats will be reserved for delegates of WTO Members in the room where the closed-circuit television broadcast will be shown. WTO delegates wishing to observe the oral hearing are requested to register in advance with the Appellate Body Secretariat.

(e) Notice of the oral hearing will be provided to the general public on the WTO website. Members of the general public wishing to observe the oral hearing will be required to register in advance with the Appellate Body Secretariat, in accordance with the instructions set out in the WTO website notice.

Geneva, 16 April 2012

Cumulative List of Published Disputes

Argentina - Definitive Anti-Dumping Duties on Poultry from Brazil

Complaint by Brazil (WT/DS241)

Report of the Panel DSR 2003:V, 1727

Argentina - Definitive Anti-Dumping Measures on Imports of Ceramic Floor Tiles from Italy

Complaint by the European Communities (WT/DS189)

Report of the Panel DSR 2001:XII, 6241

Argentina - Definitive Safeguard Measure on Imports of Preserved Peaches

Complaint by Chile (WT/DS238)

Report of the Panel DSR 2003:III, 1037

Argentina - Measures Affecting Imports of Footwear, Textiles, Apparel and Other Items

Complaint by the United States (WT/DS56)

Report of the Appellate Body DSR 1998:III, 1003

Report of the Panel DSR 1998:III, 1033

Argentina - Measures Affecting the Export of Bovine Hides and the Import of Finished Leather

Complaint by the European Communities (WT/DS155)

Report of the Panel DSR 2001:V, 1779

Award of the Arbitrator under Article 21.3(c) of the DSU DSR 2001:XII, 6013

Argentina - Safeguard Measures on Imports of Footwear

Complaint by the European Communities (WT/DS121)

Report of the Appellate Body DSR 2000:I, 515

Report of the Panel DSR 2000:II, 575

Australia - Measures Affecting the Importation of Apples from New Zealand

Complaint by New Zealand (WT/DS367)

Report of the Appellate Body DSR 2010:V, 2175

Report of the Panel DSR 2010:VI, 2371

Australia - Measures Affecting Importation of Salmon

Complaint by Canada (WT/DS18)

Report of the Appellate Body DSR 1998:VIII, 3327

Report of the Panel DSR 1998:VIII, 3407

Award of the Arbitrator under Article 21.3(c) of the DSU DSR 1999:I, 267

Report of the Panel - Recourse to Article 21.5 of the DSU DSR 2000:IV, 2031

Australia - Subsidies Provided to Producers and Exporters of Automotive Leather

Complaint by the United States (WT/DS126)

Report of the Panel DSR 1999:III, 951

Report of the Panel - Recourse to Article 21.5 of the DSU DSR 2000:III, 1189

Brazil - Export Financing Programme for Aircraft

Complaint by Canada (WT/DS46)

Report of the Appellate Body DSR 1999:III, 1161

Report of the Panel DSR 1999:III, 1221

Report of the Appellate Body - Recourse to Article 21.5 of the DSU DSR 2000:VIII, 4067

Report of the Panel - Recourse to Article 21.5 of the DSU DSR 2000:IX, 4093

Report of the Panel - Second Recourse to Article 21.5 of the DSU DSR 2001:XI, 5481

Decision by the Arbitrators - Recourse to Arbitration by Brazil under Article 22.6 of the DSU and Article 4.11 of the *SCM Agreement* DSR 2002:I, 19

Brazil - Measures Affecting Desiccated Coconut

Complaint by the Philippines (WT/DS22)

Report of the Appellate Body DSR 1997:I, 167

Report of the Panel DSR 1997:I, 189

Brazil - Measures Affecting Import of Retreaded Tyres

Complaint by the European Communities (WT/DS332)

Report of the Appellate Body DSR 2007:IV, 1527

Report of the Panel DSR 2007:V, 1649

Arbitration under Article 21.3(c) of the DSU DSR 2008:XX, 8581

Canada - Certain Measures Affecting the Automotive Industry

Complaint by the European Communities (WT/DS142);
Complaint by Japan (WT/DS139)

Report of the Appellate Body DSR 2000:VI, 2985

Report of the Panel DSR 2000:VII, 3043

Award of the Arbitrator under Article 21.3(c) of the DSU — DSR 2000:X, 5079

Canada - Certain Measures Concerning Periodicals

Complaint by the United States (WT/DS31)

Report of the Appellate Body — DSR 1997:I, 449

Report of the Panel — DSR 1997:I, 481

Canada– Continued Suspension of Obligations in the EC – Hormones Dispute

Complaint by the European Communities (WT/DS321)

Report of the Appellate Body — DSR 2008:XIV, 5373

Report of the Panel — DSR 2008:XV, 5757

Canada - Export Credits and Loan Guarantees for Regional Aircraft

Complaint by Brazil (WT/DS222)

Report of the Panel — DSR 2002:III, 849

Decision by the Arbitrator under Article 22.6 of the DSU and Article 4.11 of the *SCM Agreement* — DSR 2003:III, 1187

Canada - Measures Affecting the Importation of Milk and the Exportation of Dairy Products

Complaint by New Zealand (WT/DS113); Complaint by the United States (WT/DS103)

Report of the Appellate Body — DSR 1999:V, 2057

Report of the Panel — DSR 1999:VI, 2097

Report of the Appellate Body - Recourse to Article 21.5 of the DSU — DSR 2001:XIII, 6829

Report of the Panel - Recourse to Article 21.5 of the DSU — DSR 2001:XIII, 6865

Report of the Appellate Body - Second Recourse to Article 21.5 of the DSU — DSR 2003:I, 213

Report of the Panel - Second Recourse to Article 21.5 of the DSU — DSR 2003:I, 255

Canada - Measures Affecting the Export of Civilian Aircraft

Complaint by Brazil (WT/DS70)

Report of the Appellate Body — DSR 1999:III, 1377

Report of the Panel — DSR 1999:IV, 1443

Report of the Appellate Body - Recourse to Article 21.5 of the DSU — DSR 2000:IX, 4299

Report of the Panel - Recourse to Article 21.5 of the DSU — DSR 2000:IX, 4315

Canada – Measures Relating to Exports of Wheat and Treatment of Imported Grain

Complaint by United States (WT/DS276)

Report of the Appellate Body DSR 2004:VI, 2807

Report of the Panel DSR 2004:VI, 2887

Canada - Patent Protection of Pharmaceutical Products

Complaint by the European Communities (WT/DS114)

Report of the Panel DSR 2000:V, 2289

Award of the Arbitrator under Article 21.3(c) of the DSU DSR 2002:I, 3

Canada - Term of Patent Protection

Complaint by the United States (WT/DS170)

Report of the Appellate Body DSR 2000:X, 5093

Report of the Panel DSR 2000:XI, 5121

Award of the Arbitrator under Article 21.3(c) of the DSU DSR 2000:IX, 4537

Chile - Price Band System and Safeguard Measures Relating to Certain Agricultural Products

Complaint by Argentina (WT/DS207)

Report of the Appellate Body DSR 2002:VIII, 3045

Report of the Panel DSR 2002:VIII, 30127

Award of the Arbitrator under Article 21.3(c) of the DSU DSR 2003:III, 1237

Report of the Appellate Body - Corrigendum DSR 2006:XII, 5473

Recourse to Article 21.5 of the DSU by Argentina

Report of the Appellate Body DSR 2007:II, 513

Report of the Panel DSR 2007:II, III, 613

Chile - Taxes on Alcoholic Beverages

Complaint by the European Communities (WT/DS87), (WT/DS110)

Report of the Appellate Body DSR 2000:I, 281

Report of the Panel DSR 2000:I, 303

Award of the Arbitrator under Article 21.3(c) of the DSU DSR 2000:V, 2583

China - Measures Affecting Imports of Automobile Parts

Complaints by Canada, European Communities, United States (WT/DS339, WT/DS340, WT/DS342)

Reports of the Appellate Body DSR 2009:I, 3

Reports of the Panel DSR 2009:I, 119

China - Measures Affecting the Protection and Enforcement of Intellectual Property Rights

Complaint by United States (WT/DS362)

Report of the Panel DSR 2009:V, 2097

China - Measures Affecting Trading Rights and Distribution Services for Certain Publications and Audiovisual Entertainment Products

Complaint by United States (WT/DS363)

Report of the Appellate Body DSR 2010:I, 3

Report of the Panel DSR 2010:II, 261

Colombia - Indicative Prices and Restrictions on Ports of Entry

Complaint by Panama (WT/DS366)

Report of the Panel DSR 2009:VI, 2535

Arbitration under Article 21.3(c) of the DSU (Award of the Arbitrator) DSR 2009:IX, 3819

Dominican Republic - Measures Affecting the Importation and Internal Sale of Cigarettes

Complaint by Honduras (WT/DS302)

Report of the Appellate Body DSR 2005:XV, 7367

Report of the Panel DSR 2005:XV, 7425

Arbitration under Article 21.3(c) of the DSU (WT/DS302/17)

Report of the Arbitrator DSR 2005:XXIII, 11663

Egypt - Definitive Anti-Dumping Measures on Steel Rebar from Turkey

Complaint by Turkey (WT/DS211)

Report of the Panel DSR 2002:VII, 2667

European Communities and Certain member States - Measures Affecting Trade in Large Civil Aircraft (WT/DS316)

Report of the Appellate Body DSR 2011:I, 7

Report of the Panel - Part I DSR 2011:II, 685

Report of the Panel - Part II DSR 2011:III, 1477

European Communities and its member States - Tariff Treatment of Certain Information Technology Products

Complaint by United States, Japan and Chinese Taipei (WT/DS375, WT/DS376, WT/DS377)

Report of the Panel DSR 2010:III, 933

Report of the Panel (Annexes) DSR 2010:IV, 1567

European Communities - Anti-Dumping Duties on Imports of Cotton-Type Bed Linen from India

Complaint by India (WT/DS141)

Report of the Appellate Body DSR 2001:V, 2049

Report of the Appellate Body (Recourse to Article 21.5 of the DSU by India) DSR 2003:III, 965

Report of the Panel DSR 2001:VI, 2077

Report of the Panel - Recourse to Article 21.5 of the DSU DSR 2003:IV, 1269

European Communities - Anti-Dumping Duties on Malleable Cast Iron Tube or Pipe Fittings from Brazil

Complaint by Brazil (WT/DS219)

Report of the Appellate Body DSR 2003:VI, 2613

Report of the Panel DSR 2003:VII, 2701

European Communities - Anti-Dumping Measure on Farmed Salmon from Norway

Complaint by Norway (WT/DS337)

Report of the Panel DSR 2008:I, 3

European Communities – Conditions for the Granting of Tariff Preferences to Developing Countries

Complaint by India (WT/DS246)

Report of the Appellate Body DSR 2004:III, 951

Report of the Panel DSR 2004:III, 1037

Award of the Arbitrator under Article 21.3 (c) of the DSU DSR 2004:IX, 4313

European Communities – Countervailing Measures on Dynamic Random Access Memory Chips from Korea

Complaint by Korea (WT/DS299)

Report of the Panel DSR 2005:XVIII, 8671

European Communities - Customs Classification of Certain Computer Equipment

Complaint by the United States (WT/DS62, WT/DS67, WT/DS68)

Complaint by the United States - Ireland
Complaint by the United States - United Kingdom
Report of the Appellate Body DSR 1998:V, 1851
Report of the Panel DSR 1998:V, 1891

European Communities - Customs Classification of Frozen Boneless Chicken Cuts
Complaint by Brazil and Thailand (WT/DS269, WT/DS286)
Report of the Appellate Body DSR 2005:XIX, 9157
Complaint by Brazil (WT/DS269)
Report of the Panel DSR 2005:XIX, 9295
Complaint by Thailand (WT/DS286)
Report of the Panel DSR 2005:XX, 9721
Arbitration under Article 21.3(c) of the Understanding on Rules and Procedures Governing the Settlement of Disputes DSR 2006:XII, 5441

European Communities - Definitive Anti-Dumping Measures on Certain Iron or Steel Fasteners from China
Complaint by China (WT/DS397)
Report of the Appellate Body DSR 2011:VII, 3995
Report of the Panel DSR 2011:VIII, 4289

European Communities - Export Subsidies on Sugar
Complaint by Australia, Brazil, Thailand (WT/DS265, WT/DS266, WT/DS283)
Report of the Appellate Body DSR 2005:XIII, 6365
Complaint by Australia (WT/DS265)
Report of the Panel DSR 2005:XIII, 6499
Complaint by Brazil (WT/DS266) DSR 2005:XIV, 6793
Report of the Panel
Complaint by Thailand (WT/DS283)
Report of the Panel DSR 2005:XIV, 7071
Arbitration under Article 21.3(c) of the Understanding on Rules and Procedures Governing the Settlement of Disputes (WT/DS265/33, WT/DS266/33, WT/DS283/14)
Award of the Arbitrator DSR 2005:XXIII, 11579

European Communities - Measures Affecting Asbestos and Asbestos-Containing Products

Complaint by Canada (WT/DS135)

Report of the Appellate Body DSR 2001:VII, 3243

Report of the Panel DSR 2001:VIII, 3305

European Communities - Measures Affecting the Approval and Marketing of Biotech Products

Complaint by United States, Canada, Argentina (WT/DS291, WT/DS292, WT/DS293)

Report of the Panel DSR 2006:III, 847

European Communities - Measures Affecting the Importation of Certain Poultry Products

Complaint by Brazil (WT/DS69)

Report of the Appellate Body DSR 1998:V, 2031

Report of the Panel DSR 1998:V, 2089

European Communities – Measures Affecting Trade in Commercial Vessels

Complaint by Korea (WT/DS301)

Report of the Panel DSR 2005:XV, 7733

European Communities - Measures Concerning Meat and Meat Products (Hormones)

Complaint by Canada (WT/DS48);
Complaint by the United States (WT/DS26)

Report of the Appellate Body DSR 1998:I, 135

Report of the Panel (Canada) DSR 1998:II, 235

Report of the Panel (United States) DSR 1998:III, 699

Award of the Arbitrator under Article 21.3(c) of the DSU DSR 1998:V, 1833

Decision by the Arbitrators under Article 22.6 of the DSU (Canada) DSR 1999:III, 1135

Decision by the Arbitrators under Article 22.6 of the DSU (United States) DSR 1999:III, 1105

European Communities – Protection of Trademarks and Geographical Indications for Agricultural Products and Foodstuffs

Complaint by the United States (WT/DS174)

Report of the Panel DSR 2005:VIII-IX, 3499,4083

Complaint by Australia (WT/DS290)

Report of the Panel DSR 2005:X-XI, 4603,5121

European Communities - Regime for the Importation, Sale and Distribution of Bananas

Complaint by Ecuador; Guatemala; Honduras; Mexico; and the United States (WT/DS27)

Report of the Appellate Body DSR 1997:II, 589

Report of the Panel (Ecuador) DSR 1997:III, 3

Report of the Panel (Guatemala, Honduras) DSR 1997:II, 695

Report of the Panel (Mexico) DSR 1997:II, 803

Report of the Panel (United States) DSR 1997:II, 943

Award of the Arbitrator under Article 21.3(c) of the DSU DSR 1998:I, 3

Decision by the Arbitrators under Article 22.6 of the DSU (US) DSR 1999:II, 725

Report of the Panel - Recourse to Article 21.5 of the DSU (European Communities) DSR 1999:II, 783

Report of the Panel - Recourse to Article 21.5 of the DSU (Ecuador) DSR 1999:II, 803

Decision by the Arbitrators under Article 22.6 of the DSU (Ecuador) DSR 2000:V, 2237

Second Recourse to Article 21.5 of the DSU by Ecuador

Report of the Appellate Body DSR 2008:XVIII, 7165

Report of the Panel DSR 2008:XVIII, 7329

Recourse to Article 21.5 of the DSU by the United States

Report of the Appellate Body DSR 2008:XVIII, 7165

Report of the Panel DSR 2008:XIX, 7761

European Communities - Selected Customs Matters

Complaint by United States (WT/DS315)

Report of the Appellate Body DSR 2006:IX, 3791

Report of the Panel DSR 2006:IX, 3915

European Communities - The ACP-EC Partnership Agreement - Recourse to Arbitration Pursuant to the Decision of 14 November 2001 (WT/L/616)

Award of the Arbitrator DSR 2005:XXIII, 11667

European Communities - The ACP-EC Partnership Agreement - Second Recourse to Arbitration Pursuant to the Decision of 14 November 2001 (WT/L/625)

Award of the Arbitrator DSR 2005:XXIII, 11701

European Communities - Trade Description of Sardines

Complaint by Peru (WT/DS231/R)

Report of the Appellate Body DSR 2002:VIII, 3359

Report of the Panel DSR 2002:VIII, 3451

European Communities - Trade Description of Scallops

Complaint by Canada (WT/DS7);
Complaint by Chile (WT/DS14);
Complaint by Peru (WT/DS12)

Report of the Panel (Canada) DSR 1996:I, 89

Report of the Panel (Chile, Peru) DSR 1996:I, 93

Guatemala - Anti-Dumping Investigation Regarding Portland Cement From Mexico

Complaint by Mexico (WT/DS60)

Report of the Appellate Body DSR 1998:IX, 3767

Report of the Panel DSR 1998:IX, 3797

Guatemala - Definitive Anti-Dumping Measures on Grey Portland Cement from Mexico

Complaint by Mexico (WT/DS156)

Report of the Panel DSR 2000:XI, 5295

India – Additional and Extra-Additional Duties on Imports from the United States

Complaint by United States (WT/DS360)

Report of the Appellate Body DSR 2008:XX, 8223

Report of the Panel DSR 2008:XX, 8317

India - Measures Affecting the Automotive Sector

Complaint by European Communities (WT/DS146)
Complaint by the United States (WT/DS175)

Report of the Appellate Body DSR 2002:V, 1821

Report of the Panel DSR 2002:V, 1827

India - Patent Protection for Pharmaceutical and Agricultural Chemical Products

Complaint by European Communities (WT/DS79);
Complaint by the United States (WT/DS50)

Report of the Appellate Body (United States) DSR 1998:I, 9

Report of the Panel (European Communities) DSR 1998:VI, 2661

Report of the Panel (United States) DSR 1998:I, 41

India - Quantitative Restrictions on Imports of Agricultural, Textile and Industrial Products

Complaint by the United States (WT/DS90)

Report of the Appellate Body DSR 1999:IV, 1763

Report of the Panel DSR 1999:V, 1799

Indonesia - Certain Measures Affecting the Automobile Industry

Complaint by European Communities (WT/DS54);
Complaint by Japan (WT/DS55, WT/DS64);
Complaint by the United States (WT/DS59)

Report of the Panel DSR 1998:VI, 2201

Award of the Arbitrator under Article 21.3(c) of the DSU DSR 1998:IX, 4029

Japan - Countervailing Duties on Dynamic Random Access Memories from Korea

Complaint by Korea (WT/DS336)

Report of the Appellate Body DSR 2007:VII, 2707

Report of the Panel DSR 2007:VII, 2809

Arbitration under Article 21.3(c) of the DSU DSR 2008:XX, 8553

Japan - Measures Affecting Agricultural Products

Complaint by the United States (WT/DS76)

Report of the Appellate Body DSR 1999:I, 277

Report of the Panel DSR 1999:I, 315

Japan - Measures Affecting Consumer Photographic Film and Paper

Complaint by the United States (WT/DS44)

Report of the Panel DSR 1998:IV, 1179

Japan - Measures Affecting the Importation of Apples

Complaint by the United States (WT/DS245)

Report of the Appellate Body DSR 2003:IX, 4391

Report of the Panel DSR 2003:IX, 4481

Report of the Panel - Recourse to Article 21.5 of the DSU DSR 2005:XVI, 7911

Japan - Taxes on Alcoholic Beverages

Complaint by Canada (WT/DS10);
Complaint by the European Communities (WT/DS8);
Complaint by the United States (WT/DS11)

Report of the Appellate Body DSR 1996:I, 97

Report of the Panel DSR 1996:I, 125
Award of the Arbitrator under Article 21.3(c) of the DSU DSR 1997:I, 3

Korea - Anti-Dumping Duties on Imports of Certain Paper from Indonesia

Complaint by Indonesia (WT/DS312)

Report of the Panel DSR 2005:XXII, 10637

Recourse to Article 21.5 of the DSU by Indonesia

Report of the Panel DSR 2007:VIII, 3375

Korea - Definitive Safeguard Measure on Imports of Certain Dairy Products

Complaint by the European Communities (WT/DS98)

Report of the Appellate Body DSR 2000:I, 3

Report of the Panel DSR 2000:I, 49

Korea - Measures Affecting Imports of Fresh, Chilled and Frozen Beef

Complaint by Australia (WT/DS169);
Complaint by the United States (WT/DS161)

Report of the Appellate Body DSR 2001:I, 5

Report of the Panel DSR 2001:I, 59

Korea - Measures Affecting Government Procurement

Complaint by the United States (WT/DS163)

Report of the Panel DSR 2000:VIII, 3541

Korea - Measures Affecting Trade in Commercial Vessels

Complaint by the European Communities (WT/DS273)

Report of the Panel DSR 2005:VII, 2747

Korea - Taxes on Alcoholic Beverages

Complaint by the European Communities (WT/DS75)
Complaint by the United States (WT/DS84)

Report of the Appellate Body DSR 1999:I, 3

Report of the Panel DSR 1999:I, 44

Award of the Arbitrator under Article 21.3(c) of the DSU DSR 1999:II, 937

Mexico - Anti-Dumping Duties on Steel Pipes and Tubes from Guatemala

Complaint by Guatemala (WT/DS331)

Final Report of the Panel DSR 2007:IV, 1207

Mexico - Anti-Dumping Investigation of High Fructose Corn Syrup (HFCS) from the United States

Complaint by the United States (WT/DS132)

Report of the Panel DSR 2000:III, 1345

Report of the Appellate Body - Recourse to Article 21.5 of the DSU DSR 2001:XIII, 6675

Report of the Panel - Recourse to Article 21.5 of the DSU DSR 2001:XIII, 6717

Mexico - Definitive Anti-Dumping Measures on Beef and Rice - Complaint with Respect to Rice

Complaint by the United States (WT/DS295)

Report of the Appellate Body DSR 2005:XXII, 10853

Report of the Panel DSR 2005:XXIII, 11005

Mexico - Definitive Countervailing Measures on Olive Oil from the European Communities

Complaint by the European Communities (WT/DS341)

Report of the Panel DSR 2008:IX, 3179

Mexico - Measures Affecting Telecommunications Services

Complaint by the United States (WT/DS204)

Report of the Panel DSR 2004:IV, 1579

Mexico - Tax Measures on Soft Drinks and Other Beverages

Complaint by the United States (WT/DS308)

Report of the Appellate Body DSR 2006:I, 3

Report of the Panel DSR 2006 I, 43

Thailand - Anti-Dumping Duties on Angles, Shapes and Sections of Iron or Non-Alloy Steel and H-Beams from Poland

Complaint by Poland (WT/DS122)

Report of the Appellate Body DSR 2001:VII, 2701

Report of the Panel DSR 2001:VII, 2741

Thailand - Customs and Fiscal Measures on Cigarettes from the Philippines

Complaint by the Philippines (WT/DS371)

Report of the Appellate Body DSR 2011:IV, 2203

Report of the Panel DSR 2011:IV, 2256

Turkey - Measures Affecting the Importation of Rice

Complaint by United States (WT/DS334)

Report of the Panel DSR 2007:VI, 2153

Turkey - Restrictions on Imports of Textile and Clothing Products

Complaint by India (WT/DS34)

Report of the Appellate Body DSR 1999:VI, 2345

Report of the Panel DSR 1999:VI, 2363

United States - Anti-Dumping Act of 1916

Complaint by the European Communities (WT/DS136)

Decision by the Arbitrators under Article 22.6 of the DSU DSR 2004:IX, 4269

Complaint by Japan (WT/DS162)

Report of the Appellate Body DSR 2000:X, 4793

Report of the Panel (European Communities) DSR 2000:X, 4593

Report of the Panel (Japan) DSR 2000:X, 4831

Award of the Arbitrator under Article 21.3(c) of the DSU DSR 2001:V, 2017

United States-Anti-Dumping Administrative Reviews and Other Measures Related to Imports of Certain Orange Juice from Brazil

Complaint by Brazil (WT/DS382)

Report of the Panel DSR 2011:VII, 3753

United States-Anti-Dumping and Countervailing Measures on Steel Plate from India

Complaint by India (WT/DS206)

Report of the Panel DSR 2002:VI, 2073

United States - Anti-Dumping Duty on Dynamic Random Access Memory Semiconductors (DRAMS) of One Megabit or Above from Korea

Complaint by Korea (WT/DS99)

Report of the Panel DSR 1999:II, 521

United States - Anti-Dumping Measures on Certain Hot-Rolled Steel Products from Japan

Complaint by Japan (WT/DS184)

Report of the Appellate Body DSR 2001:X, 4697

Report of the Panel DSR 2001:X, 4769

Award of the Arbitrator under Article 21.3(c) of the DSU DSR 2002:IV, 1389

United States - Anti-Dumping Measures on Certain Shrimp from Viet Nam

Complaint by Viet Nam (WT/DS404)

Report of the Panel DSR 2011:X, 5261

United States - Anti-Dumping Measures on Oil Country Tubular Goods (OCTG) from Mexico

Complaint by Mexico and United States (WT/DS282)

Report of the Appellate Body DSR 2005:XX, 10129

Report of the Panel DSR 2005:XXI, 10225

United States - Anti-Dumping Measures on Polyethylene Retail Carrier Bags from Thailand

Complaint by Thailand (WT/DS383)

Report of the Panel DSR 2010:IV, 1841

United States – Anti-Dumping Measure on Shrimp from Ecuador

Complaint by Ecuador (WT/DS335)

Report of the Panel DSR 2007:II, 425

United States - Anti-Dumping Measures on Stainless Steel Plate in Coils and Stainless Steel Sheet and Strip from Korea

Complaint by Korea (WT/DS179)

Report of the Panel DSR 2001:IV, 1295

United States – Certain Measures Affecting Imports of Poultry from China

Complaint by China (WT/DS392)

Report of the Panel DSR 2010:V, 1909

United States - Continued Dumping and Subsidy Offset Act of 2000

Complaint by Australia, Brazil, Canada, Chile, the European Communities, India, Indonesia, Japan, Korea, Mexico and Thailand (WT/DS217)

Report of the Appellate Body DSR 2003:I, 375

Report of the Panel DSR 2003:II, 489

Award of the Arbitrator under Article 21.3(c) of the DSU DSR 2003:III, 1163

Complaint by Brazil

Decision by the Arbitrator under Article 22.6 of the DSU DSR 2004:IX, 4341

Complaint by Canada (WT/DS234)

Decision by the Arbitrator under Article 22.6 of the DSU DSR 2004:IX, 4425

Complaint by Chile (WT/DS217)

Decision by the Arbitrator under Article 22.6 of the DSU DSR 2004:IX, 4511

Complaint by European Communities (WT/DS217)

Decision by the Arbitrator under Article 22.6 of the DSU DSR 2004:IX, 4591

Original Complaint by India - Recourse to Arbitration by the United States under Article 22.6 of the DSU (WT/DS217)

Decision by the Arbitrator DSR 2004:X, 4691

Original Complaint by Japan - Recourse to Arbitration by the United States under Article 22.6 of the DSU (WT/DS217)

Decision by the Arbitrator DSR 2004:X, 4771

Original Complaint by Korea - Recourse to Arbitration by the United States under Article 22.6 of the DSU ((WT/DS217)

Decision by the Arbitrator DSR 2004:X, 4851

Original Complaint by Mexico - Recourse to Arbitration by the United States under Article 22.6 of the DSU (WT/DS234)

Decision by the Arbitrator DSR 2004:X, 4931

United States - Continued Existence and Application of Zeroing Methodology

Complaint by European Communities (WT/DS350)

Report of the Appellate Body DSR 2009:III, 1291

Report of the Panel DSR 2009:III, 1481

United States - Continued Suspension of Obligations in the EC Hormones Dispute

Complaint by European Communities, United States and Canada (WT/DS320)

Report of the Appellate Body DSR 2008:X, 3507

Report of the Panel DSR 2008:XI, 3891

United States - Countervailing Duties on Certain Corrosion-Resistant Carbon Steel Flat Products from Germany

Complaint by European Communities (WT/DS213)

Report of the Appellate Body DSR 2002:IX, 3781

Report of the Panel DSR 2002:IX, 3835

United States - Countervailing Duty Investigation on Dynamic Random Access Memory Semiconductors (DRAMS) from Korea

Complaint by Korea (WT/DS296)

Report of the Appellate Body DSR 2005:XVI, 8131

Report of the Panel DSR 2005:XVII, 8243

United States - Countervailing Measures Concerning Certain Products from the European Communities

Complaint by European Communities (WT/DS212)

Report of the Appellate Body DSR 2003:I, 5

Report of the Panel DSR 2003:I, 73

Recourse to Article 21.5 of the DSU by the European Communities

Report of the Panel DSR 2005:XVIII, 8950

United States - Customs Bond Directive for Merchandise Subject to Anti-Dumping/Countervailing Duties

Complaint by Thailand, India and United States (WT/DS343, WT/DS345)

Report of the Appellate Body DSR 2008:VIII, 2781

Report of the Panel DSR 2008:VIII, 2933

United States - Definitive Anti-Dumping and Countervailing Duties on Certain Products from China

Complaint by China (WT/DS379)

Report of the Appellate Body DSR 2011:V, 2869

Report of the Panel DSR 2011:VI, 3143

United States - Definitive Safeguard Measures on Imports of Certain Steel Products

Complaint by Brazil (WT/DS259);
Complaint by China (WT/DS252);
Complaint by European Communities (WT/DS248);
Complaint by Japan (WT/DS249);
Complaint by Korea (WT/DS251);
Complaint by New Zealand (WT/DS258);
Complaint by Norway (WT/DS254);
Complaint by Switzerland (WT/DS253)

Report of the Appellate Body DSR 2003:VII, 3117

Report of the Panel DSR 2003:VIII, 3273

United States - Definitive Safeguard Measures on Imports of Circular Welded Carbon Quality Line Pipe from Korea

Complaint by Korea (WT/DS202)

Report of the Appellate Body DSR 2002:IV, 1403

Report of the Panel DSR 2002:IV, 1473

Award of the Arbitrator under Article 21.3(c) of the DSU DSR 2002:V, 2061

United States - Definitive Safeguard Measures on Imports of Wheat Gluten from the European Communities

Complaint by the European Communities (WT/DS166)

Report of the Appellate Body DSR 2001:II, 717

Report of the Panel DSR 2001:III, 779

United States - Final Anti-Dumping Measures on Stainless Steel from Mexico

Complaint by Mexico (WT/DS344)

Report of the Appellate Body DSR 2008:II, 513

Report of the Panel DSR 2008:II, 599

Arbitrator under Article 21.3(c) of the DSU DSR 2008:XX, 8619

United States - Final Countervailing Duty Determination with Respect to Certain Softwood Lumber from Canada

Complaint by Canada (WT/DS257)

Report of the Appellate Body DSR 2004:II, 587

Report of the Panel DSR 2004:II, 659

Recourse by Canada to Article 21.5 of the DSU

Report of the Appellate Body DSR 2005:XXIII, 11355

Report of the Panel DSR 2005:XXIII, 11399

United States - Final Dumping Determination on Softwood Lumber from Canada

Complaint by Canada (WT/DS264)

Report of the Appellate Body DSR 2004:V, 1917

Report of the Panel DSR 2004:V, 1981

Arbitration under Article 21.3(c) of the DSU (WT/DS264)

Report of the Arbitrator DSR 2004:X, 5011

Report of the Appellate Body - Recourse to Article 21.5 of the DSU by Canada DSR 2006:XII, 5087

Report of the Panel - Recourse to Article 21.5 of the DSU by Canada DSR 2006:XII, 5147

United States - Import Measures on Certain Products from the European Communities

Complaint by the European Communities (WT/DS165)

Report of the Appellate Body DSR 2001:I, 373

Report of the Panel DSR 2001:II, 413

United States - Imposition of Countervailing Duties on Certain Hot-Rolled Lead and Bismuth Carbon Steel Products Originating in the United Kingdom

Complaint by the European Communities (WT/DS138)

Report of the Appellate Body DSR 2000:V, 2595

Report of the Panel DSR 2000:VI, 2623

United States - Import Prohibition of Certain Shrimp and Shrimp Products

Complaint by India (WT/DS58);
Complaint by Malaysia (WT/DS58);
Complaint by Pakistan (WT/DS58);
Complaint by Thailand (WT/DS58)

Report of the Appellate Body DSR 1998:VII, 2755

Report of the Panel DSR 1998:VII, 2821

Report of the Appellate Body - Recourse to Article 21.5 of the DSU (Malaysia) DSR 2001:XIII, 6481

Report of the Panel - Recourse to Article 21.5 of the DSU (Malaysia) DSR 2001:XIII, 6529

United States – Investigation of the International Trade Commission in Softwood Lumber from Canada

Complaint by Canada (WT/DS277)

Report of the Panel DSR 2004:VI, 2543

Report of the Appellate Body - Recourse to Article 21.5 of the DSU by Canada DSR 2006:XI, 4865

Report of the Panel - Recourse to Article 21.5 of the DSU by Canada DSR 2006:XI, 4935

United States - Laws, Regulations and Methodology for Calculating Dumping Margins ("Zeroing")

Complaint by European Communities and the United States (WT/DS294)

Report of the Appellate Body DSR 2006:II, 417

Report of the Panel DSR 2006:II, 521

Recourse to Article 21.5 of the DSU by the European Communities
Report of the Appellate Body DSR 2009:VII, 2911
Report of the Panel DSR 2009:VII, 3117

United States - Measure Affecting Imports of Woven Wool Shirts and Blouses from India
Complaint by India (WT/DS33)
Report of the Appellate Body DSR 1997:I, 323
Report of the Panel DSR 1997:I, 343

United States - Measures Affecting the Cross-Border Supply of Gambling and Betting Services
Complaint by Antigua (WT/DS285)
Report of the Appellate Body DSR 2005:XII, 5663
Report of the Panel DSR 2005:XII, 5797
Arbitration under Article 21.3(c) of the DSU (WT/DS285/13) Award of the Arbitrator DSR 2005:XXIII, 11637
Report of the Appellate Body - Corrigendum DSR 2006:XII, 5475
Recourse to Article 21.5 of the DSU by Antigua and Barbuda
Report of the Panel DSR 2007:VIII, 3109
Recourse by the United States to Arbitration under Article 22.6 of the DSU
Decision by the Arbitrator DSR 2007:X, 4163

United States - Measures Affecting Imports of Certain Passenger Vehicle and Light Truck Tyres from China
Complaint by China (WT/DS399)
Report of the Appellate Body DSR 2011:IX, 4811
Report of the Panel DSR 2011:IX, 4945

United States - Measures Affecting Trade in Large Civil Aircraft (Second Complaint)
Complaint by European Union (WT/DS353)
Report of the Appellate Body DSR 2012:I, 7
Report of the Panel (Part I) DSR 2012:II, 649
Report of the Panel (Part II) DSR 2012:III, 1251

United States - Measures Concerning the Importation, Marketing and Sale of Tuna and Tuna Products

Complaint by United States and Mexico (WT/DS381)

Report of the Appellate Body DSR 2012:IV, 1837

Report of the Panel DSR 2012:IV, 2013

United States - Measures Relating to Shrimp from Thailand

Complaint by Thailand, India, United States (WT/DS343, WT/DS345)

Report of the Appellate Body DSR 2008:VII, 2391

Report of the Panel DSR 2008:VII, 2545

United States - Measures Relating to Zeroing and Sunset Reviews

Complaint by Japan (WT/DS322)

Report of the Appellate Body DSR 2007:I, 3

Report of the Panel DSR 2007:I, 97

Arbitration under Article 21.3(c) of the DSU

Report of the Arbitrator DSR 2007:X, 4160

Recourse to Article 21.5 of the DSU by Japan

Report of the Appellate Body DSR 2009:VIII, 3441

Report of the Panel DSR 2009:VIII, 3553

United States - Measures Treating Export Restraints as Subsidies

Complaint by Canada (WT/DS194)

Report of the Panel DSR 2001:XI, 5767

United States - Preliminary Determinations with Respect to Certain Softwood Lumber from Canada

Complaint by Canada (WT/DS236)

Report of the Panel DSR 2002:IX, 3597

United States - Restrictions on Imports of Cotton and Man-made Fibre Underwear

Complaint by Costa Rica (WT/DS24)

Report of the Appellate Body DSR 1997:I, 11

Report of the Panel DSR 1997:I, 31

United States - Rules of Origin for Textiles and Apparel Products

Complaint by India (WT/DS243)

Report of the Panel DSR 2003:VI, 2309

United States - Safeguard Measures on Imports of Fresh, Chilled or Frozen Lamb Meat from New Zealand and Australia

Complaint by Australia (WT/DS178);
Complaint by new Zealand (WT/DS177)

Report of the Appellate Body DSR 2001:IX, 4051

Report of the Panel DSR 2001:IX, 4107

United States - Section 110(5) of the US Copyright Act

Complaint by the European Communities (WT/DS160)

Report of the Panel DSR 2000:VIII, 3769

Award of the Arbitrator under Article 21.3(c) of the DSU DSR 2001:II, 657

Award of the Arbitrator under Article 25 of the DSU DSR 2001:II, 667

United States - Sections 301-310 of the Trade Act of 1974

Complaint by the European Communities (WT/DS152)

Report of the Panel DSR 2000:II, 815

United States - Section 211 Omnibus Appropriations Act of 1998

Complaint by the European Communities (WT/DS176)

Report of the Appellate Body DSR 2002:II, 589

Report of the Panel DSR 2002:II, 683

United States- Section 129(c)(1) of the Uruguay Round Agreements Act

Complaint by Canada (WT/DS221)

Report of the Panel DSR 2002:VII, 2581

United States - Standards for Reformulated and Conventional Gasoline

Complaint by Brazil (WT/DS4);
Complaint by Venezuela (WT/DS2)

Report of the Appellate Body DSR 1996:I, 3

Report of the Panel DSR 1996:I, 29

United States – Subsidies on Upland Cotton

Complaint by Brazil (WT/DS267)

Report of the Appellate Body DSR 2005:I, 3

Report of the Panell DSR 2005:II- III- IV- V- VI, 297

Recourse by Brazil to Article 21.5 of the Understanding on Rules and Procedures Governing the Settlement of Disputes

Report of the Appellate Body DSR 2008:III, 809

Report of the Panel DSR 2008:III- IV- V- VI, 997

Recourse to Arbitration by the United States under Article 22.6 of the DSU and Article 4.11 of the *SCM Agreement* (Decision by the Arbitrator) DSR 2009:IX, 3871

Recourse to Arbitration by the United States under Article 22.6 of the DSU and Article 7.10 of the *SCM Agreement* (Decision by the Arbitrator) DSR 2009:IX, 4083

United States - Sunset Review of Anti-Dumping Duties on Corrosion-Resistant Carbon Steel Flat Products from Japan

Complaint by Japan (WT/DS244)

Report of the Appellate Body DSR 2004:I, 3

Report of the Panel DSR 2004:I, 87

United States – Sunset Reviews of Anti-Dumping Measures on Oil Country Tubular Goods from Argentina

Complaint by Argentina (WT/DS268)

Report of the Appellate Body DSR 2004:VII, 3341

Report of the Panel DSR:2004:VIII, 3421

Arbitration under Article 21.3(c) of the DSU (WT/DS268/12)
Award of the Arbitrator DSR:2005:XXIII, 11617

Recourse by Argentina to Article 21.5 of the Understanding on Rules and Procedures Governing the Settlement of Disputes (WT/DS268)

Report of the Appellate Body DSR 2007:IX, 3529

Report of the Panel DSR 2007:IX, 3615
DSR 2007:X, 3829

United States - Tax Treatment for "Foreign Sales Corporations"

Complaint by the European Communities (WT/DS108)

Report of the Appellate Body DSR 2000:III, 1619

Report of the Panel DSR 2000:IV, 1675

Report of the Appellate Body - Recourse to Article 21.5 of the DSU DSR 2002:I, 55

Report of the Panel - Recourse to Article 21.5 of the DSU DSR 2002:I, 119

Decision by the Arbitrator under Article 22.6 of the DSU and Article 4.11 of the *SCM Agreement* DSR 2002:VI, 2517

Report of the Appellate Body - Second Recourse to Article 21.5 of the DSU by the European Communities DSR 2006:XI, 4721

Report of the Panel - Second Recourse to Article 21.5 of the DSU by the European Communities DSR 2006:XI, 4761

United States - Transitional Safeguard Measure on Combed Cotton Yarn from Pakistan

Complaint by Pakistan (WT/DS192)

Report of the Appellate Body DSR 2001:XII, 6027

Report of the Panel DSR 2001:XII, 6067

United States - Use of Zeroing in Anti-Dumping Measures Involving Products from Korea

Complaint by Korea (WT/DS402)

Report of the Panel DSR 2011:X, 5239

www.ingramcontent.com/pod-product-compliance
Ingram Content Group UK Ltd.
Pitfield, Milton Keynes, MK11 3LW, UK
UKHW052247161225
466140UK00010B/644